MAIN LIBRARY
ALBANY PUBLIC LIBRARY
W9-COM-737

NO HANDS

NO HANDS

THE RISE AND FALL OF THE SCHWINN BICYCLE COMPANY AN AMERICAN INSTITUTION

Judith Crown & Glenn Coleman

Henry Holt and Company
New York

Henry Holt and Company, Inc.
Publishers since 1866
115 West 18th Street
New York, New York 10011

Henry Holt® is a registered
trademark of Henry Holt and Company, Inc.

Copyright © 1996 by Judith Crown and Glenn Coleman
All rights reserved.
Published in Canada by Fitzhenry & Whiteside Ltd.,
195 Allstate Parkway, Markham, Ontario L3R 4T8.

Library of Congress Cataloging-in-Publication Data
Crown, Judith.
No hands: the rise and fall of the Schwinn Bicycle Company:
an American institution / Judith Crown and Glenn Coleman.
p. cm.
Includes index.
1. Schwinn Bicycle Company—History. 2. Bicycle industry—
United States—History. I. Coleman, Glenn. II. Title.
HD9993.B544S393 1996 96-15015
338.7'6292272'0973—dc20 CIP

ISBN 0-8050-3553-2

Henry Holt books are available for special promotions
and premiums. For details contact:
Director, Special Markets.

First Edition—1996

Designed by Michelle McMillian

Printed in the United States of America
All first editions are printed on acid-free paper. ∞

1 3 5 7 9 10 8 6 4 2

Schwinn is a registered trademark of Schwinn Cycling and Fitness, Inc.

Portions of this book appeared in a different form in "The Fall of Schwinn," a two-part article published by *Crain's Chicago Business* in October 1993. Crain's granted the authors permission to use extensive excerpts and materials from its copyrighted articles in this book. The newspaper also made available its files and other resources.

To our parents

ACKNOWLEDGMENTS

This work is the culmination of reporting that began in 1992 after word surfaced that the venerable Schwinn Bicycle Company was in financial trouble and seeking an investor. Our reporting led to an investigation of the demise of the family-run Schwinn enterprise, which was published by *Crain's Chicago Business* in the fall of 1993. We soon realized there was a larger story, one that examined Schwinn not only in the context of the bicycle industry, but also in its fall as an American icon—a tale for businesses large and small.

A book is a vehicle that needs many people to steer it, and this particular project could not have happened without the guidance of numerous friends. Publisher Gloria Scoby and Editor David Snyder of *Crain's Chicago Business* offered the kind of support that journalists dream about. Former Editor Mark Miller was an early champion of our cause, and we were assisted and cheered along the way by the Crain family and corporate staff of Crain Communications, Inc., and colleagues at *Crain's Chicago Business*, including Robert Reed, Barbara

Rose, Barbara Bohn, Thomas J. Linden, Julie Hull Fournier, Marianne Rehm, Steve Leonard, Todd Winters, Lisa Goff, and Mark Mandle.

Adam Lashinsky and *The Nikkei Weekly* boosted our research efforts from Japan, and Drew Wilson aided our reporting from Hong Kong. Carol E. Rosenthal was the first person to read the entire manuscript and, as always, rescued us with her editorial instincts and eye for detail. Laurie Abraham revisited the work several times to challenge our storytelling and our writing.

At Henry Holt, our editor, William B. Strachan, always provided an encouraging word. His graceful, thoughtful pencil showed two newspaper people how to write a book. Darcy Tromanhauser and Lottchen Shivers made the publishing process smoother.

Our ally Alice Fried Martell offered an agent's infectious enthusiasm and wise judgment. Allison and Neal Rothschild provided smiles (and, in the course of the project, learned to ride their bikes), while the strength and good humor of our spouses, Richard Rothschild and Victoria Behm, made a long journey all the more enjoyable.

CONTENTS

NO HANDS

INTRODUCTION

Two distinct odors wafted across the rugged hills of California's Marin County in the early 1970s: marijuana . . . and burning grease.

Both tainted the air when gonzo cyclists raced down Mount Tamalpais on clunky old two-wheelers at speeds topping 40 miles per hour. High from the thrill, and often the dope, they'd work their brakes so hard the grease would turn to vapor, smoke spewing from the battered bikes long after ride's end.

They were hippies and gearheads, a loose fraternity of bike bums sponging off parents, holding odd jobs and literally living to ride. They drove up the dirt roads lacing Mount Tam, marveling at the misty vistas half a mile above San Francisco Bay, and unloaded their vintage balloon-tire one-speeds as the local turkey vultures flocked and watched. "Clunkers," riders called the wheels, bought for a few bucks at garage sales and flea markets and revamped with parts that ranged from motorcycle brake levers to thumbshifters off a lady's five-speed. After packing the brake drums tight with extra grease, they hopped on and pedaled off what seemed like the edge of the world.

The best trail was a screaming 1,300-foot drop that yielded five minutes of ride and a lifetime of buzz. A mean left turn known as Hamburger Helper. A rutty right called Vendetti's Face. Dirt churning at every bend. Dust coating teeth and tongue. Trees whipping and slashing skin. Riders whooping as they careened through the Triple Ripple, teetered atop Yellow Cliff, and maneuvered a breath-snatching series of switchbacks—the Cuisinart, Camera Corner, Rubbernecker's Knoll, Long Bump—before soaring over Big Rock and landing with a *whoomp* near Cascade Creek.

Not for the timid, nor for any old bike. As riders thrashed their clunkers one day and overhauled them the next, they scoured junkyards and bike shops for stronger frames, wheels, and components. The models that seemed to last longest were those big and heavy ballooners from the 1930s: curb-slammers with coaster brakes—the kind that newspaper boys used to ride, a metal monster with old-fashioned fat tires. Five dollars for the whole thing, and so ugly no one would want to steal it.

Racer Gary Fisher turned to just such a vehicle when he pieced together clunker and other cycle parts to assemble a multispeed mountain bike in the mid-1970s—a revolutionary product that pedaled up, as well as down, Mount Tam. Fisher was twenty-four and a budding entrepreneur who knew he wanted a frame with strength and style. The savvy marketer in him also demanded it be American, to complement his newer parts from around the world: an English saddle, Japanese gears, French and German hubs. Fisher found precisely what he needed at a chicken coop in the East Bay: a 1937 Schwinn Excelsior, stripped and a bit rusted, but still brawny and beautiful, ready to roll nearly forty years after it had been made. Yes, he thought, this will do the trick.

That it did. Fisher's innovation sparked a local cottage industry that drew the attention of executives at Schwinn Bicycle Company of Chicago. A team of engineers was dispatched to Marin County in the late 1970s and visited Fisher's new MountainBikes Company. But the callers from Schwinn snickered when they saw his contraption—this wasn't a bicycle, it was a mongrel. "This guy in his fifties was looking down at me like I was some jerk kid who didn't know anything," Fisher recalls. "The

Schwinn engineers were going, 'We know bikes. You guys are all amateurs. We know better than anybody.' "

Chicago bankruptcy attorney Dennis O'Dea had become a disconcertingly familiar face at Schwinn's downtown headquarters, where employees morbidly had dubbed him the "Angel of Death." Isn't it odd, someone deadpanned, how the room temperature drops when he walks by? Actually, the chill was everywhere in the unseasonably nippy summer of 1992, whether one stood outside the stylishly rehabbed industrial building, with its postcard views of the city's skyscraping peaks, or sat inside Schwinn's sleek executive conference room, accented with cycling posters and memorabilia. There, on August 26, chief operating officer Ralph Day Murray delivered the grim prognosis to a corporate advisory board that included several Schwinn family members and three outside directors. The company's negotiations with prospective buyers had turned cold, Murray told the gathering. No savior was in sight. Schwinn was $75 million in debt, and losing $1 million a month. Suppliers refused to build new bikes, shippers wouldn't allow components to leave their warehouses, and the banks were squeezing, harder and harder. Attorney O'Dea added his glum assessment. A Chapter 11 petition already had been prepared, he reported. Bankruptcy was not an if—it was a when.

Schwinn's outside directors glanced at one another, then asked for a brief caucus. Mere advisers, they were powerless. Moments later, the trio announced their joint resignations, effective immediately. Tears welled in the eyes of family leaders Betty Dembecki and Deborah Schwinn Bailey. A century-old company was dying as they watched. A proud name and business tradition soon would be the province of bankers, $200-an-hour lawyers, and other vultures of commerce. Their dividends, perks, and children's birthright . . . all would be lost. The women looked at president and chief executive officer Edward R. Schwinn, Jr., the man responsible for this mess. As usual, Ed just sat there, stone-faced and impenetrable. "We are where we are," he'd answer matter-of-factly when family or Schwinn executives pressed him on the company's deteriorating performance.

For his part, Ed had endured too many emotional meetings in the past year, ugly bouts filled with machinations and recriminations from Aunt Betty, Debbie, and all the other cousins, in-laws, and assorted hangers-on who lived off the business but weren't any better equipped to run it. He'd struggled for months as the company's fortunes faded, trying to find some way to preserve the Schwinn dynasty. Maybe he couldn't maintain the family's control, but at least members might hold on to a minority stake. It still could happen, Ed told colleagues. It never did. Six weeks later, Schwinn was in U.S. Bankruptcy Court, pleading for federal protection from creditors who seemed ready to slice up the company. Newspaper headlines across the country bemoaned the passing of an era, and by year's end, most of Schwinn's assets were sold for $43.3 million in cash to a partnership headed by high-flying Chicago financier Sam Zell, nicknamed the "Grave Dancer" by press and peers for his habit of snatching companies in the throes of death. The fourteen-member Schwinn clan pocketed a paltry $2.5 million from the deal, and Ed was sitting on the sidelines at age forty-four, pondering an uncomfortable fact: For the first time in its ninety-seven-year history, Schwinn would not be headed by a Schwinn.

No American company in recent memory offers more examples of the many forces that can bring down a family-run enterprise. And few had so much potential to thrive. *Schwinn* is synonymous with *bicycle* in many American minds—a Rosebud for the middle class—and the product was famed for its durability. Today's grandparents wax nostalgic over Schwinn's streamlined Aero Cycles and fat-tired Excelsiors; their children pine for its chrome-laden Black Phantoms; their children's children remember its super-tough Sting-Rays and Varsitys. Nevertheless, Schwinn grew too accustomed to being the big wheel, and its tumble is a saga of spectacular failure; of third- and fourth-generation family executives who lacked the passion to sustain their franchise but insisted on retaining control until it was too late; of management blunders that stretched across the globe; of giddy deal-making at the expense of good bike-making; of vengeance wreaked by former executives and Asian suppliers; of two corporate cultures—good old boys living in the past and

MBAs flow-charting the future—clashing while competitors raced by both. Most of all, it is a tale of a young CEO who alienated just about everyone he needed—from relatives, employees, and longtime dealers to lenders, lawyers, suppliers, and bidders—with a mix of arrogance and ignorance that only can be described as hubris.

It was a tortured deterioration. What follows is the story of that decline: how a Great American Company rose—and how a Great American Family failed to stop its fall.

1

"EVERYTHING IS BICYCLE"

If one word defines the Schwinn clan, it is *headstrong.* That can be a compliment, when the headstrong man knows what he is doing; it is something else when he does not.

Company founder Ignaz Schwinn always seemed to do the right thing. When the eighty-eight-year-old died of a stroke in 1948, condolences from customers and even competitors approached veneration. Ignaz was "the Henry Ford of the bicycle industry," wrote the leader of a cycle parts association. A "dean," noted the CEO of Huffman Manufacturing Company, maker of Huffy bikes. A "grand old pioneer," mourned a parts maker.

No false praise. Ignaz was a German immigrant who had seen his modest Chicago factory become one of the best-known businesses in America. He was a demanding chief executive who, with his son, Frank W., had resuscitated a lifeless industry in the 1930s with innovations that captured the imaginations of children and turned the Schwinn name into a synonym for bicycle. And he did it the old-fashioned way: *his* way, dammit. "Ignaz was a typical Schwinn—hardheaded and stubborn," says Rudolph Schwinn, a retired engineer at the company whose grandfather and Ignaz were brothers.

He was a gruff little bulldog of a man, standing five feet four inches and scowling in most photographs. He tussled with big retailers, suppliers, and just about anyone he suspected of doing him wrong. Company old-timers tell a tale of a production worker in the 1920s who wanted to buy a stripped-down frame from the boss. A suspicious Ignaz quoted the higher price of a complete bicycle. "Why so much?" the worker wondered. "Because," Ignaz barked, "you must have stolen my parts if all you need is the frame." Even his more tender moments carried bite. "My father was a stern man of the old school," Frank W. once confided to a trade magazine. "He did not spoil his children. So I was surprised, a few months after I went to work for him, when he raised my salary to what was quite a lot for a boy my age. Then he showed me a handsome new car parked in front of the plant. 'That's for you, too,' he said. 'If you're going to make a fool of yourself, I'd rather know about it now.' "

Born April 1, 1860, in Hardheim, Germany, a small town tucked in the northern hills of Baden, Ignaz was the son of a piano and organ maker, the second of seven children. His father was a gifted craftsman (a pump organ that he constructed in the early 1860s is still playable 130 years later) who died when Ignaz was eleven. The boy apprenticed as a machinist, then wandered north to the industrial center of Hamburg as a migrant factory worker. Bicycles were the hot new technology in the last quarter of the century, attracting such mechanically minded men as Henry Ford, the brothers Wilbur and Orville Wright—and young Ignaz Schwinn. "He trudged from town to town working on bicycles and bicycle parts whenever he could find the opportunity," reads a corporate history published in 1945. That headstrong nature flares here, too. Although he reached higher and higher positions in German factories, he usually left when superiors declined to embrace his ideas for improving parts or production.

Ignaz was smack in the middle of a long line of bicycle tinkerers that stretched back one hundred years to the French Enlightenment and continued one hundred years more into the California mountain bike era and beyond—a two-hundred-year-old tradition of adapting, of adding to or stripping away, of fitting this nut to that bolt, of answering the essential question, *How can I make this thing more fun?* The bicycle was developed, not invented, and its history is ruled by booms and busts, cutthroat competition, and a near-Newtonian law of innovation that rewards the nimble and punishes the bland. The basic model evolved slowly through generations of European putterings that spanned most of the nineteenth century. Yet once the instrument was more or less perfected, it became one of those ideas that changes everything. In 1895—the year Ignaz Schwinn founded his company in Chicago—an enthusiastic writer in the *New York Times* called the bicycle "of more importance to mankind than all the victories and defeats of Napoleon." That's a big claim for a little vehicle; nonetheless, the bicycle offered the common man his first practical alternative to the horse, allowing him to travel on land just about everywhere on his own power. Women, too, were emancipated by the machine, which helped unshackle the fair sex from Victorian demands on behavior and dress. An unprecedented bicycle boom in the 1890s spurred the paving of roads throughout the United States; it pushed consumer marketing and retailing to new highs—and lows; it sped the development of machinery, materials and mass production in the Industrial Age. Bicycle innovations were key to the creation of the automobile and airplane.

Not bad for a humble two-wheeler, though whom to credit for its inception is not as clear. Some historians go back to Italy, 1493. A folio tucked into one of Leonardo da Vinci's notebooks contains several childish pornographic scribblings and one crudely sketched image that may be centuries ahead of its time: a bicycle, complete with seat, handlebar, pedals, and a toothed-gear and chain mechanism to power the rear wheel. Leonardo is not the artist, and there's no evidence he constructed the vehicle, yet the gear and chain concept is found in his real drawings. This bicycle is either a draft by a young apprentice copying his master's now-lost design or a work by a modern forger wanting to endow Leonardo with more foresight than even he deserved.

Most cycling scholars begin in France, 1790. At Versailles, Marie Antoinette and coterie gathered to watch the Marquis de Sivrac mount his adult version of a child's hobbyhorse. He called the invention a *velocifere,* from the Latin for "fast" and "carry." It must have been a delightfully silly sight: two wood wheels joined by a stub of beam, saddled and shaped to resemble a horse, with de Sivrac running wildly astride it until the thing rolled fast enough to coast a few yards. Fashionable aristocrats soon were huffing across the royal gardens on their own velociferes—some machines outfitted as horses, others as lions or serpents—lifting their legs gleefully as they spun past amused pedestrians. Stripped versions were raced down the Boulevard des Italiens for wagers.

Pity the unsuspecting stroller, because the early velocifere had neither steering nor brakes. The latter problem would take decades to solve, but the former was remedied in Germany around 1816 by Baron Karl von Drais de Saverbrun, a thirty-one-year-old agricultural engineer serving as "Master of the Woods and Forests" to the Grand Duke of Baden (the home region of Ignaz Schwinn). Baron von Drais believed a serious velocifere could become a utilitarian, even revolutionary, mode of transportation. He built lighter wheels and developed a rudimentary fork for the front that could be steered, rudderlike, with a handlebar. A "belly brace" rising from the bar of the walnut frame helped a rider push the rig with his feet. The innovations made the 50-pound vehicle practical enough for road use—faster than walking and sometimes even riding a horse. A man straddling this new velocifere could move 10 miles per hour on smooth, level ground; he could walk uphill on it with relative ease and glide downhill as long as the coast was clear. The changes earned von Drais a French patent in 1818 and his vehicle a nickname, *draisienne.* The idea seeped across the Continent (the wheels at first were banned in downtown Milan) and to England, where the draisienne generally was derided as a "dandy-horse." It was introduced to America in 1819, where it became a minor rage at Harvard College and entertained crowds for a few summers in New York and Philadelphia, but the draisienne and its imitators weren't solely playthings for dandies. Clergymen and servants used iron models on their rounds. The French government supplied them to rural postmen. English enthusiasts championed the idea of draisienne teams hauling light cargo more efficiently than horses, providing jobs for the wretched poor (at least, in dry weather) and freeing pastures for farming. It never was to be, of course. The passion for draisiennes expired by the 1830s—the technician classes had shifted their attentions to steam power—and von Drais died in 1851.

Others tinkered away. In rural Scotland, around 1839, blacksmith Kirkpatrick MacMillan souped up his hobbyhorse with a series of rods and foot pedals that cranked the rear wheel. Awkward stuff, but it did the trick. This is considered the first modern bicycle, because a rider could propel the machine without touching the ground. MacMillan had liberated man from walking with a contraption whose later variations would multiply human efficiency by a factor of five, but he received no recognition for his innovation until long after he died. He attracted gawks when pedaling about the countryside (and a five-shilling fine in 1842 for knocking over a child while maneuvering through a crowd outside Glasgow), yet he never applied for a patent or reported his invention to technical journals. He simply sold his models to locals for several pounds apiece.

The popular credit for developing the modern two-wheeler goes to Ernest Michaux of Paris. In 1855, at age fourteen, he reportedly dreamed up the idea of affixing cranks and pedals to the axle of the front wheel of an old draisienne. The basic principle is still used today (it's what powers a child's tricycle), but the Michaux family's two-wheeled *velocipede* startled those who first saw it being pedaled up and down the Champs-Elysées. Young Ernest's father may have had a hand in the invention—the elder was a manufacturer of carriages—and also involved may have been an employee named Pierre Lallement, who insisted that father and son had stolen his idea. A disgruntled Lallement collected his prized parts and emigrated to America, where he and a partner in Connecticut were awarded the first U.S. bicycle patent in 1866. Money problems quickly overwhelmed Lallement, however. He sold his share of the venture and patent for $2,000 and returned to France to compete against the hated Michaux et Compagnie, which by 1868 had some three hundred workers producing four to five iron velocipedes a day for the upper class.

Early velocipedes weighed between 70 and 150 pounds, depending on how much iron stripping was used as tires. The wood wheels wobbled, the frame tended to bend and crack, and there still was that problem with brakes—no one had yet invented good ones. There was a reason this thundering machine was nicknamed the "bone-shaker" in America, where there were an estimated 5,000 velocipede riders in New York alone. "The art of walking is obsolete," *Scientific American* magazine crowed, rather prematurely, in 1869. "Manufacturers in a score of towns had all they could do to supply the demand," recalled Boston writer Charles E. Pratt in his *The American Bicycler*, one of the country's earliest handbooks for the sport, published just ten years later, in 1879. "Merchants, professional men, mechanics, college students, and even the ladies, hurried to its adoption as a pastime and a means of exercise, and also as a hoped-for instrument of practical locomotion." The newfangled machine was creeping into the popular culture, too—a Winslow Homer engraving even depicted a New Year's baby cycling into 1869. But the fad was a flash. By 1871, "not a 'velocipede' was to be found in the United States, except as junk or in the hands of a boy," Pratt wrote. "The 'mania' had subsided. The 'bone-shaker,' with all its promise in America, was laid forever by, to be brought out again only as a relic."

The putterers forged on. A new wave of velocipedes—high-wheelers dubbed "Ordinaries" by their marketers—soon rolled in.

English industrialists largely perfected the Ordinary in the 1870s, when French manufacturing was diverted by war with Prussia. It was an ironic twist, because the English had been slower than the French and Americans to embrace the previous decade's velocipede craze. ("A New Terror in the Streets," screamed a headline in the *Times* of London in 1869.) Led by cyclist and manufacturer James Starley of Coventry, the English more than made up for their recalcitrance by creating some of the most exquisitely crafted high-wheeled cycles of the 1870s and leading the development of the smaller "Safety" bicycle of the 1880s, which became the basis for the modern standard model and sparked the bike boom of the 1890s.

Ordinary may well have been short for "Extraordinary," because these custom-made machines with chest-high front wheels and knee-high rear wheels were unusual creations more finely wrought than the clunky bone-shakers. They were made of modern iron and steel, not primitive wood, and were about half the weight of the early velocipedes. Somewhat better steering and brakes made riding more pleasant. So did solid rubber tires, ball bearings in the wheel hubs to decrease friction, and threaded steel spokes that held wheels rigid and helped absorb the impact of the road. To the Victorians "it was a picture of grace itself," writes bicycle historian Robert A. Smith. The colossal front wheel may leave late-twentieth-century observers scratching their heads, but the explanation is simple. "There was no adequate chain technology in the early eighteen-seventies," notes author Andrew Ritchie. "Although there were a number of rear-driven machines being experimented with, none of them seemed to offer such a promising future as the velocipede driven by the front wheel. The best way to get more speed out of this bicycle was quite simply to make the front wheel, the driving wheel, bigger. For every turn of the pedals, the wheel thus covered more ground."

The bigger the wheel, the better the bike. Likewise, the bigger the wheel, the better the man. The cult of the Ordinary was redolent with machismo. A man's Ordinary, Bostonian Charles Pratt wrote in 1879, "is in infinite restless motion, like a bundle of sensitive nerves; it is beneath its rider like a thing of life, without the uncertainty and resistance of an uncontrolled will." Brand names like Defiance and Tension and the militaristic conceits of the cycling clubs that sprouted across the country in the 1880s underscored the philosophy that, as Pratt put it, "bicycling is manly." If manly means strenuous, he was right. Cycling an Ordinary was a feat, even for the athlete. The climb to the seat deterred most would-be riders, and, once there, he crouched atop a front wheel up to six-feet round. The tiny rear wheel could make the experience similar to traveling by unicycle. Good racers could maintain a 20 miles per hour clip, but quick turns were unwise: one's center of gravity was perched so far forward, an unexpected rut or rock could send cycle and cyclist flying. The experience was called, appropriately, a "header" in the States. It may be a major reason the Ordinary attracted only an estimated 50,000 converts here by the mid-1880s.

The undisputed leader of that flock was Boston shoe manufacturer Albert A. Pope. The former Civil War officer was among the thousands of visitors to Philadelphia's Centennial exposition in 1876 who studied the first Ordinary exhibited in America: a five-foot-high high-wheeler made by James Starley's company and ridden by an English acrobat. Colonel Pope, as he liked to be addressed, traveled to London and Coventry the next year to investigate the cycle business. By 1878, he was remaking his Pope Manufacturing Company into a bicycle factory. The colonel's initial Columbia model weighed 70 pounds, cost $313 (nearly $5,000 in 1996 dollars) and was considered the first real American-made bicycle. Among Pope's earliest moves was to hire Pratt to write *The American Bicycler* handbook to publicize both the sport and the Ordinary. The author returned the favor by describing his patron as "one of Boston's most enterprising merchants," which he was. According to historian Smith, Pope opened riding schools and sponsored cycling clubs and races, bought out or sued holders of the old velocipede patents, sought government protection from foreign competition, and underwrote litigation challenging domestic laws that curbed riders' rights to roads and parks—especially ordinances that favored horses over cyclists. He and other manufacturers pushed for street improvements, and, after helping to establish the League of American Wheelmen in 1880, funded research in highway construction at the Massachusetts Institute of Technology and lobbied statehouses for more than twenty years to construct and pave roads in cities, suburbs, and towns.

Each tactic increased the potential market for Pope's bicycles. But the real boost to his and other bike makers' business came from England, where an innovation turned the Ordinary obsolete in 1884. That year, Starley's operation began introducing a series of Safety cycles called the "Rover." Much like Kirkpatrick MacMillan's eccentric vehicle four decades earlier in Scotland, and even more like the alleged Leonardo da Vinci drawing four centuries before in Italy, these Rovers were pedaled with a chain connected to gears on the axle of the rear wheel. With the rear wheel doing the real work, the front wheel could shrink dramatically and be used solely for steering, while the seat could slide down and back to a safe perch near the middle, where a rider's feet reassuredly touched the ground. Lighter steel-frame tubing also helped make the Safety faster than the Ordinary, and most competitors in Europe and America adapted the Rover idea by the late 1880s. Additional improvements rapidly followed, most notably coaster brakes and pneumatic tires, which used compressed air to cushion the ride. By 1890, one hundred years after de Sivrac pranced his hobbyhorse across the gardens of Versailles, the job had been completed. The bicycle basically resembled what is ridden today.

Ignaz Schwinn was an early and rather lonely German advocate of the Safety, according to a corporate history published for his company's fiftieth anniversary.[1] A young man in his mid-twenties, he had worked for cycle and parts makers in the north of Germany, "saw some of the early experimental types and quickly recognized their advantages," reports the official history. "His enthusiasm and ideas were listened to respectfully, but rejected in favor of the older type" of Ordinary. The introduction in 1888 of the pneumatic tire, with its promise of easy riding on rough roads, pushed him over the entrepreneurial edge: "He was convinced that his ideas were right, and a few competent cycle men agreed with him and encouraged him in his ideas." Ignaz worked days in a machine shop in Frankfurt am Main that produced parts for high-wheelers, but he spent nights in his rented attic room designing plans for his own Safety. He presented his drawings to local manufacturer Heinrich Kleyer, who made and sold Ordinaries as a sideline, and Kleyer hired Ignaz to design and manage the production of some of the first Safety bicycles made in Germany. Business was good and, at age twenty-nine, Ignaz helped plan and oversee the building of a new factory for Kleyer that ultimately grew to become Germany's Adler Works.

Within a year, however, Ignaz wanted more. He emigrated to America with his wife, Helen, arriving in the manufacturing magnet of Chicago in 1891. The boomtown on Lake Michigan had doubled in population the previous decade to one million residents, and the number would nearly double again in the 1890s, fueled by immigration, industrialization, and the spectacles of the 1893 World's Columbian Exposition, which brought more than 20 million visitors to Chicago. All that opportunity seemed to make Ignaz restless. His first stint, with the producers of Fowler bicycles, was brief, and it was followed by two apparently unhappy years designing and opening a bicycle factory for the International Manufacturing Company. "The enterprise was not managed to his liking," explains the corporate history, "and in 1894, he severed his connection." That year, Ignaz found his angel in Adolph Frederick William Arnold, a successful Chicago investor and meatpacking executive who also served as president of Haymarket Produce Bank. Arnold was German-born, too—his hometown was Guben, about 70 miles southeast of Berlin—but he was eleven years older than Ignaz and had emigrated to America well before the Great Chicago Fire of 1871. His Arnold Brothers pork and sausage company, founded in 1864, supplied the area's largest restaurants, and though Adolph Arnold wasn't in the same financial league as Chicago meatpacker moguls Philip Armour and Gustavus Swift, his name appears in many of the "Blue Books" that listed the city's commercial and industrial baronage at the turn of the century. "He was a man of unusual business ability and of the highest integrity," according to the official Schwinn history. Arnold also was a man who knew an opportunity when he saw one. The bike business was booming, with the nation in the grip of a cycling craze like nothing it had seen before—or since.

The Safety arrived just when millions of Americans had the wealth, time, and inclination to pursue outdoor leisure activities. Suddenly there was a vehicle anyone could ride, anywhere, anytime, and the boldest bikers did just that. Newspaper readers thrilled at the Vernian exploits of around-the-world cyclists, especially (and regrettably) one Frank Lenz, a twenty-five-year-old from Pittsburgh who pedaled west in 1892 under the sponsorship of *Outing* magazine. He disappeared on the Asian leg of his journey two years later, somewhere near Kurdistan, leaving a few bike parts and half a bell.

In the States, Army General Nelson A. Miles saw military potential in this all-terrain vehicle that didn't need feeding and watering. From his command post in Chicago, Miles wheedled his skeptical superiors into commissioning the 25th Infantry Bicycle Corps as an experiment in Montana during the summer of 1896. Army brass foisted the trial on an all-black unit led by 2d Lt. James A. Moss, a white southerner who had graduated at the bottom of his West Point class. The team traveled an 800-mile round trip from Fort Missoula to Yellowstone National Park in 18 days, fording streams single-file and slogging through winds, rain, mud, and grades so steep they demanded more bike pushing than riding.

Tires punctured, rims twisted, and chains tumbled down mountainsides. But hospitable farmers helped with provisions, and elated tourists at Yellowstone snapped photos of friends and family posing with the mighty members of the 25th. "Soldiers delighted," Moss reported to Miles. "Treated royally everywhere—thought the sights grand." Although another tour was completed successfully in 1897, the discovery of gold in Alaska knocked news of the bike corps' achievements off front pages. Meanwhile, the pending war with Spain diverted the army's attention. The rides across Montana remain the only successful U.S. military experiment with bicycles. Nevertheless, other pioneering mountain bikers repeatedly proved the hardiness of the machine eighty years before their 1970s counterparts did in California. The Alaska gold rush spurred a few of the last frontiersmen to cycle the 400-mile winter trail from Dawson to Whitehorse between 1898 and 1908. Heated roadhouses dotted the route (one proprietor used a frozen horse carcass to keep his stretch plowed), but the terrain was cold-blooded. Rubber tires were stuffed with rope to ward off punctures. Bike frames were wrapped with rawhide to withstand temperatures below minus 50 degrees Fahrenheit, although falls on the ice still made metal pedals and handlebars shatter. "A long, sad, sore and eventful trip," one rider wrote wearily in his diary. Another told of tumbling headfirst into a snowdrift and later skidding his wheel down the ice-covered Big Delta River. "Our brakes would become so hot," yet another recalled, "we would have to stop and throw the machine into the snow to let it cool off." One wrote of falling through ice while crossing the Shaktoolik River, breaking his chain on the Norton Sound, and blowing into Nome using his coat as a sail. Nine members of the Yukon Nuggets hockey team also biked the trail in 1904 on their way to compete in the Stanley Cup finals.

Such stunts attracted attention, of course, but it was organized amateur and professional racing that really lured Americans to the possibilities of biking. Early curiosity was intense—nearly 100,000 spectators lined Chicago roads for an 1891 race from South Michigan Avenue to Pullman, 12 miles away—and cycling became a bigger spectator sport than baseball for much of the decade. Velodromes rose throughout the United States and Europe, and crowds roared as the *barang* of the last lap bell pushed racers into their final sprints. American fans especially relished the six-day endurance contests: 142 continuous hours of cycling around an indoor track, competitors offering "thrills and spills . . . of the highest magnitude for the urban working classes who had no visible forms of recreation," according to sports historian John Lucas. Bands played on and on while riders circled wood tracks made hazy by cigar smoke. The people, the purses, and the press were big. Chicagoan Charlie Miller established the world record (2,007.2 miles) inside a packed Madison Square Garden in New York in 1898, winning $3,800 and the hand of Miss Genevieve Hanson, whom he married just hours after the race before a raucous Garden audience. Fixes and scandals were rampant, but serious riders and fans created a valid sport through regulated individual races and team relays that became institutionalized with the first Tour de France in 1903. The turn-of-the-century's most sensational star was a black American named Marshall "Major" Taylor. Described as the "colored wonder" by the *Philadelphia Press*, Major Taylor became U.S. cycling champion in 1898 at age nineteen and world champion in 1899. Largely forgotten by history, he was the first modern black star athlete, sponsoring products by white-owned companies in the United States and spending the 1901 season netting $10,000 racing in Europe.[2]

Outside the racetracks, bicycles seemed to spin everywhere, as the public went wild for the wheel. The number of Chicago cycling clubs, for instance, swelled to 500 in 1895 from 50 in 1892. By 1897, an estimated one in seven city residents owned a bike. "Everything is bicycle," Stephen Crane wrote in the *New York Sun* following a pleasant afternoon's stroll up that town's Broadway in 1896. "On these gorgeous spring days they appear in thousands. All mankind is a-wheel apparently and a person on nothing but legs feels like a strange animal. A mighty army of wheels streams from the brick wilderness below Central Park and speeds over the asphalt. In the cool of the evening it returns with swaying and flashing of myriad lamps."

By 1899, an estimated ten million cyclists were on the road nationwide. Mass production by Schwinn and the more than 300 bike manufacturers that sprang up across the country during the decade had made the machine affordable to many middle-class Americans, who paid from

$40 to $120 for a set of wheels, often on installment plans. By the mid-1890s, when average per capita income was about $1,000, the building of bicycles had become a $60 million industry. Annual production surpassed 500,000 units, then 700,000, 800,000—one million. "Bicycle men today assert that theirs is the largest specific manufacturing industry in America," reported *Munsey's Magazine* in 1896. Colonel Pope's East Coast operation was sending a cycle a minute out the factory door, yet Chicago had become the industry's true hub: fully two-thirds of the nation's bikes and accessories were made within 150 miles of the city, according to the 1898 *Chicago Bicycle Directory.* More than thirty factories bustled along Lake Street west of the Loop, their 6,000 workers churning out cheaper and cheaper product for such major merchants as The Fair department store, which sold up to 1,000 bikes a day from its colossal State Street store, and Chicago-based mail-order giants Sears, Roebuck and Company and Montgomery Ward & Company.

All those bike riders depressed other businesses. Piano sales plunged 50 percent; theaters emptied in the spring; tavern owners watched profits fizzle. "Barbers See Daily Shave Custom Declining," read one headline of the era, "After Work, They Go Bicycling Instead." Some shopkeepers feared they were doomed, what with so many locals covering wider stretches of country on their wheels. "The bicycle sounds the death knell of the small town," argued John M. Foster, of Illinois, in 1897. Representatives of the horse industry reported the supply of horses decreased more than seven million between 1894 and 1898, blaming the decline on both the bicycle and the electrically powered street car.

Demand for bikes was so keen, buyers had to wait months for their prize, often taking cycling classes in the interim. An ad for one Wabash Avenue school in Chicago promised private lessons in the "Finest Instruction Hall in the World" with "no Falls or Bruises." Even a prim Frances Willard, founder of the Women's Christian Temperance Union in suburban Evanston, was swept away. The fifty-three-year-old Prohibitionist and suffragist spent fifteen minutes daily for three months learning to ride her bike (which she named Gladys), and published a little book on her adventure. "I found a whole philosophy of life in the wooing and winning of my bicycle," Willard wrote. "I finally concluded that all failure was from a wobbling will rather than a wobbling wheel. . . . [S]ummoning all my force, I mounted and started off alone. From that hour the spell was broken; Gladys was no more a mystery."

Young women especially took to the new cycle, for here was a rare chance to be the equal of men—and then some. "The ladies have obtained complete mastery over the wheel," observed the Country Club of Evanston's 1895 yearbook, "and it is oftentimes a matter of grave doubt whether a lady or a gentleman will first reach the destination." Frederick Law Olmstead designed Chicago's Jackson Park with separate bicycle trails for men and women. Out west, a Denver women's club named itself Entre Nous Cycliennes. It all sounds quaint today, but woman a-wheel was a radical symbol. Fin-de-siècle feminism "may well take as its emblem the two-wheeler," writes historian Patricia Marks, noting that the bicycle "helped to destroy the myth of the delicate, sickly woman that had for so long been a deterrent to her endeavor." Cycling loosened women's dress styles, ending the tyranny of the petticoat. It whisked a young lady from sitting room to new worlds in the city or countryside. It made her muscles stronger, her complexion ruddier. She grew less formal with men, more confident with women, and just plain independent. "It is nothing uncommon for a girl to be away all day, but what of it?" argued Charlotte Holt of the Chicago Society for the Protection of Women and Children in 1896. "One reason I like the wheel so thoroughly is that it has done away with the chaperone who was beginning to be foisted on us." The 1890s woman on a bike, Marks writes, decided "where she wishes to go and what she plans to do when she gets there, regardless of a male companion or lack of one. . . . [N]o other individual sport seemed to further the women's movement more radically. It could be ladylike or daring, depending on whether its rider pedaled demurely, petticoats and all, on a tricycle, or donned bloomers, tie and waistcoat and 'scorched' down the streets on a two-wheeler."

The bicycle's liberating potential did not escape the notice of more reactionary forces. Editorializing on a new courting ritual—men were accompanying ladies on rides in the woods—the *Philadelphia Taggerts Times* thundered that cycling "led young and innocent girls into ruin and disgrace." Chicago schoolteacher Gyda Stephenson was nearly fired for wearing her bloomers in her classroom. There also were physiological fears. Too much exercise made the female "brusque" and her voice "assertive," warned physician Arabella Kenealy, brooding over the "potentiality of the race they are expending on their muscles." Even worse, admonished doctor and dentist Carl A. H. Anderson in an 1895 speech to the Society for the Promotion of Rational Physical Culture, "the skin of the face, especially about the forehead and eyes, will be wrinkled, caused by the contraction of muscles about the mouth, nose and forehead necessitated by constant anxiety and observation." Eventually, however, biker women became acceptable—even admirable—as the image of the happy, hearty Gibson Girl rolled into the public psyche. "Not the least good thing that the bicycle has done," *American Life* magazine observed in 1897, "has been to demonstrate publicly that women have legs." Perhaps the ultimate endorsement: a British perfume maker sold its "Cycling Bouquet" in tiny bottles that fit neatly into a biker's purse. The scent, according to the advertising copy, "is a delicious combination of fresh country air and all the sweet odored blossoms that open their petals to drink in the warm sunshine."

One reason for the changing attitude in the press may have been the bicycle industry's enormous contributions to media profits during a decade dominated by financial panics and depressions. An estimated 10 percent of newspaper and magazine advertising in the late 1890s was bought by bicycle manufacturers, retailers, and sellers of parts and accessories, from pedal-powered electric lights to custom cork-and-leather handlebar grips to the Mead Cycle Company's handy little ammonia squirt gun ("for the vicious dog or flock of poultry that is blocking the road ahead"). Newspapers covered cycling and racing events daily, frequently in special sections. Magazines from *Scribner's* to *Harper's Weekly, Scientific American,* and *Literary Digest* devoted entire issues to the sport. "Even the billboards have surrendered," Stephen Crane wrote in the *New York Sun.* "When they do condescend to still advertise a patent medicine, you are sure to confront a lithograph of a young person in bloomers who is saying [in] large type: 'Yes, George, I find that Willowrum always refreshes me after these long rides.' " Politicians, naturally, followed the press. Five-time mayor of Chicago Carter H. Harrison

II kicked off his first campaign for the post in 1897 by pedaling a 100-mile "century" route from city to country and back. "Not the Champion Cyclist," read a campaign poster, "but the Cyclists' Champion."

Into this swirling, hurling marketplace jumped Adolph Arnold and Ignaz Schwinn. The duo incorporated Arnold, Schwinn & Company in 1895 to "manufacture, buy, sell and deal in bicycles, sulkies, wagons, carriages, vehicles, and parts for the same," according to their corporate charter, and rented a building at the northwest corner of Lake and Peoria Streets.

The consummate passive inventor, Arnold let his expert run the venture. It proved a wise decision. Ignaz was a master manufacturer, building both his own elite "World" brand and generic bikes for retailers that slapped on their labels, including Sears, one of Schwinn's earliest and biggest customers. He was hardnosed, too. Ignaz insisted, for instance, that police in Buffalo, New York, arrest a business owner who sold his bicycles in that city, according to an 1898 news brief in *The Wheel*, a weekly trade paper. (Had he cheated Ignaz? The journal didn't detail the alleged wrongdoing, but did note the grand jury declined to indict their local businessman.) Ignaz also had a flair for promotions: the diminutive 140-pounder posed for a publicity photograph with a six-foot-six-inch, 570-pound vaudeville man named Baby Bliss, suggesting the range of riders that Schwinn's products could handle. More seriously, Ignaz sponsored a World team of racers who smashed speed barriers in America and Europe and garnered press in the many cycling publications of the era, from *Wheel Talk* to *The Scorcher* ("A Hot Paper for Hot Cyclists"). At an 1896 race in Chicago's Garfield Park, *Bearings* magazine reported, "Mr. Schwinn took the liveliest interest . . . and hoped that records would be broken in the home city." Despite the notices, initial Schwinn sales hardly were out of this world—about 25,000 units annually. But, as the typically inflated copy in an early Schwinn catalog put it, "The season of 1897 finds the 'World' bicycle in undisputed possession of an established and recognized reputation for true worth, superiority and perfection of modern cycle construction, judgment having been passed by a most critical and exacting public from Klondyke's [*sic*] glacial realms to South America's Horn, from Iceland's icy shores to Africa's end of Hope, from

Siberia's snowy fields over China's Wall of Stone, under Japan's balmy skies to the land of Kangaroos." Even somewhat less self-interested voices agreed Ignaz Schwinn was going places: just three years after its incorporation, his company was identified in *The Wheel* as a "prominent" cycle maker that, like hometown competitor A. G. Spalding & Bros., "displayed a full line of its models and occupied two booths" at an 1898 Chicago expo that drew 5,000 people.

Schwinn's star was rising. Not so for most of the rest of the industry, where the too-crowded field of 300-plus cycle manufacturers soon hacked one another into oblivion. Between 1897 and 1898, the price of a top-of-the-line bike snapped in half, to $50 wholesale from $100, and the cheapest models soon were fetching $20 retail. Components of all qualities saw prices tumble even more dramatically—wood rims that commanded $2.50 a pair in 1893 sold for 75 cents in 1899. Reports of bankruptcies, receiverships, and liquidations peppered the trade magazines that year, as bicycle sales peaked at a dizzying high of 1.2 million units.

Then it all crashed. Adults stopped cycling as the automobile age revved up. By 1905, national bicycle production had dropped to 250,000 units annually. Only a dozen manufacturers survived the shake-up. "Many fortunes have been wrecked, many business reputations blasted or sorely wounded," reported *The Wheel* in 1900. "The great green public . . . has been led to believe that the manufacture of bicycles was an El Dorado or Klondike, and in some respect it does not differ from those famous gold fields: It has been frought [*sic*] with disaster and disappointment."

A deft Ignaz Schwinn fared well through the turmoil. (The corporate history later credits his "carefully and conservatively managed" approach to the business, "without loss in any single year.") He acquired the bankrupt March-Davis Bicycle Company at a receiver's sale in 1899 and moved his manufacturing operations to its factory in northwest Chicago, at the time the western edge of the city. He built a new factory nearby, and the corporate operations followed in 1901. Ignaz had settled into a cheaper location to ride out a bicycle bust that would last more than thirty years.

Just five years earlier, in 1896, the *Chicago Tribune* had looked boldly into the coming century and predicted that "as a poor man's vehicle, both of pleasure and business, the bike is going to have no rival." Bicycle makers and others already were experimenting with early stabs at the horseless carriage—Ignaz, for instance, had built an electric model in 1896 and drove it through Chicago's streets with partner Arnold at his side—but few foresaw how swiftly automobiles and airplanes would arrive. None of it would have happened when it did without the bicycle. Several bicycle innovations, such as the chain drive, differential gears, and shock absorbers, were crucial to the development of the auto. The bike boom years stimulated the production of better steels, rubber compounds, ball bearings, and tubings; they accelerated improvements in tools, machinery, engineering, assembly lines, and distribution. Cycle shop owners, such as the Wright Brothers of Dayton, Ohio, and Glenn H. Curtis of Hammondsport, New York, later pioneered in aeronautics, but it took Michigan bike man Henry Ford to drive America into the auto age and leave the two-wheeler in the dust. The beginning of the end arrived in Chicago on July 15, 1903, when dentist Ernest Pfennig bought the first Ford in the city for $850.

2

A BUST—AND A COMEBACK

A thuggish former baseball player guarded Albert G. Spalding's suite at the Waldorf-Astoria in New York, barring reporters and other intruders so the boss could do his plotting in private. It was the winter of 1899, and the head of Chicago's A. G. Spalding & Bros. had lived nearly a month in this grandest of hotels, receiving a stream of equally prominent bicycle men desperate to survive as the boom began to bust. Many had already been forced to close their dealerships and sell bloated inventories at discount to the mail-order houses and major department stores. Now, Spalding and his chummy competitor, Colonel Albert Pope, dangled a solution: form a trust to undercut and destroy the remaining independent competition, then raise prices and wallow in the profits.

The American Bicycle Company was organized that March. It claimed control of more than 75 percent of the trade, including Chicago's colossal Western Wheel Works, which produced the top-selling Crescent models, and two dozen other manufacturers and parts firms. Total capitalization was an estimated $80 million. "A Stupendous Combine in Sight," *Bicycling World* announced, almost sweating over its scoop—and the prospect of fewer advertisers. "Syndicate Has or Seeks Options On Nearly All Cycle Plants."

The last thing a man like Ignaz Schwinn would do is surrender his independence. Indeed, there's no evidence he entertained the idea of joining the trust, says James Hurd, former curator of the Bicycle Museum of America in Chicago. Ignaz was fortunate not to, because the American Bicycle Company was a fiasco. Its finances and management were so jumbled the New York Stock Exchange declined to list it. Principals joined, quit, rejoined, and re-quit. Colonel Pope's scheme to snatch up competitors' patents—so effective when he had entered the high-wheel bike business thirty years before—was a costly disaster in a time of shrinking demand. Spunky independents like Iver Johnson advertised the fact that "Our bicycles are NOT MADE by a TRUST." And the leaders of the syndicate squabbled frequently. Spalding resigned as president in 1900 and focused on other sporting goods. The treasurer left the following year with eight factories to form his own bicycle enterprise. Gormully & Jefferey used its Rambler brand to enter the auto business. By 1902, Pope and his friend John D. Rockefeller (an early cycling enthusiast) controlled the American Bicycle Company. A year later, it was bankrupt after defaulting on its bonds.

The Great Bicycle Trust had failed. Yet collusion would continue to steer the industry for thirty more years, as parts makers consolidated into their own powerful bloc and worked with Sears, Montgomery Ward, and other big retailers to keep the final costs of a bike low. The tactic caught the surviving bicycle manufacturers in a vise, squeezing their profit margins and leaving almost no incentive to improve what was a second-rate product—until a frustrated Schwinn family smashed the cozy arrangement in the 1930s.

The market for bicycles at the turn of the century offered little to cheer manufacturers like Schwinn. With adults driving autos, children were the real customers, which limited the price that could be charged. Financier Adolph Arnold bailed out in 1908, when Ignaz Schwinn bought his partner's shares and made the family sole owner (although no one bothered changing Arnold, Schwinn & Company's name until the late 1960s[1]). The bike industry's annual output between 1900 and 1930 averaged only 330,000 units, while Schwinn's hovered around 45,000, or roughly 14 percent of the market. Ignaz and his son, Frank W., focused instead on the more promising market for motorcycles. In the summer of 1910, the two traveled to Atlantic City for a trade show. The fifty-year-old father and his sixteen-year-old son scouted the offerings of Harley-Davidson, Indian, and dozens of other maiden motorcycle makers, though exactly what they were plotting isn't clear. Ignaz recently had ordered his bicycle engineers to design a Schwinn motorcycle, and the ink drawings on linen paper reveal a machine whose powerful engine and drive shaft were a good two decades ahead of other domestic models, says Jim Rogers, a historian with the American Motorcyclist Association in Westerville, Ohio. Yet Ignaz never built his brand-name motorcycle. Instead, he entered the business in a cheaper fashion by acquiring the financially ailing Excelsior Motor Manufacturing & Supply Company of Chicago in 1911 for $500,000. It was a smart buy. Excelsior and its X model motorcycles, first produced in 1905, were among the best names in the fledgling field, and the company had an estimated $200,000 in orders for the coming year. Excelsior sales zoomed in 1912, after the X became the first motorcycle officially clocked at 100 miles per hour. In 1914, Ignaz built near his bicycle plant what was then the largest motorcycle factory in the world—a 290,000-square-foot concrete showcase with touches of terra cotta ornamentation and delicate iron grillwork that recall the art of Chicago architects Louis Sullivan and Frank Lloyd Wright. Three years later, he expanded by purchasing the prominent but debt-plagued Henderson Motorcycle Company of Detroit for about $285,000. If Excelsior was considered the fastest (a young Charles Lindbergh rode a 1920 Big X), Henderson was the finest (a 1912 model was the first to circle the globe, and the luxury machines were finished in royal blue and gold). Ignaz now owned both. He merged the two logos by floating Excelsior's trademark X behind the Henderson name. His Excelsior-Henderson motorcycles soon had an international reputation for both engineering and pizzazz—especially the trade show models, accented in sparkling white enamel—and the company ranked with Harley-Davidson and Indian as the "Big Three" in the industry.

The motorcycle business had become Ignaz's passion (a Chicago telephone book in 1917 lists him as "president-treasurer, Excelsior Motor"—no word of the bike company), and Frank W. shared his father's appetite for the business. "You will have to get up early in the morning if you get to the Excelsior factory in Chicago before Frank Schwinn is at his desk," the trade magazine *American Bicyclist and Motorcyclist* reported solicitously in 1921, "for Frank is the son of his father when it comes to being on the job." A photograph taken several years earlier shows the younger Schwinn looking dashing and a little dangerous outside the factory on an Excelsior Big X. Corporate lore says the teenager talked his way out of speeding tickets by noting that his father's company supplied motorcycles to Chicago's police department. Frank W. joined the family business full-time after World War I, grandson Richard C. Schwinn said in a 1994 speech at the Mountain Bike Hall of Fame in Crested Butte, Colorado. "He went to engineering school at night for a few years," Richard added, "but his day job gave him too much practical experience to keep his interest in getting a degree."

The market for motorcycles sputtered in the late 1920s, then came the stock market crash of 1929 and the country's plunge into the misery of the Great Depression. Ignaz had "immersed himself in the financial speculation rampant in the Roaring Twenties," according to Richard, and "bet heavily on the stock market and lost almost everything." The founder soon squeezed the brakes on the motorcycle business, although the public explanation had a sunnier spin. "We are out of production," Excelsior's sales manager wrote to a motorcycle dealer in early 1931. "It is not a case of financial distress, but simply that Mr. Schwinn has been in active service for close on to sixty years and he is worn out and tired and wishes to retire. He feels that after his long service in the manufacturing game, he is entitled to a rest." Ignaz had turned seventy-one that year, yet he retained the title of president for another seventeen years, counseling Frank W. during some of the company's darkest days, representing the firm at public functions and retaining final say over major investments. With Excelsior closed, Frank W. shifted his attention to the bicycle side of the business, bringing his elite motorcycle engineers with him. The thirty-seven-year-old vice president was now running the show. Executive-level underlings even addressed him by his initials,

F.W., like some bigwig CEO in a *New Yorker* cartoon, but the picture was grim. Total U.S. bicycle sales had dropped to 285,000 in 1931 and plunged more than 30 percent a year later to 194,000—worse than the nadir of the bicycle bust three decades earlier. Schwinn sold only 17,000 units in 1931, most of them heavily discounted. F.W. had to do something, and that something was clear: Schwinn had to slap the American bicycle industry out of its stupor.

With informal consortia of manufacturers controlling bike producing and mass retailers bike selling, Schwinn and the other independents that survived the turn-of-the-century crash of the adult market[2] had spent some thirty years scrambling for "their scrap of bone from the powers that ran the industry," F.W. wrote in 1942 in a remarkably bitter collection of notes compiled for the corporate history celebrating Schwinn's fiftieth anniversary in 1945. F.W.'s vitriol was no secret within the company or the industry (his harangues against chain stores, for instance, were highlights of dealer meetings and trade show dinners after World War II), but the executive's fifty-three pages of angry musings never made it into print. Schwinn's official history was cleansed of his tale of the industry's greed and shortsightedness in the first third of the century.

Since children were about 95 percent of the market, and most retail sales were through mail-order houses and expanding department store chains that fastened their own nameplates on the product, few manufacturers saw any incentive to produce anything other than a basic model that could last a few years: a chintzy frame with spindly tires and a tinny "fuel tank," to humor a kid into imagining he was riding a motorcycle. "A bicycle was just a bicycle," F.W. sneered in describing the conventional wisdom, "and besides, the buyer wouldn't pay the increased prices needed for changes." The parts makers cemented this thinking by standardizing their products so they could keep their costs low and profit margins high. Improvements in materials, engineering, or design were avoided. "All bicycles were alike in appearance," F.W. wrote, "except perhaps that some were worse than others." For three decades, the dominant U.S. Rubber Company sold essentially one type of single-tube tire to American bike manufacturers. The New Departure Company did likewise with its coaster brakes. Same thing with the Torrington Company, which sold spokes, pedals, and handlebars. "When change was suggested to the suppliers of these items," F.W. recalled, "the suggestion was met with the condescendingly pitying smile one uses on a well meaning half-wit." Why? "Any change of any nature would increase costs."

Meanwhile, the rise of chain stores squeezed manufacturers from the other side. Ignaz Schwinn probably would not have survived the lean years that followed the turn-of-the-century bicycle bust if not for the patronage of Sears, at the time the largest seller of Schwinn-made bikes, mostly through its mail-order operations. In fact, the retail titan accounted for between 35 percent and 75 percent of Schwinn's annual sales before World War I. After that, Montgomery Ward was the major customer, with volume reaching one-third of all Schwinn sales in the early 1920s. But Ignaz, and later F.W., scorned their retail masters and the wild swings in annual business that resulted from being played against other suppliers. Around 1910, Sears management reportedly pressured Ignaz to use cheaper parts. His response was a roar: "Don't tell me how to build my bike!" Father and son saw no satisfaction and "very little money . . . wearing out men and machinery for a price so low that paying a decent wage and replacing equipment were out of the question," F.W. wrote in his 1942 notes. "Perhaps the worst of all, was the annual spell of worried anxiety about price and contract. If you lost the business, there was little or no chance in replacing the volume with other business in less than two or three years. If you got it again, it was a sorry thing at best."

As Sears and Ward's opened their own department stores and expanded their dollar-a-week time-payment plans, they dominated the trade even further through discounts that hit the smaller local retailers and independent bicycle dealers who sold Schwinn's few better-made bikes. Sears, Ward's, and other national retailers with pull, such as Goodyear Tire and Rubber Company's automotive stores, demanded ever-cheaper parts and accessories to keep the final price of the product low. They even ordered Schwinn to stop sneaking its tiny "Seal of Quality" stickers on the frames, lest customers think the bike was anyone's but the store's.

Nothing could have seemed worse—until the parts makers and the chain stores hooked up. By 1925, the two camps were trading directly with one another, arranging to have the components delivered to the bike manufacturer, who merely packaged the goods with his simple frame sets (a diamond-shaped frame and fork and cranks) before shipping the final product to stores with a limited markup. "Cycle manufacturers were completely at the mercy of these large volume buyers, aided and abetted by the principal parts makers, who were quick to see on which side their bread was buttered," F.W. wrote. He saved his severest scorn, however, for his fellow manufacturers, who "had supinely accepted the standardization of parts so profitable to the parts maker, hadn't even chirped when the parts maker sold more than half of his bicycle to his customer direct, depriving him of any profit thereon, and besides, the good little fellow was always too grateful for the bone that was left him."

Surely, things couldn't get worse, but when sales of the look-alike bikes began their plummet at the end of the 1920s, Schwinn was cornered. The existing path could only lead to bankruptcy.

F.W.'s solution was boldly simple: *Make a better bike.* Most manufacturers hadn't had such a thought since Teddy Roosevelt was elected president. Yet F.W. and his Excelsior engineers had had to think that way every year, when they rolled out the latest motorcycle models to a market that annually demanded more power, more styling, more *more.* In the depths of the Great Depression, while Franklin Roosevelt ran for president, F.W. crafted a plan to reap new profits by making bikes bigger and flashier. By making something *swell.* Something that Junior would clench his wee fists and weep for. Something that Ma and Pa would have to buy for Christmas or they'd never hear the end of it. Something that smart retailers would have to sell or watch parents drive down the street to smarter stores.

The first order of business was the wheel. The parts maker that had cornered the American rim market offered a metal-clad circle of wood. And the tires were basically the same single-tubers the Victorians had pedaled on: scrawny things that couldn't survive a spin through a surprise patch of broken glass, rider flinching and steering—too late!—as a shard sank its fang into the all-too-vulnerable rubber. The hiss could be hushed, usually by plugging the puncture with a cement-coated rubber band, but there was more glass waiting over the next hill. "[T]he tires more than all the rest had held down the sale and popularity of the bicycle," F.W. wrote, aiming most of his ire at U.S. Rubber, the firm that had monopolized the single-tube bicycle tire market. The product was highly profitable for U.S. Rubber, but unfortunately for consumers it was "a glorified piece of endless garden hose with a valve in it," F.W. cracked, adding that "every puncture sold a new tire sooner or later, and mostly sooner."

European bicycles long had used wide cord tires whose double tubes provided a softer ride and better withstood local cobblestones and rural pavement. American autos rode on larger versions of the model, too. In fact, U.S. Rubber had produced the world's first such tire, for cars, back in 1903. Firestone introduced this lower air pressure "balloon" tire to the auto public twenty years later and it swiftly became the norm. But executives at U.S. Rubber "definitely and emphatically dismissed" the sturdier product as too "silly" for the domestic bike market, according to F.W. "The argument that there . . . had been for many years nothing but such tires, millions and millions of them, everywhere else in the world was met by the same attitude Galileo ran up against when he tried to sell 'Holy Mother Church' on the idea that the world was not only round but moved to boot."

Thwarted in America, the Schwinn executive and his wife traveled to England and Germany for two months in 1932 for "some cycle research," as well as visits to the family's many relatives in Hardheim. ("I found things much improved," F.W. wrote in a letter to Ignaz that summer. "They were glad to see us and we had them all to dinner at the Rose Inn. According to the bill for the dinner, they ate 56 marks worth of food, drank 16 bottles of *wein* and 72 glasses of beer. Total damages 156.29 reichmark.") The main objective, however, was to make contact with more than thirty industry sources in Europe. F.W. purchased a carload of balloon tires and other parts that were unavailable or too expensive in the States. When he returned, his ultimatum to U.S. Rubber was blunt: "Make tires, or I'll import." U.S. Rubber relented, grudgingly, and produced a first shipment of 5,000 fatter tires. Meantime,

Schwinn worked with Firestone (a supplier during the Excelsior motorcycle days) on matching rims while the bike company widened the vehicle's frames and forks to accommodate it all. And Schwinn's sales forces persuaded enough independent bike dealers and hardware store owners to give the new product a whirl. Most other retailers, and just about all parts makers and manufacturers, were skeptical. "The industry laughed out loud," F.W. wrote in 1942. "Note: They laughed first."

Schwinn's "Super Balloon Tire Bicycle" rolled across America in 1933 on a whopper of a tread more than two inches wide, with thick knobs that pinched pavement and lasted lots longer than those piddly one and one-half–inchers the other kids rode. The balloon tire was an instant hit with children who imagined themselves steering their own version of a rich man's Duesenberg and Schwinn shipments ballooned nearly 150 percent to surpass 100,000 bikes in 1935, the year the new tire became the standard in the industry. "The heretic," as F.W. rather smugly referred to himself in his notes, had astounded his adversaries.

They hadn't seen anything yet. A string of styles and gimmicks that transformed the rest of the vehicle was introduced throughout the 1930s, chased by double-digit sales increases. In 1934 came the Aero Cycle—"built like an airplane fuselage," read the trade ads. The bike's tougher frame and tinseled accessories mimicked the streamlining movement that was raging through transportation design. It cost $34.95—twice the price of the competition—but the difference was dramatic, irresistible, like a movie changing to color from black and white. The Aero Cycle's sweeping lines, rounded tank, auto-style fenders, chromium-plated headlight, and built-in horn button offered the first real change in bike design in a generation and a half—and loudly advertised to both the trade and the consumer that Schwinn was a different kind of company. "The thing looked like it was bullet-proof," says former bicycle museum curator James Hurd. It was followed in 1935 with the Cycle Plane, an under-$30 version of the Aero Cycle with a lifetime guarantee that became the industry's most successful new product of the year. Huffman and other chastened competitors had begun touting new designs and stronger materials. Wheel-parts maker Murray Ohio Manufacturing Company even hopped on with its own line of bicycles in 1936.

But Schwinn was on a roll. It introduced the built-in Cyclelock, with cheaper theft insurance via Schwinn; the front-wheel brake for added safety; the forged-steel handlebar stem for extra strength; the "full-floating" saddle and seatpost for comfort (the suspended seat could rise and fall subtly with the cadence of the road); the "knee-action" spring fork for smoothness (similar to the coiled shock-absorbing device on the front of a motorcycle); the cantilever frame for stamina (another future industry standard); and the Paramount line of exquisitely designed lightweight European-style racing bikes for adults (the first such offering by a U.S. manufacturer since the turn of the century). All told, Schwinn was awarded more than forty patents during the 1930s, while its annual production hit 346,000 by 1941, more than twenty times what the company had sold just ten years earlier. And F.W. had done nothing less than lead the bicycle industry out of the Depression, as parents who couldn't afford the pricier Schwinns snapped up lower-cost copycats and propelled total U.S. bike sales to nearly 1.3 million units by 1940—higher than even the peak of the bike boom in 1899.

F.W. also had led another portion of the industry, the upper end of the market that was moving toward the independent dealer and away from the mass merchants. Schwinn had turned itself into the largest producer of bicycles in the country by peddling quality. "The American public," F.W. boasted in his notes, "would pay more for something if it was convinced that the value was there." Small dealers, who now had a brand that the hometown Sears, Ward's, Goodyear, or Firestone store didn't, hawked their offerings as "Schwinn-Built," turning the family name into an upscale commodity—something separate from the bike itself. Tire giant B. F. Goodrich Company discovered the power of the brand when it contracted with Schwinn in 1935 to supply bikes for its new chain of retail stores. Goodrich at first demanded its own nameplate and exclusive trimmings. "Almost immediately," F.W. wrote, "Goodrich retail stores met up with that general nuisance, the question about the Schwinn-Built Bicycle." Within two years, Goodrich's bicycles sported both the Schwinn seal and the manufacturer's lifetime guarantee. The retailer even touted those facts in its advertising campaigns nationwide. "A miracle had happened," F.W. gloated, "a chain outlet had, of its own accord, given up the alleged advantage of a private label, and was selling a nationally advertised product identified by the mark of the maker"—a rarity, at the time, for consumer goods and appliances. By 1941, Goodrich accounted for about 25 percent of total Schwinn sales, and bikes had become the retailer's "third largest dollar item," according to F.W.

The despised parts makers learned their lessons, too. Schwinn used its new clout to force suppliers to make exactly what the company wanted. F.W. relished the role reversal. "The company did its own engineering and designing and, what was worse, cost analyzing," he wrote. "When a . . . parts maker didn't see the light in quality, style or price, [Schwinn] promptly stepped out, and with its now considerable volume established new sources or made the item itself. Unheard of and unthinkably impudent impudence on the part of the bicycle manufacturer." Other sources confirm the dynamic. In its 1963 obituary of F.W., trade magazine *American Bicyclist and Motorcyclist* quoted a Schwinn competitor who years earlier had visited a supplier selling brakes to both bike makers. "They treated me like visiting royalty," the manufacturer recalled, "but I could tell whose orders they were working on. Over the inspection tables was a sign: '*Attention, Schwinn!*' "

Of course, the Schwinn-sparked bike boom had profited the entire industry, which cheered as the market for children's cycles exploded more than 600 percent in less than a decade. Even U.S. Rubber long since had seen the light, proving an eager convert to the ideas of "the heretic" and his aging father. When Ignaz Schwinn died in 1948, U.S. Rubber chief executive Noel H. Lanham eulogized his company's onetime adversary as "a great man, a worthy business associate, as well as a good friend."

Although F.W. had been de facto CEO for more than fifteen years, Ignaz had held the top title—president—until his final breath at age eighty-eight. The patriarch had stepped back from day-to-day management around 1931, and a year later, his wife, Helen, died. (Helen, says a family member, brought Ignaz his lunch every day at the factory.) The remaining time was spent living with F.W. and his daughter-in-law, Gertrude, their two sons,[3] and the occasional visiting relative from Germany in a sprawling fifteen-room house on northwest Chicago's elegant Humboldt Boulevard. Brick mansions, stone town houses, and shaded parkways graced much of the neighborhood, home to some of the city's most successful German and East European immigrants. Nearby Humboldt Park was an urban marvel, with meandering lagoons, boathouses, formal rose gardens, even a miniature prairie. Ignaz installed a turntable in his garage floor so he could turn around his car every morning, rather than trouble with backing it out to the street. Court documents filed with his will list many of the trappings of wealth: maid quarters, billiards room, old Persian and Chinese rugs, heavy oak and mahogany furniture, Steinway piano, bronze figurines, Laguna pottery, Limoges china, pearl-handled silverware, engraved crystal goblets, and, in the reception room, four leather-bound volumes of Edward Gibbon's *Rise and Fall of the Roman Empire.* Chicago dealer Oscar Wastyn, Jr., (whose grandfather was a preeminent bike designer and friend of both Ignaz and F.W.) remembers cycling past the house as a boy and spying Ignaz napping in his screened front porch.

With his cottony white hair and short, stout frame, Ignaz "looked like a little brewmaster," says former employee Gary Fusz. Indeed, he often played the role of lovable old wise man at corporate and industry functions. After employees presented him with a birthday "bouquet of the finest flowers," *American Bicyclist* reported, Ignaz reciprocated by "making the rounds of all the offices and leaving a rose on the desk of each girl employee." A 1939 photograph shows a seventy-nine-year-old Ignaz standing alertly as he congratulated a member of Schwinn's Paramount Racing Team following a six-day marathon in Chicago (the 1890s endurance contests had resurged in popularity during the Great Depression). But signs of wear can be seen in a photo five years later, when Ignaz needed a cane just to sit upright during F.W.'s acceptance of a U.S. Navy award for excellence in the production of materiel. (Schwinn designed and made artillery casings and other supplies for both the navy and army. As a navy commander explained at the 1944 ceremony: "You have kept up a high standard of quality that resulted in a need for rejecting less than one percent of your production. That makes you practically perfect." Management did its patriotic duty during work hours, according to F.W.'s 1942 notes, and spent evenings and weekends plotting corporate strategy and developing future bike models for the coming postwar market.)

Company old-timers say Ignaz was going blind and feeble, pinching a nurse's behind one moment and rambling unintelligibly the next. The signatures grew shakier with each codicil to his will. Nevertheless, when Ignaz did shuffle into headquarters, it often was at his customary early hour, and he always was escorted by his son. An *American Bicyclist* correspondent was impressed with the show of devotion. "I love that old gentleman," was F.W.'s unadorned response. Apparently, so did many others; if not love, then at least respect. When Ignaz died late in the summer of 1948, after heading the company through boom and bust and boom again for fifty-three years without posting a loss, hundreds of floral arrangements flooded the funeral home—bountiful offerings from competitors, customers, and cyclists, including a full-size bicycle made of flowers. Nineteen limousines and flower cars followed his coach. Draping the casket was a blanket of lilies bearing the single word, *Father.*

Ignaz bequeathed his two married daughters, Elizabeth and Margaret, their mother's jewelry (valued after his death at a mere $316) and left his son the house in Humboldt Park and a summer mansion in Lake Geneva, Wisconsin. The three divided the rest of the estate's official assets, valued at about $461,000, before inheritance taxes. But the real money lay in a trust their father had established in 1920 to govern the company's management and distribution of profits after his death: Each would receive one-third of the annual dividends—a tidy fortune, in those days, that could reach several hundred thousand dollars or more annually apiece. In the Old World spirit of primogeniture, however, Ignaz awarded all shareholder powers to his first son and succeeding first sons. The daughters and their offspring would enjoy the fruits of the business, but they never could have any real say in its operation. It was a provision that would lead to resentments and rivalries for the rest of the family company's history.

The year 1948 saw the passing of another tradition at Schwinn: the last private label bicycle rolled off the assembly line that year. No more making products for others to clap their names on, F.W. told his factory workers proudly. From now on, Schwinn would sell only Schwinn. He and his management team were working on creating the nation's strongest network of independent bicycle dealers, all selling premium-price Schwinns at a premium profit. Of course, no one in the industry had accomplished such a thing, but F.W. had heard that sort of refrain fifteen years before.

Not that his confidence should be confused with cockiness. Far from it, in fact. Former *American Bicyclist* publisher Stuart J. Meyers remembers meeting with F.W. in Chicago in the 1950s, not long after the young man had inherited his father's magazine. Their conversation was wide-ranging and eventually turned to the new publisher's fears about handling so many responsibilities and business problems. "I can't give you the answers," F.W. told Meyers, "but I want to tell you something important. You're probably feeling very inadequate because you've got these problems. A young man in business is in danger of thinking that some day, when he has really mastered his job, everything will go smoothly. It is never going to happen. You had better know now that business means trouble. The two words are inseparable. From now on, you won't be out of trouble until you're out of business."

3

THE OLD MAN

F. W. Schwinn hurled a pair of pliers on his desk, smashing its glass top. Investigating a complaint about defective pedals, he'd taken them apart and found they indeed were flawed. "The Old Man was shaking, he was so mad," recalls Ray Burch, sales promotion manager at the time. The boss buzzed for general manager Bill Stoeffhaas and commanded him to summon the factory's chief inspector. "You let this stuff in with my name on it," F.W. yelled at the hapless overseer. "Get out, before I say something I shouldn't."

F.W. was demanding, to say the least, and his personal and professional standards dominated Schwinn in the 1950s. The company was capitalizing on postwar prosperity and revved-up demand for consumer goods. As young veterans and their families settled into Cape Cods and ranch homes in identical suburbs sprouting across the nation, they bought Philco television sets, Frigidaire and Kelvinator refrigerators, and the latest model Buick or Chevrolet. Americans no longer purchased goods solely for function, using them until they wore out. They sought style, status, sparkle. Not just new, but *brand*-new. It was out with the old, in with the Formica. Goodbye, gabardine; hello, rayon. TV trays and boomerang coffee tables, Jell-O molds and Waldorf salads. Mom in her cashmere twin-set, plugging in the Mixmaster; Dad in his Ray Bans, plucking the maraschino from his Manhattan. And the kids? Outside in the fresh air, of course, plying the streets on their Schwinns.

The latter was no false '50s stereotype—Schwinn made one of every four bikes sold in America in 1950. This was the era of the Black Phantom, the top-of-the-line balloon-tire bike that was introduced in 1949 and gripped many a young heart for the next ten years. Schwinn's Phantom was an instant American classic. "It was like the '57 Chevy convertible," says former bicycle museum curator James Hurd. "Upon looking at it, you just wanted one." Priced high, from $80 to $90, the Phantom was a beauty swathed in chrome, its fenders gleaming as you opened the garage door. And it was built like a little truck, confidently taking subdivision curbs head-on. The bike weighed 62.5 pounds, and much of the extra heft came from the chrome—layer upon layer of it, plating the fenders and portions of the spokes, frame, horn tank, handlebars, and Styleliner headlight. The snazzy look emulated the autos of the era, just as Schwinn's 1934 Aero Cycle copied the industrial streamlining movement of its age. This time around, children wanted their own version of the family car: the chrome bumpers, big and rounded and rippling in the sunlight, the flashy trim, the whitewalls as wide as their tires, and the fins stretching out and up toward the heavens. In truth, the Phantom's "fins" were more suggested than real—the curve of the headlight, the slight flip of its fenders, end-tips jutting just so from the rear rack—but the rest of the bike loudly said, "Cadillac." A dealer could close a sale by pointing to the springed front-end and noting how it helped absorb road shocks. "Drives just like a Caddy, son. Howdja like to give it a spin?" Back home, the Phantom's lavish chrome required as much attention as a car's: While Dad washed his vehicle, Junior soaped his, wiping the saddle springs dry to ward off rust and buffing the fenders until they shone so bright they reflected the world as truly as a mirror. Pals would crowd 'round, lean in close, and watch faces stretch into funhouse shapes, giggling as their breath fogged the images into memories.

Each Phantom sale had the new owner's friends coveting their own.

The wooing of the wallet would begin: postwar parents, who perhaps had been denied their own dream bike during the Depression, often found it impossible to resist the strategic sniffles, the sad little eyes. The crush for Phantoms and other Schwinns had the company's factory producing more than 400,000 bikes a year. Although market share peaked in 1950 at 25 percent, Schwinn maintained a share in the mid-teens in a steadily growing market. The outlook was rosy: "35 million kids by 1960!" exclaimed a 1951 edition of the in-house newsletter, *The Schwinn Reporter*, citing expanding birth rate forecasts. "Everyone engaged in the bicycle business is bound to gain."

Schwinns weren't selling only on style. They were tough and durable. The frames carried "The Schwinn Lifetime Guarantee, without a parallel in the bicycle industry," according to brochures of the period. Paint "never cracks or peels," the company promised. The policy also included all parts made by Schwinn's suppliers. (A Colorado customer wrote the company in 1975, "Just wondering whether to replace the tires on my wife's 1940 Schwinn New World bike.") The company's obsession with quality was due to F.W. The "Old Man," as many veterans even today refer to him, was a perfectionist who'd blast parts makers at conventions for cheapening their products to please Sears and the other price-conscious chain stores. He was a terror—a stickler with a temper—and the factory was his province. No one knew more about the nuances of plating and painting, punch presses and screw machines, welding and heat-treating. "One day I tried to fool him," says retiree Phil Cicchino, who used to be a general foreman in the special parts department. "I couldn't set a machine, and I tried to talk my way out of it. He said, 'I'm an engineer. You can't fool me.' "

"You couldn't change the nuts, screws, and bolts on a bike without his approval," says Al Fritz, who began his forty-year Schwinn career in the factory and rose to executive vice president, the No. 2 post. It was a familiar sight to employees: F.W. dashing into his office, coat flying, hat on, buzzing for a subordinate or simply beckoning with a stern glance. Every afternoon, after the factory closed at 3:30, the Old Man would stride through, inspecting work in progress and peeking at designs still on the drawing board. If he uncovered a screwup, Fritz says, "It would hit the fan; the riot act would go." One day in the mid-1950s, F.W. was sorting through a batch of head cups, a part that holds the bearing where the fork rotates. He found a defective one, recalls nephew Rudolph Schwinn, a longtime company engineer who sometimes tagged along on the tours. "He stood by the box until they removed it from the floor. He made the engineer inspect every one. There were thousands of them, and it took days."

F.W. wasn't just concerned with nuts and bolts. Once, he asked a metallurgist to oversee the company's conversion to a new method of heat treating. The technician suggested F.W. should compensate him for the additional work. "He fired him right there, just told him to leave," says Fritz, who at the time was F.W.'s secretary. "He was so angry, he was vibrating." Still furious, F.W. said he wanted any request for a job reference on the metallurgist passed to his desk. "You know what that S.O.B. wanted from me? He tried to blackmail me," he told Fritz. "He was telling me that to undertake this new project, I would have to pay him more money. Now, if he had done the job and come to me and proven himself, well . . . yes."

The Old Man could be tough on his own sons, too. Veteran Schwinn dealer George Garner remembers writing to F.W. about troublesome brackets on the bottom of three-speed bikes that could bend too easily and cause the gears to go out of adjustment. Later, when Garner was visiting the Chicago factory and killing time in the showroom, he noticed the problem hadn't been fixed. Garner brought this to the boss's attention. F.W. leaped from his chair and sprinted into the office of his youngest son, Edward.

"What happened to that bracket I told you about?" the Old Man demanded.

"It's right here," Edward said casually, "in my drawer."

"What's it doing there?" the father roared. "It's supposed to be fixed and on the bike!" Two weeks later, it was.

Nephew Rudolph Schwinn says F.W. fired Edward twice. "But each time he came home, his wife, Gertrude, said, 'You can't fire your son.' "

F.W. had his own way of fessing up to his missteps. Sales executive Ray Burch notes an early-1950s meeting with distributors in Boca Raton,

Florida, at which the company was prepared to launch "suggested" retail prices. Burch had argued this would make Schwinn's consumer advertising more effective. Nevertheless, at the last minute, a distributor from Louisville, Kentucky, gained the Old Man's ear and counseled against it, arguing that dealers needed the flexibility to negotiate their own prices with a wavering customer. After lunch, F.W. stood up and announced, "We'll not have suggested prices at this time." Burch, flabbergasted, left the session fuming. Back at his hotel, he received a telephone call from general manager Bill Stoeffhaas: "The boss would like you to come to his house." Burch drove to F.W.'s winter home outside Boynton Beach for lunch the next day, prepared for the worst. Yet F.W., sitting on the patio and working on an engineering drawing, greeted him warmly. Over soup and iced tea, he chatted about the state of the economy—no word on the sore subject. Only as Burch was leaving did he mention, "I like the idea of suggested prices." On the drive back, Burch realized, "This is his way of apologizing." Stoeffhaas confirmed it when he called asking how the lunch went. The new pricing policy, he told Burch, had been approved.

Although F.W. cast a long shadow over the company, he was slight and frail in his later years, and he struck many close observers as something of a hypochondriac. "His drawer was full of pills," says Bill Chambers, longtime manager of dealer relations, "and he had thick books on medicine." Every Tuesday morning, a nurse would give him a vitamin shot in the buttocks. Every six months, he had a hospital physical. Newcomers to the executive suite learned to endure his impromptu lectures on proper diet and exercise.

F.W. was a slight figure in Chicago's civic scene, too. Although his family name was famous, he didn't play a memorable role among the city's business elite. Many financiers and industrialists spent their lunches hobnobbing high above the Loop in sequestered dining clubs and their evenings sealing commercial relationships with spouses at glittering charity events and fund-raising parties. Indeed, Chicago's concentrated business district ensured that corporate and civic boards were intertwined tightly. But F.W. and Gertrude would have none of it. "They were low-key all the way," says Rudolph Schwinn. "They wanted to be left alone." Adds former dealer relations manager Bill Chambers, "I never saw their name in the paper."

Rather, the Schwinns looked inward, to family and friends. They lived comfortably but not ostentatiously in the same Humboldt Park home that had belonged to Ignaz Schwinn. A live-in housekeeper cooked hearty meat-and-potatoes meals and set platters on the table for the family to help themselves. On most days, a chauffeur drove F.W. in his Cadillac to the factory two miles away. If Gertrude had the car, F.W. might ask a Schwinn worker for a lift home. "Boss, I'd drive you, but I've got an old Jeep," former parts and service manager Keith Kingbay once apologizied. Much to Kingbay's surprise, the Old Man enjoyed the ride.

"He was not given to great levity," says Charles Y. Freeman, a grand-nephew of F.W.'s wife, but he enjoyed conversation about current events, especially politics, where he tilted to the conservative and admired J. Edgar Hoover and General Douglas MacArthur. "We sat up until three in the morning when Eisenhower was elected in 1952," Rudolph Schwinn says. "He made me a Republican." F.W. was perhaps more ambivalent when it came to religion—attending church, for instance, less often than Gertrude, who came from an Irish Catholic family on Chicago's West Side. (Gertrude was one of five Walsh girls, some of whom married good names. The oldest sister wedded Fred McNally of the Rand McNally map-making clan; another married into the John M. Smythe family, at the time one of Chicago's most prominent furniture retailers. The women weren't particularly involved in each other's lives, according to Freeman. Gertrude preferred to pursue her charity work: She'd ask the priest at nearby St. Sylvester Church which families needed help, then donate money anonymously. In the late 1950s, when the aging couple decided to move to a downtown apartment not far from fashionable North Michigan Avenue, they gave their home to the church, which built a school on the site and named its cafeteria and stage area Schwinn Hall.)

Instead, F.W. found his inner peace through fishing. He reconstructed a dark-green panel truck—appropriately dubbed "The Fishin' Wagon"—so that his boat could slide down easily from the roof. Inside, the floor had been waterproofed, and a pegboard held the exotic fishing tackle he enjoyed collecting. During F.W.'s winter sojourns in Florida, he'd sometimes invite Chicago bicycle dealer and frame builder Emil Wastyn for a fishing trip. Once a year, he'd undertake a more elaborate adventure to Canada or Northern Michigan—places he liked to call "God's Acres"—with other business owners. Eldest son Frank V. Schwinn once asked Kingbay, "Pop tells those guys about this wonderful fishing spot. But there's no inside plumbing. I wonder what they think?" Kingbay answered, "They're thinking the same darn thing—that they're happy to get away where people aren't bowing and kowtowing to them."

The Old Man angled most often on Lake Geneva in southern Wisconsin, where the Schwinn family spent summers for more than seventy years. Lake Geneva was once an exclusive enclave for Chicago's leading industrialists—the "Newport of the West," it was called—and its heyday was between 1880 and 1914, when big business names like chewing gum magnate William Wrigley, Jr., and meatpacking executive Edward F. Swift owned opulent estates and imposing yachts. Summers included exuberant birthday parties and gala regattas, or just a lazy Sunday cruise to the strains of Wagner or Brahms from a Victrola on the deck. By the time Ignaz Schwinn bought in, around 1920, the houses were getting smaller, the community less exclusive. Built on four acres, the Schwinn property didn't match the twenty-acre spreads of established neighbors, but it was no shack. The home was a stately six-bedroom, six-bathroom brick mansion filled with the arriviste accoutrements of the era: Oriental rugs, English walnut chairs, a Chickering player grand piano. There was a greenhouse and caretaker quarters, a six-car garage, and more than 300 feet of private lakefront. Ignaz bequeathed it all to F.W., who built a tram from the house to the dock, since it was a steep and sometimes tricky walk for Gert, as F.W. fondly called her. In the summer, he would spend weekdays at the factory and hurry to Lake Geneva on Friday afternoons. There, he enjoyed tinkering on the estate grounds. "The Old Man was so proud of every tree," Rudolph Schwinn says. Chicago bicycle dealer Oscar Wastyn, Jr., (grandson of Emil) remembers his family driving around the area on a house-hunting trip one overcast Sunday afternoon when his father, Oscar Sr., decided it would be fun to roll by the Schwinn estate. He spotted a man inconspicuously raking leaves and asked for directions. "You're here, Oscar." It was the Old Man himself.

If Lake Geneva offered refuge from Chicago's boiling summers, Florida was the place to escape its arctic winters. F.W. and Gertrude usually set off for their home near Palm Beach after New Year's Day, traveling by train while their chauffeur, Rush Smith, drove the Cadillac. The Schwinns wouldn't return until the ice had melted in April, but the boss never stopped working. He'd regularly mail to Chicago envelopes stuffed with memos about his conversations with dealers and designs for bikes, parts, or equipment. "After a week in Florida," Al Fritz says, "the mail would come in virtually daily filled with copious notes—instructions on every aspect of the business. He phoned very frequently, too. He ran up tremendous telephone bills."

Fritz also would work with F.W. at home in Chicago or in Lake Geneva. That happened more frequently in the early 1960s, when the Old Man was diagnosed with prostate cancer. "He'd instruct me to bring this or that. . . . I drove to his house and worked with him in the bedroom. I'd sometimes get a call at eleven at night. I never knew when I'd be home."

F.W.'s hard-driving ways and relatively simple lifestyle were a contrast to those of his sisters, Elizabeth and Margaret, the other beneficiaries of the trust established by their father in 1920. Ignaz Schwinn made certain his two daughters each received one-third of the dividends, but he gave them no shareholder rights. Barred from top management, they and their offspring often did what many heirs and heiresses do: they partied.

The two sisters had seven marriages between them and delighted in society life. They also were fiercely competitive. "They had to one-up each other," says Rychie Schwinn, former wife of one of Elizabeth's grandsons. After Elizabeth bought a ranch in Wyoming, Margaret found a larger spread in Arizona. "They'd get similar jewelry, too," she adds, "but do it bigger and better. They were like princesses. They never worked a day in their lives."

"They were crazy," says Bill Chambers, the former head of dealer relations. "F.W. had nothing to do with them." But he did take care of them. The sisters often clamored for more money, telling their big brother before he declared the annual dividend that they could use a larger one this year. "Margaret," Chambers says, "could spend money faster than he could give it. She was always calling asking for money." Elizabeth, a veteran of four marriages, in her later years lived alone in a downtown Chicago apartment, bedridden with multiple sclerosis. "She could only move her eyes," Rychie Schwinn says, "but she understood everything."

Elizabeth's only son was Clarence Braun, born in 1925 and named after his father, whom she divorced when the boy was young. The senior Ignaz Schwinn seemed especially taken with his playful grandson, and Elizabeth, perhaps mindful of her father's fascination with primogeniture and first-born sons, changed the boy's legal name when he was twelve—to Ignaz Schwinn II. (The new name didn't stick; eventually everyone just called him "Brownie.") His mother would live until 1974, and when she died, her son became the single largest shareholder, owning a third of the company's equity.

Brownie began his Schwinn career humbly, working as a grinder on a welding line during the 1940s, but he always had a hankering for fun. "We beat the daily mandated production rate by one P.M.," says Fritz, who also worked on the line at the time. "We went to the john and played cards." The bylaws of the family trust excluded Brownie from top management, but few believe he had the stuff anyway. He lived fast and drove fast. Brownie lost his left arm in a motorcycle accident in the late 1940s, and over the years became a true one-armed bandit. He was an accomplished golf hustler and crack pool player, using his left foot to cradle the pool cue. "He'd psych you out—get you all unnerved," according to Bill Hill, a Schwinn dealer in Fair Oaks, California. "He wouldn't talk to you if you didn't bet." Brownie would carve himself a cushy career at Schwinn, schmoozing with dealers and taking them drinking, golfing, gambling, even skeet-shooting. His alcohol-inspired antics became legendary. While visiting New Orleans, the twenty-six-year-old Brownie, dressed as a Keystone cop, was arrested and charged with disturbing the peace. The Schwinn name made the front page of the

October 24, 1951, edition of the *New Orleans Statesman* when two officers charged that Brownie was first "pushing people into a nightclub" then "out directing traffic in the middle of the street . . . acting crazy, yelling and screaming." The newspaper quoted one officer: "I told him it was fun, but that he'd better take a walk. He said, 'No, I won't take a walk. Go ahead, arrest me. Why don't you?' So we did." Brownie told police he had been to a costume party earlier that evening. "I was just having fun, not raising my voice or harming anyone." Though he pleaded not guilty, Brownie figured he didn't have much of a case. "The judge said, 'Ten days or ten dollars.' After observing the clientele of the jail, I paid my fine."

Back in Chicago, the Old Man was not amused. "F.W. blew his stack," Ray Burch says. It wasn't as if he only had relatives in the United States to watch out for; he also took care of cousins and other family in Germany, a practice Ignaz had started. (Years earlier, during a Depression-era trip to Europe, F.W. noted in a letter to his father that he was planning a stop in Hardheim, "which will cost you considerable in presents to the nephews and nieces, as I remember there are four in Uncle Franz's family, six in Uncle Joseph's and two in Uncle August's.") Al Fritz, by then F.W.'s secretary, took care of personal bills and sent clothing and gifts of bicycles. "I bought lingerie for women, too. There were thirty to forty relatives. I had a long list, I'd be gone for hours. I bought hundreds of pounds of candy at the [nearby] Brach factory at Christmas."

F.W. could afford to be generous: Schwinn was doing well. Although the family was private about its finances, former executives estimate the company generated sales in the range of $25 million in the mid-1950s—a midsized company for its time. The business literally was cyclical, and bicycles don't carry huge profit margins, yet Schwinn was managed with a sharp eye on the bottom line and was consistently profitable.

It wasn't a bad place to work, either. As with so many family-owned businesses, Schwinn was, well, like a family. The factory dominated a tight patch in the heart of working-class northwest Chicago, and "it was common to have whole families" employed there, says retired foreman Phil Cicchino. He met his wife at Schwinn during World War II: He was working in the machine shop at night; she was inspecting artillery shells on the day shift. His brother and brother-in-law were in the machine shop, too. His sister was a secretary; his father-in-law handed out tools. Later, two daughters and a son would hold jobs at Schwinn. Then there were the five Schwartz boys—George, Freddie, Louie, Buddy, and Dempsey—and the Sikora clan: Casey and his three brothers (Fred for years ran the dealer service department); his wife, Dorothy; her brother and sister; and her brother-in-law, Tom Kujawa, who clocked nearly fifty years at Schwinn. "Basically, the whole family met their wives working there after the war," says Casey's son Bruce Sikora, who was a longtime regional sales manager in the Midwest; his brother, Chuck, was a Schwinn salesman in Minneapolis, and his wife's father, a Schwinn dealer in Kansas.

There were annual summer picnics at a state park in the far western suburb of St. Charles, turkeys at Christmas, and good food in the cafeteria prepared by local Polish women—kielbasa and pirogis, bread pudding, and "custard that was out of this world," according to Keith Kingbay. The workforce reflected the neighborhood: largely Polish, German, and Irish, with names like Rip Styczenski, Walter "Snuffy" Groth, and Nick "The Greek" Kantas. Before and after shifts, some would gather for a couple of beers and a hamburger at the Cycle Inn across the street from the factory.

Of course, life at Schwinn wasn't always an easy ride. The factory was cold in the winter and hot in the summer, when temperatures rose so furiously "the chrome on the wheels would burn your skin," according to former line worker Mary Jones. The plating department, with its cleaning solutions and hot baths, was even more grueling. Elsewhere, the roof leaked, old wood floors cracked open and the air always seemed gritty. Former national sales manager Jack Smith, who in the 1950s was in charge of the order department, had a desk in the middle of the factory floor where he calculated "piece work," or the rate workers were paid according to their daily output. Smith remembers one thing always slowing him down: "I had to dust the paper off."

Demand would rise and fall regularly, with Schwinn enjoying two or three good years, followed by three or four down years. That, along with the seasonal nature of bicycle sales, meant periodic factory shutdowns, even job cuts. "It slowed down in November and December and people got laid off before Christmas," says Stanley J. Natanek, who ran Schwinn's dealer service schools. "Frank W. would feel bad. 'What am I gonna do?' he'd ask." Many of those workers would return the following March or April, when orders traditionally picked up. But occasionally employees grew angry enough to walk off their jobs—over a pay dispute, perhaps, or an especially egregious work condition. "We were disorganized," Natanek says. "We'd go out for an hour and gather in the parking lot. People groused. Then the big wheels came out and wooed the people back in." Nevertheless, "it was a good place to work," he adds. "You could complain, but if an outsider said something bad, there was no way he could get away with it."

When there were grumblings at the factory, the fellow who often smoothed over disputes was general manager W. F. "Bill" Stoeffhaas, then the company's second-in-command. Stoeffhaas's tenure with Schwinn dated back to 1914, when he joined the family's Excelsior motorcycle business at age fifteen. Young F.W. brought Bill to the bicycle side when Excelsior was liquidated in 1931, and the two men with the transposed initials developed a sort of management yin and yang. Stoeffhaas was not product-oriented like F.W., but he was considered a first-rate administrator, handling matters from import competition to the company's bowling league. Stoeffhaas also was courtly and soft-spoken, often playing the comforting elder who smoothed frayed edges after one of F.W.'s tirades. "I don't think I ever heard him raise his voice," Al Fritz says. "He was well respected and well liked. An excellent complement to Mr. Schwinn." When Stoeffhaas died in 1969, "there was a parade of factory workers around the block of the funeral home wanting to pay their respects," says dealer Oscar Wastyn, Jr.

In their later years, both F.W. and Stoeffhaas delegated increasing responsibility to Al Fritz, who took over product design and manufacturing and became one of the most influential executives at Schwinn. Fritz, along with marketing guru Ray Burch, often are credited for many of the company's triumphs in the '50s, '60s, and '70s. Yet Schwinn family members would come to begrudge the men's success. F.W.'s grandson Richard Schwinn once grumbled to a Chicago dealer that Schwinn had made Burch and Fritz wealthy. To which the dealer retorted, "They made millions for Schwinn."

Fritz started his career at Schwinn in October, 1945—a cocky twenty-one-year-old with a full head of wavy hair and plenty of stories to tell. He was just out of the army, where he had served as a staff sergeant at MacArthur's headquarters in Brisbane, Australia. Now he was a lowly welder, but he had a twinkle in his eye. "Bill," he told Stoeffhaas after the general manager had returned from vacation, "it's not a good practice for us both to be away at the same time," as if he were of equal ranking to the executive. Stoeffhaas failed to see the humor. (There always would be some awkwardness between the two: Fritz's older brother had been married during the war, but his wife, who came to work at Schwinn, later had the marriage annulled and wed Stoeffhaas.)

Fritz was raised in a bungalow in northwest Chicago, the seventh of eight kids. He had studied to be a court reporter and knew typing and shorthand, so when he was told of an opening in the Schwinn office, he jumped at the opportunity. It turned into a front-row seat: secretary to the Old Man. "When F.W. died, Al was so entrenched; he knew the whole operation," Wastyn says. The velvet-voiced Fritz would prove to be an innovator in his own right. He is given credit for Schwinn's wildly successful Sting-Ray, with its high-rise handlebars and banana seat, and the company's novel stationary exercise bicycle, the Air-Dyne, which helped prop up corporate profits when Schwinn was losing money on bikes in the late '80s. Retired now, Fritz's eyes still brighten when he talks about his forty years with the company, at least when it comes to the good years. "I woke up running," he says. "I was anxious to get to work."

His right-hand man was Frank Brilando, Schwinn's top engineer, who could fit Fritz's sometimes far-out design schemes to the confines of factory production. Brilando was more technician than visionary, but he was the man who ultimately made sure Schwinn bikes lived up to their lifetime guarantees. It also helped that he was a good-natured target of ruses or practical jokes by Fritz, who rarely resisted taking advantage of Brilando's narcoleptic tendencies during work trips.

A down-to-earth, hands-on guy of few words and solid form, Brilando grew up building and racing bicycles with his brother on the South Side of Chicago. He became enamored with racing at fourteen, in the late 1930s, a time when biking shorts were cotton, not Lycra, and helmets were made of leather. Racing still was exotic stuff in America then—Brilando had to build his own derailleur bikes, because single-speeds were about the only style available—and he'd attract considerable attention whizzing through the neighborhood or riding long distances through farmland outside the city. He made the 1948 U.S. Olympic team at trials in Milwaukee, and the twenty-three-year-old kid was excited when he traveled to London to represent his country, but disaster struck when he got a flat tire during his 100-mile race. "I was pretty down," Brilando says today, "but I got over it." After earning a mechanical engineering degree, Brilando started at Schwinn as a draftsman in 1951. During his forty years there, he accumulated fifteen patents, including one in the 1970s for an added feature to quick-release wheels that prevented them from popping off inadvertently. "I thought I'd be interested for a few years," he says. "Then I found a home."

Rounding out this trio was Ray Burch, the marketing chief whose greatest contribution to the company would be overhauling Schwinn's unwieldy distribution system (industry press actually called him the "Master of Selective Distribution") and prodding bicycle dealers to clean up their erstwhile grimy act.

Burch was born in Austin, Texas, in 1912 and grew into a man who struck most people as naturally friendly and just as naturally driven. After finishing the University of Texas, he dabbled in department store retailing and aircraft manufacturing in California before establishing, in the mid-1940s, a successful career at motorbike maker Whizzer Motor in Pontiac, Michigan. Whizzers were motorized bicycles that could zip along at up to 35 miles an hour. The company sold its motors and parts to Schwinn dealers, who put them together using sturdy Schwinn cantilever frames. Thus, Burch already knew the players when Bill Stoeffhaas called one day in 1950 to ask if he wanted a job. "I had great respect for Schwinn," recalls Burch. "They were as well known as Coca-Cola." He offered to work for his same salary, around $17,000 a year, but Stoeffhaas said, "We don't pay like that over here." Burch cut a deal: He'd chop his pay and work at Schwinn's price—$13,000—for one year, but after that, "I'll get my price or I'll go." The odds were not in his favor; a parade of men had held the sales promotion manager's post being offered. When one Schwinn distributor joked at a meeting that he was awarding Burch a 21-day pin for longevity, F.W., sitting in the back of the room, said sternly, "Let's get on with the meeting." A year later, Burch got his price.

4

DEALER AND ÜBERDEALER

"Why do you want to be a dirty old bike mechanic?" George Garner's sister would ask. She wasn't the only one. In the late 1940s, most bicycle shops were dingy places, more often run from a greasy garage or backyard than a Main Street storefront. Mothers dreaded the prospect of herding their children inside when a bike needed repairs. Schwinn's top brass shuddered at the thought, too. "Joe's Bike Shop" was the catchall term they coined to describe the typical back-alley dealer. Unshaven and scratching his T-shirted gut, drinking beer with his buddies while some kid fixed flat tires in the dirt, old Joe wouldn't attract the new suburban family willing to pay a premium for Schwinn bikes.

Fresh out of the Marine Corps, George Garner vowed his store would be different. "I felt they should be cleaned up and made attractive, so people would want to come in. I liked bicycles; I didn't like people saying what a terrible business it was. I felt bicycle people needed more respect."

This he achieved, and more. Garner's earliest stores, in Southern California, were clean and orderly, brightly lit and efficiently run, and sales popped off the charts, drawing the attention of Schwinn headquarters. Executives realized that in Garner they had their prototype for a new kind of Schwinn dealer—not just the man's store, but the man himself. Fit, friendly, and faithful to all things Schwinn, Garner was transformed by the company's marketing machinery into *überdealer*, the kind of superbusinessman all good Schwinn dealers should strive to be. He was the company's No. 1 seller for 17 years in a row, and he held the top sales spot for 19 of 21 years, peddling as many as 10,000 bikes annually from his various stores. No dealer personified Schwinn more than Garner, and no dealer felt as crushed—betrayed, even—when the family enterprise crashed.

Garner grew up during the Depression in his grandparents' house in North Hollywood, California, the youngest of four children abandoned by their father. His mother helped make ends meet by baking and selling fruitcakes at Christmas. Young George did odd jobs, too, but there was nothing he liked better than working at the local bike shop, tinkering with hubs and handlebars, digging deep into boxfuls of parts and finding the right fix for a stubborn mechanical problem. It was something most other boys couldn't do, or most adults, for that matter. Garner usually hung out at the shop while playing hooky. Sometimes he made 25 cents an hour, sometimes nothing. One week, he earned $40. That kind of money made high school even less inviting, and his formal education ended in the eleventh grade. "They asked me to leave," Garner recalls, with some regret. "I was never there."

He became a marine during World War II, serving as an infantryman on Iwo Jima and a brig warden in occupied Japan. Returning home, Garner set his sights on opening his own bike shop. He had saved $300, mostly from war bonds, and he borrowed $1,200 from friends and $1,500 from a local bank, where the president seemed impressed by Garner's determination. That bought out the lease of a modest 10-by-60-foot hobby shop on a side street in the swelling San Fernando Valley town of Van Nuys. The store already sold bikes, but it also stocked lawnmowers and model airplanes, which Garner considered an annoying distraction. "I hated taking the model airplane kits out of the boxes and putting them back. One day a kid came in and asked to see one. I said, 'Here, you can have it. It's a gift.' " Other youngsters heard about the windfall and Garner gave away the entire inventory—more than 500 kits—in three days. "It was the best thing I ever did."

And so was born the modern bike store. Garner renamed it Valley Cycle, and sales built steadily as he honed his retail instincts. He sought ways to make his shop more appealing, studying the displays at Bullock's department store in Los Angeles, for example, and noticing that a neutral background made the merchandise stand out—a technique that worked well for showing off his store's colorful bikes. His experiments were proven beyond expectation—at an inviting store, the bicycles would sell themselves. At first, Garner sold several brands—Schwinn, Raleigh, and lesser-known labels—but he soon shifted totally to Schwinn because he liked the dealer-friendly sales terms and policies. Besides, the company's Paramount racers and middleweights (larger Americanized versions of the English three-speed bike) didn't stay in the store for long. Schwinn's longtime California bicycle distributor, Harry Wilson Sales Agency, was impressed, and president Bob Wilson put out the word: Here's a guy to watch.

Sales promotion manager Ray Burch visited from Chicago, and he rigged up a microphone and tape recorder to discern the secret of Garner's success. The first and somewhat typical transaction of the day told it all.

A twelve-year-old boy came in with his father and pointed to a Schwinn Traveler, a middleweight that was becoming popular in Southern California.

"This is the one, Dad."

"How much is it?" the father asked.

"$79.95," replied the low-key Garner.

"$79.95!" said the father, in mild sticker shock.

"Dad, all the kids have it."

"There was no sales talk," recalls an admiring Burch. "Zero. Little selling. Just a beautiful store."

No grubby mechanics at Garner's place; they wore white smocks and worked in a meticulous space partitioned from the selling floor. No excavating for oily spare parts; they were polished and encased in glass, like jewels at Tiffany's. Garner's standard offer to less-than-satisfied customers: "What can I do to make things right?" Basic merchandising by today's standards, but almost unheard of in the bike business at the time. Over the next decade, Schwinn's marketers repeatedly would trumpet Garner's recipes for success: big bright stores with picture windows on the main drag of town; spotless, systemized, and stocked with row after row of shining bikes beckoning passers-by to come on in and give 'em a ride. Schwinn's marketing literature called this new breed of retailing the "Total Concept Store," not just a bike shop, but an "ultra-modern Schwinn Cyclery."

Garner's store was just what Burch had been searching for as he set out to tame Schwinn's unwieldy distribution system. By the early 1950s, the decades-long shunning of most chain stores had exacted a price: Schwinn now was selling to almost anyone—some 15,000 outlets of varying ilk, including pool halls, gas stations, barber shops, even funeral parlors. The problem, as Frank W. Schwinn saw it, was that too many bikes were being handled by people who didn't know or care much about the product. That led to faults in assembly or repair and a chorus of customer complaints, potentially disastrous for a company touting a "no time limit warranty." These unsavory shops also didn't offer the proper assortment of models and styles the Old Man believed his customers deserved. Most significant, the fragmented distribution made it difficult to gain the undivided loyalty of aggressive dealers who held the key to boosting Schwinn sales, especially in the face of growing competition from lighter-weight European imports. "We cannot hope to have that measure of security," F.W. wrote in a 1950 memo outlining Burch's mandate, "until we bring some rhyme or reason into this picture and the dealer feels that he is safe and secure in building his business around our product."

The premise wasn't an easy sell even within Schwinn. General manager Bill Stoeffhaas and sales manager Paul Oberlin were skeptical that bike shops alone would provide enough volume to keep the factory going. Yet Schwinn's market share already was slipping from its commanding 1950 high of 25.5 percent of all bicycles sold in the United States. The figure slid to about 22 percent in 1951 and 1952, when competitors began catching up with their own Phantom-style offerings. Then imports began flooding the market after bicycle tariffs were reduced, soaring from 11 percent of total U.S. sales in 1952 to 40 percent in 1955. Schwinn's market share tumbled to 18.5 percent in 1953 and dropped even further before bottoming out an alarmingly low 13.7 percent in 1955, when F.W. and other chief executives of domestic companies pressured the federal government to reintroduce tariffs.

Ray Burch quickly amassed anecdotal evidence of the distribution and retail chaos that reigned. During a Schwinn training session at Marshall Field's mammoth State Street department store in Chicago, for instance, the salespeople "would sit and gab," he remembers. "They were toy department people, interested in dolls and toy trains. You couldn't make bike people out of them." Elsewhere, Burch and F.W.'s oldest son, vice president Frank V. Schwinn, called on a dealer in Louisiana and found a cruddy hole-in-the-wall. The owner had box after box filled with Sturmey-Archer three-speed hubs, yet he didn't know how the contraptions worked. When repairing bikes, he stripped out the gears, threw away the cables and levers, and turned them into single-speeds. "We realized," Burch says, "that even mechanics didn't know what they were doing."

The next step was to quantify the entire dealer mess, a project stymied by years of atrocious record-keeping. Who knew how many of the 15,000 accounts on Schwinn's mailing lists were active? Distributors supplied virtually no information about the dealers who handled the bikes. There were no sales analyses, no market-by-market breakdowns. "We didn't know where the bikes were going," says Bill Chambers, who would become Burch's aide-de-camp in developing the dealer ranks.

Chambers's experience with dealers stretched back to his boyhood job in a bike shop on Mackinac Island off Michigan's Upper Peninsula—a lucrative business, since cars are banned on the tourist haven. He served in the U.S. Coast Guard during World War II and returned to his hometown in 1946 with a day job on Schwinn's assembly line and college at night. He advanced to timekeeper in the cost department, and was preparing to take an oil company job paying $75 a week (almost 50 percent more than he was making at Schwinn) when Burch, needing help with his fledgling franchising program, called Chambers into his office.

"I hear you're leaving the company."

"Yeah," Chambers answered. "I wanted to get into sales, and I'm not making enough here."

"Hell, I'll give you $75."

Chambers already had earned a reputation as an up-and-comer. He was energetic, amiable, and had a keen memory. Those traits ultimately would serve him well in the powerful position of dealer relations manager: he could make friends easily and remember the names of a dealer's wife and children. Chambers also provided strong guidance to store owners, especially when it came to finding a site or obtaining financing. In some instances, Chambers handled the dirty work—he was the one to break the bad news that a dealer's franchise was being terminated. "He was real direct," says Burch. "But Bill had more friends than foes."

Chambers's first order of business under Burch was to decipher Schwinn's arcane record-keeping. He piled on the hours, often working until ten or eleven at night. The results: he discovered that 27 percent of Schwinn's retailers accounted for 94 percent of its sales.

The company sold most of its bikes through 22 independent distributors catering to the industry, while another 200 wholesale hardware distributors were responsible for just 13 percent of sales. They sold to any friend or connection, such as a cigar-store owner who wanted a Phantom for his twelve-year-old at a wholesale price. In some cities, there were only two dealers selling more than 50 bikes a year and as many as 230 "dealers" that were inactive. In Madison, Wisconsin, one hardware distributor sold 600 bikes annually to 1,200 dealers—an average of a half a bike per shop. Yet each name on Schwinn's master list of dealers was sent catalogs and other company material throughout the year. Bundles would be returned after every mailing, marked "Improperly addressed," "Moved," "Out of business," "Not listed at this address." Young Frank V. Schwinn, then overseeing sales and finance operations, found the duplication appalling. Perhaps it reminded him of his days as a procurement officer during the war—all that paperwork and waste for the simplest requisition. Why spend the family's money on thousands of people who aren't serious about Schwinn?

The solution, as fashioned by Burch, was to certify a corps of several thousand credible dealers and drop the undesirables. Schwinn executives called it franchising, although the parent company never collected fees or royalties on the Schwinn name. But they did control the rules of the game, approving store locations (with care, so that a new shop wouldn't nibble sales from an established dealer nearby) and supervising layouts and service standards—all in the name of maintaining quality. "If a guy can't make a living from you, you have no clout," Burch reasoned. "You want him to make a living, offer the chance to make him a millionaire."

The task at hand was to cut off the unproductive sellers, such as the hardware distributors and remaining department stores. Yet some executives wondered if Schwinn could justify its so-called selective distribution from a legal standpoint. Schwinn was restricting its distribution—did that also mean Schwinn ultimately was restraining trade and price competition? Burch had found much to be heartened about. A Chicago producer of laundry equipment called Thor Corporation had reported an impressive increase in sales after slashing its dealer base to 7,000 from 20,000. Burch also was encouraged after a two-hour meeting with a Federal Trade Commission official in Washington who acknowledged that manufacturers had the right to eliminate undesirable accounts, as long as the policy was openly stated and the company was evenhanded in enforcing standards.

The federal government later would argue otherwise. On April 26, 1957, the Department of Justice filed a massive antitrust case, charging the company with price-fixing and restraint of trade through its control of who did—and did not—sell Schwinns. Also named as defendants were the twenty-two independent distributors of Schwinn bikes to various outlets, as well as B. F. Goodrich Company, Schwinn's largest retail customer. The seriousness of the issue startled Schwinn executives, especially Burch. "My God," he thought. "The Old Man will say, 'You finally did it.' Better get my pencils together." Burch met with F.W. the following day, but the president was philosophical. "I don't want you to feel bad about this, Ray. You didn't do anything I didn't approve." Burch was relieved—and grateful. "He put the blame on his shoulder. I loved him for that."

F.W. was not going to let the government tell him how to run his business. He ordered into action his lawyers at what is now Chicago's Keck Mahin & Cate. To handle the crushing demand for legal documents, Schwinn rented an office three stories below the law firm's LaSalle Street suites and eventually filled twenty-seven five-drawer file cabinets with documents. "It took all our time, day and night, seven days a week," Chambers says. Schwinn managers and Keck lawyers who worked on the case met daily for lunch downtown in the LaSalle Hotel. The case lasted an astounding ten years, and would boil down to a single issue before the U.S. Supreme Court: whether Schwinn could restrict the sales of its independent distributors.

While the lawyers ground away, F.W. continued winnowing marginal dealers and narrowing his base of wholesalers. Schwinn already had eliminated fly-by-night shops, such as the shack on Chicago's West Side that sold bikes in the summer and Christmas trees in the winter. "We wrote a letter and I signed it," Chambers says. "If they called, I'd say: 'I see you aren't buying bikes. I can't afford to do business with you.' " It proved harder to break bonds with the hardware wholesalers. Some had ties with Schwinn dating back forty years, to the days of Ignaz Schwinn, who turned to hardware stores and other general retail outlets for salvation whenever his relationships with Sears or Ward's soured.

Paul Oberlin, Schwinn's imposing but genial sales manager, reluctantly broke the news to many longtime clients with his lip quivering. "I can't sell you any more."

"That's all right, Paul," one distributor consoled him.

"The guys almost felt sorry for us," Chambers says.

It would take more than a decade to purge all the troublesome retailers, and Schwinn's relationship with its remaining chain-store customer, B. F. Goodrich, ended when Goodrich signed a consent decree shortly before the government's antitrust trial finally started in the fall of 1962. (The chain sold its last Schwinn bike a year later.) Independent Schwinn dealers frequently had complained about unfair competition from Goodrich's automotive and appliance stores, which began selling Schwinns in the mid-1930s and accounted for nearly 25 percent of the bike company's total sales until the early 1950s. To Goodrich, Schwinns were a valuable loss leader—a retail term for a product that offers the proprietor little or no profit but draws customers into the store, encouraging them to linger long enough to be smooth-talked by salesmen with higher-margin goods in mind. Goodrich dangled discounted Schwinn tricycles in a store's front windows and lined the colorful two-wheelers just off the entrance. They were the first thing the kids saw when Mom and Dad dragged them along on a Saturday shopping errand. While children played *vroom-vroom,* parents bought tires or auto parts or household appliances. In these days before retail credit cards, Goodrich also offered long-term payment plans for Schwinns that ensured buyers would return to the store each week to make their $5 and $10 cash installments. That was a luxury few independent dealers could afford. They often griped to Schwinn representatives that Goodrich was almost giving away bikes, while they caught the brunt of customer complaints later if the Goodrich cycle wasn't assembled properly and needed repair.

George Garner regularly battled with a Goodrich store two miles away in Panorama City, California. The manager called and reproached Garner for offering too much on a trade-in. "It's a free country," Garner replied.

"I'm gonna come down and punch you in the nose," the angry competitor threatened.

"I'm here," Garner replied casually. The tire man never showed up.

When Goodrich finally severed its tie with Schwinn, some 1,700 retail locations were eliminated in a pen stroke. Burch's selective-distribution plan further whittled the total number of outlets to less than 3,000 by 1967, and finally to around 1,700. Schwinn parted with its last hardware wholesaler in the 1960s and funneled all sales through the twenty-two regional distributors, such as Chicago Cycle in Chicago, Harry Wilson Sales Agency in California, and Hans Johnsen Company in Dallas.

As Schwinn made the dealer pipeline smaller, it turned up the pressure by exhorting mom and pop retailers to become bigger and better merchants—and yanking Garner into the corporate limelight. He had never hesitated to pick up the phone and call Chicago to complain about a flaw in design or construction, so, in 1963, Schwinn's top guns flew him in for a week at the factory. "They picked me up at seven A.M. and dropped me off at ten P.M.," Garner says. "There were constant questions and answers. Burch was a master at picking people's brains. I was exhausted, but I really enjoyed it." Then Burch asked Garner to present the story of his success before a meeting of one hundred Schwinn salesmen and distributors at a Chicago hotel. Garner had never made a speech before—he was a high school dropout, after all. He agonized over the 25-minute script for a month, and was fidgety the night of the event as he waited for a motivational speaker to finish his spiel. He accidentally kicked the leg of the table. "Whatsamatter, George, you nervous?" teased F.W.'s younger son, Edward R. Schwinn. Garner began smoothly enough, but he soon lost his place in the script. "Everything was a blur. I stopped." The audience was sympathetic and he regained his composure. "I found my place and read it, slower. It went over well. People lined up to shake my hand."

Burch asked permission to reprint the speech and mail it to dealers, then he persuaded Garner to sign on as a consultant. Finally, he told him about a failing shop that was for sale in the fast-growing Chicago suburb of Northbrook. It was only 25 miles from the factory, and it could be used as a model store for out-of-town dealers who were visiting headquarters. Schwinn could arrange the financing. Interested?

Garner moved east to refurbish the store as a state-of-the-art bike-retailing mecca, right down to the 1890s cycling-motif wallpaper in the bathroom. (He'd later open similar stores in other towns around Chicago's toney North Shore.) Soon, the company's sample invoices and other order forms for business cards, signs, and promotional products all were stamped with the George Garner Cyclery logo. "Schwinn built me up as an image," Garner says today, but the relationship wasn't all PR. Garner was still a dealer in the thick of the marketplace. He could be counted on to dispatch his views from the trenches—good and bad—to the suits in Chicago. "We used to argue a point; I lost a lot, won some," he says. "One time I finally conceded, 'You win. I'll get going. You don't need me.' Burch answered, 'That's why I've got you, you're not a yes man.' "

By no means was Garner the only dealer with merchandising flair. In Santa Monica, California, Helen Throckmorton had fought the stereotype of Joe's Bike Shop since the late 1930s with her family's large and well-appointed shop. Even the name, Helen's Cycles, was chosen so that women would feel comfortable walking in. Throckmorton hired an architect in the early 1960s and opened a striking freestanding store with an open beam ceiling and floor-to-ceiling glass windows. "She was many years ahead," says former employee John Turner, now a West Virginia dealer. In New Orleans, Henry C. Bentz also was ahead of his time. A 1937 photo shows his Oak Street outlet in which nearly a hundred bikes were displayed in a clutter-free space, with white walls and ceiling and indirect lighting. Expensive models were placed up front. Tricycles were lined neatly on a shelf above cases that exhibited parts and accessories. Bells and sirens jangled from a wood pole.

But these were rarities. Garner's shop become the format, and dealers from Arizona to Massachusetts embraced the "Total Concept Store," usually with happy results.

In East Providence, Rhode Island, Robert Foulkes, Jr., had sold and repaired bikes out of a converted garage since 1951. He had never seen Garner's showcase store, but Schwinn's East Coast sales representatives articulated the program well enough that Foulkes was willing to make the investment, substantial as it was. (A conversion in the early '60s could cost a dealer as much as $40,000.) "Schwinn took them by the hand and explained the benefits of modern merchandising," says Foulkes's son, Robert III, who now runs East Providence Cycle. Chicago headquarters made it easier by pricing the fixtures low and sending a layout specialist to take measurements. "Dad was proud of how it looked and the response it received from customers, that he started with so little and was able to achieve this."

Pictures of other "ultra-modern" shops were featured in a sales manual to inspire those who weren't yet with the program. A night view of Bernie's Schwinn Bicycle in Trenton, New Jersey, was dazzling: A motorist could see an array of cycles sparkling behind a wide expanse of glass—"a sight that will impress every prospect who sees it." At John's Bicycle in Pasadena, California, the corner entrance was made even more attractive with planters and greenery—"an invitation to come on in and get out of the sun." This, no doubt, was the wave of the future. At a Schwinn get-together in Texas, one Fort Worth dealer approached Burch and said, "Ray, Pearl and me, we've been thinking. We'd like to get us one of them Total Concept Stores."

Schwinn spread the gospel through its sprightly house organ and marketing tool, *The Schwinn Reporter.* The monthly publication was filled with news about production, sales trends, and foreign and domestic trade issues. Burch penned F.W.-esque editorials blasting the ruthless chain stores for selling cheap goods and not treating customers properly. Garner wrote a monthly column on retailing. Perhaps most important were the down-to-earth advice and inspirational dealer success stories. Read the legend on one 1952 article: "Put 'em on the bike, feed 'em with the info, watch 'em buy . . . is the sales technique employed with zest and honesty by Scotty's Bike Shop, Compton, Calif., a 100 percent Schwinn dealer."

The tales continued throughout the '50s, '60s, and '70s. Frank's Mend-It Shop in Salt Lake City sold an average of two Schwinns daily before turning Total Concept; four to five Schwinns daily after. Pruitt's Pet and Garden Supply in North Palm Beach, Florida, was transformed into Pruitt's Schwinn Cyclery. Mulhaupt's Schwinn in downtown Lafayette, Indiana, poured $148,000 into a colossal renovation. Moore's Southwestern Wheel-A-Rama (next door to the Skate-A-Rama) opened to crowds in Oklahoma City. John's Cyclery in St. Albans, West Virginia, installed indoor-outdoor Spanish Gold carpeting by Ozite ("That interior decorator look is here," *The Schwinn Reporter* gushed). Monsey Cycle Shop in Spring Valley, New York, went from a barn to a 60-foot-wide store to a berth in the venerable 1,000 Club, the wealthiest stratum of Schwinn sellers, who sold that number of bikes or more in a year. The owner of Mineola Bicycle Service on Long Island had a private plane. And on and on. The Total Concept formula worked, judging by the rising ranks of dealers making a middle-class living from selling

Schwinn—and the growing number of wives wearing furs in photos of regional dealer meetings. In 1963, only 48 dealers were members of the 1,000 Club; by 1968, 455 dealers belonged. All told that year, a record 701 stores were in the 1,000 Club or 500 Club—the latter being the benchmark for making Schwinn one's main source of income. Average sales volume was $100,000 that year, with 30 percent of all dealers selling 66 percent of the 1.03 million Schwinns sold.

Schwinn pitched directly to consumers, too. In the 1940s, stars such as Lana Turner, Bing Crosby, Bob Hope, and Ronald Reagan posed for publicity pictures with Schwinns (Reagan's contract demanded both payment *and* the bike). "Lovely Rita Hayworth," slobbered one caption, "lets her Schwinn-Built bicycle carry her smoothly and swiftly away from it all . . . for a pensive pose in the great outdoors." The celebrity connections continued well into the 1970s, some of them strained: Dr. Paul Dudley White (Dwight D. Eisenhower's chief medical consultant after the president's first heart attack) recommending bicycling as good exercise; Georgia governor Lester G. Maddox (a trick cyclist who could ride backwards) and his wife on a tandem; actress Carol Channing atop a ten-speed Suburban; bubble-gum pop star Bobby Sherman hunched on a Schwinn in a photo from his 1971 album cover. ("This kid is with it," *The Schwinn Reporter* admired. "He's a young fast-driving performer who's in tune with the 'in' things of his many fans, like bike riding.") And, of course, the annual Playmate of the Year, straddling her prized Schwinn "especially painted Playmate Pink."

Most of the company's publicity and advertising, however, were geared toward kids. Schwinns were touted in comic books as early as the 1930s, and an ad filled the back cover of *Boys' Life* magazine every other month. The biggest bang came from children's television character Captain Kangaroo (actor Bob Keeshan), who beginning in 1958 regularly encouraged young viewers to buy Schwinn. His amiable sidekick, Mr. Greenjeans, often would roll out this week's model—a Bantam, perhaps, or an older child's Jaguar or Hornet—and the Captain would extol its design and safety features, concluding each spot with the kicker, "Schwinn bikes are best!" The campaign was highly successful: two of three Schwinn dealers could trace bike sales directly to Captain Kangaroo, according to a 1963 company survey. The show's core audience was under six, barely on the cusp of handling a two-wheeler, but Schwinn's interest was in building for the future, "to make Schwinn synonymous with a bike," Keeshan says today, "so that by seven or eight years old, they'd be asking not for a bike but for a Schwinn." It was a pillow-soft sell by some current standards, Keeshan adds, as were his for-hire minglings at special events. "Distributors and dealers would ooh and ahh," says Ray Burch, "especially if they had kids with them."

Dealers appreciated the advertising efforts, which also included sample radio scripts for local commercials. But Schwinn really made its mark with training and assistance that no other competitor offered, from confidential analyses of a dealer's balance sheet and operating statement to group-rate medical plans and a mutual fund for retirement savings.

During the 1950s, parts department worker Stan Natanek casually began helping dealers who visited the Chicago factory, showing them how to repair three-speed hubs or shifters. "They didn't know what to do, and they would soon as sell a guy a new hub or new wheel rather than repair it," Natanek says. "They didn't want the consumer to know they didn't know what to do." Then he started a school in a cage tucked underneath a staircase, teaching the art of bicycle maintenance to four or six dealers at a time. "Kind of cramped, kind of dumpy," he recalls. By 1959, he had started a company-sponsored road show—rolling workshops for small groups of dealers and their mechanics. "They'd show you how to take apart a Sturmey-Archer three-speed hub, or a Bendix two-speed," says John Mooy, a bike mechanic in Santa Barbara, California. "They would throw all the different types in a box and you would have to sort it out. It was great fun. It was *the* bicycle mechanics school. You could say you were a *factory trained mechanic.* 'I went to Schwinn factory school.' People would raise their eyebrows and say, 'That's cool.' " Natanek also explained how to fix a derailleur, the gear-shifting mechanism on multispeed bikes. That kind of valuable and practical information helped dealers demystify and popularize ten-speeds in America, although they wouldn't really catch on until the late 1960s, in the form of the Schwinn Varsity. As his mechanic-training program expanded, Natanek would pack tool sets in wood boxes and ship them to the different parts of the country he'd be visiting. He was always on the road, receiving a 100,000-mile plaque from United Airlines in 1962—long before the era of frequent-flier miles. At year's end, the tools would be shipped back to Chicago for refurbishing. "Jerry Fritz [Schwinn's controller] used to scream about the freight bills," Bill Chambers says. Natanek also would put his repair wisdom on paper in *The Schwinn Reporter* and, later, in a comprehensive service manual coveted by dealers selling rival brands. There were step-by-step instructions for aligning a frame, adjusting brakes or replacing a saddle. Natanek used to joke that he had the most-photographed hands at Schwinn.

While Schwinn was turning its dealers into skilled mechanics, it also was turning them into businessmen. A roving sales school was established, headed by regional sales manager Harry Delaney, who hung out in Garner's newly opened Northbrook store to learn from the master. Delaney traveled the country staging three- or four-day programs in distributor warehouses or banquet halls. He began with simple lessons ("Keeping the Customer Happy" or "Ten Ways to Close Your Sales Talk") and moved on to what came to be called "The Schwinn Commandments." On prices: "Never apologize for your price," Delaney wrote in 1961. "Your product is *better* and commands a higher price because of the way it's made." On prestige: "Things that other people in business who have less prestige do, we cannot do," he argued in 1962. "The way each salesperson acts in private life, as well as in public life, all help to contribute to that prestige." He also backed up his homilies with useful sales pitches: Were parents reluctant to invest in a pricier Schwinn bike for Junior? They shouldn't be. Their son *should* learn to ride on the safest bike around. And a Schwinn at $49 would outlast all five kids and still have trade-in value. A competitor's version at $39 just couldn't take the abuse.

Delaney graduated to more complex subjects, such as inventory management. "Some guys never knew what a profit statement was," Chambers adds. He and Delaney also set out to champion the financial benefits of the Total Concept Store. "We convinced dealers they made more money doing it our way than their way," Chambers says. He'd usually arrive at the seminar on the last day to sum things up—and advocate that sales at a Schwinn cyclery could be twice or more those of Joe's Bike Shop. The math could be compelling. A store in the early 1960s selling 750 bicycles a year at an average price of $100 could generate gross sales of $125,000 (counting another $50,000 or so in repair work and revenues from parts and accessories). As long as expenses were kept in line, the dealer could see a net profit of 15 percent to 17 percent, or about $20,000—a good living for a small-business owner at the time.

The goal was 100 percent Schwinn sales, and the company often succeeded: Approximately 75 percent of its 1,700 dealers sold Schwinn exclusively by the late 1970s. Not all dealers would be—or could be—100 percent Schwinn, especially in sophisticated East and West Coast cycling markets, where consumers first began turning to foreign three-speeds and ten-speeds in the '50s and '60s, then to the competition's BMX and mountain bikes in the '70s and '80s. Still, the minimum requirement was 50 percent of floor space devoted to Schwinn, according to the dealership agreement. The company's sales and marketing forces religiously pressed dealers to up their Schwinn counts, mostly through persuasion, but sometimes through bullying. During an unexpected rush for English three-speeds in 1950s Michigan, for instance, non-Schwinn distributor Detroit Cycle was offering Raleigh's popular Dunelt model. Much to Schwinn's dismay, some of its dealers started displaying the enemy. Sales reps retaliated by counting a store's units to make sure Schwinn was at least half of the mix—and warning dealers that they risked cancellation if they embraced the rival brand. Such tactics could work in the short run, but only when Schwinn followed up by introducing models that matched or bested the newest competitor. Decades later, the company's heavy hands were forced to yield to the market's invisible hands.

5

COOL? AND HOW

On a wintry Saturday morning in 1963, Al Fritz received a telephone call from West Coast sales manager Sig Mork. "Something goofy is going on," Mork said. "The kids out here, they're buying used twenty-inch bikes and equipping them with Texas longhorn handlebars."

"Send me the handlebars," Fritz said.

Schwinn's Southern California distributor, Harry Wilson Sales Agency, already had sold thousands of the long-forgotten handlebars (probably designed in the 1940s to help paperboys carry wider loads) to dealers in San Diego, where the fad seemed to have started. It also was selling an elongated red and white saddle—called the Solo Polo—made by Ohio manufacturer Richard Persons in the late 1950s (on the flawed premise that bicycle polo would be a hot game). Persons had unloaded his inventory on a California parts distributor named Peter Mole, who occasionally sold them to bike dealers for $1 per seat. Suddenly, in 1963, sales of the strange-looking saddles started picking up. Mole asked Persons to haul out the old mold for the part that would come to be known as the banana seat. "We had to give him a minimum order," Mole says. "He didn't want to get stuck with them again."

Back in Chicago, Fritz was getting more involved in design work at Schwinn. He had to, for F.W. was ill with prostate cancer and less involved in day-to-day operations. After two major surgeries, and several months in a sickbed, the autocrat whose quest for two-wheeled perfection put his family name into households across America died on April 19 at age sixty-nine. A three-paragraph obituary appeared in the *Chicago Tribune,* underscoring F.W.'s low profile in the city. Yet the funeral at Chicago's Holy Name Cathedral was a who's who of the bicycle business: distributors, dealers, competitors, suppliers, trade book editors—several hundred in all. "He followed no one," Stuart Meyers wrote in an issue of *American Bicyclist* that included nearly fifty eulogies from industry leaders. "Frank was 'Mr. Bicycle,' " according to competitor H. P. Snyder Manufacturing Company, maker of Rollfast bikes. "It may be a long time before we find a man to match his vision, his inspiration and his dedication," wrote the chief executive of Huffman. As several others hinted, F.W.'s company never would be the same.

During F.W.'s final weeks, Fritz worked on Schwinn's prototype of the bike inspired by Southern California's road culture. The tires were wide and smooth, like those on a drag racer. At the back of the banana seat, a curved steel-tube extension that the kids called a "sissy bar" let you lean back like an easy rider. The whole package looked like a good time, Fritz thought. He combed the dictionary for ideas on a name and stopped at a picture of a stingray. "It reminded me of the bike," he says. On the morning of F.W.'s funeral, Fritz invited three visiting distributors from the East and the South to look at this new thing called the Sting-Ray. "I took the bike into the paint shop and they rode it. They were smiling and they were laughing, saying, 'You're out of your mind.' "

On the West Coast, Southern California distributor Bob Wilson urged him along, promising to order 500 at the start. "It's going to sell," Wilson said, but Fritz still had to convince skeptics closer to home. He was loading the prototype into the trunk of his car at the end of a Friday when Frank V. Schwinn walked by.

"What are you doing?" the company's new president asked. "What have you got there?"

"I have an appointment," Fritz replied. "Tomorrow morning, at Chicago Cycle [Schwinn's biggest distributor at the time]. I'm going to show them this new model, the Sting-Ray."

Frank V. looked at the bike, then shook his head.

"Frank," Fritz insisted. "This is gonna be the Number One seller in the line this year. I'll bet you we sell at least twenty-thousand." Selling 10,000 units of any model was big volume back then. "You've got a bet," Frank V. said. "Twenty dollars."

It took Fritz eighteen months to collect on the wager, but sales of the Sting-Ray more than compensated Frank V. for his loss. Schwinn sold 45,000 units in the last six months of 1963. "We were drained clean of bikes," one dealer told *The Schwinn Reporter.* Another described his total 1963 sales as the "best in twenty years." "We could have sold more," Fritz says today. "But we didn't have enough molds for the unusual balloon tire."

Schwinn at first had some regional competition with what the industry soon would call, generically, the "high-rise" bike. Peter Mole, the California parts distributor who rekindled sales of banana seats, had contracted with Huffman to build his Penguin brand high-rise at its Los Angeles Huffy plant. The bikes, sold to independent dealers, proved far too popular. By Christmas of 1964, Huffy's mass merchant customers were clamoring for a similar, but less expensive version, "and my exclusive went out the window," Mole recalls wistfully. "Schwinn was giving its Sting-Ray a lot of hype and pretty soon the whole country knew about it. They had a field day and it put them on top of the pole."

The Schwinn model, which more dreamily mimicked the era's hot-rod craze, turned out to be hot stuff among children, who snapped up nearly 2 million Sting-Rays between 1963 and 1968. The '64 Christmas season was so heated, some dealers even ran out of gift certificates. Priced at $70 to $140, the Sting-Ray was expensive for a kid's bike, but still within reach. The wild look of the wheel was irresistible to your average nine-year-old. "I dig the crazy styling," a Milwaukee buyer scribbled on a dealer's comment card in 1964. "You're not cool unless you have a Schwinn," another wrote in 1965. Cool? And how. Here was a vehicle made for popping wheelies—hike that front wheel high into the air, scootch back into the sissy bar for extra balance and pedal for block after block, like the biker dude you were meant to be. The Sting-Ray was perfect for carting a pal on the handlebar—or a girl on the back of the banana seat. The smooth, tread-free balloon tires painted streets with the deepest skid marks (two, three, even four cars long) after you slammed the coaster brakes at top speed.

The Sting-Ray style of bike was a uniquely American creation. Not as important as, say, jazz, but a cultural phenomenon nonetheless. Not every observer was enthralled with it, however. "What are we to make of these . . . flamboyant, ill-proportioned grotesques which are beginning to dominate the American bicycle scene?" wrote sociologist Arthur Asa Berger (a fan of the more "austere and basic" ten-speed). "In its garishness and vulgarity, it stands for the chrome-plated, plastic-coated ugliness that is so widespread in American culture. . . . But it also symbolizes a perversion of values, a somewhat monstrous application of merchandising and salesmanship that . . . has led to grave distortions in American society."

If the Sting-Ray and other high-rises symbolized anything, it was the value of fun. And because of that sales flowed, or, more accurately, gushed. During the mid-1960s, the high-rise style accounted for more than 60 percent of all bikes sold in the country. Bike giants Murray, Huffman, the American Machine & Foundry Company (producer of the AMF Roadmaster brand), and the Columbia Bicycle Company (created from the remains of Colonel Pope's old firm) sold millions through chain stores and dealers. Schwinn's dominance was so strong, however, children often referred to any high-rise by the copyrighted Sting-Ray name. The company held its lead in the market throughout the decade by presenting variations on the theme: the Slik Chik for girls; the Fastback five-speed stick shift, attached to the frame; besparkled banana seats called "Glitter Sitters"; curling ram's horn handlebars; and the wildly popular Krate series, featuring the vibrantly painted Orange Krate, Apple Krate, Lemon Peeler, Cotton Picker, and Pea Picker.

The Sting-Ray wasn't bad for Fritz's career, either. He was promoted to vice president in 1965, as the sixty-six-year-old Bill Stoeffhaas, now chairman of the company, delegated more responsibility in engineering and design. That year Fritz also was appointed to the board of directors, joining Frank V. and his brother, Edward Sr., their cousin Brownie Schwinn, and non-family members Stoeffhaas and attorney Bob Keck.

The Sting-Ray fad faded by the late 1960s, but Schwinn had its sturdy, ten-speed Varsity to pick up the slack. The company had introduced racer-style multispeeds as early as 1938, with the premium Paramount cycles for adults. Sales of the high-priced product always had been meager, even unprofitable, but F.W. never seemed to mind. "I think he needed to have his name on a bicycle representing the highest state of the art," former trade magazine publisher Stuart Meyers explains. Simpler and less expensive New World models (named after Schwinn's 1890s World brand) followed in the 1950s; they proved somewhat more successful, yet ten-speeds and their unfamiliar European trappings failed to catch on with most American adults, much less older children who were closer to eying their first car than their next bike. Many dealers were uncomfortable with them, too, but with Schwinn's service schools teaching a generation of mechanics how to assemble the derailleur, and articles in *The Schwinn Reporter* championing the beauty and the bucks in ten-speeds, "we convinced dealers you could sell derailleur bikes to kids and survive," Ray Burch says.

The Varsity finally proved them right. With its drop handlebars and absence of kiddie fenders, it was the first multispeed bike produced in large numbers (selling at a relatively affordable $69.95) and was Schwinn's first product aimed squarely at twelve- to fourteen-year-olds. Then there was the more-upscale Continental, which, for a $10 to $15 premium, offered a superior wheel, tire, saddle, and pedals. Because the bikes were built for bigger children, the company made the ten-speeds durable and dependable—not like those skinny European models you occasionally saw whizzing down the street. A surly teenager could ride the crap out of his Varsity, dumping it on the driveway in a defiant heap or taking it off the beaten suburban path—the woods behind school, perhaps—to hook up with friends and sneak a smoke or a beer.

Schwinn would produce 400,000 Varsitys a year by the early '70s. It already had become the dominant manufacturer of derailleur-equipped bicycles, accounting for 80 percent of those produced in the United States. When imports are considered, one in every four derailleur bikes sold in 1969 was a Schwinn. Though both the Varsity and Continental would get bad raps when trendier and lighter racing bikes became de rigueur later in the '70s (they would come to symbolize what Schwinn stood for: durable but dull), many in the business still look back on them fondly. "They were the best bikes made and designed for kids," says Chicago dealer Oscar Wastyn, Jr. "It stood up—a workhorse, a great bike."

It wasn't just the Varsity and Continental that screamed quality. The strength of all Schwinn bikes was almost mythical. Fritz tells of a southern Illinois dealer who often stood on the chain guard of a child's bike to show that it wouldn't crumple. Local competitors soon complained—customers doing comparative shopping were experimenting on *their* bikes in a similar manner, and the chain guards were collapsing.

Schwinn enjoyed the loyalty of Middle American families, like the McCarthys of Palmer Woods, a middle-class section of Detroit. During the '60s and '70s, each of the twelve McCarthy kids had his or her own Schwinn. As the older half accumulated new bikes for Christmas, the younger half got the hand-me-downs. The five- or six-year-old learned to ride a two-wheeler on a vintage model with cracked paint that the McCarthy family dubbed "Old Blue." The collection even included a tandem and a unicycle. The bikes filled the garage; cars were relegated to the driveway. And a Schwinn was considered a status symbol at a time when there were few coveted brand names aimed at kids. "We wouldn't be caught dead riding a Huffy," recalls Anne McCarthy, the No. 8 child. In eighth grade, she used $129 from baby-sitting earnings to buy a bronze Continental. McCarthy, now a *Fortune* 500 public relations executive, remembers a chicken fight with a childhood rival on a non-Schwinn bike. "Our spokes connected, and his front wheel crumbled. The Schwinn came out unscathed."

Customers around the country were true believers. "A Schwinn is as American as a hot dog," a New Jersey patron wrote on a comment card in 1964. "A strong bike that could stand a rough boy," a West Virginia buyer penned. Consumers had long memories, too. "Bought Schwinn because of your prompt attention to my request for replacement of a broken frame eighteen years ago," reported a loyal New York fan.

That sort of fervor helped Schwinn pass a milestone in 1968. For the first time, it produced more than one million bikes in a single year. Just weeks before Christmas, more than sixty managers and shop supervisors paused for a commemorative photo on the factory floor. The celebrity bike, fresh off the assembly line, was an Orange Krate. "We did it," read a poster.

There was no higher calling than working for Schwinn. "You were playing for the Yankees," says Allen Singer, former president of Midwest sales operations. "It was the pinnacle," adds Jim Burris, a Sunnyvale, California, bike dealer who in 1972 took a 60 percent pay cut to join Schwinn's West Coast sales force. "I wanted to work for Schwinn so bad. They were like IBM. You got prestige. You got respect. You *commanded* respect."

Presiding over all this prosperity was F.W.'s oldest son, Frank V., who assumed control in 1963 at the age of forty-three. The V. stood for Valentine, and as the middle name suggests, he was about as different from dad as a son could get. Frankie, as he was called by colleagues, was studious, introverted, and "showed some of the marks of being the son of a very strong father," says Stuart Meyers. "He had a slight stammer. He was quiet—very serious, and very serious about the company." Frankie attended Northwestern Military Academy and Beloit College in Wisconsin and served in the U.S. Army Air Corps during World War II. At Schwinn, he shared an office with his father, making finance and marketing his specialty. He maintained copious records of Schwinn's volume and profitability stretching back to the 1890s, and painstakingly hand-colored maps of the United States—county by county—to analyze marketing data and determine which Schwinn dealers and distributors did their jobs and which didn't.

Like his father, Frankie was unpretentious. He drove an Oldsmobile, freeing up the corporate Cadillac and chauffeur for his mother, Gertrude. In 1964, he married Nancy Wilson, daughter of Schwinn's high-flying California distributor Bob Wilson, but she was about ten years

Frankie's junior, and it seemed an odd union. She was outgoing and contentious, while he appeared uneasy around women. "She was out to have fun; he was not the kind to party," says Dennis Morgon, who worked at Bob Wilson's distributorship. "But some people thought, 'Maybe that combination will work.' " The marriage lasted less than six months. "He didn't say much," according to Bill Chambers, "except that it cost him a pile of money."

On occasion, Frankie could emulate F.W. and grandfather Ignaz and take a strong stance. In 1971, during an unanticipated boom in bike sales throughout the country, he threatened to cancel a dealer's franchise after several customers complained of rude treatment. "I must tell you most frankly," he wrote in a letter excerpted in *The Schwinn Reporter*, "I will not tolerate discourtesy in the sale of a Schwinn bicycle under any circumstances by any Schwinn dealership, regardless—I repeat, regardless[—]of volume of business."

But most contemporaries describe him as a soft-spoken, hands-off manager. Frankie was compassionate, perhaps overly so. During a 1968 meeting at a downtown Chicago hotel, he was riding in an elevator with the wife of a Michigan dealer whose credit had been shut off. When the dealer's wife began crying, Frankie hushed her and agreed to set aside the shop's balance due, so they could again start buying bicycles. The shop later went out of business.

He was always accessible—the kind of guy you could corner at a cocktail party. If a kid wrote complaining about a faulty bike, the Schwinn president often wrote a lengthy, heartfelt response in longhand, which was then typed by his secretary. That amazed and puzzled staff members, who figured they were paid to handle such routine grievances. Shouldn't the chief executive's time be spent on more lofty concerns? His workers found him oddly sentimental, yearning for a bygone era. If they stopped in his office on a business matter, Frankie often would lapse into reminiscences of better times twenty-five years earlier. That made for awkward moments. "I had work to do," says former national sales manager Jack Smith, "but I didn't want to insult him." Compared to his father, whose inspiring stump speeches still give old-timers goose bumps, Frankie just couldn't measure up. "He was a cold fish—a terrible public speaker," says retired Northern California dealer Robert J. Letford.

Frankie seemed happy to stay out of the limelight and let the employee shine; he rarely paid the restaurant or bar bill if he joined an underling entertaining a client. "He'd slip you money, made sure you have enough," according to Keith Kingbay, a former parts division manager. "He let you look as if you were in control. He'd build up your morale, your spirit." During his tenure, Frankie ceded management powers to the polished Fritz and outgoing Burch. Some observers credit the third-generation Schwinn for recognizing his limitations and gaining the loyalty of top-notch managers, but there would never be another Schwinn as chief executive with F.W.'s drive and stature.

There also would never be as strong an advocate for the Chicago factory as F.W. The white-collar-minded Frankie hadn't labored much inside the plant; having worked with Burch to build selective distribution, he was geared to finance, marketing, and sales. As the company spent more and more time and money fighting the Department of Justice's antitrust case, the factory, run by F.W.'s gregarious but increasingly frustrated younger son, Edward, began to take a back seat. Indeed, the antitrust battle would prove to be a turning point for the entire company, dramatically changing the way it did business.

After five years of evidence-gathering and pretrial wangling—and a record 70-day trial in the fall of 1962—Schwinn prevailed in the lower court (although it was found guilty of an antitrust violation involving the allocation of distributor territories). "The evidence is abundantly clear," U.S. District Court Judge J. Sam Perry ruled, "that Schwinn's practice of eliminating dead timber, useless and active accounts . . . has greatly enhanced trade in Schwinn bicycles and has in fact been the salvation of Schwinn . . . and has actually made for genuine competition in the bicycle manufacturing industry" by providing a strong alternative to chain stores.

The government chose not to take issue with Schwinn's exoneration on price-fixing through franchising, but it appealed the restraint-of-trade verdict directly to the Supreme Court. Arguments in *United States* v. *Arnold, Schwinn & Co.* started more than four years later on April 20,

1967. Bill Chambers, who had led much of the company's research efforts and by this point was intimately familiar with the facts of the case, bought a vest for the occasion and sat at the defendant's table. Schwinn attorney Bob Keck winked and called him "Judge Chambers."

The issue before the high court seemed simple: Could Schwinn tell its independent distributors whom to sell to? Yet the arguments were not simple: Lawyers sent a 22,000-page record of the case, one of the thickest the justices ever had to contend with. At the crux of the constitutional case were the twenty-two bicycle distributors. Under a structure termed the "Schwinn Plan," about 75 percent of the company's sales flowed directly to the dealer from the factory, with the distributor basically acting as order-taker for headquarters and receiving a commission as the original sales agent. The remaining 25 percent of sales directly involved the distributors, who'd buy bikes and parts from Schwinn and then resell them on an as-needed or fill-in basis to authorized dealers only. Here, ultimately, was the heart of the matter: whether Schwinn's practice of prohibiting its distributors from reselling to unauthorized dealers (a practice known as "bootlegging") was a reasonable restraint in pursuit of a larger good—in this case, the ability of a small manufacturer and its retailers to compete against more powerful mass merchants. "We are concerned when the safety valve which such phenomena as bootlegging represents is closed off completely," asserted Justice Department attorney Richard A. Posner, noting that excluded outlets might compete vigorously in price with authorized dealers if they could get the product.

The long-awaited decision, handed down on June 12, 1967, was a 5–2 ruling (two justices did not participate) written by Justice Abe Fortas. He did not take issue with the part of the Schwinn Plan where distributors acted as mere agents to authorized dealers and collected commissions. But the court found Schwinn could not dictate the terms of resale in the 25 percent of sales made directly to the distributors. In fact, although the two sides had argued whether the restraint could be considered reasonable, the majority further raised the constitutional stakes by ruling that the curb was illegal per se. The key distinction, Fortas wrote, was that a manufacturer couldn't tell its distributors whom to sell to. "Such restraints are so obviously destructive of competition that their mere existence is enough," he argued in what would be called the Schwinn Doctrine. "Once the manufacturer has parted with title and risk, he has parted with dominion over the product."

The Schwinn Doctrine was controversial.[1] But Schwinn had been preparing for this day. Within seventy-two hours of the decision, the company announced plans to open its own regional distribution centers in Illinois, New Jersey, Georgia, and California. "Thus," it said in a press release, "we can retain title on all our Schwinn bicycles until they are sold direct to our franchised sales-and-service dealers." The company would have to bid farewell to its longtime distributors. "One guy sat in my office and cried," Burch recalls. "We thought it was the end of the world," says Steven Duncan, head of warehouse sales at Houston distributor Herbert L. Flake Company.

Many of the distributors eventually closed. The survivors (including Flake) turned to competing brands. "Schwinn hoped we'd go out of business," remembers Dennis Morgon, who took over California's Harry Wilson Sales Agency with a partner when the Wilson family bowed out and renamed it Wilson Bicycle Sales. "Sales are not close to what we used to do," Morgon says today, then shrugs. "We're making a living." Nevertheless, some fared well with the new brands. "We were able to put our bicycles into 50 percent of the dealers we had been selling Schwinn to," recalls Howard Johnsen, president of Dallas distributor Hans Johnsen Company. And one distributor—Service Cycle Supply of Commack, New York—was transformed under chief executive Harry Manko and grew to become a direct competitor to Schwinn when it acquired the popular Mongoose BMX brand in 1985. (Service Cycle went public in 1993 as American Recreation Holdings Company, and merged in 1995 with helmet maker Bell Sports Corporation.)

Whatever sentiments the Schwinn family may have had for the Wilsons, Johnsens, and other colleagues, direct distribution turned out to be highly profitable for the company, which shipped goods more efficiently through four centers than twenty-two warehouses. "In many respects, it was a boon to Schwinn," says the distributors' lawyer in the antitrust case, Earl Pollock. "It expanded its U.S. parts business and benefited from establishing direct relations with retailers." Yet there was a subtle cost, as headquarters became more inbred. With the distributors, Schwinn had a rich source of market intelligence for each region of the country. As independents, they could be candid. "We could tell Ray Burch or Al Fritz they were wrong," Howard Johnsen explains. "An employee who answers to Al Fritz would have to choose his words carefully if he's telling his superior that he's off-base."

6

LET THE GOOD TIMES ROLL

Schwinn had spent an estimated $1 million combating the government's antitrust charges—significant money, back then, for a modest manufacturing operation—and in the five years following the Supreme Court ruling, it would sink millions of dollars more into opening the regional warehouses. Meantime, the sales and marketing divisions won a growing share of the company's investments, amplifying their power and prestige. And rightly so, the salesmen and marketers reasoned—they were the ones bringing home the bacon. The domain that got short shrift was the Chicago factory—a shift in corporate vision that might have seemed nearsighted to a technocrat like F.W. As grandson Richard C. Schwinn noted in a 1994 speech: "Even in the recession of '38, Frank, with the help of one last investment from Ignaz, invested in the first automatic screw machines ever made. His new machines had serial numbers seven to twelve. The first six went to General Motors."

It was a gradual detour, hard to put your finger on. Sure, you could wring another year or two out of an old screw machine, but the lack of investment would catch up. By the late 1960s, Schwinn desperately needed new equipment, like bigger punch presses and automated crank machines that the Germans and Japanese were using. The screw machines were so ancient, replacement parts were nearly impossible to find: managers had to scavenge—or make them at the factory. Manufacturing head Jack Ahearn usually would receive the machinery on his urgent list, but there never seemed to be enough capital for equipment that really could give the factory an edge. Ahearn tried to persuade Frank V. of the need to change. "I would go in the office thinking, 'If I could just get him for five minutes.' He'd start talking about the old days."

The neglect also bothered Frankie's brother, Edward, who joined Schwinn in 1944 at age twenty-one as vice president of operations and later oversaw manufacturing from an office he shared with Fritz. Edward came to resent what he saw as extravagant budgets for the sales and marketing units, which had risen to $3.5 million annually by the 1970s. "He complained that the marketing department had money to spend," Bill Chambers says, "and he didn't have money for machines."

Like Frankie, Edward had toiled in the shadow of his domineering father, but he was much more entertaining—"a panic," recalls Stuart Meyers. Edward owned a beaverskin coat, was fond of performing vaudeville numbers, and once drove an army vehicle through downtown Chicago. He'd talk in an ersatz German accent—"*Vat eez der meenink of zees?*"—imitating Grandfather Ignaz. "Ed was more of the wild kid," says Oscar Wastyn, Jr., whose father was a close friend. "He'd come to the store in his leather jacket at five o'clock and say, 'What time you close, Oc? Think you can handle it? Your old man and I are heading off.' They'd go to the tavern, shoot pool. Just regular guys."

Although Edward was well liked in the factory, many of the more button-down types in administration didn't take him seriously. Named executive vice president after F.W.'s death and Frankie's ascension, Edward thought the marketing department's dealer outings and dinners and happy hours were wasting the family's money. But he didn't have the clout to change spending priorities. His only recourse was to grouse privately. When Burch in 1965 set up a model bike store at headquarters, which he punningly named "Frank's Schwinn Cyclery," he soon felt Edward resented the ploy and had complained to his big brother.

"Frankie started backing away from me," Burch says. "I realized that I was the cause of problems for Frankie."

Frankie protected Edward and treated him with affection, yet Burch sensed Edward's family "bugged Frankie and wore him down." Edward developed leukemia and died in February 1972 at age forty-eight, leaving his widow, Mary, his twenty-three-year-old son, Edward R. Schwinn, Jr., and four younger children. "Friends and associates will especially remember his warm and gentle manner," read the obituary in *The Schwinn Reporter.* "No one had to stand on rigid decorum or protocol . . . to see him or to seek his advice." Edward's mistrust of the ascending sales and marketing executives bubbled within his family—and it especially stuck in the craw of Ed Jr. when he succeeded his Uncle Frankie as president in 1979.

Burch shrugged off the criticism. Marketing, especially the franchising and selective distribution program, had been the company's salvation. Besides, Schwinn's work-hard, play-hard culture reflected the way much of America did business in the '60s and '70s. The drinks flowed freely (Fritz preferred Stolichnaya on the rocks, straight with a wedge of lemon; Burch opted for Old Fitzgerald or Old Granddad on the rocks, with water on the side), the recreation of choice was golfing, not cycling, and executives caucused with suppliers at posh settings like Pebble Beach in California or Greenbrier in West Virginia. The confabs usually included morning business sessions, then afternoons on the links while the wives went shopping, followed by long evenings at the 19th hole. Regional meetings to honor dealers who sold 500 or 1,000 Schwinn bikes in a year always featured steak dinners, plaques, and diamond or ruby lapel pins. The rallies bloated as more and more dealers prospered via Schwinn. In February 1968, the company hosted its first nationwide meeting for 500 Club and 1,000 Club dealers at Chicago's deluxe Conrad Hilton Hotel. Chambers loaded dealers onto buses in subzero temperatures to tour the factory, then warmed them up at the bar later that night. A motivational speaker at dinner urged shop owners, "Don't sell the steak, sell the sizzle!" Scantily clad girls from Chicago's Gaslight Club put on a Gay Nineties show. Five years later, the company produced another lollapalooza for its top dealers at the Fontainbleau Hotel in Miami Beach. With cocktails and a dinner dance for 1,990 people, and entertainment by singer Anita Bryant, the tab came to more than $35,000.

Schwinn enjoyed something of a Hollywood connection through its Southern California distributor, Bob Wilson, a vivacious partier who loved to hobnob with celebrities. Wilson was friends with John Wayne, accompanying the actor on boating trips to Baja, and television fixture William Frawley (Fred Mertz in *I Love Lucy*), who'd stop by the office to crack jokes with the boss. He'd visit well-known watering holes and eateries—the Brown Derby, Cocoanut Grove, Chasen's—and talk to anyone, says Dennis Morgon, who worked for Wilson at the time. "The [restaurant] manager would introduce him to the stars." Wilson introduced his chums to the Schwinn crowd, too. Andy Devine, host of a popular children's television show that featured a frog puppet jumping out of a box with a "Hiya kids, hiya!," was master of ceremonies for one awards dinner.

The biggest party animal, however, was Brownie Schwinn, whose main job at the company was to drive about the country entertaining dealers, his golf clubs and skeet guns tucked in the trunk of an El Dorado (his two Browning shotguns, with fitted cases, were worth around $8,000). The loss of his left arm in the 1940s hadn't slowed Brownie, who rarely, if ever, played a game of golf, pool, or gin rummy without betting. He pursued his vices with gusto. "Taking your wife to Las Vegas," he once told a Chicago dealer, "is like taking a ham sandwich to a banquet."

Brownie could afford the smorgasbord. In prosperous times, annual dividends to the Schwinn family trust that owned the company ranged from $800,000 to $1.2 million, and Brownie got a full third of the trust after his mother died in 1974. In addition, he earned an upper-middle-class salary (estimated at about $45,000 in the 1970s), and had a bountiful expense account. "He was in clover," Chambers says. Although Brownie was a company director, he wasn't at the center of decision making—being just a little too risque for his straighter and narrower cousins. Nevertheless, he could be influential and served as a goodwill ambassador to other family members, especially when the dividend wasn't as generous as expected. If he wasn't on the road wining and dining dealers, he might be in the company cafeteria jabbering with employees.

Usually tan, wearing a turtleneck under a tweed sport coat, Brownie cut a dapper figure. His license plate was 14W ROS (for "Real Old Stinker," he joked), and his driving could plunge passengers into a cold sweat, especially when he hit 90 miles per hour on a highway, steering with his knees as he ostentatiously lit a cigarette. "How can he drive like that, with one arm?" dealer Oscar Wastyn, Jr., once asked Edward Sr. "If he had two arms," Edward replied, "he'd go 180."

Brownie owned a surprisingly nondescript three-bedroom ranch home in the western Chicago suburb of Medinah. His showplace, though, was a Wyoming ranch that his mother, Elizabeth, had built in the 1950s, 12 miles from the postage-stamp-sized town of DuBois. Two lakes on the spread inspired the name Blue Holes Ranch. Brownie owned fifteen quarter horses—he made a saddle for one horse with sterling silver studs—and grew hay and alfalfa. When he refurbished the ranch after his mother's death, he left a cross over the entrance that suggested a church, but inside, the place was hardly sacrosanct. He set up the family room Vegas-style, with slot machines and tables for blackjack, roulette, and pool. When he wanted the real thing, he'd take off for Nevada on a moment's notice. Ray Burch remembers Brownie partying at Medinah Country Club outside Chicago, getting drunk and heading to a plane for Las Vegas with fellow club members. "He squandered vast sums at craps, at the blackjack table," Burch says. After one long night of blackjack, Brownie confessed he had lost "five big ones."

Former Schwinn employees remember Brownie as a gracious host, often starting a day of golf with a champagne breakfast and continuing the round with a bottle of Dry Sack discreetly tucked into his golf bag. The day ended with a steam bath, more drinks, and dinner with wives invited. The one catch: you had to bet. "He would bet the *dealers*," Fritz recalls. "There was nobody sacred. He'd be happy if he won five dollars." The betting got arcane and goofy, maybe $1 a point to start, but after doubling, then redoubling, "you'd be up to twenty, thirty, or forty dollars a point," Fritz says. "His income was obviously a lot bigger than a lot of the people he'd be playing." (Brownie's manipulations on the links bothered Fritz, who had a handicap of 10 to 12, compared with Brownie's 20 to 25. But Fritz maintained that Brownie had a phony handicap—no pun intended—based on the relatively difficult course at Medinah. That enabled him to make a strong showing on easier courses. "I stopped betting him on golf," Fritz says.)

Brownie reveled in pleasing his friends, but he wasn't much of a family man. His first marriage, to Katie Ruth Schwinn, ended in divorce in 1949. He married again two years later, but his thirty-year relationship with Jean Y. Schwinn was stormy. Sometimes, after drinks at the country club, the couple would get into tempestuous arguments, oblivious to embarrassed friends and shocked onlookers. An even darker side of Brownie is suggested in a 1971 divorce complaint filed by Jean. Her husband had beaten her twice during the past two years, she charged, adding that in the most recent incident, four months earlier, two of her ribs were broken. Brownie had insulted or ridiculed her in front of friends and relatives; he often had left town without notice, leaving no funds for the family to live on and forcing her to borrow money from friends, the charges read. Jean asked the court for possession of the family's 1970 Cadillac Fleetwood, complaining that Brownie sometimes took the car and parked it where she couldn't find it. Her husband denied all the charges. The beating incidents, Brownie responded to the suit, were started when Jean attacked him and he tried to defend himself. Nor was it imperative, he said, that she have use of the Fleetwood.

Jean soon dropped the matter, but she remained unhappy and increasingly sought solace in drinking. "She felt if she divorced, she'd end up with nothing," explains Rychie Schwinn, who married Jean and Brownie's son Robert in 1975. With his never-ending road show, Brownie often wasn't home for his children, six by his two marriages. They rarely took vacations together, according to Rychie; during family dinners, Brownie usually excused himself from the table and retreated to his room. Former executives still express dismay. "The way he treated his family was atrocious," says Fritz. Most of his children did not earn college degrees nor, it seems, did they formally prepare for life without a Schwinn dividend check. The rule of succession written by their great-grandfather Ignaz had barred Brownie's side of the family from top management, but the heirs were confident that they would not want for money.

As the children matured and moved away, Jean spent more time alone at Blue Holes Ranch. Despite her doctor's warnings, she continued drinking, according to Rychie. Her liver and kidneys failed, and she died at the Mayo Clinic in September 1982. Shortly after Jean's funeral, Brownie was diagnosed with lung cancer. Months before, he had treated his grandchildren to a summer picnic. It was uncharacteristic, even a bit bizarre. "He became a loving grandfather," Rychie recalls. Still, Brownie never gave up his gift of the grand gesture. On New Year's Eve 1982, he flew in his children for a gala at Medinah Country Club. Brownie rented a tuxedo and arranged for an ambulance to pick him up at the hospital. "He couldn't walk, so he lay on a stretcher—grinning," Rychie says. "He had a balloon tied around one ear." Brownie even made the most of his final hospital stay, ordering steak or seafood feasts from downtown restaurants. He died ten months after Jean, and is buried next to her in Blue Holes.

Brownie left his children the ranch, oil well leases, investments in subsidized housing, and a collection of diamond jewelry he had given to Jean, including a splendid brooch and pendant combination, bangle bracelets studded with sapphires, earrings, and rings. (Brownie's daughters fought over the spoils, according to Rychie, who notes that two who vied for the same bracelet agreed to cut it and divide the diamonds.) Always in character, Brownie bequeathed $10,000 for a final bash. One year later, a crowd of a hundred toasted their old cohort at a restaurant near Medinah. Lobster, steak—whatever you wanted from the menu—and drinks, of course. "Quite a few people got smashed," Chambers says. "We did it up, Brownie-style."

During Brownie's heyday, Schwinn could afford to be lavish. It—and the rest of the industry—was in the middle of a nationwide bicycle boom that saw annual production more than double, from 6.9 million bikes in 1970 to 15.2 million in 1973. Suddenly, everyone seemed to want bikes. Not just kids or college students, but adults, too. In fact, for the first time since World War I, American consumers in 1972 purchased more bicycles (13.9 million units) than new automobiles.

"Shades of the 1890s," observed *American Bicyclist.* The bicycle had indeed become fashionable again. In the ten years preceding the 1970s boom, only one of twenty bikes was purchased for an adult. Between 1971 and 1973, however, more than half of all bikes sold nationwide went to adults. No one thing explains the sudden crush. As a sport for getting and staying fit into middle age, bicycling preceded the tennis and jogging crazes of the later '70s. Social activism had magnified awareness of the environment, with the first Earth Day celebrated in April 1970, and the bike was being touted as the ultimate in environmentally friendly transportation, not requiring an ounce of gasoline. (As North Vietnam's military had proved so effectively: many of its supplies were biked along hidden trails.) The 1973 Arab oil embargo didn't hurt—cycling to work was one way to avoid those interminable lines for gas. And college students, in particular, embraced the bicycle. They toured the countryside on lightweight French models made by Gitane and Peugeot, out for an easy 10-mile jaunt or a more ambitious cross-country trek.

Whatever the reasons, almost everybody had to have one. Like Cabbage Patch dolls in the '80s or Rollerblades in the '90s, it was the craze of the moment. By the early '70s, Schwinn's factory was cranking out nearly 1.5 million bicycles annually. In 1971 it sold out—in May. "We stopped taking applications for dealers," Fritz says. A year later, the factory was turning out 6,000 bikes daily. "It's easy to spot a Schwinn dealer this January," Ray Burch wrote at the end of 1972 in *The Schwinn Reporter.* "He's the guy with the glassy-eyed dreamy grin on his face, a warranty check in one hand and a travel folder in the other, and he sags a little on the side where he carries his wallet." More than 500 dealers were inducted into the 1,000 Club (master merchant George Garner had sold an astounding 10,000 bikes) and the factory ran three shifts, as employment swelled to 2,000 workers. Bursting at the seams, Schwinn spent $2.5 million to open a satellite plant for welding bicycle frames near its northwest Chicago complex. "Quality suffered tremendously," notes former national sales manager Jack Smith. "There was poor paint and construction because of the speed with which we were getting the bikes out. It was not a fun time for the factory."

Just the opposite for Schwinn dealers. In towns across the country, crowds lined up waiting for stores to open. Bikes arrived from the factory by the trainload, most already presold. "It was like sale day at Macy's—people fought over the same bike," says Chris Travers of La Mirada, California. "You didn't have to know how to sell a bike," adds Terry Gibson of Normal, Illinois, "all you had to do was have one." Larry Parker of Pasadena, Texas, remembers working in his family's store when a customer who'd just bought a Varsity returned for another. "What happened?" Parker asked. "I tied the bicycle to a tree," the customer answered, "and someone cut down the tree."

The good times indeed were rolling: in 1974, the company earned a record $6.2 million on sales of $135 million. But there were whispers of troubles to come. Schwinn for decades had told its dealers that the company could supply all their needs, from parts to finished product. It had been the standard-bearer in quality, with little domestic competition in the independent dealer market. Now, the overstretched Chicago factory couldn't supply enough bikes. Schwinn's dealers were on allocation and begging for more. Frankie had to tell them, *Get bikes wherever you can.*

To some extent, many Schwinn dealers in more cosmopolitan East Coast and West Coast markets always had done just that, but for 100 percent Schwinn dealers, especially those in the heartland, it was a taste of forbidden fruit. They brought in Raleigh, Peugeot, Asian names like Nashiki—anything they could grab. "They found there were other bikes out there, and that the other bikes were not all that bad," says Allen Singer, former president of Schwinn Sales Midwest, one of the company's regional distribution arms.

Around Christmas 1973, cancellations of orders began trickling into headquarters. By mid-1974, the Chicago warehouse was receiving 100,000 a month. Schwinn still sold a record 1.55 million bikes that year, but in 1975, nationwide sales cracked in half, to 7.3 million units. "It took [only] four years to get our garages full of bikes," figures Pat Murphy, Singer's deputy at Schwinn Sales Midwest. Many of those bikes remained in those garages, too. Older adults often found little fun in the ten-speed style, hunched over the handlebars and straining necks to look up at the road ahead. Their bikes gathered dust as America turned to other leisure activities.

Schwinn had a good ride while it lasted, yet few executives realized that their business had been changed dramatically. During the boom, Made-in-America Schwinn quietly began importing its first bikes from two Japanese factories. The genie was out of the bottle, according to California importer Michael L. Bobrick, whose company got its start procuring Japanese bikes. "That legitimized us and others," he says, "and took away the Schwinn mystique."

7

THE HANGOVER

The 1970s bike boom revolutionized the industry in at least one way: it brought new blood into the business—investors and cycling enthusiasts lured by the call of manufacturing profits or the sight of mom-and-pop bike shops making fifty, sixty, even a hundred thousand dollars a year. "Everyone thought we were geniuses," says Jeff Allen, a Schwinn dealer in the Chicago suburb of Villa Park.

Schwinn executives thought they were pretty smart, too, judging by the backslapping in photos documenting corporate outings to golf and beach resorts. "We had the world by the tail on a downhill pull," says Ray Burch. Yet something else seems clear in the pictures of middle-aged men filling out Banlon sport shirts and kelly green slacks: It had been a long time since some of these fellows had been on a bike.

Leaner and hungrier competitors already were developing and marketing new styles and technologies that, like Schwinn's Sting-Ray a decade before, sprang from the garages of California kids. In the San Fernando Valley, a cottage industry was making motorcycle-style bikes for children with cast aluminum wheels that could survive the muddy poundings of an off-road bicycle motocross, or BMX, race. About 400 miles north, in Marin County, adult ten-speed racers and mechanics were reconfiguring 1930s Schwinns and other fat-tired clunkers to tear down local mountain trails.

Schwinn wasn't watching its backyard, either. Some 100 miles northwest of Chicago, in the Wisconsin hamlet of Waterloo, the founders of Trek Bicycle Corporation were beginning to prove there was more money in the upper end of the business than Schwinn had imagined.

In the early 1970s, however, Schwinn's more immediate headache was the foreign-made, skinny-tired lightweight bike. The boom had flung open the door to imports, which zoomed to 37 percent of the market in 1972 from 26 percent the year before. Serious young cyclists soon became enamored of European names —Peugeot, Gitane, Motobecane, Cinelli—in addition to Raleigh, maker of the fabled English Racer and until 1971 the only large established importer in the United States. The overseas models weighed as little as 23 pounds, nearly 40 percent lighter than Schwinn's sturdy Varsity, and that difference helped a rider go farther, faster.[1] The leading component makers also were Old World: France's Huret and Maillard and Italy's Campagnolo. The Continental craze culminated in the popular culture with the 1979 American movie *Breaking Away,* in which the working-class college-town hero leads a quirky fantasy life as an Italian cyclist, losing the girl but winning the big race. By that time, however, European bikes had become too expensive and were being overtaken by high-quality Asian brands such as Nishiki, Fuji, and Centurion.

Centurion was one of a raft of foreign labels that splintered a market Schwinn once had owned, enriching entrepreneurs who eventually would grow big enough to challenge the company's dominance. Romanian-born Mitchell Weiner was working as a sales agent for Japanese manufacturers in the late 1960s, when he started on an innocent enough project: helping Raleigh Industries of America import a Japanese knockoff of the Grand Prix bicycle made in Nottingham, England. When Raleigh's British parent angrily nixed the plan ("How could an English bike be built in

Asia?" executives sniffed), Weiner was stuck with 2,000 bicycles. Fortunately, the boom was accelerating. He slapped the label Centurion on the ten-speeds and sold them in 60 days at a good profit.

Santa Monica bike store owner Michael Bobrick was intrigued. "What's your plan?" he asked Weiner in 1971.

"I don't have a plan," Weiner confessed.

Bobrick sold his store and became Weiner's partner in Western States Imports. He spent six months a year in Japan, working with small suppliers eager to bargain. That offered him a cost advantage over Schwinn, which recently had hooked up with the two most established Japanese factories. The duo sold their Centurions to growing numbers of bike shops, including Schwinn dealers. "The dealer made an extra ten percent over Schwinn," Bobrick recalls, "and it was cheaper to the consumer, too." The arrangement also benefited Western States. The modest importer would expand to become an important player in the independent retail market in the 1980s and would be an antagonist of Schwinn at the time of the bankruptcy.

As Centurions and other brands came to market, so did new shops to sell them, particularly in college towns like Boulder, Austin, Berkeley, and Bloomington, Indiana (the location for *Breaking Away*). Some retailers were lured solely by the profit potential, others were hippies out to save the world with ecologically correct bikes. Then there were the cycling nuts, just happy to be tinkering. Schwinn was still the Big Kahuna, but a shopkeeper didn't need a Schwinn franchise to raise a shingle. He could nibble around the edges, selling Raleigh and other imports, even the high-priced American upstart Trek. "I couldn't be a Schwinn dealer," remembers frame builder Ron Boi, who opened a shop in the wealthy Chicago suburb of Winnetka in 1974, down the street from an established Schwinn franchise. "So I asked, 'Who else is out there?' " The answer, for him, would be Trek.

Boi and hundreds more comprised a new breed of seller: the non-Schwinn dealer, and executives at the company disdainfully labeled these sellers and their bikes "Brand X." As younger buyers began embracing the competition, Schwinn for the first time since the early 1930s found itself on the defensive. Its sales had exploded during the '70s boom, but market share was slipping, from 13.8 percent in 1968 to 10.2 percent in 1972. The growing popularity of lightweights—accounting for three-quarters of total U.S. bike sales by 1974—mostly came at the expense of the beloved children's high-rise Schwinn had pioneered with the Sting-Ray. And while Schwinn had sold between one-fourth and one-third of all ten-speeds in 1970, its share of that market would fall more than half, to 14 percent, by 1977.

Schwinn executives could accept that mass merchants like Sears were bound to capture the sales of the most price-conscious customers. (The chain stores traditionally account for two-thirds of all units sold in the United States and half of domestic revenues.) What galled them was losing chunks of the Cadillac segment that their company had dominated for so long. It was an inexplicable situation to many in management. After all, Schwinn *was* the market.

But not this new market. Schwinn had geared its image and products to kids: if you won a youngster's heart at seven, you'd keep him for life, and he'd want a Schwinn for his kids, too. These consumers were different. They were young adults buying bikes for themselves. Increasingly, their choice was Brand X. "When cycling became serious, people didn't think Schwinn," says Tom Ritchey, a Palo Alto component designer and one of the first custom builders of mountain bikes.

The irony was rich. For decades, Schwinn had led the American industry in championing the benefits of adult cycling, from its public relations stunts with movie stars in the '40s to its hiring of Dr. Paul Dudley White as a spokesman in the '50s, to its lobbying for urban biking trails in the '60s and '70s. Its engineers believed their factory built the best product for kids *and* grown-ups. Why, those European imports seemed flimsy. It was Schwinn, they'd boast, that had set the standard for lightweights in the States, with its high-design Paramount line, then its hardy New World models and Varsitys. Hell, those bikes could ride forever.

Unfortunately, durability was less of an issue in the '70s. The new and lighter steel alloys were just as strong as the old technology that Schwinn used. Adults also wanted more sophisticated colors and graphics than the primary reds and blues that had worked so well for Schwinn in the past. In addition, the new breed of enthusiast was a little too alien to

Schwinn folks who had grown more accustomed to putting than pedaling. "I got kidded for being a 'bikie,'" says former product manager Chuck Gillis, who started as a twenty-four-year-old sales representative in 1975. The company was blinded by the complacency that often afflicts businesses at the top of their fields. Just as General Motors was once wedded to gas-gulping cars, and IBM to unwieldy mainframe computers, Schwinn executives were clinging to the formulas that had brought glory; they scoffed at internal pleas for change and were contemptuous of competitors. "We figured because it said 'Schwinn,' people would buy it," says Brian Fiala, former vice president of human resources.

Established Schwinn sellers already were feeling the heat. As customers asked for lighter road bikes, even Middle American dealers picked up some of the import lines. Headquarters, however, refused to acknowledge the shift in demand. When a dealer at a sales and management session in the early '70s criticized the lack of lightweight offerings, Harry Delaney, the head of Schwinn's sales school, retorted, "Are you gonna ride it or carry it?" The comeback had become corporate mantra, reflecting a newfound insecurity. Sales reps later suggested that dealers use scales to weigh bikes in front of customers and show that Schwinns weren't significantly heavier than the new competition. If that failed to impress, "they always had the excuse, 'Well, once you got that bike rolling, weight didn't matter,'" scoffs John Pelc, owner of a Schwinn shop in Lincoln, Illinois, a downstate town that is as heartland as they come—no locks on bikes parked outside the historic county courthouse.

Al Fritz complained that some rival marketers misrepresented the weight of their bikes. And what about those hippie types who wore heavy boots and chains around their waist? That certainly didn't lighten the load. Fritz commissioned a Cornell University study showing properly inflated tires were more critical to bicycle performance than the overall weight of the vehicle. It didn't work. "When people thought 'Schwinn,' they thought 'tank,'" says Marin County dealer John Lewis.

Executives struggled to understand dealers such as Oscar Wastyn, Jr. His links to Schwinn stretched back to his Belgian-born grandfather, Emil, a prominent Chicago bicycle designer who crafted early Paramount and New World models for Ignaz and F.W. The Wastyns used to sell Schwinns to elite clientele, such as the chairman of the Chicago Board of Trade and members of the Chicago Symphony Orchestra. Now, the third generation was offering Peugeot and Motobecane.

"When are you going to get rid of that stuff, Oscar?," Brownie Schwinn would ask. "Isn't it easier to write one check at the end of the month?"

"No," Wastyn retorted. "That doesn't distinguish us."

Vice president Jay Townley later wondered why Wastyn carried the Cinelli Italian racing bike, rather than Schwinn's version of a Rolls-Royce, the Paramount. "That's all they make," Wastyn explained. "It's like owning a Lamborghini."

As dealers diversified, Schwinn sometimes tried to throw its weight around, rather than adapt and meet the competition. For years, Gary Sirota's Brands Cycle in Wantagh, New York, had been one of the nation's ten biggest sellers of Schwinns, although the name accounted for only 30 percent of bike sales at his bustling Long Island store. In the middle of the 1978 season, Schwinn stopped shipping him bikes. "They'd yanked my dealership," Sirota says. Headquarters gave an ultimatum: Sell a minimum of 80 percent Schwinn next year. "I said, 'OK,' and signed on the dotted line. And the next year, we kept our word." But the experience left a sour taste. "They thought beating me up was the way to sell more bikes here. I knew in my heart it was wrong."

Schwinn sometimes lost the battle in the trenches. Its sales reps—the guys who took dealer orders—pulled up in Oldsmobiles and Buicks; competitors drove Toyotas and Datsuns. Schwinn reps wore suits; Brand X preferred khakis. Schwinn salesmen were schooled in business and professional matters, how to advertise or turn inventory; they sold a broad line of bikes, parts, accessories, and, later, exercisers, so their technical knowledge about any single model was limited. Competitors who sold smaller lines were more focused: brimming with information on the latest derailleurs and brakes, they swapped racing and repair tips with younger employees in the back of the shop. It was a gap that would plague Schwinn for the next fifteen years. "They were weakest on product knowledge," says former sales rep Gillis. "What's the geometry?"—

the angles on the frame, which vary by type of bike—"They couldn't tell you."

There was a final indignity. Schwinn's longtime spokesman, Captain Kangaroo, could no longer pitch the bikes personally on his show. Critics of children's television for years had argued that childhood celebrities like Bob Keeshan unduly influenced youngsters with their commercial endorsements. In anticipation of stricter government control, the National Association of Broadcasters adopted a new code for children's shows requiring better separation of programs and product plugs. Schwinn introduced its commercials on the Captain Kangaroo show with an actor playing "Mr. Schwinn Dealer." It never was quite the same.

If Schwinn was lagging, much of the lapse could be blamed on the aging Chicago factory, which lacked new technology for lighter bikes. The Varsity was manufactured by electro-welding to seal joints under high heat. That required relatively thick-walled steel tubes and resulted in a heavier bike. In contrast, Japanese firms had developed lug-frame technology, in which the joints were connected by a separate fitting. This method used brazing, accomplished at lower temperatures, and opened the way for thinner-gauge steels and, ultimately, a lighter bike. It didn't take long for the American market to embrace the new technology, from the tiny Wisconsin start-up Trek to the larger East Coast rival Ross, whose parent, Chain Bike Corporation, saw sales grow after building a modern factory in Allentown, Pennsylvania.

The central building of Schwinn's Chicago plant was constructed at the turn of the century—and looked it, with wood floors and a leaking roof. The place reminded downstate Illinois dealer John Pelc of a sweatshop he had worked in as a young man after World War II. "And I was on a tour—they were showing us the good parts!" Even management cringed. In early 1980, new president Edward R. Schwinn, Jr., asked his just-recruited vice president of finance, John Barker, to name the first thing he needed. "An arsonist," Barker quipped.

Schwinn had expanded its manufacturing complex during the boom, adding a new rim mill and warehouse. The result was a hodgepodge, with no continuous production line. At the main plant, a mill fabricated steel tubing for the bicycle frame from flat steel, while other components were stamped or machined. The pieces were placed in steel bins, loaded on one of the company's fleet of trucks and ferried just over a mile to a new satellite facility, where the frame was welded and primed. Back again on special racks, the frames were returned by truck to the second floor of the main plant for final assembly and painting.

Some of the manufacturing, such as the electrostatic spray-painting operation, was modern, but the wheel assembly was primitive. Workers attached spokes to hubs by hand, then laced them into holes in the rim before passing the part to a machine for alignment. Throughout the complex, there were twists and turns, nooks and crannies. The whole fractured mess led to inventory literally being tucked away and forgotten. "When a model was discontinued, twenty million dollars worth of hidden stuff vomited up," says former product manager Carl Cohen, who arrived in 1982. "We found Shimano coaster brakes that had been airfreighted five years earlier and were never used."

Inside the executive suite, Schwinn struggled to cope with the public's changing tastes. Marketing chief Ray Burch walked into the office of Al Fritz and pounded on the desk. "Why can't we make bikes as light as Peugeot? We've got to come out with a lighter bike."

Burch and Fritz long had been rivals, albeit friendly ones. The former rarely missed an opportunity to poke the latter—asking, for instance, why a broken part or process was "on the Fritz." Colleagues say Burch was shaken in 1972 when Frank V. Schwinn elevated Fritz to executive vice president, the No. 2 position, after Ed Sr.'s death. The promotion made sense: Fritz had been close to the Old Man; he'd come up through the ranks, possessed a broad knowledge of the company, and had a wide following. With his new status, Fritz oversaw manufacturing, engineering, and purchasing, and was chairman of the executive committee. Burch says he never complained, but soon after the appointment, he and chief financial officer Al Selkurt were named senior vice presidents, each reporting to Frankie.

Then in 1974, the fifty-four-year-old Frankie suffered a heart attack. Never the activist president, he became even more withdrawn. Burch and Fritz hashed out their differences in private and usually emerged on the same track. "The structure gave us problems at times, made for uncomfortable moments, yes," Fritz says. His own authority was limited; he could influence, but he couldn't single-handedly call the shots. The result: power became even more diffused in a company that faced tough issues.

Although Burch and the marketers had gained preeminence at the expense of the factory, Schwinn's engineering group still was powerful. The men who had pioneered the innovative designs of the 1950s now were twenty years older and still proud, rightfully, of the factory's sturdy bikes. Engineer Rudy Schwinn today shows off a 1975-era Town and Country cycle hanging in his garage. "It looks like new," he says. "That bike will last you a lifetime—two lifetimes!" But success made some of them imperious: *Are you gonna ride it or carry it?* The attitude wasn't from lack of exposure. Chief engineer Frank Brilando had traveled the world, visiting the newest lug-frame bicycle plants and components factories. Brilando was deft at adapting technology: introducing measures to shave manufacturing costs in Chicago, for instance, or simply to make an older part better. But the mild-mannered Brilando was practical and conservative, not the big-picture type or one to lead the charge in a new direction. "In lug frame, Schwinn was slow," Brilando concedes. "It should have been done sooner. It was hard to be competitive on price. We could [import] them and make more profit than if we did it ourselves."

Certainly, Schwinn was not alone on this score in the early '70s. U.S. auto companies, steel mills, and machine tool builders also were under siege from cheaper Japanese competition. It was part of a long, painful period of industrial decline that by the mid-1980s would nearly halve the number of manufacturing jobs in Chicago alone and litter much of the Midwest with the rusting carcasses of once-mighty, smoke-belching factories. Would Schwinn be another casualty? As an interim measure, executives decided to import lug-frame bikes from Japan.

The company recently had started to buy Japanese components, but importing a complete cycle was another story. Japan's bike companies had adopted a voluntary quota following pressure from American-made

Huffy, Columbia, and other mass-market competitors of Schwinn. Those allocations were calculated according to prior-year sales. Since Schwinn was a newcomer, it wasn't entitled to a single bike. Fritz, the point man on the project, pushed ahead, arguing that selling to Schwinn would enhance Japan's prestige. Although the country's cars were starting to make their mark in the United States (and, after the Arab oil embargo of 1973, cause fits among domestic auto makers), Japanese bicycle manufacturers at the time were selling mostly lesser quality products to big American retailers. But Schwinn offered something no other company had. "The message I repeated each time was that the image of Schwinn Bicycle Company was Number One in the U.S." Fritz says. "The image of Japanese bicycles in the U.S. was very poor. We would reverse that image."

It took six trips to Japan over the course of a year, including lengthy negotiating sessions with officials of the Ministry of International Trade and Industry. Schwinn finally was granted an exemption from the quotas, and Fritz made a deal with Japan's two largest bicycle builders (the only two that could supply the volume Schwinn needed): Bridgestone Cycle, a unit of the giant tiremaker, and Matsushita's National Bicycle Company, also known as Panasonic. Then came detailed haggling on pricing and delivery. Fritz's personal translator was Yoshizo "Yoshi" Shimano, the youngest of three brothers who headed the components manufacturer Shimano Industrial Company, a family firm that was striving for cachet in the American market. Yoshi was an articulate and astute salesman in charge of Shimano's U.S. territory who constantly pushed Schwinn for more business. Indeed, Shimano later would become *the* bicycle industry powerhouse, with a virtual monopoly on the market for derailleurs, hubs, pedals, shifters, brake cables, and other key parts, but for now Yoshi was happy with a front-row seat, privy to Schwinn's sales and production forecasts. He, in turn, helped Schwinn, knowing both English and the language of bicycles. Schwinn executives, like many of their counterparts in American industry at the time, had a cultural disadvantage. Recalls Fritz: "I used to talk for three minutes, and I'd say, 'Yoshi,' and then Yoshi might talk for ten minutes. Why did it take him so long to translate?" After one such meeting, Fritz teased his translator. "Yoshi, one of these goddamned days I'm gonna learn to speak Japanese, but you're not gonna know it."

Schwinn imported its first model in 1972, a basic lug-frame road bike under the World label, and soon brought in an upgraded European-style touring bike, appropriately called the LeTour. The made-in-America tradition demanded some finessing. The first Japanese cycles neither appeared in the catalog nor carried the Schwinn name; later versions had a tiny "Schwinn Approved" sticker on the tubing. By 1975, however, Schwinn was importing 200,000 bikes annually from the new suppliers. The Japanese-made World model sold for about $130 retail—close in price to the American-made Varsity. It was an improvement over the Varsity, too, although still a far cry from the sleek French models that were so much in vogue. (By the late '70s, Schwinn finally installed in Chicago a factory line for manufacturing lug-frame bikes—the LeTour and Super LeTour.) With diminished domestic production after the boom, imports now represented more than 20 percent of the company's sales.

Importing helped satisfy some of the new marketplace, but Schwinn still needed to tackle the larger issue: what to do about the aging factory. "The repercussions of Schwinn's inability to meet dealer demands are still being felt," the company's marketing staff wrote in a plaintive 1978 report.

Two years earlier, a task force had been formed to study the idea of building a new plant. Heading the project was Frankie's twenty-seven-year-old nephew and corporate heir, Ed Schwinn, Jr., who had joined the company after finishing college at the end of 1972, ten months after his father's death, and had been named vice president of corporate development in late 1974. Accounting firm Peat Marwick Mitchell was hired to study financing and site selection. The location that won the popularity contest at Schwinn was the then-fast-growing oil patch city of Tulsa, Oklahoma, which offered plenty of reliable power and water, a central location, and a friendly business climate.

One of Tulsa's biggest boosters was Jack Ahearn, vice president of manufacturing and leader of the team charged with the nuts and bolts of pulling off the move. In 1977 Ahearn wined and dined factory foremen and their wives, who wanted to know about Tulsa's housing, schools, and crime. Schwinn was prepared to move nineteen foremen and twenty-five supervisors, many of whom had fifteen to twenty-five years' tenure. "We had them on board," Ahearn says.

For engineering and design, Schwinn hired a Houston firm that proposed an 800,000-square-foot plant with manufacturing consolidated under one roof—a more efficient alternative to the scattershot situation in Chicago. Schwinn's board of directors authorized the $700,000 purchase of 140 acres in an industrial park and asked the design consultants to develop a state-of-the-art bicycle plant. That was the rub, Ahearn says. In retrospect, the Schwinn board was prepared to fund nothing of the sort.

(Meanwhile, talk of a move to Tulsa created unease among the rank and file. Word spread to state government officials, who were eager to preserve local jobs—and keep a famous name in Illinois—possibly by offering the company tax breaks and other economic development goodies. The black Checker car of Governor James R. Thompson frequently was parked in front of the corporate offices, and his daughter rode a Schwinn Pixie in the building's halls.)

Ed Schwinn was a strong advocate for Tulsa, wanting to build a case that growing demand for bicycles justified the new factory. He predicted sales soon would rise to 2 million units from the peak 1.5 million units sold in 1974. Instead, business was rolling to a halt in the years immediately after the boom. "I made a conservative [sales] estimate and Ed was incensed," Ray Burch says. "He thought I was trying to kill the deal."

Jack Ahearn was a bit nervous when he began a formal presentation to the Schwinn board in June 1978. The blistering price tag: nearly $50 million. The directors, including Frankie, Brownie, Ed's mother, Mary, and attorney Bob Keck, "almost fell out of their chairs," Ahearn says. He went back to the plant designer to discuss ways to mitigate the family's financial burden. In a second presentation in early August, Ahearn suggested that the project be tackled in stages, perhaps over two years. But the directors, he says, already were murmuring about the "bond market going to hell" and "Frankie was shaking in his boots."

The price tag proved too daunting for the closely held company. In addition, Frankie wouldn't consider taking on minority investors to help fund this kind of project. Coming out of the boom, Schwinn was ripe to be acquired. "We got letters from people offering to buy the company, or a stake," Al Fritz says. "If we sold twenty-five percent, we could get twenty million dollars. But Frankie said, 'I'm never going to sell.' " It was a critical juncture. The company needed new capital to grow, yet it was unwilling to make the moves needed to gain the financing: seek long-term borrowing; sell stock to outsiders or to the public; sell all, or a piece, of the company to private investors. In the headstrong Schwinn tradition, Frankie told Burch, Fritz, and others he didn't want outsiders telling him what to do. "The family was religious in the belief it wanted to own the company," according to Bob Keck. "You couldn't get them to think otherwise."

Frankie's decision merely had put off the day of reckoning—the day Schwinn would have to build a new plant or close its old one. The company, which had been inching away from its manufacturing legacy for more than a decade, now was just another decaying Rust Belt metal-bender. "Our intention is to keep Chicago open," Frankie announced to employees after the fateful board meeting, "although we will review our operations on a year-to-year basis." That kind of corporate-speak was a not-so-subtle signal to worried workers. The plant and its jobs were at risk.

The Tulsa fiasco laid the groundwork for a final struggle between the defenders of the factory, who wanted to preserve Schwinn's manufacturing tradition, and the marketers, who argued that the company's too-heavy bikes were dinosaurs. Given rising labor costs and growing government interference, the latter argued, the company would do better as an importer.

Selling a minority stake so Schwinn could build a modern plant and still control its destiny might have been prescient, but plans for the Oklahoma factory called for using the fading welded-frame technology. Although lug-frame imports had been the hot topic at Schwinn, Ed and other planners figured the big numbers still were in steel-welded frames. The plant would have become a white elephant the day it opened.

When the board formally rejected the Oklahoma project "Eddie went ballistic," Burch recalls. The young executive roared down the hall, confronting the marketing manager whose lower sales projections had helped doom the deal.

"Tulsa is dead," Ed said. 'You better get off your ass and sell bicycles."

Burch says today, "He never forgave me for it."

8

"WEIRD AND FREAKY STUFF"

Only a few scenes stand out in the otherwise dreadful 1971 documentary on motorcycle racing, *On Any Sunday*. There's a bloody crash, of course; some shots of a dusty Steve McQueen tearing up the California desert; and a brief but remarkable episode that shows a pack of boys speeding their Sting-Rays off-road through a vacant lot, emulating their gutsy heroes with the simulated sounds of motorcycles shifting gears.

"Hn-hnnurrrrrrrrrrrrrrrrr. Hn-hn-hnnurrrrrrrrrrrrrr."

These ten-year-olds are among the first BMXers captured in action. For some time, children on bikes had been racing through a motorcycle park in Valencia, California, after the real Sunday shindigs were finished. Their cameo in the film introduced thousands of other kids to the potential thrills awaiting them off the street in a subdivision's undeveloped parcels. From the San Fernando Valley to Orange County, children began racing each other through suburbia's most hostile territory, pounding their Sting-Rays, jumping across gullies and bulldozer trenches, flying 15 feet or more before landing on a precarious wheelie or tumbling into the dirt. Out of Southern California's garages came reconfigured high-rise models that could withstand the clobbering. With their 20-inch wheels, these were still kids' bikes—Schwinn's bread and butter—yet, unlike the pre-Sting-Ray era ten years earlier, when the company jumped on a hot fad out west and spread it nationally, Schwinn steered clear. Those hair-raising BMX exploits, Frank V. warned his staff, inevitably would result in accidents and lawsuits; the company couldn't risk losing its reputation for safety.

Schwinn would lose, all right, but only because it sat on the sidelines. By 1982, bicycle motocross was so entrenched in the national landscape that the obligatory chase scene in the movie *E.T.* featured kids transporting their extraterrestrial friend back to his landing site on BMX bikes, scorching the suburban terrain and then miraculously flying to safety.

Many parents didn't share Frankie's schoolmarmish fears in the early '70s. They embraced the new sport, if for no other reason than that supervised bike racing on closed-circuit courses was safer than unsupervised competition. Other parents were getting their thrills vicariously, gravitating to "the speed, the competition, the rough and tumble, the thrills and spills," explains BMX pioneer Skip Hess, whose Mongoose line of bikes would dominate the new market. "It was no place for sissies. This is part of the action and mystique of the sport." Big business welcomed the action, too. Yamaha Motor Company, the Japanese motorcycling giant, was one of the first sponsors to put together bicycling teams and stage competitions. By the summer of 1974, there were an estimated 130,000 BMX-style bikes and more than 100 tracks in California alone. The fad spread eastward. Miami Schwinn dealer Ray Knapp told *The Schwinn Reporter* in 1977 that motocross accounted for 55 percent of his gross sales. Nationwide, sales surged that year to 1.75 million units, representing nearly 20 percent of all U.S. bicycle purchases. World championships in Oklahoma City drew 2,000 participants in 1982, when BMX sales peaked and accounted for nearly one-third of U.S. bike sales.

The races usually were two laps around a one-eighth-mile course, including a series of jumps and turns, and there often was a wheelie contest to test how far a rider could travel balanced on the bike's rear tire. It was marvelously thrilling, just a bit dangerous and utterly cool. The meets became all-day family affairs—"like a 'hip' Boy Scout outing," according to sociologist Jeffrey E. Nash in a 1986 article on the phenomenon in the *Journal of Popular Culture.* Parents packed the kids, bikes, tools, and picnic into the van for a day at the BMX park, where the competitors (usually ages ten to sixteen) would strut their stuff, wearing racing pants, or "leathers," with knee pads and tapered ankles and sporting professional-style jerseys emblazoned with the colorful logos of local sponsors. Most excellent were the high-tech wonder bikes—"backyard engineering marvels," Nash calls them—costing a then-unheard-of $500, $1,000, or more. When equipment like shoes, pads, goggles, dust masks, and helmets were added, it was not an undertaking for the needy.

The early models were products of a garage-based industry spurred by the inevitable results of treating an old Sting-Ray like a little motorcycle. The standard high-rise frames or forks broke; the wheels crumpled. Just as the bike boom wrought changes by attracting new blood, the BMX craze in particular lured backyard mechanics fascinated by the possibilities of applying automotive and even aerospace technology to upgrade the garden-variety bike. There were frame makers, welders, rogue dealers, and riders from the motorcycle- and auto-racing fields, many of whom were BMX parents who also organized teams and races. These entrepreneurs started making custom metal frames and added heavy motorcycle wheels and tough components that could take the abuse of a race. Webco, a motorcycle distributor near Malibu, was one of the first BMX frame builders. Northridge-based Redline, which started making front forks, expanded into frames, and later, full bicycles. Mike Bobrick and Mitchell Weiner of upstart Western States Imports hopped on the trend relatively early, too. They funded a racing team and called their BMX model Diamond Back, a name that honored the rattlesnake (whose cousin can eat a mongoose) and later would describe the company's full line of bikes. "The BMX," Bobrick says, "was a breath of fresh air."

One of the best known apostles of the movement is Mongoose founder Skip Hess, a ten-speed racer in his youth (he was California state champion in the early 1950s) who grew up to become chief engineer at a car accessory business and a professional drag racer for a Ford Motor Company team. Hess was eager to upgrade the primitive technology that his children and their friends were riding. He developed a wheel that wouldn't collapse: a one-piece cast-aluminum "Motomag," which he began selling in 1974. Soon, every kid in the sport *had* to have a Motomag. "They never bent, never were out of true," boasts Hess, now a consultant. He sold his hot wheels everywhere: to the mass market bike makers Huffy Corporation[1] and Murray Ohio Manufacturing Company—so kids who couldn't afford a high-end model for $129 could approximate one with an $89 Huffy—and even to Schwinn, which didn't use the wheels on its own bikes, but sold them as after-market parts to dealers. "We infiltrated their distribution with products they didn't care to offer," Hess says. "The people in Chicago only heard the echo."

Frankie did hear the noise, but he saw nothing but potential problems. "He thought it was his duty not to subject Schwinn buyers to a dangerous sport," says Fred Teeman, Schwinn's product manager for BMX and mountain bikes in the early 1980s. The fear was not unfounded: the Consumer Product Safety Commission in 1973 published a study of accident injuries that described bicycles as "the most dangerous consumer product in America." Schwinn's former California regional sales manager Dave Staub remembers escorting a group of commission officials and Schwinn executives to a BMX track near Los Angeles. The visitors seemed horrified at the thought of children being catapulted over their handlebars in mid-race. "This is hardly a good time to start promoting dirt biking and stunt riding, which do involve increased risk of injury to the rider," Ray Burch dutifully wrote in *The Schwinn Reporter* in October 1973. "We believe everyone in the bicycle industry would be well advised to concentrate on other kinds of bicycle business rather than dirt biking. It may not disappear overnight, but on the other hand, I doubt it will find a permanent place in the sport of bicycling. There are too many better ways to enjoy bicycle riding. And to those few Schwinn dealers who have encouraged us to build special bikes for dirt biking, we say, 'Sure . . . we can beef up Sting-Ray frames, forks, wheels, and handlebars. But how do you beef up kids?' "

Many at Schwinn thought the trend was too strong to ignore. While a child might fall face down in the dirt and lose a tooth (researcher Nash counted five serious injuries—including a concussion and a broken rib—among fifty races he attended, and he calls lesser cuts and bruises "commonplace"), was bicycle motocross any more risky than football or wrestling? Besides, California Schwinn dealers were under fire: their customers were clamoring for a good BMX. "Schwinn kept popping out Sting-Rays past their prime," says La Mirada retailer Chris Travers. "We took Sting-Rays, changed the handlebars and wheels, and sold buckets of them."

A few miles north, in the San Fernando Valley town of Canoga Park, bike shop mechanic Russ Okawa also was overhauling Sting-Rays. For added strength, he expanded the number of spokes on the wheel—to 36 from 28—and created a hub that more likely would be found on a full-size bike. "That was a cool-looking wheel," Okawa recalls. Next he adopted a knobby tire, then he replaced the longhorn handlebars with lower and flatter motorcycle-style bars that offered riders better control. Okawa and others in his boss's shop taught local BMX racers how to reconstruct the high-rise bikes. "We set them up in a production line in the back of the store," he says. "We paid them, and that financed their racing." The souped up Sting-Rays cost between $84 and $94, a stiff premium over the $64 ticket of the original. "We thought, 'That's way too much. No one will buy these,' " Okawa says, but people did, accounting for 80 percent of all Sting-Rays sold at the store.

Schwinn's timid stance created a sore point with some dealers. If Sting-Rays were modified into BMX bikes—a use they weren't intended for—the lifetime warranty would be void, the company warned. Yet lots of kids were bringing broken frames to the Canoga Park shop for replacement. While most young customers, if not all, had jumped the bikes and added stress to the frames, Schwinn's quality control had been off for several years because the company had been pressured by the bike boom to crank out product. Sometimes the welds on the bikes were weak, Okawa notes, which gave dealers a bit of bargaining power with the factory. Many of the frames ultimately would have failed anyway, Okawa argues; racing them BMX-style merely "made them fail in a month."

It was difficult for a national company like Schwinn to hop on a regional grass-roots movement like BMX. Bikes were built on Fridays, raced on Saturdays, and reconfigured on Mondays. "Innovation came from guys that race and can build stuff in their garage—weird and freaky stuff," Okawa says. Yet the company could have embraced the trend as its own and starred on the national stage, just as it had done with the Sting-Ray. Instead, it allowed competitors like Skip Hess to establish strong brand names.

By 1976, Hess had a $3 million business in Motomag wheels and was plowing his earnings into a nearby factory to build complete BMX models. His Mongoose Bicycle Company, named after a drag-racing pal, became the first domestic firm to seriously commercialize BMX, churning out 200,000 vehicles annually by the late '70s.[2] Like the makers of European road bikes, Hess used an alloy of steel, chromium, and molybdenum, called chrome-moly, for a stronger frame. (Until then, most U.S.-made bikes were carbon steel.) Instead of painting the frames, he plated them with nickel or chrome, for a bejeweled appearance. Mongoose fielded its own racing team, yet the majority of buyers were suburbanites who simply wanted a cool ride to school. "Most of our bikes," Hess notes, "never saw a track."

A chastened Schwinn finally had scrambled to get into the market the year before, with the introduction of a motocross model dubbed, appropriately, the "Scrambler." Ray Burch conceded in the January 1975 *Schwinn Reporter* that the company was making "an about-face," but he observed that helmets and padding, limited speeds, and soft dirt at tracks had made the sport "not as dangerous as many of us anticipated." Unfortunately, the Scrambler was a lame entry in the BMX sweepstakes. Like the Varsity, it was heavy steel—one reason Schwinn's marketers preferred to tout its strength and rigidity, not its weight. "It was a cross between a Sting-Ray and a street bike," scoffs veteran California Schwinn distributor Dennis Morgon. "It was not what kids were looking for. Schwinn was pussyfooting along." By 1977 Schwinn was stuck with a "minimal" 5.6 percent share of the BMX market, according to an internal marketing report, and was setting its sights on a modest 7 to 8 percent by 1980. In the late '70s, when independent dealers were selling an estimated 750,000 BMX models annually, Mongoose would become No. 1 in the market. "Schwinn's decision not to enter into the BMX market at its inception allowed other manufacturers to not only enter, but dominate this portion of the market," the company report lamented. "As a consequence, Schwinn has been fighting an uphill battle to establish itself in the BMX market."

Schwinn did have a modest success in the Sting, a top-of-the-line BMX model intended to "sting the competition," but the bike was good mostly for bolstering Schwinn's sagging image. The $525 product was handmade at the Chicago factory of chrome-alloy steel and its joints were sealed by a melted fillet of brass. "It was well received—a primo bike," says Fred Teeman, at the time Schwinn's thirty-four-year-old head of consumer affairs, who ringmastered the company's BMX racing team. Nevertheless, the factory could produce no more than 1,000 of its prestigious Stings a year.

Only in 1983—ten years after the fad took off—did Schwinn become a force in BMX. That year, the company began marketing the Taiwanese-built chrome-moly Predator (so named because a predator presumably could chew up a mongoose). "First track bike built for the streets," Schwinn's trade announcements bragged. "Catch it. Before it catches you." The Predator actually caused major problems for Skip Hess's American-made Mongoose because the Schwinn import was as much as 30 percent cheaper than Hess's bikes, and the pressure forced Mongoose to shift its production overseas. That, plus the cost of liability insurance for BMX makers, Hess says, contributed to his decision to sell Mongoose in 1985 to New York's Service Cycle Supply, the former Schwinn distributor that had been dumped following the Supreme Court decision, but had thrived and become a competitor.

A few years later, the BMX craze petered out, falling to about 15 percent of bicycle sales. Both Mongoose and Western States diversified into a full line of products, including the mountain bike (which Hess still insists on calling "an adult-sized BMX"), while Schwinn moved on to other challenges that would prove even more difficult. The damage would be lasting, however. Just as Schwinn had lost its edge in the adult market to imports, it had lost its lead in the kids' market with the BMX. Children now were as likely to yearn for, say, a Mongoose under the Christmas tree as they would a Schwinn.

9

"JUST BEING A KID"

Just as the BMX sprang from the soul of a Schwinn—the fading Sting-Ray—the mountain bike was created from an earlier generation Schwinn—the long forgotten balloon-tire bicycle. Like the Southern California BMX builders, the Northern California mountain bike pioneers were relentless tinkerers who'd pulverize their wheels on weekends and rebuild them, stronger and smarter, during the week. That kind of inventing is difficult, though not impossible, for a larger company. "When you're Number One, you don't have to try things," explains former Schwinn product manager Fred Teeman. "When a new segment emerges, there is an infant, experimental stage. For every mountain bike, ten fads fall by the wayside."

This was the wrong fad to ignore. The mountain bike and its urban offspring would prove to be the most important bike trend of the 1980s, accounting for nearly two-thirds of the adult market by decade's end. Again, Schwinn would find itself left in the dust. It was too absorbed with its own manufacturing and management problems and still too arrogant to acknowledge that others were setting the trends. "If they didn't think it up, it wasn't worth making," says John Lewis, a Schwinn dealer in the Marin County town of Mill Valley whose shop was a frequent haunt of the early mountain bikers. Instead, it would fall to imported parts salesman Michael Sinyard and his Specialized Bicycle Components—an upstart firm with no excess baggage—to bring the mountain bike to the mass market.

Riding off-road is still considered something of a cutting-edge sport, making its Olympic debut, for instance, at the 1996 Atlanta games. Yet casual bikers embraced the vehicle in the mid-1980s because it was user friendly. The upright ride was more comfortable than that of the skinny-tire ten-speeds, where you slouched toward the handlebars on a hard narrow saddle. The fat knobby tires also absorbed the shock from a pothole. Between 1975 and 1985, many aging buyers of ten-speeds hung up their road bikes in garages, not far from the fondue pots and Pocket Fishermans. The mountain bike, however, proved irresistible. Sociological minds theorized that the sport offered baby-boomers the chance to break loose from their structured routines and again become the nonconformists they'd thought they were in the 1960s. Biking up a hill was faster than hiking up (and far more fun on the trip down), yet the vehicle was slow enough and silent enough for the at-one-with-nature types. Of course, the expensive mountain bike also fit nicely into the fashion- and status-conscious '80s economy, alongside BMW sedans and Krups coffeemakers. Actually, mountain bikes probably were more akin to a Jeep Grand Cherokee or Chevy Blazer—a much more rugged vehicle than the average suburbanite ever could need, but ever so cool.

The guys who invented the mountain bike were cool, too. Gary Fisher, his rival Joe Breeze, their compatriot Charlie Kelly, and frame builder Tom Ritchey all were a generation or two removed from the World War II vets who had built up Schwinn. "We joked about the Midwest dealers—fat guys chewing on cigars, selling lawnmowers, too," says Charlie Kelly, an early chronicler of the trend. "You know, 'Would you sell a mountain bike to these guys?' "

Kelly and cohorts hailed from Marin County, where a culture of casual affluence looms as large as Mount Tamalpais, the local peak that rises 2,600 feet above the Pacific Ocean and towers over the Golden Gate

Bridge, beckoning everyone from Cub Scout troops and yuppie backpackers to New Age mystics and Baptist picnickers. Joe Breeze was a preschooler when he asked his father, "Is it the tallest mountain in the world?" At age ten, Breeze was hiking Mount Tam's trails and cycling its paved roads. He was encouraged by his dad, who designed and raced sports cars and would lecture his son about the importance of vehicle efficiency. Young Breeze rode a three-speed English model with fenders and upright handlebars and graduated to a Dawes Galaxy British racing bike. None of his friends had Varsitys—too middle-class, in many Marin minds—although he remembers coveting a purple number when he was in seventh grade. "My dad said no. It was not a proper bike." As a teenager, Breeze and buddies borrowed younger children's Sting-Rays and clobbered the wheels on dirt paths. "We trashed 'em bad—bent forks, rims, flat tires. We'd promise to fix 'em up, same or better. Riding in the dirt was a lot of fun. Just being a kid." Breeze also was becoming an accomplished distance racer, starting with 100-mile treks through Sonoma County, then a 200-mile trip to Lake Tahoe, and finally a 1,400-mile jaunt to Washington state at age sixteen. Breeze soon was competing in the highest men's class in both traditional road racing and European-derived cyclo-cross, an older and considerably more refined version of BMX for adults that uses lighter, skinny-tired bikes and pit crews on a manicured dirt course.

With hair down to his shoulders, Breeze conformed to the style of the day, but he was not as enraptured of the '60s counterculture as mountain bike adversary Gary Fisher, who got a kick out of flouting authority. Fisher, the son of an architect, had been riding competitively since he was twelve, yet he dropped out of racing in high school after the Amateur Bicycle League of America expelled him because he wouldn't cut his hair. A fan of Jefferson Airplane and the Grateful Dead, he moved to San Francisco's Haight-Ashbury district and staged light shows for rock acts at the Fillmore West and the Avalon Ballroom. Fisher quickly was disillusioned about the profit potential, however; too many competitors were selling their services at a loss. "They just wanted to go backstage and meet the rock stars," he says. Fisher resumed riding and racing in 1971 and joined a Marin County collection of maverick road racers called Velo

Club Tamalpais. They scorned the established cycling order—"geeks," as Fisher describes them—who wore jerseys with patches and helmets with rear-view mirrors. "We were too cool for that." Fisher and friends became self-styled bike activists, whizzing by gas lines and mocking the tortured motorists for queuing up. He was still hanging out with rockers—living with members of the band New Riders of the Purple Sage by bartering his housekeeping services for rent—when he met a kindred soul in Charlie Kelly.

Then twenty-eight, Kelly had been a National Merit Scholar who had flunked out of college and become a sound man and piano hauler for a rock group—the "1960s equivalent," as he puts it, "of a circus roustabout." He was a bicycle devotee out of necessity: while working for a band called Sons of Champlin, he discovered it was pointless to own a car because any vehicle became community property and promptly was driven into the ground. Tooling around Marin on his Peugeot, Kelly heard tales about the long-haired cyclist Gary Fisher, nicknamed "Spidey" because he was tall and skinny, all arms and legs. One day, Fisher was cycling with his pal, John Cullins Dawson III (better known as Marmaduke, lead singer for the New Riders), on a jaunt to Jerry Garcia's Grateful Dead office in San Rafael when Kelly pedaled by. "Are you Spidey?" he asked, matching Fisher to the description, and Kelly joined the expedition. Fisher, who was tiring of his setup with the New Riders, soon moved into Kelly's house in Fairfax.

The decor was early bicycle. An assortment of frames hung on hooks, functioning as room dividers, and race posters splattered the walls. A workbench dominated the dining room. A thundering rock 'n roll speaker system blasted day and night. The pad became national headquarters for the cult sport of "clunking."

A wild and woolly clique from Larkspur called the "Canyonites" had been ripping through cast-off balloon-tire bikes they'd found at salvage shops—Shelbys, Huffys, and Columbias, but mostly Schwinns. Models from the late 1930s were best equipped for hill-riding. The thick prewar frames were harder to crack, and the upright handlebars at first offered better control. The old bikes became known, affectionately, as "clunkers." "Soon," Kelly wrote in a 1979 article in *Mariah/Outside* magazine, "the canyon gangsters were doing such stunts as riding at 40 miles per hour under a . . . gate (with two inches of clearance above the handlebars) to maintain enough speed to launch the bike off a sharp crest for a 40-foot jump."

At first, Joe Breeze turned up his nose. He was working at an upscale bike shop in Sausalito and pedaling a fine roadster. "I would never ride something like that," he scoffed. "It's not efficient." Yet Breeze had also begun restoring turn-of-the century bikes, and he often scouted for parts at time-worn shops. In 1974, Breeze and friend Marc Vendetti (a member of Velo Club Tamalpais who had ridden ballooners) were rummaging through a bike shop in Santa Cruz that was rumored to house a treasure trove of antique parts. Alas, there wasn't much. The booby prize was a 1941 Schwinn-built B. F. Goodrich ballooner. "I've ridden these," Vendetti said. "They're kinda fun. Offer five dollars."

The bike was slathered with red paint. There was a big basket, chrome fenders, a metal chainguard. The Schwinn had so much . . . character. "Soulful," Breeze says today. "I was amazed how great it felt. A solid feeling. You could run it over anything. It didn't jolt you like a road bike." He went home, stripped the fenders and basket, oiled the chain and scraped off the paint to uncover the original blue and ivory featherhead motif. He hitchhiked a van ride to the top of Mount Tam and zoomed down the trails.

Meantime, Gary Fisher had purchased a one-speed ballooner at an East Bay chicken farm. His passion at the time was traditional road racing: Fisher was a top-class competitor and cycled up to 500 miles a week. But clunking tugged at his soul, too. Fisher began buying old frames, building a pile of fifty to piece together better clunkers. Charlie Kelly, traveling with the band, combed the countryside for parts. He found rare Schwinn cantilever brakes in Stockton and Bendix coaster brake two-speed hubs in Denver. His biggest coup was in Los Molinas, where he stumbled across a farmer with a yard of rusting bikes. Some Fisher and Kelly sold, others they pulverized, since even a durable old Schwinn frame would buckle after enough rides down Mount Tam. Riders coming off a hair-raising spin—their hands and faces scratched, their sneakers and jeans caked with mud—would stop by Gary and Charlie's place to fix a part or discuss ways to improve performance. Fisher loved to turn people on to clunking for the first time. "Their eyes would be this big," he says, widening his thumb and forefinger. "There was a sense of mystery and discovery." A collection of regulars cruised the hills in the afternoons, from trust fund kids to a San Francisco firefighter. Some, like Fisher, arranged their bike mechanic jobs so there'd be plenty of time to ride. A hit from a joint often enhanced the experience. "It was a bunch of stoners," Kelly says.[1] "Not all were marijuana farmers. Some were." All had time on their hands and "no discernible agenda," according to Kelly, who became a sort of Boswell to the mountain bike set with his own publication, *Fat Tire Flyer*, and numerous articles written for *Outside* and cycling publications.

There was just one downside to all this fun. The rider had to get his clunker up the mountain. "You were riding twenty percent of the time and pushing eighty percent—or getting a [van] ride," Fisher recalls. That spurred him to tinker with gears. At a flea market, he bought a Schwinn tandem for its enormous and sturdy drum brake. The brake, transferred to his ballooner, enabled him to mount a derailleur. Now, Fisher had a five-speed that could climb a hill, reversing the drudgery ratio to 80 percent riding and 20 percent walking, and though it was heavy—more than 50 pounds—it worked. "He rode away from us," Kelly says.

Marin County bike shops were besieged by clunker riders in search of the obscure tandem drum brake. Mill Valley Schwinn dealer John Lewis, whose storefront often doubled as a pit stop for hitchhiking bikers needing a ride up Mount Tam, ordered the part from a French supplier. Within weeks, he and other dealers throughout Marin were displaying the pieces prominently and, no doubt, selling more than the rest of the country combined. Lewis also was doing a brisk business in motorcycle brake levers and heavy-duty brake cables that could handle the rigors of the new sport. Schwinn's West Coast sales reps reported back to Chicago on the strange goings-on. "I don't think they noticed," Lewis says of headquarters.

By 1976, a burning question arose: Who was the fastest down Mount Tam? A mass start was out of the question. Clunker riders instead would use a time trial on a two-mile trail that descended 1,300 feet. The morning races came to be known as "Repack"—because the intense pressure on a coaster brake vaporized the grease, requiring the rider to repack the hubs with goop—and the Mount Tam course was dubbed "Repack Road." (The name was a bit of a misnomer by this point. Most clunker riders had added sturdier motorcycle brakes, so it was rare to see a smoking hub at the time.) The races grew in popularity, and Repack Road became a forum for showing off innovations in rims, handlebars, crank sets, seatposts, saddles, gears, pedals, and stems.

Breeze and Fisher were the biggest rivals on Repack Road. The meticulous Breeze, dubbed the "Mad Scientist," would chart the course in advance and mark an "X" on maps for where there was a bad turn. Both men claim to have won the most races. Fisher holds the course record (4 minutes, 22 seconds); Breeze (lagging by two seconds) has the No. 2 slot. Yet the conflict was deeper than athletic. Much like Michaux and Lallement a century earlier in France, Fisher and Breeze each would claim to have invented a unique vehicle, and each had a different view of what constituted the ideal clunker. Fisher had grafted road bike components and other parts onto his ballooner frame in his quest to master the rugged terrain; Breeze was happy riding his clunker in its original state. "My interest was in the old bikes staying the way they were," Breeze explains. "Some people, myself included, were 'One speed or die.' Let the road bike ride on the cutting edge of technology and the clunker remain an outlet for your primitive side." Fisher saw it another way: "They were purists," he sniffs. "They were superior—'no gears.' "

Most clunker riders clamored for better equipment. The newer gears and brakes helped, but the old steel frames didn't hold up after awhile. Besides, they were awfully heavy, and the day of the $5 find at a flea market was disappearing. In the spring of 1977, Kelly finally persuaded Breeze to build a frame from scratch that was tailored to mountain riding. Breeze tackled the project with his customary eye to detail. His wheel base was longer than a road bike's, to lend stability; there were twelve gears, to tackle the intonations of mountain turf; the angles of the tubes on the frame (or the "geometry") were borrowed from the stalwart Schwinn Excelsior. Breeze used thinner-gauge chrome-moly steel, then nickel-plated it, like the new BMX bikes on the market, and discarded

Fisher's big drum brake in favor of a cantilever brake, which lightened the load. Still, he had to use heavy tires and steel rims and his "Breezer"—the first custom bike built specifically for mountain riding—weighed 38 pounds.

Breeze completed model No. 1 that September and kept it for himself; the second went to Kelly the following winter. He paid Breeze $750, pennies per hour for all that labor. Breeze completed eight more bikes by spring, assuming he'd built enough to satisfy world demand. Yet other devotees of the growing sport were covetous. "The people who owned them handled the ups at nearly Jeep speed and the downs like fine ski racers," rider and writer Craig Vetter reported in *Outside*. Now it was Fisher, with his Excelsior mixed breed, who was behind the curve, continually rewelding his more tender steel frame.

Fisher shunned the Breezer and instead found a promising supplier in a hot shot Palo Alto racer and frame builder, Tom Ritchey, who had bought a milling machine at sixteen (with a loan from his father) and a lathe two years later. College hadn't seemed necessary—Ritchey earned nearly $40,000 the year he turned eighteen and set up shop 75 miles south of Marin, largely unaware of the Mount Tam scene. In January 1979, Breeze stopped by with his first Breezer, and the twenty-year-old Ritchey was impressed. He went to work on his own version, modifying Breeze's design and lightening the load nearly 25 percent to 28 pounds. Yet Ritchey continued to putter: When his two-piece handlebar slipped during a Repack Road ride, he designed a one-piece or "bullmoose" handlebar, which became widely copied. In the following months, Ritchey knocked out three of his own mountain bikes and sold one to Fisher. Weeks later, he called Gary: "I made nine more; can you help me get rid of them?"

Fisher and Kelly no longer were roommates, but they had remained friends. The pair opened a checking account and appropriately dubbed their new company MountainBikes. Ritchey supplied unpainted frames; Fisher and Kelly assembled the components, advertised, and sold the bikes at $1,300 a pop. The frames bore two brand names: Ritchey and MountainBikes. "We were the Rolls-Royce guys," Kelly says. "No one else was close. Doctors and lawyers would call in and treat you like an equal." Kelly spread the gospel of mountain biking. His *Fat Tire Flyer* offered race results, product reviews, riding tips, and musings about the up-and-coming sport. Fisher raced, to show what the machine could do. "I was the marketing device," he says.

Mountain biking was not yet registering on the Schwinn radar screen. "Schwinn didn't know there were mountains west of the Rockies," cracks Pat Murphy, a former manager of the Midwest sales arm. For the Chicagoans, the more important trend out of California came from the southern half of the state, where surfer dudes cruised beach towns on funky old ballooners, many of them refurbished to their pristine state, complete with ersatz gas tank and rubber handgrips with streamers fluttering in the breeze. The retro image appealed to hipster instincts, and the bikes were eminently practical. A rider could carry a surfboard in one hand and steer with the other. The wide tires could even traverse packed sand. They were silent—no clicking to spoil the pure sound of the waves—and they were cheap. (Until Santa Ana collector Leon Dixon helped send prices for finished Schwinns and other vintage bikes surging to $1,000 and more with trade show appearances and magazine articles.)

Hoping to profit from the trend, Schwinn in the late '70s introduced a product called Klunker 5, a five-speed, fat-tired model that wasn't meant for mountain riding, but with its hefty tires, showed up in Marin County Schwinn shops anyway, looking like a deformed cousin of the mountain bike. The Klunker's caliper-style front brake wasn't brawny enough for mountain riding, and the model had chintzy rubber (instead of stronger metal) pedals. Although no one in Marin had claimed ownership of the word *clunker*, Charlie Kelly was irritated that Schwinn had appropriated the hallowed name for such a clearly inferior bike. He wrote to Schwinn's California sales subsidiary in 1979, offering suggestions, and received a letter from none other than Ray Burch. The popularity of balloon-tired bikes seemed confined to California, Schwinn's marketing chief wrote. "At this point we do not see sufficient demand for more sophisticated Clunker-type bicycles to justify tooling up for high volume runs of such models. Accordingly, we believe the demand which does exist probably can be adequately supplied by the small producers." The Klunker 5, Burch added, had been discontinued.

The following year, Schwinn brought out the King Sting, a variation of the high-end BMX Sting. It was closer to the real thing—made of chrome-moly steel, with alloy parts and hand-brazed joints—yet there were not enough gears to mount an honest hill, it had the same weak brakes, and the handlebars weren't well positioned. "The components were off the mark," concedes former product manager Fred Teeman, who in addition to BMX was handling mountain bikes and other oddities of the era. The problem now facing Schwinn: Asian manufacturers were mass-producing bikes with chrome-alloy frames, but since Schwinn's Chicago factory was geared to heavy steel, it could produce only a chrome-moly bike by hand and position it as a top-of-the line model. In 1982, Schwinn tried again, this time with the Sidewinder, but it was all steel—basically, a Varsity with huge tires. The factory simply could not mass produce a lightweight bike. "It wasn't something to pay much attention to," Kelly says. "The Stumpjumper, now, that was something to pay attention to."

The Stumpjumper was a Japanese-made model designed and marketed by Michael Sinyard's new Specialized Bicycle Components, and it was serious stuff. Priced at $750 (three times as expensive as Schwinn's Sidewinder), the Stumpjumper was a credible mass-produced version of the pricier custom wheels that Charlie Kelly, Gary Fisher, Tom Ritchey, Joe Breeze, and others were producing. Mike Sinyard was equally serious: quiet and cagey, but ferociously competitive. As a kid in San Diego, Sinyard had repaired bicycles (his father was a machinist) and rode motorcycles in motocross races. During high school and college, he'd buy old bikes at flea markets, refurbish them, and sell them for a tidy profit. After graduating from San Jose State University with a business degree, Sinyard spent three months bicycling through Europe in 1974, riding his English Holdsworth and sleeping in youth hostels. In Milan, he met a woman with ties to Italian parts manufacturers Regina and Cinelli. Sinyard, twenty-four at the time, asked for a meeting. "They said they would be glad to sell to me," he told *Entrepreneur* magazine years later. "I couldn't believe it when they said that. I knew I was on to something."

Sinyard ordered $1,300 worth of handlebars, racing saddles, and other parts and air-shipped them back to the States. He stored the pieces in his mobile home and started phoning contacts at local bike shops: "Would you be interested in high-quality Italian components?" Although the parts sold quickly and Sinyard made money, he didn't have much capital left. Determined to make a go of his tiny operation, Sinyard asked his customers for advance payment. They obliged—and he was in the importing business.

By 1976, business had increased enough for Sinyard to move his upstart Specialized Bicycle Components and his single part-time employee to a 4,000-square-foot warehouse in San Jose. What caused his sales to ignite, however, was a skinny, high-performance tire for racing that he called the Turbo. The slimmest tire at the time was 1¼ inches, and an even thinner model would offer less weight and resistance. Schwinn earlier had introduced a narrow 1⅛-inch tire for road racing that would hold high pressure, but never marketed it properly. Sinyard saw the potential and made the most of it. "That put Specialized on the map," Joe Breeze recalls.

Sales soared from $228,000 to $3 million, giving Sinyard the capital for his next big product: a Marin-style mountain bike made in Japan, which already was manufacturing his Turbo tires. By 1980, Sinyard was two steps ahead of the nascent competition when he ordered four cycles from Fisher and Kelly's MountainBikes, which was one of Specialized's customers for tires, brakes, and crank sets.

"Your bikes are cool," Sinyard told Kelly. "Some of the guys here want to ride them."

While Sinyard was known for playing his cards close to the vest, Kelly, Fisher, and frame builder Ritchey say they never suspected how close.

Having sold 160 bikes in 1980, MountainBikes had an 85 percent share of its market, yet their little company was a marginal operation. "We were hippies doing everything wrong," Fisher says. "We were barely making money. We had a ton of back orders. We were not well organized."

Fisher mentioned the order from the larger Specialized to Ritchey. "Isn't it great?" he enthused. Then, in late 1981, Fisher saw the new Stumpjumper while buying parts at Specialized's headquarters. "Whoa," he thought. "That's *our* bike."

Every component was the same, except for the brake levers and the handlebars. The frame's angles were identical, he says, and it was nearly the same metallic blue.

We've been had, Ritchey thought when he first saw the Stumpjumper. His proof: a glitch in assembling Sinyard's four MountainBikes had produced a fork slightly longer than it should have been, which made going uphill a little more difficult. The longer fork initially showed up on the Stumpjumper, Kelly says. (Today, Sinyard says he doesn't think the early fork was too long, but he does credit Ritchey: "Tom was the originator. We did copy some of his designs." As for the similar components, Sinyard notes that Specialized had been selling those parts to Fisher and Kelly. "They bought them from me.")

Sinyard took his Stumpjumper to a February 1982 trade show in New York and sold 500 in 20 days. "Specialized set the world on fire with that one," says Mill Valley dealer John Lewis. "Sinyard saw the opportunity to mass produce and he capitalized on it." Schwinn's reluctance to jump into the budding market would puzzle Sinyard. "I thought, 'Maybe this is the way a big company acts.' "

Back in Chicago, most Schwinn officials still viewed mountain biking as an elite, radical sport.[2] Adult lightweight road bikes ruled the day, accounting for two-thirds of sales. Product manager Fred Teeman knew that to market a credible mountain bike, he needed a chrome-moly frame. Schwinn was subcontracting with Murray Ohio, the mass market bike maker, to produce children's models and other lines, including the Sidewinder, at a factory in Tennessee, but Murray, too, was unable to make the alloy frame. It took Teeman another year to win approval to go offshore. Schwinn's Taiwanese-made chrome-moly High Sierra hit the market in 1984. The bike was an instant hit, doubling in sales three years in a row, but it was two years after Sinyard's Stumpjumper and five years after Fisher and Kelly's MountainBikes. "I was late," Teeman ruefully admits. "Schwinn was changing its sourcing, and it looked like it didn't know what it was doing."

Two companies that had been tracking the mountain bike cult more closely were the Japanese component makers Shimano and the SunTour unit of Maeda Industries. They sent engineers to study the Marin

County bikes, attending races, examining the various hybrids, interviewing the visionaries, taking notes, and snapping photos. "They came over here in droves and checked it out," Fisher says. "Ten guys at a time from Shimano."

One of the more colorful entrepreneurs attracting their attention was Charlie Cunningham, who had built a superlightweight aluminum mountain bike in 1978. His custom product was the priciest around, selling for up to $3,500. Like his bikes, Cunningham is not standard fare. He sleeps in an unheated lean-to, a short ladder climb from his main house, which includes a goldfish pond and a pet rat. His wife, accomplished rider Jacquie Phelan, founded an early all-female racing group called Wombats (for Women's Mountain Bike & Tea Society). Shimano's chief engineer was Cunningham's house guest and the two toured the Marin hills. Cunningham was flattered by the attention, gratified that the sport he loved was gaining acceptance. He marveled at the idea that a component that took him two days to machine by hand could soon be purchased off the shelf.

By 1982 both Shimano and SunTour had come out with complete component groups for mountain bikes, including thumbshifters, cantilever brakes, special hubs, motorcycle-style brake levers, and derailleurs capable of a wide range of speeds. It soon became clear that it wouldn't be the Marin entrepreneurs who'd cash in on the mountain bike. Japanese firms, quick to spot a good idea and never shy about copying one, would come to dominate the market for the components. Shimano would emerge the winner, with a near monopoly in the market for gear-shifting systems. Many of the Californians, today in their forties, still blister at the turn of events. Cunningham, for instance, says he licensed a brake design to SunTour and struggled to collect royalties.

Few, if any, of the early bike builders had the inspiration or financial resources to patent their inventions—after all, the mountain bike had evolved by riders and designers sharing and improving on each other's ideas. Those days came to an end. "If you can't afford to protect your ideas, it's not your idea," Cunningham's partner, Steve Potts, gloomily told the *San Francisco Chronicle* in 1987. "The little guy is at the bottom of the pile," concluded Cunningham. "We were pretty naive."

Things were not going so well at MountainBikes, either. Gary Fisher and Charlie Kelly tried unsuccessfully to trademark their company name in 1980. They say their lawyer told the government the MountainBikes name simply was descriptive of a bike to be ridden in the mountains and the application was denied, because generic descriptions can't be trademarked. A pity, because their product was more than that. It might have been described in the application as a one-of-a-kind vehicle to be ridden on a mountain, on a beach, on city streets, anywhere.

By 1983, Fisher was growing disenchanted. He considered Ritchey's frame prices too high and feared that MountainBikes was vulnerable by having a single supplier. Specialized now was on the scene, and the market was more competitive. In Fisher's mind, he was in essence working for Ritchey, putting the noted frame builder's name on the bike and marketing the hell out of it. "He never appreciated what I did," Fisher says.

The real rub: partners Fisher and Kelly were behind in their payments to supplier Ritchey by an estimated $70,000. "Where's the money?" Ritchey asked. Fisher began looking for other sources of frames.

Ritchey also felt vulnerable. He says Fisher didn't appreciate how he had capitalized the company, buying raw materials and turning them into marketable frames. His work was being well received, he was in demand, but Fisher, who controlled sales, distribution, and marketing, was building an empire and wanted *his* name on the bike. Worse yet, Ritchey wasn't getting paid. Why should he keep producing frames for MountainBikes?

Meantime, Fisher and Kelly split up that June. The former posed the option: "You can owe your half, or let me buy you out cheap."

"Gary was ahead of me," Kelly says today.

"Charlie was no businessman," Fisher grouses.

With Kelly gone, the dispute between Fisher and Ritchey came to a head the following January at a trade show in Anaheim. "Gary Fisher" decals were pasted to bikes using Tom Ritchey frames. Ritchey was stunned: "It's like Ritchey never existed. I was like a man without a country."

He sued Fisher for the money owed, and though the pair eventually settled, it was a nasty falling out. "To this day," Kelly says, "you don't want those guys together at dinner."

Fisher reorganized his firm as Gary Fisher Bicycle Company and had his bikes built by Asian suppliers. In the late '80s, he sold his company to a manufacturer with a reputation for handling high-end bikes, Taiwan's Anlen Bicycle Company. Fisher received a lucrative management contract, but relations soured as Fisher and Anlen fought over financial goals, pricing, production, quality problems, and mounting inventories. Anlen was forced to liquidate in 1992, and Wisconsin-based Trek Bicycle Company purchased the Gary Fisher name the following year. "Gary is not a businessman; he's an inventor, a bike guy," says one Trek manager. Fisher today is president of the subsidiary that bears his name, designing the line and enjoying a legacy as king of the mountain bike. "He knows bikes in a native, unschooled way that's truly awesome," Kelly says. "Only one guy can be Gary Fisher."

His Repack Road challenger, Joe Breeze, built more custom Breezers in the early 1980s. By the middle of the decade, he contracted with a small Minnesota frame maker to build the "American Breezer," and in 1990, with a Japanese backer, he started designing and marketing a line of $1,100 to $2,600 bikes. At mid-decade, he paid tribute to the Schwinn legacy with a $700 cruiser called the Breezer Ignaz X—the X being associated with the Excelsior bike that first inspired mountain biking.[3]

Of the foursome, the highly focused Tom Ritchey has had the most business success—his Redwood City company generates annual sales estimated at more than $15 million. Ritchey works a half-hour away from headquarters in a converted garage at his log-cabin-style home, where he designs rims, tires, pedals, and pocket tools sold to manufacturers, distributors, and retailers. Ritchey also builds more than 500 custom frames a year. "He made money," Fisher says. "I'm envious."

Then there's Mike Sinyard's Specialized, which had grown to a $170 million company in the early 1990s—larger than Schwinn. Sinyard's products were strong technically and he marketed them brilliantly, cultivating a high-end image by pouring money into team sponsorships. That produced the coveted "halo effect"—riders who couldn't afford the Stumpjumper ($750 to $1,400) still could buy a bit of hot technology in the Stumpjumper's less expensive offspring, the Rockhopper ($400 to $700), and later, the Hardrock ($275 to $400). "Specialized had the enthusiast's cachet," says John Lewis, the Marin County dealer. The company polished its ultra-hip image with the bad-boy motto, "Innovate or die," while publicists touted the fact that Sinyard and his designers rode a 25-mile loop around their Morgan Hill headquarters every day at lunchtime. "Innovation here isn't a job," intoned a company catalog, "it's a religion." By the time of the first world mountain-biking championships in 1990 in Durango, Colorado, Specialized bought a congratulatory and slightly patronizing full page ad in the program, crowing, "Hey Breeze, Kelly, Gary, Charlie [Cunningham], Tom, did you guys ever, in your wildest imaginations, think mountain biking would come to this? Neither did We. But it's pretty cool, don't you think?"

As for Schwinn, the Mountain Bike Hall of Fame in Crested Butte, Colorado (another early center for the sport), inducted two new members in the summer of 1994: Ignaz and Frank W. Schwinn. Those long-dead Schwinns had developed the father of mountain bikes—the Excelsior curb slammers that had inspired Joe Breeze, Gary Fisher, and other pacesetters. Most important was the balloon tire that Schwinn had introduced to the broader U.S. market in the early 1930s. "If this durable, shock-absorbing, sure-footed fat tire had not existed, the idea of a bike such as a mountain bike would probably not have surfaced for many years," Breeze explained at the induction ceremony. "Theirs is a legacy," Ignaz's great-grandson Richard C. Schwinn told the audience, "that is shared by every tinkerer who ever picked up a wrench and tried to make that bike work just a little better."

The irony. Certainly, Schwinn had cranked out hundreds of thousands of perfectly respectable mountain bikes during the '80s, but these never were a product Schwinn could call its own like the Varsity, Sting-Ray, Black Phantom, Excelsior, or Aero Cycle. Schwinn had struggled to catch up on lightweight bikes in the '70s, then it dragged its feet on BMX. Mountain bikes became an even bigger sensation. Schwinn, once ahead of the pack, had become halting and skeptical, doubtful that adults would shell out so much money for what was, after all, a toy. Yet Schwinn for decades had championed, more than any American company, the idea of developing an adult bicycle market in the United States—from Lana Turner on her New World to Bobby Sherman on his ten-speed. When a real adult market finally hopped on the mountain bike, the company was looking the other way. That left an opening for a raft of aggressive competitors—not only Specialized, but other important new names, such as Univega, Cannondale, and Diamond Back. Like Schwinn's biggest BMX competitors, Mongoose and GT, they weren't selling to Kmart and Wal-Mart; these were upscale bikes—not just a Cadillac, but a Mercedes—aimed at the better bike shop customer. Meanwhile, Schwinn had become a Chevy, squeezed between its longtime rivals selling to the mass market and its new up-market competitors.

A wall at the back of John Lewis's California store reinforces the fact. Rows of engraved plaques from the '60s and '70s repeatedly rank him among the country's biggest sellers of Schwinns. Suddenly, in the early-1980s section, similar honors from other companies appear, mingling with the Schwinn commendations. By decade's end, Schwinn plaques were rare, while Specialized dominated. "I didn't want customers going elsewhere," Lewis explains. "The cosmetic appeal of Schwinn was not good. You got a better engineered bike in Specialized for the money."

Perhaps it was understandable that Schwinn's Chicago headquarters would have a hard time comprehending a hippie-inspired sport springing from faraway California, but regional differences explain only part of the story. Another formidable competitor was emerging near Schwinn's home turf.

10

TREKKING

While Gary Fisher and Joe Breeze were racing down Mount Tam on their clunkers, college students halfway across the country were enamored of a different kind of biking. Touring was the rage in the Big Ten university town of Madison, Wisconsin, where undergraduates had more time than money. Young riders meandered the back roads, their bikes and bodies strapped with packs and camping gear. From Dairyland's dells to Austria's alps, it was a fine way to explore the world, to connect with the countryside. If cycling a sleek roadster was akin to racing a Ferrari, pedaling a touring bike was like traveling by Volkswagen bus.

Manufacturers displayed plenty of packs and racks at trade shows, but there weren't many good touring bikes in the U.S. market until South African émigré Bevil Hogg and Milwaukee appliance salesman Richard Burke joined forces in 1975 to establish Trek Bicycle Company. Their venture ultimately would supplant Schwinn as the top brand name among independent bicycle dealers.

Hogg was a mere twenty-three at the time, yet he was importing a line of French road bikes and selling them through his chain of shops in

Madison; Champaign, Illinois, and other college towns. Retailing was more grueling than he had expected, however, and European bikes (like European cars) were becoming noncompetitive in price and quality compared with Japanese models. Hogg sold his five stores—"with great relief," he says—to the then forty-one-year-old Burke for about $100,000, most of it for assumption of debt.

Burke had a history of good timing. The native of Chicago's West Side graduated from Milwaukee's Marquette University in 1956 and three years later was credit manager at Roth Corporation, a local distributor of stoves and other appliances, when the owner died of a heart attack. The highly disciplined and single-minded Burke bought a 30 percent stake in the company for $25,000 and soon gained operating control. "I was in the right place at the right time," he says. Burke had considered jumping into the bicycle distribution business during the early-1970s boom, but concluded that middlemen—such as the former Schwinn distributors—faced a shaky future. Bicycles were still on his mind when he met Hogg. At first, Burke thought Hogg's stores could be made successful with a cash infusion and the elder's instinct for structure and organization. The two soon acknowledged their future was not in retail (they sold the stores) but manufacturing. "We need to create an American bicycle company," Hogg had argued. Burke was enthusiastic, in part because Hogg was so persuasive and charming—the perfect dinner companion. "A visionary," says Burke's son, John. "Bevil Hogg is the John DeLorean of the bicycle business."

The child of a civil engineer who worked throughout Africa building roads, Hogg as a teenager moved to Europe to study in Switzerland and France. He started an import-export company and moved to America during the bike boom to sell French cycles. After some minor success, he was introduced to a company in Minnesota that had made a fortune selling snowmobiles. Seeking to diversify the seasonal business, the company ordered a shipment of bikes in the unlikely colors of chartreuse and purple. Hogg says he had the dubious task of selling the models to North Woods snowmobile dealers with beaver pelts on their shop walls. "They looked at me pretty blankly." The chartreuse bikes didn't sell, but he earned enough cash to open his shops. Now, with Burke providing a new source of financing, Hogg was determined to beat the European bike makers at their game.

Tom French, a University of Wisconsin liberal arts graduate who was managing Hogg's shops, suggested the name "Trek," to connote the essence of touring. The new company's bike frames would come with eyelets for mounting a rack and threading a pack. The wheels would be farther apart (the opposite of racing bikes) to help riders balance their loads. Most important, the product would be American-made, presumably an important selling point at a time when Japanese cars and bikes were starting to pour into the U.S. market. With a starting price of about $279, the Trek would be $100 more expensive than a midpriced Schwinn road bike from Taiwan. No matter. "A Schwinn," French explains, "was not something a Trek buyer would have considered as an alternative anyway."

Burke put up some $150,000 in seed money. He and Hogg agreed to open a factory midway between Milwaukee and Madison, a rolling stretch of countryside dotted with dairy farms. On a snowy day in 1975, Hogg and French found the perfect spot: a 5,000-square-foot carpet warehouse in rural Waterloo. While both men had a strong grasp of the marketing side of the business, the manufacturing side was another matter. Their factory was using the new lug-frame technology, but it was difficult to find workers experienced in the low-temperature silver brazing of chrome-moly steel. "We had to figure out how to make paint stick to chrome-moly tubing," says French, who functioned as sales manager. "It wasn't obvious then."

Trek feverishly promoted its light chrome-moly frame: "It is the heart of the bicycle," French told dealers. It was surrounded by some of the world's best parts: derailleurs from Japan, rims from France, tires and saddle from America. Trek sold fewer than 1,000 bikes its first year of production and about 2,500 in 1978. Volumes were so low, it was nearly a custom operation. Yet Trek quickly found cult status. "It was handmade—built in Wisconsin, where there are cows," says a droll Burke. The company enjoyed the luxury of courting only cream-of-the-crop cycleries. Sometimes, they were Schwinn stalwarts: Trek's charter dealer was Penn Cycle near Minneapolis, a major Schwinn seller. Other times, they were Brand X: Ron Boi, in the Chicago suburb of Winnetka, was selling custom bikes and begged Hogg for a Trek dealership. "In the first year, I sold ninety, while they only produced nine hundred," says Boi. "The second year, I sold three hundred. It was fun to watch them grow." North Shore customers usually stumbled upon Boi's small shop asking for Schwinns. "We've got Trek," he'd answer. "They're lightweight," he'd insist. "Ride it." Skeptics became converts.

On the West Coast, Harry Spehar was a manager of a non-Schwinn dealership in a college town outside Eureka, in Northern California's redwood country. Spehar sold Raleighs, Gitanes, Peugeots, and custom framesets. A woman rolled in with her Trek, and the shop's frame builder was impressed, telling Spehar, "This is a great bike." Coincidentally, Trek sales rep Tom French showed up the next day. Spehar rode a Trek model and was smitten. The bike was custom quality, but half the price; it was more stable than most French frames and handled well, absorbing the harshness of the road. Trek never caught up with the demand during these early years. Spehar would order every two weeks, yet nothing came. Then, one August, everything arrived at once: five to ten bikes for each size. "As a result of that mistake," he says, "we were one of the largest Trek dealers in the country." But the bikes sold. "Someday," Spehar thought, "I'm going to work for Trek."

In the bicycle world that Trek entered in the late 1970s, Schwinn still was king of the hill. While the Chicago company had left a gaping hole in the upper end of the market, it enjoyed a broad, deep, and financially sound dealer base. Its long-established programs to help dealers, such as the mechanic schools and service seminars, continued to pay dividends in retaining loyalty. Trek's sales reps were in awe, not so much of Schwinn's offerings, but of its size, reach, and capability. "Schwinn had provided good quality products, a decent value, delivered on-time to the customer," says Trek's Pat Sullivan, who started as a purchaser of the Wisconsin company's parts and accessories and eventually became national sales manager. "They had the best service, by far, in the bicycle business. No one was as generous to dealers as Schwinn." Richard Burke's son, John, remembers calling on Rocky Mountain shops in the early 1980s: "They would boast about the way Schwinn was taking care of them."

Trek made gains in those early days, although they weren't at Schwinn's expense. Sales of $16 million early in the decade were too small to seem threatening, and Schwinn executives viewed the manufacturer as an oddity filling an enthusiast's niche. "They left us alone," says Harry Spehar, who finally joined Trek as a sales rep in 1981 and was promoted to product manager two years later. "As close as we were geographically, we had free reign in our own little playpen."

By 1984, Trek's name was on the map. The company, however, had troubles stemming from its double-digit growth. The Waterloo plant was inefficient and lacked adequate systems and controls, so quality and service were inconsistent. "People would say, 'I'll ship today,' knowing they couldn't ship it for a week," says sales manager Sullivan. Sometimes, Trek would ship the bike anyway, with IOUs for missing parts. "It was like a car going faster than it ought to," Hogg says. "Bits and pieces start to fall off." But lulled by its early status as a hot name in bikes, Trek was becoming haughty. Charles Bonten, a large Detroit-area dealer who was having run-ins with Schwinn over his insistence on selling Raleigh, says he briefly considered taking on Trek. After a single meeting, he found the Trek sales reps to be surprisingly "dictatorial" and later opted for other lines. John Burke concedes, "We were not customer friendly."

In Waterloo, tensions increased. Although Hogg was an industry trailblazer, he could be an autocratic manager. When Sullivan considered joining Trek, colleagues warned him, "Don't go there. They chew people up and spit them out." Spehar felt like he was "walking on eggs. . . . You worked under a lot of fear. Small mistakes were unacceptable. You felt your job was on the line." Hogg concedes he might have been harsh, but points to other factors, too. The breakneck pace, for instance, wore down many workers, and some employees just weren't up to snuff. A great regional sales manager would become a mediocre national sales manager, Hogg says. "We were Peter Principling out."

Trek wasn't just driving hard, it was going in different directions. The touring market had dried up by 1984, as '70s college students settled down. Mountain bikes were gaining market share, but Trek (much like Schwinn) was constrained by its own factory. The Waterloo plant used lug-frame technology for its road and touring bikes. Yet mountain bike frames were manufactured with even higher-tech TIG welding (for "Tungsten Inert Gas"), a method that welds chrome-moly steel tubes without lugs—a Star Wars–age version of Schwinn's old-fashioned electro-welding of frame pieces. Hogg and Richard Burke discussed importing mountain bikes, but how? And how many? "It was not a very clear picture," Hogg says. Then they dreamed up another idea to spark growth: Why not acquire Schwinn?

At the time, Schwinn was coming out of a painful financial crisis. Burke made the contact through an outside director who had a connection with Chicago's Harris Bank, Schwinn's main lender. A group of Schwinn managers was meeting at headquarters when they heard that Burke had telephoned. The consensus in the room: Trek wants to sell. "It couldn't be any other way," recalls Bill Imielski, a twenty-four-year-old assistant product manager back then. Imielski, however, impudently suggested to colleagues that maybe Trek wanted to buy Schwinn. He received only glares. "It was like, 'Shut up. You're an infant.' " President Ed Schwinn, Jr., and his vice president of finance, John Barker, grudgingly met with Richard Burke and summarily rejected his overture. "It didn't surprise me," Burke says. In retrospect, Hogg adds, Trek wouldn't have known what to do with Schwinn. "It was hot air mostly. And Schwinn was not about to be bought by a whippersnapper up the road."

The friction between Burke and Hogg was increasing. The elder partner was far more pragmatic than the younger; he wasn't visionary, he was after money. And he wasn't always appreciative of the creative touches that Hogg fussed over. (Burke's top two choices for the early venture's name were National Bicycle Company and American Bicycle Company.) Hogg was much more of a techie. He was running a back-room "skunk" project that experimented with high-strength carbon-fiber frames and produced an aluminum racing bike using aerospace adhesives. Trek unveiled its aluminum model in 1985, but the first bikes weren't strong enough. "What we built didn't work, and we couldn't build a new one," Burke says, still angry ten years later. With the company at about $30 million in revenues, selling 60,000 bikes a year, Hogg wanted to slow down and burnish Trek's image. He believed the disarray stemmed from Burke's insistence, via his offices in Milwaukee, on continued rapid growth. Complains Hogg: "He was saying, "Drive it any way you like, as long as you drive it at ninety-five miles per hour.' Well, if you're dictating, you'd better be behind the wheel." Burke, of course, has a different view: "We had to grow to justify the resources we put into the plant and equipment."

The aluminum bike screwup, as well as high inventories from Trek's disappointing 1984 line and other operating problems, sparked two years of losses. Hogg had to be replaced, Burke says. "I had banks, directors all over me." (Hogg merely cites "different visions" between the two founders. "It seemed totally reasonable that we'd part.") The pair hammered out a severance agreement in February 1986. Hogg remained an additional six months to help smooth the transition, and cashed in his stock options. He moved to California to start a carbon-fiber bicycle company with his old sales sidekick, Tom French, who had left Trek in 1982 to become general manager of Blackburn Designs, a West Coast maker of bike racks and cages for water bottles.

Burke assumed control of troubled Trek. He assembled his managers at a midday meeting in the company's lunchroom and laid out three options.

Plan A was to sell the business. Burke noted, however, that in its current state Trek wouldn't bring what it really was worth. (In fact, Burke already had tested the market, even inviting a bid from Ed Schwinn during a Saturday morning breakfast at Chicago's regal Drake Hotel. "He was cordial, but not interested," Burke recalls. "Things were going well for them in 1986." Burke also sounded out Mike Sinyard of Specialized. "Trek was not very attractive back then," Burke says. "We were a pretty ugly kid.")

Plan B was to close the factory. That was not feasible, Burke added, because he would still have to pay off the equipment, mortgage, and other fixed costs associated with the Waterloo property.

Plan C was to turn around Trek. This, he said, was the only viable alternative. The company needed to return to some fundamental precepts: deliver a good bike on time at a competitive price; provide a healthy working environment; and return a profit to the owners. Basic stuff, he admitted, but Trek was falling short on all counts.

Now there was a sense of urgency. Employees knew there was more at stake—and more for which to strive. "I left the meeting pretty pumped up," Pat Sullivan says. "People dug right in and started working." Burke set up an office at Waterloo. To run operations, he brought in Tom Albers, a former vice president of finance at bike maker Huffy who had been handling financial matters at Burke's holding company, Intrepid Corporation, since 1982. Son John transferred to headquarters from his post in the Rockies to become chief of customer service (and later was elevated to vice president of sales and marketing). Burke's daughter Mary would start a European operation. The new administration boosted Trek's sales force and service team. It diversified the product line and expanded distribution. From a base of 500 dealers in 1987, Trek added 200 shops a year, including more and more Schwinn dealers. Meantime, Burke shored up the supply side. A cloutless Trek was paying top dollar for cycling components purchased through the Japanese trading company Mitsui. Burke traveled straight to the source, hoping to establish a direct link with component colossus Shimano. Trek was still a small player, but vice president Keizo Shimano agreed to a deal. "They believed in us," Burke says. Fortunately for Trek, market demand was strong. As it gained a larger percentage of dealers' business, the name became easier to build on, particularly in the Midwest and West. "Things started turning around real fast," Sullivan says.

Like Specialized, Trek cultivated the lofty end of the market. (It became known among cycling fanatics, for example, for the adhesive bonding technology—which Bevil Hogg had prematurely pushed—used in aluminum and carbon-fiber bikes, and it ultimately converted much of its production to TIG welding.) But Trek loyalists were quick to point out what Specialized lacked: a made-in-America tradition. Having established his company in the upper tier, Burke, like Specialized's Sinyard, could begin selling lower-priced products that would share in Trek's glossy image. And in moving down-market, Trek would aim directly at Schwinn. In 1986, Trek imported 7,000 bikes from a Taiwan company that also made models for Raleigh and Mongoose. For Harry Spehar, competing with Schwinn still was a game of "Godzilla versus Bambi." Any day, he worried, Schwinn would launch a line of high-end bikes. "We were waiting for the big foot to come down—for them to get serious."

11

ED TAKES CHARGE

On the morning of April 15, 1980, Max Scott was tending to his usual duties as vice president of sales and marketing at the Schwinn Sales West office in Southern California, when Ed Schwinn, Jr., dropped in unexpectedly. The new president wasted no time with pleasantries.

"Max, I'm here to ask for your resignation. We'd like for you to leave the company, right now. You can come tomorrow to get your belongings. That's all I have to say."

Scott, who had worked at Schwinn for fifteen years, was devastated. "I was fifty-eight," he says. "I never worked again."

He was one of several longtime managers who were fired, retired, or demoted after a thirty-year-old Ed assumed control of the company in October 1979, following the withdrawal of his Uncle Frankie from active management. Ed was targeting the old-timers who had overstayed their welcome—in particular, the senior sales and marketing executives. Many insiders thought the new president was missing the point: the real problem was in design and manufacturing, especially at the outdated Chicago plant. Ed saw it differently: His first mission was to clean the corporate house.

As a young vice president in the mid-1970s, Ed had been critical of Ray Burch and his marketing staff. "Look, if it will make things easier, I'll resign," Burch said at one stormy board meeting. Frankie, ever the peacemaker, dismissed the suggestion. In 1977, however, he began to quiz Burch about his retirement plans. Burch was sixty-five, but told Frankie he wanted to stay a few more years. "Fine," the chief executive assured him. The question came up again in 1979. This time, the industry's master of selective distribution said he was ready to leave.

Ed seized the opportunity of Burch's retirement to overhaul the marketing department. He often had groused in the '70s that sales executives at the autonomously managed regional offices were spending too much of the family's money on themselves and their favored dealers, whom Ed suspected of taking advantage of Schwinn's largess. The salesmen, for instance, earned a maximum 15 percent of their salary in profit sharing, while managers back at headquarters earned a much smaller percentage. Rightly so, argue former sales executives: the sales companies were highly profitable, while the Chicago factory was losing money on a number of its bikes. Gun-shy from the decade-long antitrust battle, Frankie had sought to keep the four regional sales companies at arm's length from the parent. Now, Ed grabbed them by the scruff of the neck. To replace Ray Burch, he went outside the marketing ranks and tapped John Nielsen, who had headed the company's profitable parts department. Things changed swiftly. While salesmen had enjoyed considerable latitude—granting payment terms to dealers, for example—such decisions now had to be approved by Schwinn's chief financial officer. Top executives at the regional sales offices, who had always hung out with suppliers at annual conventions, no longer were invited to the gatherings. When Schwinn staged a big meeting at a hotel near Chicago's O'Hare International Airport to explain the changes, Allen Singer, head of Schwinn Sales Midwest, turned to his lieutenant Pat Murphy and said, "We're in trouble." Indeed, Singer was ordered west in the spring of 1980 to lead the California-based sales arm, only to retire a year and a half later. Murphy was elevated to head of Schwinn Sales Midwest, the company's most productive warehouse, but was dismissed at the end of 1980 when he clashed with the new regime.

New faces entered the scene, like Peter Davis, Ed's twenty-five-year-old brother-in-law who had married Ed's sister Mary and was named director of corporate planning in 1979. Some colleagues found Davis overly image-conscious and annoyingly self-important in conversation. He had a master's degree in marketing from Northwestern University and a few years of management consulting experience. "He and Ed were like schoolkids, running around," says former chief financial officer Mike McNamara. "They didn't know what they had." Ed and Davis frequently huddled with Frankie at the Lake Geneva mansion sipping cognacs in front of the fireplace as they reconfigured operations. But as the duo sought young managers with MBAs, the world of regression analysis clashed with the glad-handing good-old-boy bike culture. There was no middle ground at Schwinn. "I did sophisticated planning, econometric models," Davis remembers. "And Frank V. said, 'All that matters [regarding sales] is how many days of rain we get in April.' "

Since his 1974 heart attack, Frankie had become even more disengaged. Ed's hard-driving mother, Mary, began to push her heirless brother-in-law to name her oldest son president, according to Ray Burch. Frankie finally did in 1979, although he retained the titles of chairman and chief executive until his death at age sixty-seven in 1988. Much of his retirement was spent in Lake Geneva, enjoying an easy chair and a large-screen television. He was an early connoisseur of cable, having set up a satellite dish that could scan 300 channels, and he passed the hours watching oddball programs. He was entitled to relax. Frankie had helped pioneer the development of Schwinn's dealer network in the 1950s; he had presided over his company's stunning growth in the 1960s. He'd been a likable guy, too—compassionate, a good boss. But, ultimately, Frankie bears much responsibility for the company's deteriorating position. Schwinn had been too passive during the '70s onslaught of new rivals that introduced lug-frame lightweights and BMX racing bikes. The creaking Chicago factory no longer was competitive. Frankie had little stomach for conflict, but wouldn't cede authority to a tougher manager. "If they had given [No. 2 executive] Al Fritz full reign, we'd have been a lot better off," says Jack Ahearn, former vice president of manufacturing. "But the Schwinn family couldn't allow anyone to be top dog—unless their name was Schwinn." Nor would Frankie give up equity in exchange for the chance to grow. Grandfather Ignaz's company must remain family owned, no matter what.

A new generation was in charge as Schwinn entered its eighty-fifth year, with young Ed unequivocally out to make his mark. Shortly after he took over, Ed summoned vice presidents and division heads to the conference room. "I am not my grandfather," he warned. "Not my father. Not my uncle."

"It was a tough I'm-the-boss speech," Ahearn says. "The kid was showing he had control."

Ed also made a point of showing the Schwinn family who was chief. Shortly after cousin Brownie's death in 1983, he invited the entire clan, kids in tow, to an overnight gathering at the Lake Geneva retreat. Rambunctious as Brownie was, he had functioned as an elder statesman who also represented his side of the family's interest on the company's board. Now, Brownie's one-third stake would be divided among six children, but no one would assume his seat as a director. Ed's aunts and cousins urged that each of the three branches be represented, yet Ed refused, pointing out that the beneficiaries possessed no voting rights. "He was very cold about it," recalls Rychie Schwinn, former wife of cousin Robert Schwinn. Ed promised to keep in touch, "which he never did," Rychie asserts. He would keep a distance from his relatives, declining, for example, to attend another cousin's wedding several years later, although his wife, Leslie, showed the flag. "Ed did not like to be around the family," Rychie says. "They would try to get information out of him."

While Ed didn't concern himself too much with family dynamics, he seemed to enjoy the freedom and status of his new job. He drove a Jeep Cherokee with the vanity license plate "BIKES." And he starred in a 1981 American Express television commercial, riding various bicycles, tricycles, and tandems on- and off-camera, teasing, "Do you know me?

I'm one of the biggest names on two wheels . . . three wheels . . . and four wheels." He was pleased with the recognition, even showing a videotape of the ad years later to a supplier visiting his home. "I think he was very proud of the Schwinn name and the Schwinn company," says Stephen E. Codron, executive vice president of China Bicycles, a major supplier of bikes in the 1990s. "And to be recognized by American Express—you know, you have to be someone." Ed was a confident public speaker and a feature attraction at industry conventions, where attendees asked for autographs from a real live Schwinn. Did the attention go to his head? Sympathetic voices say no. "He's fun to talk to," says competitor Mike Sinyard of Specialized. "He's so blunt. He's a character that way." Gladstone, Missouri, dealer Ralph Litten adds, "He was always extremely approachable at conventions. If you wanted to stop and talk to Ed Schwinn, he'd talk to you. You always felt like you were important to the operation." Neither was Ed one to shrink from having a good time. He enjoyed vodka-and-tonics, single-malt scotch, and was known to pair a Heineken with a double cognac. "A party with Ed was always fun," says Nai-Wen Kiang, a former Schwinn purchasing manager. "He tells stories. He can handle drinks."

Yet to many other observers, Ed exhibited all the arrogance of a fourth-generation scion who was destined to be boss. One might say he was born with a silver spoke in his mouth. Heir to a dynasty whose business was a household name, he carried himself in the Schwinn vein—proud, stubborn, comfortable with his celebrity status—yet he possessed neither the drive of great-grandfather Ignaz nor the genius of his grandfather Frank W. Schwinn. He seemed to enjoy tweaking the graying dealer establishment when he wore a polo shirt or Bermuda shorts to awards dinners, which were designed to be dignified affairs. When Ed arrived at a weekend regional meeting at a suburban Chicago hotel in golf shirt and jeans, the daughter of a Wisconsin dealer turned to Fritz and snapped, "Al, that's insulting." One Chicago-area merchant recalls a 1985 meeting in Mexico where hungry Schwinn executives and top dealers milled impatiently outside a readied banquet room. "Everybody stopped, because he had to lead the way into dinner," the dealer says. "The way I looked at it was, *we* should've been leading *him* in there." Maybe some didn't like the way Ed played the ceremonial game, but what really bugged many dealers was his lack of empathy, a sense that he wasn't interested in making connections with people, that he just didn't care. Chicago dealer Oscar Wastyn, Jr., was accustomed to calling Fritz or another honcho directly when he had a complaint. His family, after all, had basked in a special relationship with the Schwinns that stretched back to Ignaz. Until the antitrust case, the dealership had enjoyed a price break by purchasing directly from the factory. Wastyn felt he could always call with a suggestion. "The only reason you did was because you cared," he explains. Now, when Wastyn phoned Ed with a complaint about a faulty model, he received a cold response: "We have people and engineers who know what's good," Ed said. "We don't need dealers calling us telling us what's wrong." Wastyn still seethes at the memory: "That was the last time I called." Ed was more tolerant of überdealer George Garner, who wasn't shy about pointing out problems. Still, one day Ed snapped, "Don't you ever say anything nice?" Garner made a point of complimenting him the next time he called.

Ed knew almost all his life he'd be the big wheel. He grew up on a lovely tree-lined street in privileged Winnetka during the 1950s and 1960s, a North Shore kid with one of the most famous last names in America. "I remember him having a swaggering attitude," says one of his Winnetka neighbors, now a Chicago businessman. "Every kid rode a Schwinn bike, and he was a Schwinn." A classmate from Winnetka's private Faith, Hope and Charity Elementary School remembers Ed for his angelic "altar boy look," yet recalls he was gawky, as young boys will be. "He was not outgoing," she says. "He hung back a little."

Sometimes fame brought trouble. When Ed was nine, he and his brother, Richard, and sisters, Lisa and Mary, were threatened in an amateurish extortion plot by the adopted son of a North Shore minister. The unnerving incident occurred one evening two weeks before Christmas in 1958, when an anonymous caller instructed, "I want five thousand in cash or else one of your children will be harmed—and don't call the police because they cannot do you any good," as his father, Ed Sr., recounted the story to Winnetka police. The shaken parents made arrangements with school officials to ensure the children never were unattended. Fortunately for the Schwinns, the plotter was faint-hearted. When he phoned the following evening, and was told the family had contacted the police, he backed down. "Well, you might as well forget the whole thing. You're safe, you're lucky." *Click.* Two months later, Winnetka police arrested a nineteen-year-old from neighboring Glencoe, who readily admitted to the attempted crime, adding, "I had thought about this deal for a bit and decided that I wouldn't go through with it."

Although Ed was raised amid conversations about pedals and derailleurs, he wasn't a cycling enthusiast. "He didn't look like he rode a bike," says California mountain bike builder Steve Potts, recalling a meeting with Ed at a trade show. Old-timers say he didn't work much in the factory in his youth, preferring to spend summers working on boats on Lake Geneva. With his love of the water, it was no surprise that he excelled at swimming. "He was a natural, talented athlete," recalls Dick Shiman, Ed's freshman coach at Loyola Academy in neighboring Wilmette. "I was disappointed that he didn't continue." While sports was a forte, academics were not. Ed attended three high schools in five years, spending three years at Loyola and a fourth at Augustinian Academy in St. Louis (both private schools) before finally graduating from the North Shore's public New Trier High School in 1968. "He was not a scholar by any means," says his New Trier adviser, Harold Severns, "but he was a plugger." Otherwise, Severns adds, Ed was amiable and clean-cut, memorable for his flaming red hair. Nearly five years later, he received his bachelor's degree in marketing from the University of Denver—several months after Ed Sr. died of leukemia at age forty-eight. The son joined the family business straight out of college at twenty-four as assistant to Al Fritz. "It was obvious he was not serving an apprenticeship," Fritz deadpans. A group photograph from a Pebble Beach sales meeting, published in *The Schwinn Reporter,* hints at the tension: a dour Ed, his hair well past his ears, stands with his hands behind his back, an odd extra space between the heir apparent and the old squares around him.

The real thorn in Ed's side was Fritz, who, along with Ray Burch, essentially had been running the company for the past fifteen years. Fritz knew it all: every corner of the factory, every worker's name. He had extensive contacts in the industry and was highly influential. Worse, he aggravated Ed by undiplomatically calling him "Junior." Ed eventually repaid the kindness. With the help of Uncle Frankie and brother-in-law Peter Davis, he banished the No. 2 executive to suburban Northbrook as head of Schwinn's new Excelsior Fitness Equipment Company, a division that would sell the Air-Dyne exerciser Fritz recently had been championing.

Fritz was interested in exercise bicycles as early as the mid-1960s, when the company introduced a run-of-the-mill stationary bike. The hope was that exercisers would help level the peaks and valleys of Schwinn's seasonal bicycle business. Not much happened in the market, however, until the summer of 1978, when engineer Lindsay Hooper, from Australian manufacturing concern Repco, stopped by for a surprise visit. Fritz had met Hooper several years earlier during a business trip to Melbourne. Now the Aussie was in Chicago, dragging a contraption that he dubbed the "Bionic Bike." Hooper seemed dejected. He'd been attempting to sell or license the exerciser to a handful of American firms, including Chicago giant Sears, and each had turned him down. Little wonder, Fritz thought. It looked like a Rube Goldberg contraption, with its square tubing and a bicycle wheel with fan blades that displaced air to create resistance. Frank Brilando, Schwinn's chief engineer, and Sam Mesha, the vice president of purchasing, laughed as Fritz climbed on. A minute or two was all he needed to be sold. The motion was natural, like walking or jogging, and the moving handlebars enabled the rider to exercise arms and legs at the same time. "This is unique," Fritz told Hooper. A Repco representative soon flew to Chicago to negotiate an exclusive deal: Schwinn would receive worldwide distribution (except for Australia, New Guinea, and New Zealand) and pay a royalty of 10 percent on the first 5,000 units, 5 percent after that.

Frankie and other board members grimaced when they saw the peculiar exerciser Fritz was calling the "Air-Dyne" and touting as the next big thing for Schwinn—a product that would spark sales as demand for cycles plateaued following the bike boom. "They told me I was crazy," Fritz says. Some thought the agreement with Repco was too liberal. Longtime counsel Bob Keck was worried that the Food and Drug Administration was planning to regulate the advertising of exercisers and urged Schwinn to lay low. Fritz was frustrated. Not being able to say exercise is good for you, he recalls in classic Schwinn-speak, "was like selling the steak without the sizzle."

Fritz looked for an ally in the newly installed president. "Junior, we've gotta get the rag out," he told Ed. "We've got to do something about this exercise business. We've got to get moving on it. We've got to promote it. We've got to sell it."

Ed agreed, although not in the way Fritz expected. The pair pitched a more aggressive marketing program for Air-Dynes at the company's December board meeting, then Fritz spent the Christmas holiday at his condominium in Sarasota, Florida. When he returned to work the first Monday in January, Ed invited him to dinner with Frankie, Peter Davis, and Bob Keck.

Fritz was the first to arrive at a downtown Chicago club and was directed to a second-floor dining room. Behind the private bar was a blown-up photograph of himself, 3 feet by 5 feet, with a sign that read, "Excelsior Exercise Company." Holy Christ, he thought.

Fritz hustled back downstairs and feigned nonchalance when the others arrived. "Now we walk up to the room," he says, "and I've got to act surprised. 'Am I being asked to retire or what?' "

As the group sat down for drinks, Ed explained that Fritz was being named president and general manager of Excelsior, a start-up christened after Ignaz's long-folded motorcycle business, one of the company's most venerable names.

"Wait a minute," Fritz insisted. "I've never had my own company. I've never had any aspirations to start up a company. I think I'm reasonably good—I'm doing a reasonably good job in the job that I have—but I don't know that I want to take on something like this."

"Baloney," Davis said. "There's not that much to it."

Attorney Keck chimed in, "You know, you're the one who's been promoting this exercise business. You've made your own bed, now you've got to lie in it."

Keck had emerged as a mover and shaker in Chicago legal circles, having made his name as an antitrust specialist in both the Schwinn case and a long-running battle between the government and Chicago wallboard producer U.S. Gypsum. His surname took lead position at his law firm in the 1970s (it is now Keck Mahin & Cate, the fourteenth incarnation in a history that stretches back to 1886) and he served on more than a dozen corporate boards. "He was a commanding figure in the firm," one associate says, "a tough guy." His law firm's relationship with Schwinn dated from the 1920s, and Keck fiercely supported Ed in public. "He felt it was his fiduciary duty to protect the family," says Ray Burch, suggesting that Keck could have provided more pointed counsel. "The kids relied on him."

Ed certainly had depended on Keck in paving the way for Fritz's ouster. At dinner that January night, Ed produced a labor contract.

"I've been with the company since 1945," Fritz said. "What do I need a labor contract for?"

"This is for your protection!" was the reply.

Fritz scanned the document, and turned to Frankie, who was sitting on his left at a round table. Ed was on his right.

"Frank, do I have any option here?"

"No!" Frankie and Ed answered in unison.

Despite Fritz's hesitance, his Excelsior division soon became a roaring success. Annual sales of fitness equipment grew dramatically—to $24 million in 1986, when the company sold nearly 67,000 Air-Dynes. More important, the exercisers, which sold for $595 at the time, were immensely profitable. Gross margins for the company would rise to more than 50 percent by mid-decade, versus 20 percent to 30 percent for bicycles. Dealers loved them: "You can take profit margins up to forty percent to forty-five percent with the bells and whistles, the heart monitors and such," says Joe Russell, a merchant in rural Washington, Illinois. Schwinn's Taiwanese supplier, Giant Manufacturing, expanded its factory to build the Air-Dyne, and although Giant was reliable,

Schwinn's corporate managers were skeptical of the optimistic forecasts from Excelsior. As a result, Fritz says, "we never had enough exercisers."

Although the Air-Dyne was hot, Fritz was not. He had worked at the side of the legendary F. W. Schwinn, developed the Sting-Ray, and risen to the No. 2 post under Frankie, but that meant little to Ed and his hand-picked advisers. "They elected to get rid of me, Japanese-style," Fritz says.

First, there were slights: dealer meetings to which he wasn't invited or, worse, a gathering where Ed left the room as Fritz walked to the podium. By 1985, Fritz was enraged that he and his staff had not received raises. His last pay increase was in 1978, yet he had been told in the 1980 meeting that if the exerciser business performed well, he'd be rewarded.

"I don't think I will be contradicted when I say that I am sure these returns exceeded even the wildest expectations of any of the directors," Fritz told Ed and other Excelsior board members at a meeting in May.

His plea was not well received. By July, Fritz was predicting to his lieutenant, Gerard O'Keefe, that he'd be fired.

"We've been hearing rumors that you want to retire," Ed told Fritz that month.

Fritz laughed. "I don't know where you heard that. I can't afford to retire. I still feel I'm making a contribution to the business, and I'm enjoying what I'm doing. The rumor's not true."

Ed's face reddened. "Well, we *want* you to retire." The dismissal, Ed noted, was "at the request of the family."

"Why?" Fritz demanded.

"You're not performing the way the family wanted you to perform."

Fritz retired August 1, 1985, at age sixty, nearly forty years after his first day on the Chicago factory's welding line. The message rumbled throughout headquarters: It was the end of the old Schwinn. Outsiders heard it, too. Repco was especially concerned—the Australian company's royalties on Air-Dynes were as high as $750,000 a year. Repco executive

Neil H. Domelow flew to Chicago to find out what was going on. He says the most revealing explanation came from finance vice president John Barker, who told Domelow, "There's not room for two bosses."

In the years that Al Fritz ran Excelsior, John Barker was becoming the real power at Schwinn. Both Barker and his main rival, marketing vice president Bill Austin, had been recruited by Ed in the early 1980s. They were not invested in the old corporate culture and they seemed to enjoy shaking the company out of its lethargy.

A freewheeling, cigar-smoking dealmeister, Barker both knew the numbers and saw the big picture. He had a zest for crisis and combat—he always seemed to have a scheme—and he thrived on chaos. Young managers admired his creativity and enjoyed working for him. His taste for fine food, vintage wines, and first-class travel would become legend at Schwinn. "He had a lot of Barnum in him," says Mike McNamara, who answered to Barker in the early '80s as Schwinn's treasurer.

Barker grew up in a modest neighborhood in northwest Chicago. His father died when he was young, according to a friend, and he was raised by his mother, aunt, and uncle. He graduated from a Christian Brothers high school and received a degree in business administration from John Carroll University near Cleveland in 1963. "He was not a bookworm," says college classmate Joe Glunz, Sr., heir to a prominent Chicago wine distributorship, who helped turn his friend into a connoisseur of burgundies. "He had an outstanding palate." Barker began his business career at Canadian farm equipment maker Massey-Ferguson, holding financial positions while studying for his MBA from Drake University in Des Moines, Iowa. In the '70s he held posts in Switzerland, the United Kingdom, and Australia, gaining the grounding in international business that would become his forte. He was the thirty-nine-year-old vice president of international finance at Bell & Howell Company in the Chicago suburb of Skokie when Schwinn hired him for its top financial job in May 1980.

Barker was flamboyant. He drove BMWs and carried wads of cash in his pocket, which served him well getting around Third World countries. He immediately clicked with his younger boss, and Ed seemed to be taken with his gregarious recruit. The pair dined out several times a week, often with their wives, at Stefani's, a cozy Northern Italian restaurant on Chicago's North Side. "He made it a point to make the relationship important," observes former controller Don Gilliard. Indeed, some subordinates felt Barker worked hard to make sure no one was as close to Ed as he. Nevertheless, they delighted in the ride. "John spent time making sure others were happy and taken care of," Gilliard says. "He was interested in the people who worked for him." The best part was the travel. In Paris, Barker favored the famed Hotel George V near the Arc de Triomphe; in Hong Kong, the Peninsula or Mandarin Oriental, where rates approached $300 a night. It was unusual for him to select a bottle of wine for less than $50 off a menu, and his hotel room doubled as Schwinn Central, stocked with the best scotches, cognacs, and liqueurs for clients and colleagues. In Hong Kong, he once ordered a round of 1945 Armagnac that cost $28 a shot. "I noticed the date," says former marketing director Byron Smith, "because it was the first time I'd put something in my body older than I was." Barker always seemed to know the place for treats: the steak at Smith & Wollensky in New York, the pastry at Gerbaud bakery in Budapest, the chocolates at the Peninsula's candy boutique. "It doesn't cost that much more to eat well," he once told Mike McNamara.

Schwinn never had scrimped on travel, and Ed was not about to impose austerity on his hires. Most executives flew first class and they were encouraged to stay in the best hotels, because there was a successful image to maintain. Product manager David Karneboge, who traveled to Asia four times a year, says he would have been as content with a business class flight—a savings of $2,000. "Listen, Kathy," he told Ed's assistant, Kathy Sieczko, while planning a trip to Osaka. "I'll fly business class. I just want to go a day early so I can check in and get a good night's sleep." Even with the extra night's stay, Karneboge calculated he'd save the company more than $1,500. Yet when the tickets arrived, they were first class, as usual.

Like John Barker, vice president Bill Austin helped shake up the old order when he took control of the marketing organization. But he was more conservative than his counterpart in the finance department. "He was a professional, *Fortune* 500–style," says Carl Cohen, who worked for Austin as a product manager during the 1980s.

Austin was raised in New Jersey, the son of a quality control engineer in the needle department at Singer Sewing Machine Company. His years at Rutgers University were storybook: he was an All-America football tailback and president of his fraternity. After a three-year stint in the air force, Austin became a sales trainee at General Electric Company's housewares division in Bridgeport, Connecticut, selling toasters, irons, and clocks. He thrived on developing and carrying out marketing strategies, and moved into top sales positions at other companies, first at cookware maker Revere Copper & Brass Company in New York, then at International Silver in Connecticut. Austin was vice president of sales and marketing at Aladdin Industries, a Tennessee manufacturer of lunch boxes and thermos bottles, when he was tapped by an executive recruiter for the top marketing post at Schwinn in September 1981. For the forty-three-year-old Austin, "It was a new business for me—a company in trouble, a top-notch brand name. They needed a lot of help."

Austin was regimented and systematic, bringing new rigor to the marketing process. When the general managers of the distribution subsidiaries came to Chicago for monthly sales meetings, he quizzed them immediately: "How many pieces did you sell? How'd you do in parts? What's next month's number?" He added new positions—product managers—to serve as specialists who'd live and breathe particular bikes, gauge market demand, and tell the manufacturing side of the business exactly what was needed. Previously, Schwinn's "product managers" were one man: Al Fritz. Austin also tried to motivate dealers using updated incentives, like annual trips for the top 50 retailers to Acapulco and Nassau, and he tended to them carefully. Product manager Carl Cohen remembers a 1984 Puerto Vallarta meeting where Austin didn't want his Chicago workers wandering off by themselves. He assigned each of his staff members to stations, so he'd know where to send a dealer with a gripe or question. "My location was at the intersection of two pools, where the margaritas were," Cohen says. "From ten A.M. till five P.M."

In comparison with the more even-tempered John Barker, Austin could be cruel—publicly dressing down a subordinate, for example. Some attributed his periodic dark moods to his diabetic condition. Austin shrugs and acknowledges, "I'm demanding." But both Barker and Austin brought new vitality to Schwinn, helping to engineer a revival in the 1980s. Soon, however, they would become rivals. Barker, who so skillfully captivated Ed, gained the edge, whispering his grand schemes into the boss's ear.

12

ONE STRIKE AND YOU'RE OUT

It was late on a chilly March evening in 1980—ten o'clock—when the Chicago factory's second shift finished voting. Jack Ahearn, the vice president of manufacturing, and Lee Meader, vice president of human resources, telephoned chairman Frank V. Schwinn with the news: The hourly employees had chosen to affiliate with the United Auto Workers.

Frankie was shaken. He felt betrayed, he told Ahearn and Meader, especially by the old-timers. Schwinn had always taken care of its own. Observes UAW negotiator Carl Schier, "The company thought the world was coming to an end."

That cozy world had ended long before the vote to unionize. Labor relations had deteriorated from the paternal management style of the 1950s and 1960s, when factory workers were represented by in-house committees rather than outside unions. "Before, it was like a family," says Henry Mahone, who headed Schwinn's internal shop union. "Everyone knew everybody's business." But the relationship changed during the 1970s boom, when employment rose to a peak of 2,000 workers. From management's perspective, there were fewer familiar faces as the ethnic mix in Schwinn's northwest Chicago neighborhood shifted from Polish, German, and Irish to black, Hispanic, and Korean. By mid-decade, the workforce had become divided between the older whites and the younger minorities. Longtime factory hand Nick "The Greek" Kantas, for instance, blames the abrupt end of the company's tradition of summer picnics in suburban St. Charles on a Puerto Rican guest who reputedly flashed a knife during a quarrel.

The arrival in 1975 of human resources chief Lee Meader further changed the tone of business. Meader, a former director of personnel and industrial relations for Johnson & Johnson's Chicago operations, was Schwinn's first experienced professional in the job and bargaining suddenly became more sophisticated. "The workers were frustrated, not able to accomplish as much as they wanted," says Meader's assistant, Brian Fiala. "They were feeling outgunned."

The mild-mannered Henry Mahone seemed an unlikely labor leader—hardly the type to infuse the rank and file with righteous indignation. "It took a lot to get him riled," Fiala says. Mahone had headed the shop union since 1969 and remained something of a compromise choice among old and new. Meader and Fiala found dealing with Mahone on even routine matters taxing. As soon as they thought an issue had been settled, Mahone would return and ask for a change. Meader called dealing with Mahone a "string bet," meaning there was a string attached to every deal. Clearly, he was not firmly in control of his troops.

From the workers' point of view, management had become adversarial. "Before, the supervisors were nice, considerate; they thanked you," says Mary Jones, a twelve-year veteran of the factory. "Then, management changed. A bunch of dogs. There wasn't that kindness for the people." It was understandable that workers were uneasy about the future. Schwinn had been importing bikes from Asia since the early 1970s, and talk of relocating to Tulsa, Oklahoma, hardly comforted them, either. "There was a feeling that, as an independent [in-house] union, they weren't as able to be as powerful as they would like," says Schwinn's labor attorney, John McDonald. "They wanted the protection of an outsider who would come in and make sure nothing bad ever happened to them."

Although there had been some minor and unsuccessful attempts to organize the factory in years past, the issue that finally made Schwinn workers receptive to the UAW was the lack of a pension plan—a concern critical to an aging workforce. By September 1979, 70 percent of the hourly workers had signed petitions in favor of holding an election. Schwinn fought the push at every step with legal maneuvers. "The family had an attitude about bankers and unions," observes Pat Murphy of the Schwinn Sales Midwest distribution arm. "They didn't want people telling them what to do." Schwinn didn't want a union, and it didn't want the powerful United Auto Workers in particular, with its history of rabble-rousing and restrictive work rules at General Motors, Ford, Chrysler, Caterpillar, John Deere, and the like. (In fact, the UAW had been growing weaker by the time it organized Schwinn; in the late 1970s, with the union's ranks being depeleted by layoffs and plant closings, many large industrial companies already were asking for—and winning—concessions from organized labor.)

The National Labor Relations Board scheduled an election for March 28, 1980. Management stubbornly waged a campaign for no union representation at all, not even the old in-house committees; the company was still furious at Henry Mahone and other shop leaders for trying to bring in the UAW. Yet the attack was not high-pitched—there were no hip-hip-hooray rallies or conveniently timed raffles, for instance—because management was afraid of alienating old-timers. Instead, there were earnest letters signed by Frankie or Al Fritz and ribbons with the pithy slogan, *Win with Schwinn. Vote no.* Manufacturing chief Jack Ahearn met with small groups to reiterate management's position. "I said, 'Some companies that took the UAW went out of business.' No one would say a word. Henry Mahone wouldn't say a word."

The final tally was close: 747 for the UAW, 566 for no union at all, 79 for keeping the old system. Workers elected Mahone president of UAW Local 2153. Yet management, according to Mahone, stonewalled when it came time to negotiate a contract. "They were not serious," he says. The company had agreed in principle to start a pension plan, but negotiations bogged down over a cost-of-living pay increase and basic work rules, such as layoff procedures and shift assignments by seniority. That September, workers voted to authorize a strike. A month later, some 1,400 people walked off their jobs.

Negotiators for management believed the UAW wanted to pick a fight, especially with a nationally known company like Schwinn. "The union wanted to take over and show us they were tough," labor lawyer McDonald says. "The UAW had won over the independent [union] on the theme that they were going to be more powerful. So they had to start kicking us around." Chief negotiator for the UAW was Carl Schier, a former machine operator at farm equipment maker International Harvester Company. He was in his early sixties but still a firebrand. "He was religiously into the labor movement," McDonald says. "Practical solutions were hard to come by." With contract talks deadlocked, the UAW brought in a second negotiator, Dick Shoemaker, who was an alumnus of Deere and a rising union star. After the Schwinn strike, Shoemaker would move on to top posts at the UAW's Solidarity House headquarters in Detroit, where he served as an executive assistant to then-president Owen Bieber, negotiated agreements for the U.S. plants of several Japanese auto manufacturers, and became a union vice president.

As strikes go, it was a quiet affair. McDonald says he watched one worker fake an injury by pushing himself into Lee Meader's running car. "The guy was lying at the rear of the car with his eyes closed. There were fumes coming out of the rear of the car, and the man looked uncomfortable." McDonald told Meader to turn off the car, "but because the guy was pretending to be hurt, he couldn't get up. They took him to the hospital, but there was nothing wrong with him. Zero."

Schwinn had revved up production in the months leading up to the walkout, when bargaining was at a standstill, and had stashed thousands of bicycles at a warehouse next to a frame-building plant. Picketing strikers propped wood sticks against the warehouse doors, so they would know if anyone entered the building, but Jack Ahearn and a half-dozen supervisors would slip in at 2:00 A.M. on Fridays and Saturdays and pile the bikes onto trailers. "The loading docks were inside, so we couldn't be seen," Ahearn recalls, and his crew carefully replaced the sticks before they left. "Where did those bikes go?" one union committeeman asked him after the strike. Ahearn shrugged. "I don't know."

Before the strike, Schwinn had been importing 20 percent of its product—mainly from Japan—and was buying about 100,000 models a year from Giant Manufacturing, an ambitious start-up in Taiwan. When the union went out, Schwinn purchasing vice president Jay Townley asked Giant's president, Tony Lo, if he could step up production. Lo returned an answer within 24 hours: "A friend in need is a friend indeed." Giant agreed to pump out bicycles for Schwinn—it shipped about 80,000 units over the next five months—with the understanding that the gravy train would halt when the strike was over. It proved a smart move on Tony Lo's part. Giant impressed Schwinn with its quality, service, and delivery. The Americans would be back.

The strike was settled four months later, in February 1981. Workers won a modest pension plan, a wage increase, and some beneficial labor rules. "A tough strike with a determined adversary," negotiator Carl Schier reminisces. "We got a good first contract." If the union won the battle, however, it soon would lose the war, because the strike laid the groundwork for the closing of the Chicago plant.

Before the vote to unionize, older workers had argued that the Schwinn family would never tolerate such a move; that if they ever organized, the factory would be closed. Yet the family had already doomed the plant by failing to upgrade it over the years. Now there were new pressures, such as low-priced foreign competition and increased government regulation. The union movement was the final nail in the coffin. The presence of the UAW virtually ruled out future investments there, says Peter Davis, former director of corporate planning and Ed Schwinn's brother-in-law. Shortly after workers embraced the union, Ed, Frankie, and Davis began hatching plans for an out-of-town factory far from Schwinn's labor troubles. The company again turned to consultancy Peat Marwick, which had helped plan the failed Oklahoma initiative years earlier. Davis even hired one of its Young Turks, Hank Russell, as group vice president of manufacturing—essentially Al Fritz's old job—and a task force headed by Davis and Russell secretly worked to find a site. They came up with Greenville, Mississippi, whose prime attraction was that Mississippi, as a right-to-work state, wasn't hospitable to unions. "They found a county where the sheriff knew what to do with labor organizers," jokes marketer Jay Townley.

Nevertheless, the drawbacks proved plentiful, and the Greenville plant, which opened in mid-1981, almost seemed designed to fail.

The new factory sat 75 miles from the nearest interstate. (In contrast, Wisconsin-based competitor Trek had located its rural Waterloo factory about ten miles from Interstate 94.) And traveling to Greenville from Chicago required a flight to Memphis, Tennessee, then either a connecting commuter flight ("the kind where the pilot moves the passengers around to best distribute the weight," says personnel executive Brian Fiala) or a nearly three-hour drive. Weather problems often delayed departures from Memphis (Schwinn purchasing manager Mark Marusarz amassed a collection of Elvis Presley memorabilia from his layovers there) and the standing joke among managers in Chicago was, "You could get to Hong Kong faster than you could get to Greenville." It wasn't simply a matter of getting people to Greenville; there was the logistical nightmare of importing bicycle components from halfway around the world. The Mississippi River town was a barge center, but Asian components weren't brought in that way. They were shipped to the West Coast, then hauled by rail to Memphis and finally trucked to Greenville—a voyage of at least two months duration. Parts from Japan could arrive at a Taiwanese bicycle factory in a matter of days. It was quicker to import a container of finished products.

Because Greenville wasn't a center for metal manufacturing, there was a scarcity of skilled machinists and experienced metal workers. Attracting upper management was difficult, too. There were three plant managers during the factory's ten-year life. Few executives in Chicago were willing to move to Greenville, and Ed Schwinn initially didn't force the issue by, say, assigning rotating stints. Some did volunteer, like cousin Robert Schwinn, who spent seven years as a quality control engineer there, but the company's tooling engineers remained in Chicago, working with product managers to design and build the systems for making new bikes in Greenville. The engineers would ship the equipment and train the operators; a reasonable process, until a glitch occurred. It could take days while a Greenville worker tried to fix a tooling problem, called headquarters for a diagnosis, and waited for an engineer to catch a flight to Memphis.

Production was also scheduled in Chicago, and coordination was wanting. In the early months, bike frames piled up and front forks were ready to go, but the correct components hadn't arrived on time. The frames would be stored in a back room, but the paint would harden during the long wait and decals wouldn't stick, so the frames had to be stripped.

Then there was the question of what models to build. Trek manufactured with some success in the United States because its bikes sold at a premium. (Later, it would manufacture costlier models and import less expensive ones). Schwinn's leaders proposed moving to Greenville the production of midpriced ten-speeds in the range of $250 to $300. Manufacturing vice president Jack Ahearn objected; those models were costly to produce and vulnerable to competition from Japanese and Taiwanese companies. Rather than relegate a profitable line to a new plant, he suggested, why not produce the troublesome kids' bikes that were labor intensive and price sensitive? Ed Schwinn and Peter Davis decided it would be ten-speeds. A frustrated Ahearn remained to get Greenville's equipment up and running, then retired in May 1981 at age fifty-five.

Finally, there was the matter of paying for the plant. Schwinn wanted to finance the Greenville purchase using attractively priced industrial revenue bonds, but its lenders wouldn't allow the company to incur additional debt. "We thought the banks would let us do it if we got a good rate," says Mike McNamara, Schwinn's treasurer at the time. "But the banks wouldn't budge." So, the Ignaz Schwinn Trust, which owned the company's stock, guaranteed a bond issue of about $2 million, used the money to build the plant, then leased it back to the bike business through an entity called Schwinn Development Company. "It was a fair-market-value lease," McNamara adds. "Schwinn Development made money on it, but not a lot." (For a brief period in the early 1990s, the trust raised the bicycle company's rent to compensate for dried-up dividends, although the banks soon squashed that scheme.) The Mississippi plant, with all its woes, would become a nightmare for the family trust, which would be saddled with liability for lease payments after the company filed for bankruptcy in 1992. In the early 1980s, however, most of Schwinn's top executives were optimistic about their new facility. The Greenville factory produced 60,000 bikes in 1982 and was slated to expand to 200,000 units a year. It seemed time to turn management's attention to the dinosaur back in Chicago.

There Ed was at the center of a struggle between the manufacturing loyalists and the marketers, who favored importing and its higher profit margins. He previously had sided with the former, ruling that Schwinn must remain committed to making bikes in America. His decision struck some observers as emotional; it reflected his family's legacy, from great-grandfather Ignaz to father Ed Sr., a long-ignored proponent of the factory in the 1960s. Now that Schwinn had a new plant in Greenville, Ed Jr. could jettison Chicago and remain a U.S. manufacturer. The hometown factory started to die a slow death.

After the strike, the Chicago operation, under consultant-turned-manufacturing exec Hank Russell, had boosted production to shrink the average cost per bike and make the plant more profitable. (Schwinn had barely broken even in 1980, and it would lose more than $5 million in 1981.) Russell assumed the mantle as defender of the factory's honor. He even became somewhat possessive of it. "The optimal output of my factory is forty-five hundred bikes per day," he told Carl Cohen, former product manager for the Varsity. "Why can't you sell it?" Unfortunately, not enough customers wanted the Varsitys and Continentals that Chicago was cranking out at the rate of more than 3,000 a day. Long after other American companies had become more market responsive, Schwinn was still mired in the mindset of manufacturing dictating to marketing.

Schwinn had been stockpiling bikes into warehouses since before the strike—a painful time to carry too much inventory, because interest rates were so high. By 1981, group vice president John Nielsen, who had succeeded Ray Burch in the top marketing post, realized that Varsitys and Continentals were stacking up. "You're right," Nielsen told his lieutenant, Jay Townley. "We can't sell these bikes.' "

When the imposing Nielsen presented his unpleasant assessment to Ed at a managers' meeting, the president flew into a rage. "If you can't sell them," he shouted, "I'll get someone who can."

"Don't talk to me that way here," Nielsen finally told Ed. "I'll see you in your office."

Nielsen stormed out of the room. Days later, he resigned.

Today the retired Nielsen notes that the issue of unsold bikes merely contributed to his decision to leave Schwinn. More frustrating, he says, was the cultural change sweeping the company, as Ed recruited cocky MBAs who clashed with the veterans. "They were long on theory, short on reality and practice," he says. "This was not what Schwinn was all about."

Nielsen was replaced in September 1981 by no-nonsense Bill Austin, who, along with finance vice president John Barker, cast a cold eye on the factory. Schwinn "had four warehouses full of merchandise," Austin says. "I pulled the sales and marketing people together for a two-day meeting and asked them, 'What do we need?' " The bikes Schwinn needed, attendees answered, couldn't be produced by the Chicago factory. "Don't worry about the factory," Austin assured his troops.

The new Asian suppliers also strengthened the case against Chicago. Buying bikes abroad was becoming an economic imperative. It was cheaper to purchase a Taiwan model whole and ship it to California than to buy the raw materials for a bike made in Chicago. It wasn't simply labor; everything was more expensive in the States. By importing, Schwinn could earn a profit of $25 to $40 per bike, instead of losing $5 to $20 on the domestic version. In this instance, time was on Austin's side. As the plant's limitations became increasingly obvious, Ed began to examine the facility more critically. In February 1982, Austin formally presented his case to Ed and other executives. Here is what we need, he said, to bring Schwinn back: BMX for kids and mountain bikes for adults, with chrome-moly TIG-welded frames. Austin and Jay Townley wanted the company to experiment with a BMX model imported from Taiwan's Giant Manufacturing to revitalize Schwinn's battered name in the children's market. "Manufacturing said, 'You're gonna shut us down, you're gonna kill us,' " Townley recalls. But Ed said, "Go." Giant delivered about 130,000 BMX Predators in the fall of 1982. "We got market share and became players," Townley says.

Between the second half of 1982 and the third quarter of 1983, Townley (with the new title of assistant to the president) headed a task force charged with closing sections of the plant and sourcing production elsewhere. Once that strategy was set, the factory's days were numbered. Austin's staff would design a bike and ask for a price quote from Giant—and from Chicago. Giant could make a chrome-moly lug-frame bike with alloy wheels that could retail for under $200. "The factory couldn't touch it," Austin says.

Hank Russell, the embattled champion of the factory, left the company in 1982, as did Peter Davis. In what is described by Schwinn managers as a failed "palace coup," the brother-in-law tried to sway attorney and board member Bob Keck to his view that he was better equipped to run the company than Ed and should have the top job. Word quickly got back to Ed—and Davis soon departed. Both Davis and Keck later denied the story, but Davis concedes, "It was no secret that Ed and I disagreed. . . . I chose to take a different career path."

Just as Schwinn's engineers had turned over blueprints to Japanese manufacturers for the company's first imports during the '70s bike boom, they now shared designs with Giant. Former head engineer Frank Brilando acknowledges he had "misgivings," but notes that Schwinn employees were obliged to share details with their Taiwanese counterparts to ensure they manufactured high-quality bikes.

The Air-Dyne exerciser was the last to go. With the knowledge that the factory might be shuttered, Al Fritz asked Giant's Tony Lo for a quote in September 1982 during a meeting in Taiwan. "I hope I don't have to buy from you," he told Lo. The following February, Lo arrived at Excelsior's suburban Chicago office with his numbers. He could land the Air-Dyne in Los Angeles for less than Schwinn's current cost of raw materials. Lo's price would boost Excelsior's bottom line by $3 million annually. Fritz thought Ed would be delighted; instead, the president was furious. He was planning to continue exerciser production at the factory because "we've got to keep a presence in Chicago." While the exercisers were profitable, Fritz doubted they could support the overhead of the entire factory. Headquarters and the Air-Dyne division spent several months dickering over which exercisers should be manufactured in Chicago and which should be imported. A few months later, Schwinn decided to shift its entire exerciser production to Taiwan and close the Chicago plant. Lo built an addition to Giant's bicycle factory to make the lucrative Air-Dyne. Equipment and parts were packed and shipped, and Schwinn engineers again shared their drawings. Engineer Rene Mraz was worried. Townley assured him, "We have no choice." At first, there were problems with tolerances and other technical snags, but Giant quickly impressed the Schwinn engineers. "Tony Lo made a sensational product," Mraz says.

Not all Schwinn production went to Giant. In September 1982, Schwinn contracted with mass-market competitor Murray Ohio to produce about a third of its bikes—mostly the unprofitable 16-inch and 20-inch kids' models, but also the venerable Varsity—at Murray's plant near Nashville, Tennessee. (Schwinn also assigned its mountain bike to Murray, much to the dismay of product manager Fred Teeman, since that factory couldn't produce the chrome-moly frame he needed.) Schwinn moved its welding equipment to Tennessee in order to make the bikes at a lower cost and improve profitability. Although the Schwinn product was a step in quality above the Murray model sold to a chain store, the bike still was too heavy, says Carl Cohen, former product manager for the Varsity. Schwinn, he argues, should have melted the welding equipment and contracted its children's bikes to Giant immediately. "No one would pay a $20 to $25 premium for an electroforged bike," Cohen says.

With the announcement of the Murray deal, Schwinn laid off 300 Chicago workers. The following July, another 211 were furloughed.

"As early as February 1981, at the bargaining table, I began to get the sense they would shut Chicago," says the UAW's Henry Mahone, noting that after the strike, Schwinn had called back only 65 percent of the hourly work force. "They made comparisons between what they could import and what they were paying Schwinn workers here."

The mid-1983 layoff left only 400 employees at Chicago locations. Ed attributed the cutback to a seasonal downturn in production. "Our business is cyclical," he told the *Chicago Tribune*. "It happens every year."

The end was inevitable. Factory hands watched more and more production transferred offshore. Soon, there were just 200 workers, then 92. "When I left," Mahone says, "there were four to five maintenance people."

The factory was shuttered by Christmas 1983. Newer portions were sold, but now most of the plant is a vacant lot covered with weeds and broken glass. Schwinn executives wouldn't allow the Varsity to be manufactured overseas, so, after its brief stint at Murray, the cherished name that had served Schwinn so well died, too.

At one point, as manufacturing was being shifted to Asia, the UAW charged that the plant was doomed once the workers voted in the union. In a complaint filed with the National Labor Relations board, the UAW said that management had failed to disclose its intention to close the factory and therefore hadn't bargained in good faith. "They've had a master plan to stop manufacturing in Chicago all along," Mahone said in the *Tribune*. "They've just been going through the motions with the union." The company's response—that its decision was made in stages and not predetermined—ultimately was accepted by the labor board. "The UAW gave us too much credit," says attorney John McDonald. "Schwinn was trying to figure out how to make the next buck; they were not long-range planners." Brian Fiala, who later succeeded Lee Meader in the top human resources post, puts it this way: "The planets were in juxtaposition. The union made it easier to go down that path. . . . You're going to go down that path anyway. It was timing as much as anything."

Surely, Schwinn's failure to upgrade sealed the factory's fate well before workers embraced the union. Ed stated the obvious in 1983, when he told the *Tribune*, "It would have been too expensive to retool. . . . We would have had to tear it down."

Ed had beaten the union, but he couldn't have devised a more Pyrrhic victory. With the closing of Chicago and opening of Greenville, Schwinn was stuck with a two-pronged strategy. Although it designed its own bikes, it essentially was an importer—a distributor highly dependent on its overseas suppliers. Yet with the Greenville factory, it was still a manufacturer. The company would remain torn between its roles, and the perceived need to control manufacturing would lead Schwinn into a series of joint ventures that would sap its limited resources and dilute its focus.

There was a more immediate threat, however. The closing of the Chicago factory plunged Schwinn into a financial crisis that would push the company to the edge of bankruptcy.

13

THE DIFFERENCE O'DEA MADE

Almost anyone who cared about Schwinn in 1983 would have cheered. The albatross of a plant in Chicago was gone, the company finally could design and sell bikes that consumers demanded. Everyone cheered, that is, except Schwinn's bankers.

The company's balance sheet lay in ruins. Because of operating deficits and special charges associated with closing the Chicago factory, Schwinn had posted three consecutive years of losses. Its net worth plunged from $43.8 million in 1980 to $2.7 million in 1983, and it owed nearly $60 million to the banks. The lending institutions demanded collateral, sparking a financial crisis that nearly sent Schwinn into bankruptcy. "The loss of hard assets changed Schwinn's character as a borrower," says Keck Mahin & Cate lawyer Dennis O'Dea, who was Schwinn's bankruptcy attorney in 1992 and handled the 1983 financial restructuring spurred by the lenders' demands. "Ironically, the banks saw the company as a credit risk, even though it was more efficient and competitive."

Until the early 1980s, Schwinn had enjoyed a casual and open-ended relationship with its two main lenders, Chicago's Harris Bank and Northern Trust Company. "They called me and asked, 'How much are you going to need?' " says former treasurer Mike McNamara. "We paid interest once a month." There was no credit agreement, no security. The bank's standing was no different than that of a components supplier or any other trade creditor.

In 1980, however, Schwinn was marginally profitable. Inventories had been built up to accommodate a 1979 burst in demand and swelled further in anticipation of the strike. That's an expensive strategy when the manufacturer's revolving loans to purchase components—repaid after the finished product is sold—carry interest rates of nearly 20 percent. As Schwinn began to post operating losses, the banks grew concerned. Then Schwinn closed the Chicago plant, requiring the company to set up reserves for write-offs of obsolete inventory, equipment, and buildings. Schwinn also faced severance costs and had to establish a reserve for future pension payments. "The banks wanted a blanket lien" on Schwinn's assets, says O'Dea. "No terms and conditions." That would give lenders the ability to claim the company's assets if it defaulted.

O'Dea was a thirty-four-year-old bankruptcy specialist and former George Washington University law professor when he joined Keck Mahin & Cate as a partner in 1980. Bob Keck asked the new recruit for help. "I've got a company you should talk to," he said. "They're running into trouble with their banks." O'Dea met the equally young Ed Schwinn and was impressed by his pride and ambition to preserve his family's enterprise. The two walked through the plant, then in its last days, and Ed showed him the company's substantial collection of antique bikes, which even included models from the days of the draisienne and velocipede. "He had a sense of being the inheritor," O'Dea says.

The lawyer prepared his client for the tumult ahead as meetings with senior officers of the two banks grew acrimonious. Northern Trust sent the Schwinn loan to its workout department, where troubled accounts are dispatched coldly, with little sentiment for a years-old relationship.[1] Northern wanted out, but Harris Bank was committed to Schwinn and wanted Northern to stay. Northern's Bart Wilson played bad cop to Harris's Ed Lyman, the good cop who wanted to work out a refinancing, almost as though the negotiations were scripted.[2] According to O'Dea, "Bart's job was to be difficult, so Lyman could look like a hero." Whether it was part of a script or not, Bart Wilson seemed to take an instant dislike to Ed Schwinn, who goaded the banker in return. "Ed and Bart sat at opposite ends of the table," says a participant. "Ed called him by his real name—Harry—which no one did."

If a negotiating session was scheduled at Schwinn's northwest Chicago headquarters, executives who drove company-owned Mercedes or BMWs would park them discreetly inside the shuttered factory next door so that the visiting bankers wouldn't get the wrong idea about their supposedly threadbare client. Downtown, there were meetings in smoke-filled rooms that went late into the night. Attorney Terry A. McIlroy of Chicago law firm Chapman & Cutler, which represented Harris Bank, would line up a half-dozen cigars on the table in preparation for a marathon session. Banker Lyman one night slept on a couch at Harris.

Some of the parrying resembled theater of the absurd. During one early morning session at Chapman & Cutler's offices, Ed Schwinn and John Barker, the vice president of finance, sat at one end of the table, munching on a pile of candy. McIlroy commented that the Schwinn team was beginning to perk up from the sugar boost, but Ed and Barker wouldn't share their bounty with their adversaries. The bankers sent someone to fetch their own goodies. (Barker actually missed some of the sessions because of hip surgery. Don Gilliard, who had been hired in the fall of 1983 as controller, visited Barker in the hospital where he was recovering. "I didn't think it was going to be this bad when I hired you," Barker told the newcomer.)

Amid the games, the biggest stumbling block was that there wasn't enough equity to sustain the kind of borrowing Schwinn needed to continue buying inventory. The bankers would have to recognize intangible assets, mainly the sterling Schwinn name. But how much value to attach to the country's most famous brand of bike? Talks broke off one afternoon as the two sides reached an impasse. The lenders left the room knowing that Schwinn had a bankruptcy petition ready. What a shame, they muttered, to have it all end like this. But the banks were unsecured creditors—they had a stake in a settlement. Harris's Lyman called Ed later that day, suggesting that cooler heads might prevail. The two sides got back together and, over the next few days, hammered out the basis of an agreement that expanded the asset base to include the Schwinn name and the company's trademarks and patents. "Everything was pledged," former treasurer Mike McNamara says. "They started with nothing and got everything."

Although Ed could be flippant with the banks—hardly ingratiating himself with the lenders he needed to keep his business running—he received high marks from O'Dea for his handling of the crisis. "He was courageous, focused, and resolute. He was willing to put the time in and listened to advice."

Now Schwinn had a credit agreement, but it was on a tight lending leash: the company had to file weekly reports showing its cash balances, inventory, and accounts receivable. When the agreement expired in 1986, McNamara lined up a new one with a different bank syndicate, which enabled Northern Trust—long disenchanted with Schwinn's prospects under Ed—to exit the credit picture. Although Schwinn had returned to profitability, the new bank group imposed even tighter covenants and more onerous conditions. The syndicate was composed of Harris, nearby LaSalle National Bank and the Chicago outposts of Detroit's NBD Bank, Tokyo's Mitsubishi Bank, Hong Kong Shanghai Bank, and Pittsburgh's Mellon Financial Services, which specialized in asset-based lending, where a borrower's earnings and other assets are monitored closely through daily reports and quarterly audits. That kind of scrutiny aggravated Ed and John Barker, who didn't feel they needed the controls. "Schwinn viewed us as a thorn in its side and couldn't wait to get us out," says a former Mellon banker. (Mellon departed in 1988 as Schwinn's fortunes improved, and was replaced in the lending group by what is now New York's Chemical Bank.)

The crafting of the 1986 bank syndicate agreement also had its moments. The night before the closing, as Schwinn attorney O'Dea reviewed the paperwork, he discovered the company's base of assets was short by $20 million. Thousands of bikes, it seemed, had been shipped into Schwinn's four regional distribution centers, but had not yet found their way onto the books. Human resources vice president Lee Meader started telephoning managers at their homes in the middle of the night: "*Find those bikes.*" In the East, groggy employees counted, verified, and recorded the entries; at one center, a worker inadvertently tripped the burglar alarm. Within hours, the emergency swing shifts had tallied a whole new set of inventory.

"What's this," quipped Mellon lawyer Scott Pickens, "the Lazarus borrowing base—back from the dead?"

O'Dea winced. "We found a lot of bikes last night."

Even with the restrictive borrowing conditions, Schwinn faced brighter prospects in the mid-1980s. By shifting production overseas, mostly to Taiwan's Giant Manufacturing, Schwinn was able to upgrade its unimpressive line of bikes. Even better, its profit margins zoomed.

After a series of false starts, product manager Fred Teeman finally got the nod to have a chrome-moly mountain bike made at Giant. The Sierra and High Sierra models, introduced in late 1983, were a hit: sales doubled three years in a row.

The company's long-suffering parts and accessories department also enjoyed a boost. During the '70s, Schwinn had imported tires, rims, and other hardware and taken a markup before selling them to the regional distribution centers. The warehouses added their own charges, so Schwinn priced itself out of the market and sales tumbled by half to $23 million. After the Chicago factory closed, there were no more unique Schwinn parts. "You could get them anywhere," says former product manager Carl Cohen. Marketing chief Bill Austin had his protégés overhaul the pricing system to make the parts less expensive, then added more profitable items, such as helmets and speedometers. Sales nearly doubled to $42 million by 1987. Schwinn's parts and accessories division was competitive again.

Most impressive was the Air-Dyne juggernaut, which continued to roll after Al Fritz's departure in 1985 and was folded into Chicago headquarters. Unit sales of 66,700 in 1986 would almost double again to 123,600 in 1989, with the help of Chicago-based radio commentator Paul Harvey, who began hawking the exerciser in 1985. Schwinn spent $1 million a year for the radio ads, in which Harvey, a master of the pregnant pause, would segue seamlessly into the inspiring tale of a . . .

satisfied . . . Air-Dyne . . . customer. Sales would jump after such spots. "He has a lot of credibility," notes former marketing executive Byron Smith. Even more credible were the profit margins on Air-Dyne exercise equipment: a fat 50 percent, which turned the exerciser into Schwinn's cash cow. By the end of the '80s, the company would become perilously dependent on Air-Dyne, as the fitness division covered the shortcomings of the bicycle business.

For now, however, the financial picture was encouraging. In 1984, Schwinn rebounded from three years of losses, posting a profit of $3 million on sales of $134.4 million. Earnings peaked in 1986: $7 million on sales of $174.5 million. Not a spectacular margin for many industries, but it was the best Schwinn had performed in more than a decade—since the height of the bike boom in 1974, when the company had earned a then-record $6.2 million. Bicycle volume soared to 985,000 units in 1986, up 64 percent from the 600,000 units sold in 1981. Inventories had been cut by more than half in the same period. Schwinn commanded nearly one-third of the 3 million bikes sold by independent bicycle dealers (who accounted for about 30 percent of the domestic industry's sales and half its revenues). "I think we took a look at our business and met the challenge," Ed said in a 1985 interview with *Crain's Chicago Business*, "and we're prepared to reap the benefits right now."

One of the perquisites of the newfound prosperity would be a move to more stylish digs. Schwinn executives had been laboring in gritty offices across the street from the closed factory, in a neighborhood where street corners are tagged with graffiti marking the territory of the local Latin Kings gang. While many U.S. bicycle companies made do with modest offices in industrial parks adjacent to their warehouses, Ed sought stylish accommodations for his new headquarters. Schwinn rented fashionably rehabbed industrial space west of Chicago's Loop for $600,000 a year, near a collection of trendy restaurants and nightclubs. Renovations exposed the brick walls, and bicycles were suspended whimsically from ceilings. One Chicago newspaper's real estate section gushed at the setup and its impact on the gentrifying neighborhood. Some executives even got a piece of the action—Ed, John Barker, and head engineer Frank Brilando bought small shares in the partnership that owned the building.[3]

Everything seemed to be going right. Twenty-eight-year-old mountain bike racer Ned Overend surprised the sport's elitists by winning the Pacific Suntour Series in 1984 with a stock bike—a $300 Schwinn High Sierra. "It was reasonable, not a bad bike," Overend recalls. He raced professionally under the Schwinn banner for four years, switching to a custom Paramount model with which he nabbed the national championships in 1986 and 1987, and Schwinn sold a Ned Overend signature frame set until he defected to Specialized in 1988.

Mountain bike racing was still in its infancy compared with road racing, which received most of Schwinn's marketing resources during the decade. Schwinn made an advertising splash in 1980 by signing as a spokesman five-time Olympic gold medalist Eric Heiden, who was turning his sights from speed-skating to cycling, and Heiden became the centerpiece of a team that Schwinn co-sponsored with the 7-Eleven convenience store chain. Although an accomplished cyclist, Heiden never gained the fame that he'd had on the ice, and Schwinn's marketers never could prove that his presence helped sell more bikes. Schwinn also couldn't afford to keep pace with 7-Eleven's multimillion-dollar spending, and the two companies parted ways. David Karneboge, who oversaw the racing effort for Schwinn, pleaded with marketing executive Jay Townley for $250,000 to field a competitive four-man team. Karneboge repainted the old 7-Eleven van, rounded up a quartet of top amateurs, and was thrilled when Schwinn finished among the top three in a national team trial in 1982. "Our goal was to finish in the medals," Karneboge says. "And we did it."

Many dealers enjoyed the good times, too. Typical was Jeff Crittenden, who in 1979 bought a store in the fast-growing Chicago suburb of Crystal Lake, then added shops in the west suburban centers of St. Charles and Elgin. So what if Schwinn designs weren't on the cutting edge? During Crittenden's first nine years in business, his worst performance was a 22 percent increase. This was prime Schwinn territory: Middle America, not California, more interested in a solid value than the latest technology. Crittenden consistently was in the top 50 group of dealers nationwide, winning trips to Hawaii, the Bahamas, and Mexico, where he played volleyball and came home with a trophy for his winning sales record. His peak was in 1988, when he sold 5,000 bikes and ranked as the No. 12 Schwinn dealer in the country. Trek asked Crittenden if he'd be interested in taking on its line. "We said, 'No, we're one hundred percent Schwinn. We can't see straight, we're so busy.' "

Schwinn reveled in the 1980s prosperity. It was the power tie heyday of junk bond–financed hostile raids and leveraged buyouts. Banks and savings and loan associations were delighted to extend credit. Why assume equity when you could take on debt? Perhaps that go-go climate contributed to a thawing of tensions between Schwinn and its lenders. The company still had debt, but it was doing better. "The banks took Ed to skyboxes" at sports events, lawyer O'Dea recalls. Schwinn "got on the A list."

In 1988, treasurer Mike McNamara scored a coup. With earnings still strong, the banks were willing to release some of the assets that had been pledged as collateral. McNamara remembers the moment of triumph with a smile: "I got the name back."

14

LAND OF THE GIANT

With the Chicago factory closed, Schwinn management saw new worlds to conquer. Supplier and manufacturing deals soon stretched from California's Silicon Valley to the Far East to Eastern Europe—and, in many cases, stretched the resources of the thinly capitalized company. Yet Ed seemed captivated by the global action, particularly in Asia. He'd listen to Chinese-language tapes during long flights across the Pacific. He even purchased a one-of-a-kind Chinese junk in Hong Kong from a bankrupt U.S. steamship line for an estimated $50,000, then spent another $10,000 to send the 80-foot wood ship by freighter to New York and through the Great Lakes to a slip at the Chicago Yacht Club. Ed's junk, used to entertain clients and friends, easily was one of the odder crafts plying Lake Michigan.

Despite his worldly enthusiasms, Ed bungled his dealings with his major Asian suppliers, souring relationships to the point where his biggest suppliers, Giant Manufacturing of Taiwan and China Bicycles Company of Hong Kong and Shenzhen, ultimately hastened the fall of Schwinn. The two companies recruited former Schwinn executives spurned or angered by Ed and became his competitors—as well as his largest creditors. When Schwinn filed for bankruptcy in late 1992, the alienated suppliers had their knives sharpened, and they were aiming at Ed's throat.

Schwinn's new Asian relationships were skewed almost from the start, when the company became perilously dependent on its first overseas ally, Giant, after the Chicago plant was closed. By 1986, Giant was producing about 700,000 bikes for Schwinn—more than 80 percent of Schwinn's product. A stupendous share. And a stupid one. "You can be important to a supplier with 200,000 units," observes Bernie Kotlier, president of Schwinn competitor Service Cycle Supply, the marketer of Mongoose bikes. "You can be monumental at 400,000 units. At 800,000 units, you should own it." Despite its interdependence, the relationship between Schwinn and Giant had always been uneasy. By rushing into Giant's arms, Schwinn had given the Taiwan company early credibility in the cycling industry, and eventually helped it become the biggest bike manufacturer in the world (annual revenues by the mid-1990s reached $380 million). "At the start, their name was a joke," Kotlier says. "They were no 'Giant.' "

The company was launched in 1971 by thirty-eight-year-old King Liu, an engineer with wide-ranging interests whose eel farming business was destroyed by a typhoon. Liu and his partners raised $100,000 to start a small bicycle factory in Taichia, a town outside the steamy port city of Taichung, and soon was joined by Tony Lo, a twenty-four-year-old entrepreneur whose trading company acted as the sales arm for Giant. Lo sold his firm to Liu and became an owner and key manager of the bike manufacturer.

The two men complemented each other. Liu, whose family was native Taiwanese, was educated in the Japanese language and customs during the tail end of Japan's fifty-year imperial rule of Taiwan. Largely self-taught, he enjoyed tinkering with machinery in the factory. Lo was born on mainland China; his father was a pilot in the Chiang Kai-shek regime and became a teacher in Taiwan. Lo was educated in business management at Taiwan University, spoke English fluently, and proved to be a perceptive strategist and negotiator as head of sales and marketing.

They started with a few small accounts, producing, for example, the Nishiki bike for California importer West Coast Cycle, which was growing disillusioned with the rising costs of Japanese factories. Giant was an unsophisticated operation back then. At the start, there were few tools—just hammers and wrenches. Bicycle frames, usually aligned on a steel plate, were pressed against the concrete floor. The paint booth consisted of workers with spray cans, and the end result could be peeled off with a fingernail. West Coast Cycle founder Joel Davis was underwhelmed. "Tony," he told Lo, "a factory should flow like a river; this one goes here and there." Liu and Lo were never sure when the next job was coming. The latter often would walk the factory and caution the thirty or so employees, "Don't work too fast."

Lo began wooing Schwinn's Al Fritz in 1973 by inviting him and other company representatives to visit Giant's plant. Schwinn, which had started importing bikes from Japan a year earlier, had begun purchasing accessories and replacement parts in Taiwan. For Giant, a Schwinn order would be prestigious, propelling the factory into the big time. Schwinn was *the* bike company, Liu and Lo figured; if it bought from Giant, others would follow. Schwinn executives, however, weren't impressed with their first glimpses of Taiwanese technology. "It was a small factory," Fritz remembers. "One kid was holding a part, the other was welding." He rebuffed the overture, explaining that Giant wasn't qualified. The plant lacked sufficient capacity, he told the partners, and quality wasn't up to par. (Some ten years later, Fritz recalls, Liu and Lo in an emotional discussion "thanked me for the turndown—for not having acquiesced to buying bicycles at the time they wanted to sell us. I would have jeopardized them, because they couldn't have lived up to Schwinn. It would have been a very short, unsatisfactory relationship.")

Time was on Giant's side. Taiwan's gross domestic product had posted average annual growth of more than 10 percent for the ten years leading up to 1973, manufacturing had grown more than 21 percent a year, and exports had soared a spectacular 40 percent annually. Industry prospered under a variety of arrangements—direct foreign investments, joint ventures, licensing deals—and locals itched to get in on the boom. "Everyone wants to be chairman of his own company," observed histo-

Cover, 1896 Schwinn catalog—The "World."

Logo, circa 1920.

In 1996 the "World" imagery continues under new owners, with the company out of bankruptcy and celebrating the start of its second century.

Ignaz Schwinn.

Young F. W. Schwinn looking dangerous.

F. W. Schwinn *(center)* with sons Edward Sr. *(left)* and Frank V. *(right)*.

F.W. honored for factory efforts during World War II, as Ignaz looks on.

Ignaz "Brownie" Schwinn around 1963.

Ed Sr. and his wife, Mary.

Season's greetings card from Edward Schwinn family: Captain Kangaroo on bike with Schwinn children.

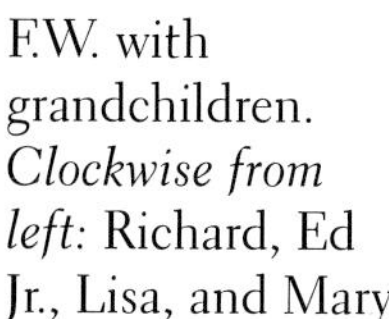

F.W. with grandchildren. *Clockwise from left*: Richard, Ed Jr., Lisa, and Mary.

Detail of Aero Cycle, circa 1934. Top-of-the-line child's bike mimicked the era's streamlining movement with simulated gas tank and headlight.

Girls model, circa 1940, featured lots of metal.

An American classic: the 1950 Black Phantom.

The ultimate bike of the 1960s: the Sting-Ray. Here, an Orange Krate with five-speed stick shift.

The Varsity, geared to older children, was the ten-speed to buy well into the 1970s.

Everything old is new again: shock absorbers at work on a 1950s Black Phantom and a 1990s mountain bike.

Marketing to children and adults in the 1930s.

Hollywood's Buck Jones on his Schwinn.

Schwinn's "fat tire" bikes changed the industry.

The company's ads encouraged children to beg for a Schwinn under the Christmas tree.

In the late 1970s the growing adult market forced Schwinn to play up the lighter aspects of its bikes—with the help of a *Playboy* model on a pink ten-speed.

Executives and factory workers celebrate a milestone in 1968. *(Courtesy of Ray Burch)*

Superdealer George Garner. *(Courtesy of Steve Leonard/*Crain's Chicago Business)

Ray Burch *(left)* and Al Fritz. *(Courtesy of Ray Burch)*

New owners Sam Zell *(left)* and David Schulte. *(Courtesy of Steve Leonard/*Crain's Chicago Business)

Dennis O'Dea, Schwinn bankruptcy lawyer.

Edward R. Schwinn, Jr., the day after the bankruptcy filing. *(Courtesy of Michael Marcotte/*Crain's Chicago Business*)*

Richard Schwinn in 1992. *(Courtesy of Guy Moeller Photography)*

Edward R. Schwinn, Jr., in 1985. *(Courtesy of Mary Herlehy/*Crain's Chicago Business*)*

Michael Sinyard, founder and CEO, Specialized Bicycle Components.

Richard Burke, founder and chairman of Trek Bicycle.

Tony Lo, president, Giant Manufacturing.

Jerome Sze, founder, China Bicycles Company. *(Courtesy of Cycle Press)*

Bill Austin, Jr. *(left)*, former Schwinn marketing vice president and former president of Giant USA.

John Barker *(right)*, former Schwinn executive vice president, now at China Bicycles.

rian Thomas B. Gold. Factories sprang up to produce everything from men's shirts for Arrow to bathing suits for Jantzen to televisions and consumer electronics for Japan's Matsushita and Sony. By 1977, what once was an expanse of rice paddies and farmhouses had become a sea of apartment complexes and industrial parks. Taiwan benefited from its low-wage labor pool—cheaper in 1972 than South Korea's, Singapore's, Hong Kong's, and, of course, Japan's. That year, the average wage for a skilled worker in Taiwan was $73 a month, compared to $272 in Japan. Yet Taiwan's labor efficiency ranked just below that of Japan and the United States.

Much to Giant's favor, rising costs were making basic Japanese bikes prohibitively expensive. By the mid-1970s, Fritz thought Schwinn's suppliers in Japan were pricing themselves out of the market. One negotiating session with Bridgestone Cycle at an Osaka hotel was aborted after only an hour. "We just can't accept it," Fritz said of the proposed price schedule. He and purchasing manager Sam Mesha returned to their hotel and contacted one of the Asian trading companies that Schwinn hired to buy and ship parts. Fritz's instructions: "Start looking for other sources."

Ambitious and determined, Liu and Lo had continued to upgrade their factory (abandoning the spray cans, for example, and adding electrostatic painting equipment), yet they persuaded Schwinn to add them to its list of qualified suppliers largely through pricing: Giant could sell bikes for 25 percent to 30 percent less than the Japanese. Their goods would displace production mostly from Bridgestone Cycle. (Matsushita's National Bicycle Company would continue as a supplier, mostly of high-end bikes, through the 1992 bankruptcy.) As negotiations were wrapping up, it looked like a coup for Liu and Lo. But the two men feared one potential hurdle: What if Schwinn should ask for equity ownership in their factory? They badly wanted to boost production for Schwinn—an order for 100,000 units would double the plant's output. They also had to consider their biggest competitor, Merida Industry Company, owned by Taiwan's Tsun family and a manufacturer of bikes for Raleigh. If Schwinn's order went to Merida or another competitor, Giant would be seriously, perhaps fatally, weakened. Giant's board agreed in principle that it was prepared to give one-third of the equity, says one source close to the company. Fortunately for Giant, Schwinn never asked.

By 1977, the Giant factory produced its first lug-frame steel road bike for Schwinn, under the World label. It was a gold-colored ten-speed with a smart white band that sold for about $130. The Schwinn name was left off, because the American company's marketers were uncertain how their customers would react to Taiwanese goods. "But the quality was so good," remembers former Schwinn regional manager David Staub, "it seemed silly to leave the name off." Then came the upgraded World Sport and a more expensive Traveler model with a chrome-alloy frame. Schwinn boosted its business with Giant to 100,000 units by the end of the '70s, with models retailing from $150 to $200.

The Taiwanese bikes were a bargain for Schwinn, and Fritz was impressed with Giant's desire to please. He especially enjoyed working with the urbane and polished Lo, whose English was so good he was appreciative of American slang and jokes. Lo entertained his prospects graciously, too. "Not the same grandeur as in Japan," Fritz notes, "but always first class." Schwinn's engineers also were delighted with Giant's responsiveness. Supermechanic Stan Natanek recalls an early trip where he saw workers lacing wheels in their laps and tightening spokes with a manual screwdriver. "Why don't you get a bit?" he suggested. They did so immediately. On another occasion, engineers were having problems with the alignment of a chain. Natanek said he needed a washer, but there was none to be found. The Giant engineers tooled up overnight to produce the part. The Taiwanese and Americans cemented their relationships at local nightspots. Drinking in Taiwan often was a game of endurance and one-upmanship, and both sides usually were up to the challenge. "The Giant people would toast the Schwinn guys—'*Gam bei!*'—and everybody had to drink it down," Natanak says. "Then the waitress would refill your glass."

The 1980 strike provided Giant's big opportunity. Liu and Lo, still worried that Schwinn would find another Taiwanese supplier, took a shrewd gamble and built a massive new plant covering more than 400,000 square feet. Giant doubled its business with Schwinn during the Chicago walkout, to the annual rate of 200,000 bikes, and an empty field that Lo had shown Fritz became a two-story factory addition for the Air-Dyne exerciser. "Giant picked up huge volume," says Schwinn's Nai-Wen Kiang, a Chinese-American raised in Taiwan who was hired as an engineer and promoted to a post overseeing relations with Asian suppliers. "Everyone made money." Schwinn's marketers, who at the time were struggling with the Chicago factory loyalists, also were impressed. Why keep cranking out money-losing heavy-welded bikes when you could profit by importing sleek and well-made models from Giant? In May 1982, top marketing executive Bill Austin led a Schwinn delegation to Taiwan to negotiate price and specifications for the planned BMX Predator. The two sides spent an arduous day around a U-shaped table in a sparsely furnished conference room. Product manager Fred Teeman had a precise frame geometry in mind, but the Giant team was doubtful. The Schwinn group was discouraged when they adjourned for dinner at 6:30, but the following morning offered a pleasant surprise: sitting on a metal table was a prototype of the desired bike. "We lit up like Christmas trees," Teeman says. "It was exactly what we wanted." The Schwinn reps quickly learned that their Giant associates didn't always say what they were thinking. In this case, they hadn't wanted to disappoint, and delighted in surprising their prominent customer.

Groups of young Schwinn managers, as many as ten on a trip, would fly to Taiwan to hammer out the specifics of components and frame design—and to negotiate price. Giant whisked them to its headquarters in a customized imported van for sessions that would last well into the evening. During the mandatory round of drinking and partying, the Giant factory's night shift would swing into action, whipping up samples from the day's drawings and instructions. However hung over, the Schwinn crew was required to show up at a 7:00 A.M. hotel breakfast in suit and tie. "Learn to play hurt," vice president Jay Townley counseled. Lo often entertained his Schwinn guests at restaurants (in later years, he took them to the fancy watering holes owned by his wife, Mimi) and would lead them through glasses of single-malt scotch, proceed to Taiwanese wines (which to some American palates tasted like vinegar), and top off the night with cognac. Lo exuded success in his 300-series Mercedes Benz. He also impressed customers with his grasp of manufacturing and knowledge of world markets. "He could quote from memory statistics on country-by-country sales," says former marketing executive Byron Smith. The Americans didn't know King Liu as well, largely because his English was halting. Yet Liu still was good for a comeback. When the chauffeured chairman purchased a limited edition, white Cadillac convertible, Schwinn managers teased, "Hey, King, are you going to drive it or sit in the passenger seat?" His answer: "I'll drive it. And my driver will drive another car following me."

Giant made it all seem so easy for Schwinn executives who had been wearied by the strike, Ed's overhaul of top management, and the trauma of the Chicago plant closing. Schwinn upgraded its product line, made meaty margins, and enjoyed efficient delivery—all of which helped the company bounce back to profitability.

Schwinn, for its part, had helped Giant rise out of nowhere. The Americans had shared their technical know-how and provided a vehicle for Giant to gain distribution, expand production, and drive down its costs. By 1984, Giant was shipping 500,000 bikes a year to Schwinn, accounting for about two-thirds of its customer's sales, and its share of production would grow larger still.

Some at Schwinn didn't see a problem in the increasing dependence. Giant was efficient and competitive, friendly and cooperative. Why spoil a good thing? Others suggested it was all too seductive. "Listen, fellas," said Boston consultant Peter Gerstberger, who was hired in 1984 to help Schwinn mull strategic questions. "You are engaged to Giant. You'll have to go one way or another—get married or have a divorce." By blindly depending on one manufacturer, Gerstberger warned, Schwinn was giving up the opportunity to play off one source against another—a classic gambit that can ensure the best price for the best service. When Giant supplied only 10 percent of Schwinn's production, the U.S. company controlled marketing and distribution. But as the Taiwanese company handled a majority of Schwinn's bikes, the buyer was losing leverage. It would be difficult for another manufacturer to gear up quickly to produce as many bikes. "You're putting a lot of your future in the hands of a single supplier," Gerstberger cautioned. Finance vice president John Barker also was worried that Schwinn was ceding too much power to

Tony Lo. That year, he persuaded Ed to propose purchasing an equity stake in Giant. Lo and King Liu wouldn't consider it. "There was no interest on their part," Barker says. Perhaps Schwinn might have been successful in acquiring a stake in the mid-1970s, when Giant was hungry for Schwinn's business, Barker concedes, but now the tables were turning.

Giant no longer was the underdog. Lo had been honored by Taiwan's government as one of the top ten business leaders of 1982. Two years later, Giant was completing construction of a gleaming six-story office building (with atrium) adjacent to its factory. By 1985, it would hit the 1 million annual bike-production benchmark. When Schwinn broached the idea of an equity stake, Giant responded with a proposal to acquire a stake in Schwinn. Chicago swiftly rejected any such thought, and the scenario still amuses executives in Taiwan. "They'd like to invest in Giant, but they don't want Giant to invest in Schwinn," says Lanty Chang, a high-ranking Giant manager.

Ed had cordial relations with Lo, entertaining him at the prestigious Chicago Club and local restaurants (occasionally selecting the best Chinese restaurants on Michigan Avenue, which, although not up to Taiwanese standards, were not an embarrassment, either). The two men were contemporaries, born only two years apart, but where Ed was the inheritor, trying to preserve an increasingly fragile dynasty, Lo was the self-made millionaire, hungry and aggressive. Lo clearly posed a challenge by the mid-1980s, and Ed, by now wary of Giant's newfound wealth, didn't trust him. Lo could be hard to read, according to others at Schwinn. He seemed interested in learning more than he gave out. Nai-Wen Kiang once kidded Ed, "At first, Giant was a nice little kitty. You hold a kitty and sleep with it. When it's bigger, it's a tiger. Can you sleep with it? No." Schwinn still was operating from its shabby northwest Chicago headquarters when Ed visited Giant in 1985. The new office tower perturbed him. "Look what we built for Giant," he blurted to marketing chief Bill Austin. Later, Ed would bluster, "We put Giant in the business!" No matter that Giant had helped bail out Schwinn during the 1980 strike. Ed seemed to believe that Giant wasn't respectful, that no one should be stronger than Schwinn.

After the idea of swapping equity stakes was dismissed, Giant broached a more serious topic: a joint distribution venture. Just as Schwinn's consultant had warned about overdependence, Giant's own consultant was urging diversification. Giant wanted to expand its brand name, which accounted for less than 15 percent of worldwide sales, and lessen its dependence on private-label sales to Schwinn. It was a universal business concept that, in the bike industry, went all the way back to Ignaz and F. W. Schwinn chafing at the dictates of Sears and other early masters. Yet Taiwanese industry historically did not grow brands as effectively as, say, Korean manufacturers, which nurtured such well-known names as Samsung and Hyundai. An undaunted Lo plowed ahead, opening a Taiwanese sales company in 1981 and launching a Giant brand in Europe five years later. Although the notion of a joint Schwinn and Giant brand would have been heresy years earlier, the two sides in late 1985 began to negotiate the terms of a venture in which Schwinn would distribute a second label. The Chicago company would own a majority of the operation and take the profits from distribution; Giant would make its money on the manufacturing. Schwinn even dispatched a half-dozen managers to Taiwan to work out details.

Advocates argued that a second line would maintain Schwinn's leverage with its dealers, many of whom had taken, or were considering, a second brand. And perhaps this was an opportunity to move into non-Schwinn—or the dreaded Brand X—dealers. If Giant was set on entering the market, they argued, why not control the venture and make some money out of it? "Schwinn could have sold two sides of the street and combined to have fifty percent to sixty percent of the [independent] bike market," says former Schwinn product manager Fred Teeman, who later went to work for Giant. "It would have been awesome."

Still, the idea was controversial at Schwinn. Many marketers, including the old-timers of the Ray Burch era, came up through the ranks believing Schwinn could fill all of a dealer's needs. (Some retailers were dismayed that a company with such a strong Made-in-America tradition had moved offshore in the first place.) Others argued that a second line, requiring more nurturing, would sap resources from the flagship brand.

As the weeks went by, Ed's interest waned, and the scenery changed.

In May 1986, a frustrated Bill Austin, who had supported a joint venture, left Schwinn to become president and chief executive officer of Nappe-Babcock Company, a Virginia marketer of bean-bag chairs. Schwinn executives link Austin's departure to the elevation of his corporate rival, John Barker, to executive vice president, the No. 2 post. Austin responds, "That never entered my mind." It's clear, however, that the politically savvy Barker had captured Ed's imagination with his deal-making skills and vision to diversify Schwinn's sources of bikes on a worldwide scale and sell them internationally. Meanwhile, the more distant Austin apparently had been left on the side.

Barker and Ed soon shifted their focus away from Giant and toward China Bicycles Company, a fast-growing firm run by energetic Hong Kong entrepreneur Jerome Sze in the up-and-coming Chinese province of Shenzhen. This time, Schwinn recognized the chance to buy equity in a manufacturer and Ed snatched it.

Sze had been running a factory in Hong Kong that manufactured and exported inexpensive kids' bikes when he began exploring the possibility of shifting production to neighboring Shenzhen, an area targeted by the Communist Chinese government as the country's official testing ground for free market economic reforms. "One day, I'll have the biggest bike factory in the world on this site," he told customer and future partner Stephen Codron in 1979. Shenzhen was a fishing village then, but it would become a boomtown, "combining the business acumen, technology and capital of Hong Kong industry with the bottomless pool of cheap Chinese labor," according to an admiring *Forbes* magazine. Just as Taiwan had usurped Japan's place in bicycles, China would be the next Taiwan.

Sze established China Bicycles in 1984 in a joint venture with a local government agency, Shenzhen Municipal Light Industry Company, and his own holding company, Hong Kong (Link) Bicycles, and built a mainland factory in 1985. While other state enterprises would turn out drab single-speed heavyweights—so-called "iron mules"—China Bicycles would court Western markets with flashy designs. At a trade show in Italy, Stephen Codron invited several Schwinn executives to visit Shenzhen. When Schwinn's Nai-Wen Kiang traveled to China with product manager Brad Hughes in October 1985 to scout potential suppliers, the duo saw mostly dirt floors and thousands of black bicycle frames. "We had been in China two weeks," Kiang remembers, "and it was pouring like hell. We were sick of the food." Their final stop was China Bicycles. "This factory was not too bad, in comparison. Not good enough, but better. We wrote a good report."

A month later, Ed and John Barker opened negotiations with Sze—not just about a supply arrangement, but about an equity deal. It's doubtful Sze needed the money, since his factory was already built and selling more than 900,000 utilitarian bikes a year in China. The Schwinn name, however, would lend prestige and access to the U.S. market for big volumes. "Go put on your best suit," Sze told Codron. "You're going to see Schwinn."

The bargaining would last nearly eighteen months. In the end, Ed would spend $2 million to buy a one-third interest in the China Bicycles plant (the other two-thirds was split between Sze's holding company and the Chinese government). He won the exclusive right to import the factory's bikes to North America and agreed to decrease his company's business with Giant so that China Bicycles would become Schwinn's leading supplier.

By 1987, rumors were circulating in the Asian side of the industry about a Schwinn deal with China Bicycles. A reporter from Japan's major bike-trade newspaper, *Cycle Press International,* called Giant's Tony Lo to ask what he knew. Lo posed the question to Ed via fax. "He said the rumor was not true," Lo recalls, "and that we could tell the press so, and we did."

Former Schwinn executives today say their hands were tied. "We were trying to nurture a new situation and not cut off an old one," explains ex-controller Don Gilliard. John Barker insists he told Lo "at the very start" that Schwinn was planning a deal with China Bicycles. Perhaps Barker told Giant only part of the story, for when Schwinn finally acknowledged the China Bicycles arrangement the following month, Lo was furious. Not just because Schwinn hadn't been straight, but because he had denied the rumors in print and now Giant looked foolish. "We didn't think we'd been treated right, because they kept us in the dark," Lo says. "Our two companies had a very important relationship."

Ed and Barker maintained at the time that the investment in China Bicycles was defensive—that Giant had pulled the trigger first by preparing to introduce its own brand to the U.S. market, with or without Schwinn. Whichever it was, Lo clearly had global ambitions. He was already selling the Giant brand in his home market and in Europe, where it would emerge as one of the top labels, and he wanted to infiltrate the U.S. market using the Schwinn distribution system for a quick and low-cost entry. Ed's rejection of a joint venture and subsequent alliance with China Bicycles either hastened Giant's move, as Lo explains it, or was the excuse Giant needed to launch a full bore attack on Schwinn on its home court.

Bill Austin was sitting in his Nappe-Babcock office in Richmond, Virginia, at 6:30 on a Wednesday evening when he received a telephone call from Tony Lo. With Schwinn leaving, Giant still had a big factory to keep busy, Lo told Austin. What was he going to do?

"You have to control your destiny," Austin responded.

By late summer, Giant had formed a unit to launch its brand in the United States—and Bill Austin was named the following spring as the man who would head the venture.

The new president and chief executive of Giant's U.S. marketing company would sell the line with a vengeance. Austin's sales people had a compelling pitch: Giant bikes were made by the same factory that had made Schwinns, but could retail for 10 to 15 percent less. "The first Giants mimicked Schwinn exactly," says now-retired San Diego Schwinn dealer Michael H. McKittrick. Giant also took a page from Schwinn's approach to dealer relations that hearkened back to the days of Ray Burch and set up a similar distribution system. It even hired longtime Schwinn hands, such as veteran product manager Fred Teeman. Giant also shrewdly offered dealers a better profit margin—about 36 percent, compared with the 34 percent typical for a Schwinn. In the modest low-margin world of bicycle retailing, those extra two percentage points could make a difference. Giant's growth was startling: within four years, its U.S. arm was selling 300,000 units annually—more than half of Schwinn's sales of 543,000 bikes in 1992.

By investing in China Bicycles, Schwinn had gained its independence from Giant, but that move had a cost. "Schwinn created a monster," says competitor Bernie Kotlier of Service Cycle Supply. "A monster that came back to haunt them."

15

SCHWINN MEETS CENTRAL PLANNING

After completing the pact with China Bicycles, Ed Schwinn entered a second overseas joint venture, acquiring a controlling stake in a battered old bicycle factory on the industrial island of Csepel in Budapest, Hungary. The madness of the move became painfully apparent just a few years later, when Hungarian managers advertised their new Schwinn-Csepel bikes with posters in Budapest streetcars that, roughly translated, declared, "They're not as bad as you think."

At first blush, it seemed a bold and brilliant stroke. Communist Eastern Europe was in the midst of economic upheaval and democratic reforms that would culminate with the toppling of the Berlin Wall in November 1989, and Hungary was considered the most progressive of the Warsaw Pact nations. Translating American free market standards to a state-run bicycle plant would be tricky, but if successful, Csepel could serve as Schwinn's springboard to Western European consumers and later to Hungary's neighbors who were awakening from their own Marxist stupors.

The project at Schwinn became the pet of purchasing vice president

Jay Townley and now–executive vice president John Barker, who dreamed of Schwinn as a global power that would manufacture and sell bikes and fitness equipment around the world. The notion was appealing to their boss, too. Shell-shocked from his experience with Giant, Ed was determined to wield greater control over new suppliers by acquiring equity stakes in the plants that made his bikes. "John knew how to 'wrap it' for Ed," Townley says. "He sold Hungary by telling Ed he'd get a march on the competition in Europe and that he'd get it at a great price."

While Barker reveled in cutting still another deal, he may not have considered fully some of the longer-term problems. Investments behind the former Iron Curtain required capital and manpower—an easy thing for deep-pocketed multinationals such as General Electric and Sara Lee Corporation, which entered Hungary around the same time. Yet it didn't make sense for a weaker company like Schwinn, which was still operating under the tight scrutiny of its bankers and was already stretching itself too far with commitments in Shenzhen, China, and Greenville, Mississippi. Budapest would be a boondoggle.

The idea for the venture was hatched by Hungarian émigré Willy Ehrlich, who was flipping through an economic publication about the Warsaw Pact nations in 1986, when an article caught his eye: "Hungarian Bicycle Factory Must Improve or Go Out of Business." Ehrlich telephoned Hungary's minister of industry, introduced himself as a bicycle industry consultant in the States and asked, "Are you interested in upgrading the Csepel factory?"

Ehrlich was familiar with Csepel Works, part of a century-old industrial complex on a twenty-mile-long island in the Danube River that was the historical center of Hungarian manufacturing. During the German occupation of World War II, Csepel Works produced machine tools and electric transformers, as well as engines for Messerschmitt fighter planes. After the war, the sprawling smokestack operation was nationalized by the government, which raised a statue of Lenin outside its aging gates.

Ehrlich also had another advantage—his considerable survival and storytelling skills. Colleagues marvel at his background: a young Jew who escaped from concentration camps, joined French Liberation forces, and played professional soccer in France before returning to his homeland in

1948 for a Christmas-time visit. It turned out to be no holiday, however. Ehrlich's name was listed among the war dead, and he was arrested on charges of spying for the West. Fortunately, he was released from prison three months later—perhaps, he explains, because "people looked favorably at me as a soccer player." He ended up at a small Hungarian bike factory that purchased components from Csepel Works and finally escaped the country in 1956—the year of the uprising quashed by Russian troops—by driving a company truck to the Austrian border and giving bicycles to peasants in exchange for help in negotiating the mine fields. Ehrlich arrived in the United States on December 31, and soon landed at Chain Bicycle Company, the East Coast maker of the popular Ross brand.

Ross was a bicycle dynasty not unlike Schwinn. The Ross family, however, was somewhat more prescient. At the start of the bicycle boom, they closed their old plant in Rockaway Beach, New York, and built a lug-frame factory with new brazing technology in Allentown, Pennsylvania, which Ehrlich, as vice president of manufacturing, helped design. Sales, mostly through mass merchants, soared to a peak of 800,000 units in 1974.[1] Ehrlich ran the factory with an iron hand and often was on the floor from 7:00 A.M. to 7:00 P.M. "He got one hundred and twenty-five percent out of everyone," says Fred Drenhouse, who managed purchasing for Ross and later worked at Trek. "He was a hard, driven man, but he made money for Ross."

Ehrlich departed in 1980, after twenty-three years, because he had run afoul of the family, which didn't appreciate his newfound commitment to outside endeavors, such as creating an American soccer league. Ross family members snapped, according to Drenhouse, when they discovered Ehrlich had used their factory to make goalposts for his local team.[2] Ehrlich consulted for a while, then persuaded investors to fund the start-up of Bicycle Corporation of America, opening an assembly plant in Bethlehem (not far from the Ross factory) and selling moderately priced models to independent dealers and mass merchants. Hungary's Csepel Works piqued his interest as a potential source of frames, rims, and components that was both cheaper than Taiwan and a way to distinguish himself from the competition. So, Ehrlich returned to his native country thirty years after he had fled. There was little trouble at the borders this time—Hungary had become the first Eastern bloc country to allow joint ventures with the West in 1972—but the Csepel bike factory was another story. "A disaster," Ehrlich says, "The equipment was old, everything was old." It was selling coaster brakes for five dollars that could be purchased from Japan's Shimano for half the price; its paint shop was second-rate, too. "As long as the bike was black, it was OK," he says. "But you can't export black bikes." In addition, only half of the Csepel factory produced bikes; the remainder was dedicated to making lousy sewing machines. It took Ehrlich a year and a half to persuade the Ministry of Industry to concentrate solely on bicycles, yet that sparked a new problem. Instead of room to produce only 120,000 models, the plant now had the capacity to make nearly 500,000. Ehrlich needed a Western partner that could market the extra product and invest money to upgrade the plant.

The Ross family wasn't an option, but there was an even bigger name in Ehrlich's Rolodex: Ed Schwinn, who had sold Ehrlich some old wheel-making equipment after the Chicago factory closed. Ed was noncommittal at first, but in 1987 dispatched a team to Hungary that included the internationally minded Jay Townley and top engineer Frank Brilando. Townley was enthusiastic and found an important ally in John Barker. The two pulled out maps of Europe and plotted strategy. Months later, during a trade show in Reno, Nevada, Ed assembled the management team in his hotel suite to debate the merits of a Hungarian venture.

Townley and Barker argued in favor of the project. Here was an incredibly cheap way to enter Western Europe, primarily Germany and Austria, and provide a base for the nascent Eastern European market. In addition, Csepel would have a pricing advantage against Asian producers because it wouldn't have to pay European duties. Townley envisioned Schwinn purchasing large quantities from Csepel: 50,000 bikes in 1989; 100,000 in 1990; and 150,000 the following year.

Those were huge and dangerous commitments, countered Gerard O'Keefe, who had been Al Fritz's deputy at Excelsior and had succeeded Bill Austin as group vice president of marketing. Spend the company's money repairing the money-losing Mississippi plant, O'Keefe urged. He and his allies reminded Ed that Schwinn was still rebounding from its financial crisis with the banks and flirtation with bankruptcy. The initial outlays didn't worry, but the possible future drain on resources did, as did the potential damage to Schwinn's brand name if the factory made sub-par bikes.

Ed stared out the window, not looking at anyone. "OK, I've heard enough of this discussion. We're going to table this decision. Now is not the time to do Hungary."

O'Keefe and Byron Smith, recently hired as marketing director from Chicago's Quaker Oats Company, were relieved. Less than a month later, however, Hungary was pronounced a done deal. The persuasive Barker was tight with the boss, and the pliable Ed seemed to agree with the last person who had his ear. O'Keefe and Smith looked at each other in disbelief.

The transaction was closed in late 1988. It called for Schwinn to invest $958,000 for a 41.5 percent stake in Csepel, including $235,000 in painting equipment from the old Chicago factory—out-of-date for a U.S. plant, but high-tech in Hungary. For his legwork, Ehrlich would receive 9.5 percent of the venture's profits and have future travel expenses paid in return for consulting services. Schwinn controlled the votes of his friendly 9.5 percent stake—effectively making the Chicago company 51 percent owner of Csepel—with the remaining shares held by two Hungarian government agencies.

The Schwinn-Csepel project generated enormous attention in Hungary as one of the first major industrial joint ventures with the West. It would be a grand experiment in capitalism, one of the most progressive undertakings in the former Eastern bloc. "The promises were big," Ehrlich says. Coverage in the *New York Times*, *Chicago Tribune*, and other American media generally lauded Ed's vision.

Then came reality.

To run the factory, the venture tapped Laszlo Nogradi, who had been a top bureaucrat at Csepel's state-owned parent company, Rugev, and spoke little English. Nogradi was given a large salary (Ehrlich estimates it as the equivalent of $1 million in Hungarian purchasing power) and a company car; he flew to Chicago first class. "Before Schwinn, the Hungarians hadn't traveled on planes," Ehrlich quips. "Schwinn wanted to project the image of Number One, which it was, but it created a situation where the Hungarians thought gold was coming out of Schwinn."

As with Greenville, Schwinn found few Chicago executives willing to relocate to Budapest. General Electric would send a fleet of forty-five managers to launch its joint venture manufacturing light bulbs; Schwinn sent Steven Bina, an Iowa-bred middle manager who had held posts at headquarters in finance and purchasing. Bina was elevated overnight to the exalted position of director of European operations. Since Hungarians were running the plant, Bina's job was partly diplomatic, although he also handled purchasing and sales. He was aided by German-born engineer Rudolph Schwinn, who commuted to Budapest for four years. "I went for two weeks a month," Rudolph Schwinn says. "I wasn't going to live there."

Things quickly went downhill. Ehrlich says he didn't mind giving up his 9.5 percent vote to Schwinn, but he did object to paying Schwinn a markup on the frames produced by Csepel for sale to his Bicycle Corporation of America. He bought his frames from Taiwan instead and sold finished bikes in Hungary. An even bigger mistake, Ehrlich says, was Schwinn's decision to assume all responsibility for marketing, knocking out the former Hungarian sales arm. "They knew nothing about Hungary and Europe," he complains. Meanwhile, the volume that Jay Townley had predicted so confidently never materialized. Schwinn purchased no bikes during the first year, although the factory sold 120,000 units with the Csepel brand name in Hungary, and it bought only 10,000 bikes in 1990 and 53,000 in 1991.

Turning around a wheezing government factory also proved more difficult than anyone thought. Water leaked through the roof and splattered on inventory. "It was one of the most inefficient factories you ever saw," says Chicago lawyer Arnold Dratt, who visited the site twice during his stint as Schwinn's bankruptcy-turnaround specialist. Overhead was high. (Although labor rates were not that exorbitant, social costs—for insurance, unemployment, and sick leave—accounted for 45 percent of salaries.) Managing the Hungarian workforce posed special challenges, too. Factory workers often painted the chain guard one shade and the frame another. "No, no, *no*," Rudolph Schwinn would yell. "It should look like *this*, not like anything else." Productivity was lacking, because many Hungarians worked more lucrative endeavors on their own time. "They'd basically snooze through the day, then hustle off to their black-market jobs and earn three times more money," says Schwinn's Mike Martinsen, who was hired in 1989 to expand international sales from Chicago headquarters.

Martinsen found the idea of supplying Western Europe from Csepel to be flawed. The Budapest factory produced a limited line of BMX models, lower-priced Woodlands mountain bikes and retro Cruisers (Schwinn's low-tech, coaster-brake version of the old beach-friendly ballooners resurrected by Southern Californians). He had some modest success selling the American-style Cruisers to European distributors and the Woodlands at U.S. military bases, but Csepel was caught in a squeeze. It needed larger volumes to reduce costs and gain economies of scale, yet it was difficult for the plant to secure major orders. It didn't have the capital to purchase large inventories of raw materials—a prerequisite for assuring prompt delivery and adequate volumes to a potential customer. It also lacked the money to finance imports of components. Csepel's Hungarian bank sparked an emergency in 1989, when it threatened to pull its loan, and the lender soon imposed impossibly restrictive terms. The factory had no choice but to buy its parts at a premium through Schwinn. At one point in 1991, Csepel owed $3 million to Schwinn for parts (although the obligation later was paid back in bikes).

Meanwhile, competitors already had made inroads in Europe: Giant, which imported its own brand from Taiwan, and the American ski equipment marketer Scott Sports Group, which was selling mountain bikes made in Asia. Many European mass merchants were also buying through factories in Taiwan and China. Csepel ended up selling mostly to the Hungarian domestic market—and to Schwinn, which peddled much of the Csepel product in the States. Things went from bad to worse when 20,000 Woodlands mountain bikes shipped in 1991 had to be recalled. Brownie Schwinn's son Tom, working in quality control at the Schwinn Sales Midwest distributorship, discovered that the studs holding the front cantilever brakes had a tendency to fall off. The flaw potentially could cause the front wheel to stop turning and hurl the rider over the handlebars. "It was a nightmare," Martinsen says. "We had three warehouses full of them." The fiasco was followed by the inevitable finger-pointing. Schwinn blamed the factory; Csepel insisted it was Schwinn's fault for purchasing a bad part. The problem cost Schwinn at least $1 million and was a drain on the staff at the Hungary factory.

As money for the venture tightened, Schwinn stopped paying Willy Ehrlich's travel expenses in 1990, but he remained involved. Ehrlich says Csepel manager Laszlo Nogradi did not challenge Schwinn's dictates. For example, the Hungarian factory invested to produce a variety of Schwinn models, but the volumes never justified Csepel's outlays. Also, when overdue Schwinn bicycle parts arrived, Nogradi sanctioned overtime or a second shift, which Ehrlich says was absurd for a factory running so far below capacity. "He became a Schwinn man," Ehrlich says. In mid-1991, Ehrlich helped pave the way for Nogradi to be replaced in the top job by Gyorgy Podolak, a former party boss of the Csepel industrial island and a manager at parent Rugev. (Nogradi remained, only in a lower post.)[3] Podolak had good intentions and political skills, but was learning capitalism overnight—his previous position at Rugev was as overseer at another state-run operation of Csepel Works. The revolving door whirled again when Schwinn's Steven Bina, the young director of European operations, resigned in December 1991 after being told his position would be eliminated (although the company soon sent a new emissary in his place). Bina's departure raised some eyebrows in the expatriate community, because he had also served as president of the American Chamber of Commerce in Hungary. Today, Bina says Chicago management "was tired of me telling the truth" about the operation's limitations. "The time was right, the place was right, but Schwinn had other problems."

The biggest boosters of the Csepel deal, Barker and Townley, in hindsight say the project was doomed when Barker was pushed out of Schwinn in 1989 and Townley exited the following year. "The plug was pulled," Townley says, referring to the company's waning interest in Hungary after he left.

To other managers in Chicago, Schwinn was overreaching to the point of flailing. Even though he'd never been to Hungary, "I hated the place," says marketing executive Byron Smith. Schwinn didn't have enough management power to oversee those difficulties and other projects—then go home and design good, marketable bikes. Still others ascribe the Csepel disaster to poor communications and unrealistic expectations on both sides. The Hungarian managers "thought they might get from Schwinn what they had with the ministry: somebody telling them what to do, just like in the old central plan," Csepel sales manager Melina Cseh told the *Chicago Tribune* in 1993, following Schwinn's bankruptcy and sale to outside investors. "The Americans thought they were getting a company that would be able to manage itself and make decisions. But they never discussed this with each other."

Hungary, for all its miscues, was a sideshow. In the end, Csepel was no Giant or China Bicycles, creditors with the power to decide a bankrupt Schwinn's fate. But the Hungarian operation crimped Schwinn's cash flow, and total losses from Csepel exceeded $2 million. It was an adventure Ed Schwinn simply could not afford.

16

THE CHINA SYNDROME

The Hungarian venture would also antagonize Schwinn's manufacturing partner in Hong Kong. The Csepel factory, after all, was a potential opponent in Europe for the fast-growing China Bicycles Company. Schwinn's John Barker tried to calm founder Jerome Sze. "It's not as big a threat as you might think," Barker said, in what turned out to be a considerable understatement.

Schwinn's relationship with China Bicycles would become very different from what Barker and Ed had envisioned. The Chicago firm's one-third stake in Sze's company proved to be an excellent investment, especially as a bargaining chip among players in the bankruptcy, yet the Shenzhen factory at first could not match the quality and reliability of Taiwan predecessor Giant. Frustrated Schwinn managers wondered why Ed had obligated his company to buy large volumes so quickly from China Bicycles. "We got too dependent on that facility before it was proven," says Byron Smith. As a part-owner, it was in Ed's interest to ensure that China Bicycles had the necessary volume to succeed; unfortunately, his U.S. company paid dearly for the experience. Just as had happened at Giant, the rush for a large-scale commitment diminished Schwinn's leverage and influence. It became more dependent, not less.

Chastened by his experience with Giant, Ed wanted, perhaps above all else, equity ownership of his suppliers. His family's near-one-hundred-year-old manufacturing pedigree dictated as much. "*We* are a manufacturer, *we* control our destiny," he told Mike Bobrick, president of competitor Western States Imports, in 1985. "*You* are a marketing company." Yet Ed failed to manage shrewdly his alliance with China Bicycles. The initial exclusivity for North American distribution was frittered away, and China Bicycles, like Giant, eventually became a foe when Jerome Sze purchased fast-growing Western States and its Diamond Back label in 1990. While Ed was wary of Giant, he seemed enamored with his new partners. Maybe it was as simple as Hong Kong being more comfortably Occidental than Taiwan. Whatever the reason, there would be a naïveté to Ed's dealings with China Bicycles. Without the wily Barker, who left Schwinn two years after the deal was signed, Ed would be consistently outmaneuvered.

Shenzhen was still a backwater when Schwinn representatives started traveling there in 1987, six years after the Communist Chinese government had made the area a special zone for foreign joint ventures and economic reforms. It was dank and buggy, with dirt roads and more taxis than cars. Managers who didn't want the hassles of commuting to neighboring Hong Kong would stay at the new hotels in Shenzhen, where assertive prostitutes would knock on their doors in the middle of the night. The place had the hallmarks of a company town: workers for China Bicycles, for instance, lived in clean but cramped dorms, two to four bunks to a room, and cardboard bicycle cartons served a dual purpose as clothes closets and dividers for privacy. Nevertheless, China Bicycles and other Shenzhen factories attracted mobile workers in their twenties who could afford to leave family farms. The privately run bike plant offered good wages for China: about $160 a month for a factory worker and $200 for a manager—nearly twice the going rate at a state-owned plant in southern China. There were other benefits, such as free housing and board, and the cafeteria served fresh vegetables, steamed fish, soup, and rice. After a bit of saving, workers could send home color televisions, radios, or refrigerators.

Within a few years of its 1981 anointment by Beijing, Shenzhen was booming. Banana plantations and rice paddies were bulldozed to make way for factories, roads, and apartment towers. The growth was not unlike Chicago's when it was a bicycle center in the 1890s—only far more furious. Shenzhen's population of 50,000 in 1980 exploded to 1.7 million ten years later, as migrants flocked to China's mecca of capitalism. (Shenzhen's population was estimated at about 2.5 million in the mid-1990s.) Industrial output surged to $3.8 billion—80 percent of it exported: bikes, toys, electric fans, down jackets, shoes, and watch parts. Shenzhen genuinely arrived when the first McDonald's restaurant opened in October 1990.

Into this raucous atmosphere strode Jerome Sze and Stephen Codron, polar opposites in just about every sense of the phrase.

Born in China's coastal Fujian Province during World War II, Sze was educated in the Philippines and in his early twenties emigrated to Hong Kong, where he started a bike-making business. Since founding the larger China Bicycles in 1984, he has branched out into real estate projects on the mainland. There his political connections, fueled by philanthropy to worthy Communist Party causes, have become exceptional. Sze is one of three dozen or so expatriates recently made members of the prestigious National Committee of the Chinese People's Political Consultative Conference, an advisory group that meets in Beijing's Great Hall of the People and apprises government officials on Western thinking and business practices. Some observers find him friendly and casual—an approachable teddy bear of a guy who smokes too much. Others see him as soft-spoken and introspective—a man known to sit through meetings sketching intricate landscapes. Still others consider him stone-faced and impenetrable.

Sze wasn't fluent in English when he started China Bicycles, but he didn't need to be. He had the London-born Codron traveling around the world marketing the factory's bikes. (Codron says he logged more than 900,000 miles in 1994 alone, which was fine with Sze, who hates to travel.) A twenty-year-old Codron had moved to Hong Kong in 1977 to work for a British garment company, but after a year struck out on his own. "I loved Hong Kong," he recalled in a bicycle trade publication in 1994. "I thought it was magic." In 1978, Codron was talking to a business associate from Sweden who was marveling over the demand for American-style BMX bikes in Europe. Did Steve know any suppliers? Codron, who had met Sze only months earlier at a racetrack luncheon, began to buy BMX models from his company, Hong Kong Bicycles. Soon, he was exporting 12,000 units a year to Sweden. By 1984, he had signed on with Sze as his director of marketing. Fast-talking, status-conscious, and usually ready with a joke, Codron was the supreme salesman, says Nai-Wen Kiang, Schwinn's former director of Asian operations. "You'd ask, 'How much does it cost?' and he'd say, 'How much do you want to pay for it?' " Codron tended to his important new American customer, visiting Chicago every two months and often hanging out with Ed at the family's weekend home in Lake Geneva. "We'd put our shorts and T-shirts on and go cycling," Codron says.

China Bicycles was manufacturing nearly 700,000 units a year, mostly for European customers, when it teamed up with Schwinn in 1987. Sze had high aspirations, although he didn't necessarily make the best bike. Veteran engineer Frank Brilando, sixty-two at the time, moved to Hong Kong for four years, renting a house in a British and Australian neighborhood and driving across the border daily to Shenzhen in a Mercedes. Sometimes he shared rides with Sze, who lived nearby. Brilando provided technical assistance on machinery and manufacturing processes. "I was there a year before we would take a chance on letting them produce our bicycles," he says. Though the two sides never worked out written production commitments, Schwinn verbally had agreed to shift a large volume of its production to China Bicycles, up to some 450,000 bikes a year, according to Codron. Schwinn started by transferring from Giant the less-expensive models, such as its 16-inch girls' Pixie and entry-level ten-speed Sprints and Calientes. The biggest problem lay in uneven paint jobs that led to chipping and flaking. At first, no paint-stripping tank was available, so, if there was a flaw, the bikes would be repainted. Some units ended up being shipped with multiple coats.

Further complicating matters, production of several models was split between China Bicycles and Giant. When the bikes arrived at a U.S. dealer, the finish and quality of a comparable Giant model would be better. Dealers were peeved; they were paying the same price, at least at the start. Schwinn tried to ship China Bicycles and Giant products to different parts of the country, but the problem continued to crop up. Sometimes Schwinn had to offer sales or special rebates on bikes from China Bicycles. Other times, the shipments were late, and that hurt Schwinn two ways. A bike scheduled for March delivery (the start of the spring selling season) that didn't land until June meant a sale lost to other brands; meantime, the late arrival was obsolete in a dealer's eyes, and it could be purchased only as a closeout—at cost or below.

Those problems, plus the spiraling costs from ventures in Budapest and Greenville, would obliterate Schwinn's profit margins by the end of the decade. The company's net margin sank to 23 percent by 1990, down from 29 percent in 1986 and a far cry from some competitors' 32 percent. Schwinn, with its commanding volumes, should have enjoyed economies of scale that would give it the best margins, not the worst, but that wasn't possible with so many costs to juggle around the globe.

Because Ed had guaranteed that Schwinn would purchase from China Bicycles, many managers felt their company was regarded as a captive customer by its new supplier. Schwinn, they grumbled, didn't appear to be accorded the same attention as European buyers, who were being courted to expand China Bicycles' customer base. Schwinn executives were scrambling to fit into the factory's production schedule—not the other way around—and complaints about late delivery and quality didn't seem to carry the same weight that a supplier might feel if the customer had demonstrated it was willing to take its production elsewhere.[1] Of course, Schwinn really couldn't go anywhere else, unless it was willing to inflict pain on an operation of which it owned one-third.

An inevitable result of the shift to China Bicycles was a less friendly tone at Giant, which still produced a peak of 82 percent of Schwinn bikes the year after the deal and 56 percent in 1989, as well as the Air-Dyne exercisers. Workers were much cheaper in China than Taiwan, but labor costs had dwindled to represent only 6 percent of the manufacturer's price of a bike. The substantial expenses lay in raw materials and the plant. "Even if Ed goes to China and gets free labor, I can [still] outperform him," Giant's Tony Lo boasted to Byron Smith in 1988.

Lo and Sze had been antagonists since the early '70s boom, when their then tiny companies were scrapping for just about any customer. Little had changed between them as they grew. At a U.S. dealer meeting in January 1988, the contingents from China Bicycles and Giant were seated on opposite sides of the room. "We knew there would be some uncomfortableness," explains former West Coast regional manager David Staub.

When Giant saw that Schwinn was committed to reducing production, if not pulling out of Taiwan altogether, it became less accommodating on price and service. Schwinn was less reliable, too, sometimes dragging its feet on decisions involving graphics or changes in components. Understandably so, argue some former Schwinn executives, noting that Giant now was a competitor, with its U.S. sales arm and European operations, and could have chosen to copy a new Schwinn frame design if it were so inclined. Since Giant was the manufacturer, it also had one less step in the distribution process, meaning it could make changes in its models faster. And Bill Austin and his new marketing staff at Giant knew virtually every Schwinn dealer in America and were offering a less expensive product made by the same factory that produced Schwinns.

In the spring of 1990, Ed returned from a visit to Hong Kong and announced to his executive committee, "The island of Taiwan is sinking." Senior staff, he instructed, should plan immediately for a complete shift out of Giant, with more production going to Greenville and Japan's National, but mostly to China Bicycles. Several committee members were surprised. Certainly, Ed's analysis was correct over the long term: Production naturally would flow to the market with the cheapest labor pool, and labor rates and other costs were rising in Taiwan. But why rush the forces of economics? Taiwan's Giant and its local rival, Merida, still were efficient low-cost suppliers that produced first-rate bikes. Exports from those factories were growing, while China Bicycles was not ready to handle so much of Schwinn's volume.

"A couple of us sat on the side and said, 'This can only mean one thing," recalls Mike Martinsen, former director of international business development. "And that is, Jerome Sze is trying to put a dagger in the heart of the relationship between Schwinn and Giant and take over all of Schwinn's business."

"Don't do it," Nai-Wen Kiang warned Ed. "China Bicycles cannot handle it now."

Ed went ahead, but the plan backfired. With customers in the States, Europe, and Asia, China Bicycles was up against its capacity. It couldn't get enough bikes to Schwinn, and the Chicago company had to crawl—"tail between our legs," as Martinsen puts it—back to Giant in June 1991.

"Schwinn asked Giant to help," Tony Lo says today, "and we agreed." Lo and Giant founder King Liu met with Ed and other top managers at the Chicago Club later that month, not so much to help their customer turned rival out of a bind, but to boost Giant's own sales, which had slipped below target that year.

(Through all of this, Ed had managed to maintain cordial relations with Lo, even cooking a dinner of Japanese beef with garlic and green onions for him, Liu, and Nai-Wen Kiang at his Chicago home. Lo faulted the long-gone John Barker for some of the bad turns and saw Ed somewhat removed from the fray. Still, cordiality could take the relationship only so far. "I'll always want to have dinner with him," Lo told Kiang after the bankruptcy, "as long as I don't have to talk about business.")

There were other things about Schwinn's association with China Bicycles that didn't add up. As part of its initial investment in 1987, Schwinn had won the exclusive rights to import the Shenzhen factory's bikes to North America. But only a year later, the factory began selling bikes to Western States Imports, the California concern that started during the bike boom and jumped on the BMX craze with its Diamond Back label. Much to the chagrin of some Schwinn managers, China Bicycles was running off Diamond Backs as Schwinn was awaiting shipment of its first bikes. "There was no heat from Schwinn," says Western States' Mike Bobrick.

John Barker and Ed's brother, Richard, visited Western States to gauge the rival's intentions and were convinced that its purchasing from China Bicycles wasn't necessarily bad for Schwinn. The Californians were already a competitor and making Diamond Backs provided revenue for the Shenzhen factory that otherwise would go elsewhere. Moreover, Western States could provide product-quality assistance to bring the factory up to speed, just as it had done with other Asian suppliers.

Schwinn, however, could have collected royalties on the bikes, according to some observers' readings of the original agreement with China Bicycles. It never pressed the point. "The exclusivity got dropped somewhere along the way," Bobrick says.

Barker had already left the company when members of the executive committee learned about a special stock deal with China Bicycles' Stephen Codron. At the time of the original agreement, Schwinn had agreed to sell back to Codron at a later date some 20 percent of its China Bicycles stock, or about 5 percent of the total. Schwinn hands were mystified. "Why are we selling him stock?" finance vice president Mike McNamara asked Ed.

"It was agreed to," the president replied.

Codron wired the money, but it was for the same price Schwinn had paid two years earlier—about four cents a share for 9.9 million shares. "Our stock is worth more than that," McNamara said. "This is crazy."

"Then figure out what it's worth," Ed suggested.

Codron paid additional money, for a total of more than $867,000, or nearly nine cents per share, yet the transaction never made sense to managers in Chicago. If Codron was going to get a piece of the action, why did it have to come out of Schwinn's side? Why not allocate it equitably among the three shareholders: Schwinn, Jerome Sze, and the Chinese government?

But the most perplexing deal was China Bicycles' 1990 purchase of Western States. The California importer's fifty-four-year-old major shareholder, Mitchell Weiner, had been shaken by heart surgery, a divorce, and a company financial loss in 1989. He was ready to sell. A sale was fine for Bobrick, too, who owned 15 percent of the stock. He could cash out and win a lucrative management contract. Bobrick was clever, hardworking, and caustic. He had a tempestuous relationship with Weiner. "A day wouldn't go by that Mike wouldn't blame Mitchell, or Mitchell wouldn't blame Mike," says a former employee. Western States had done well, emerging as one of the top five distributors to independent dealers by 1990, selling an estimated 250,000 bikes that year and generating sales in the range of $55 million. Its crackerjack product manager, Cozy Yamakoshi, was plugged in to the Japanese components market, and his choice of parts had helped put the company's bike designs on the enthusiast's map—its heavily advertised Centurion Iron Man triathlon cycle (licensed from organizers of the grueling annual event in Hawaii) had taken off in the mid-1980s.

Bobrick put out feelers, and China Bicycles emerged as the most logical buyer. Its factory was manufacturing private-label bikes for Schwinn, Sears, and European distributors. Following the example of Giant, China Bicycles could develop the Diamond Back name as its own brand and export the product worldwide—even to Europe, where Schwinn was attempting to get a toehold through the Hungary venture.

At first, Ed didn't like the idea. "I want nothing to do with this," he told Asian liaison Kiang. Could he have blocked it? Perhaps with a little more planning, but Kiang counseled that Ed also risked being outvoted by fellow shareholders Sze, Codron, and the Chinese government. "If you vote in, you have a chance to say a few words, try to negotiate a better deal."

Soon, Ed was talking up the advantages of China Bicycles' acquisition of Diamond Back and he dispatched finance executive Mike McNamara to Western States' offices to handle due diligence for Sze. At one point, Ed announced to employees in the cafeteria that China Bicycles was buying Western States. Good news, he said. Because Schwinn owned almost one-third of China Bicycles, it also would own a chunk of Western States and control two brands—Schwinn and Diamond Back. "We'll work out the synergies," Ed told the group. "The obvious potentials are to share warehousing expense and pool customer service. Sales reps, don't worry. We're not going to fire you and hire the Diamond Back guys. We're going to keep them separate for a while."

In Hong Kong, Sze and Codron were seething that Ed was portraying himself as a new owner of Diamond Back. They say Ed never came up with the money to fund the purchase. Instead, Sze's own holding company, Hong Kong (Link) Bicycles, and not China Bicycles, acquired Western States in May 1990 for an estimated $13 million. "Ed knew full well that he had to come up with the money," Codron says. "This was agreed in a board meeting . . . [with] all board members, including Ed." Adds Sze in a letter defending his actions: "Ed Schwinn was personally involved in the negotiations. Schwinn, until the final moment, was a partner with China Bicycles in buying [Western States]. . . . It was only when the funding for the project came about and Schwinn could not raise the necessary capital did Schwinn drop out of the group that bought [Western States]."

Former Schwinn executives insist Ed never mentioned having to pay for Schwinn's slice of Western States. In an embarrassing aftermath, Ed continued to call Mike Bobrick with grand ideas for Diamond Back, sometimes from his car phone. "He didn't understand why I was noncommittal," Bobrick says. "I said, 'Ed, you need to talk to Jerome.' " When Ed finally did, "he was stunned," Bobrick adds.

Had Ed botched the basics of the deal? Or was he the victim of a double-cross? Ed never offered a clue as to what actually happened. Martinsen says members of the executive committee wanted to ask, " 'Ed, did you misunderstand or were you just bullshitting us?' But you didn't have that kind of conversation with Ed. It was never appropriate."

No one but Ed has the real explanation. Maybe he thought China Bicycles would go ahead with the purchase without Schwinn's contribution. Perhaps China Bicycles suspected that Schwinn, which was running into financial difficulties, wouldn't be able to come up with the funds. Whatever the answer, it's clear Ed's partnership with China Bicycles suffered from a lack of care and feeding after Barker's departure in 1989 and withered further following the Western States deal in 1990. Ed had taken over primary management of the China connection, but he didn't visit Shenzhen as much as the globe-trotting Barker had. "Ed didn't want to be involved in the business," Codron says. "Ed would always inform us through a third party that he was coming, or we'd hear from someone else, 'Ed's coming.' It would be twenty-four hours' notice, and then he wouldn't come."

After Barker's departure, there was jockeying among the remaining executives to win Ed's favor—tension that surfaced at the annual bike-buying negotiations in Hong Kong. "There was internal bickering at the company which we would see at the table—I mean, there was shouting," Codron says. "You should never bicker at a meeting in front of others. Never! There's something in Chinese culture called 'keeping face.' You always have to keep face in public."

Nevertheless, Ed was mindful of some of the other etiquette of doing business Asian-style. He would ask about the appropriate dress code for a particular meeting or event, and when representatives of Asian suppliers visited Chicago, Ed could spend half an hour organizing the seating plan around the table. "He didn't want to be incorrect," says Bevil Hogg, the co-founder of Trek, who would later sell his carbon fiber bicycle company to Schwinn and work for the company.

(The same attention to Asian feelings wasn't always true of Ed's brother Richard, who was becoming more involved in decision-making at home and abroad. Richard attended a 1988 dinner given by Sze at a luxurious Hong Kong restaurant that featured jade spoons and waiters hovering attentively over almost every diner. The table of ten was served the expensive Chinese delicacy shark fin soup, to which Richard remarked enthusiastically, "It tastes like vermicelli!" Sze's face dropped. "Excuse me, Mr. Schwinn. We wouldn't serve you with that cheap food.")

Ed had begun his unions with his two Asian suppliers with many cards—namely, the leverage of a lot of orders—yet he never played them. By buying a stake in China Bicycles, Schwinn had roused an angry Giant, then Ed allowed his partners in China Bicycles to become adversaries. That last turn is particularly puzzling, because Ed acceded to aggressive moves by China Bicycles that didn't make sense for Schwinn. Now he had two suppliers turned competitors. Once Schwinn was in Bankruptcy Court, each would be both creditor and competitor. Having Schwinn survive intact was not necessarily the top item on their American agenda.

Ed's sourcing strategy had been determined not by a quest for the best price, the best quality, or the best way to play off various vendors. He was driven by the premise that he needed to own a piece of his suppliers. "Schwinn couldn't cut the umbilical cord to manufacturing," says Bill Austin. Just as Ed Sr. had championed the factory during the 1960s, Ed Jr. was determined to preserve Schwinn's manufacturing tradition. It was an emotional decision, a judgment on which Ed bet the company—and lost.

17

THE OTHER *S*

Schwinn was at the top of its form when Japanese components maker Shimano was struggling in the 1960s to find a market for its parts in the United States. Schwinn was the prestige nameplate, the coveted customer, but it never became entangled with Shimano the way it did with Giant and China Bicycles. Shimano's story is important for a different reason. The Japanese family firm would grasp the mantle of industry leadership from Schwinn in the next generation. Just as Schwinn in its heyday was revered for innovation and enjoyed exceptional power and prestige, so would Shimano.

The two at first worked together closely. Al Fritz found the Japanese company more responsive and energetic than many longstanding European suppliers. In addition, the cultured and gracious Yoshi Shimano served as his translator during negotiations with Japanese bike builders in the early 1970s. The arrangement offered Shimano an exceptional window on Schwinn's thinking; Schwinn, in return, often got one-year exclusives on new Shimano designs that were labeled "Schwinn approved."

Yet the companies were on different courses: one on the way up, the other on the way down.

Shimano's rise eroded the power of all bike manufacturers, not just Schwinn. As was the case with U.S. Rubber during the days of Ignaz and F.W., the industry's true clout would be wielded by a components company. Only this time, the parts maker so deftly created a market for its wares that knowledgeable riders soon were purchasing bikes not for the name on the frame, but for the Shimano pieces. Shimano would achieve a virtual lock on the market for gear-shifting systems; there simply would be no other place to go. Bicycles would become near-generic commodities, as manufacturers and marketers discovered they had less leeway to distinguish themselves and instead were forced to play up frame designs, colors, graphics, and the cachet of their names. Suburban Chicago dealer Jeff Crittenden points to two competing models—a Schwinn and a Scott—each priced at $399. "They have the same hubs, gear-shifter, pedals, and cranks," he notes. "Pick a color." Shimano came to be dubbed "the Intel of the bicycle industry," dominating its field the way the microchip maker drove the early-1990s computer industry. "Shimano saw a void," says former Schwinn engineer Marc Muller, "and drove a truck through it." That was a long way from Schwinn's glory years, when F.W. could force vendors to develop components no competitor could match. And if outsiders couldn't do it right, or had grown too strong in their arenas, Schwinn made its own parts in the interest of self-sufficiency. When that proposition became inefficient, the company imported components from a variety of suppliers, including old-line European names such as France's Huret and Maillard and Germany's Fichtel & Sachs.

Shimano has its roots in the ancient swordmaking center of Sakai, a port town on the southern side of Osaka Bay that spawned small forging operations and evolved into a center for the Japanese bicycle industry. In 1921, twenty-eight-year-old Shozaburo Shimano opened a machine repair shop there, but dreamed of selling bicycle freewheels—the cluster of sprockets on the rear wheel that works with the chain to shift gears. Imported freewheels were superior, however, so Shozaburo studied heat-treating technology and metallurgy to make his freewheel harder and longer wearing. Quality improved to the point where he offered two free replacements for every one found defective. The young Shimano no doubt was driven: he was married in 1927 in a ceremony at his house on the factory grounds and was seen working in the plant with his new bride the morning after the wedding. Shozaburo had six children, including three sons who would single-mindedly expand the business following their father's death in 1958: Shozo, the oldest and chairman, who historically handled the firm's finances; Keizo, proficient in engineering and technology; and Yoshi, the youngest, who would head U.S. sales operations, based first in New York, then in Irvine, California.

The company experienced turbulent times after World War II, when its factory had been reduced to rubble. It experimented in derailleurs and three-speed hubs with limited success and survived a financial breakdown in 1954 only after Shozo persuaded customers to loan money, with inventory serving as collateral. Shozo realized that to grow, the business needed to tap the American market. Starting in 1962, the brothers visited leading companies to show off their three-speed hub. Few were impressed, but, like its compatriots in the auto and electronics industries, Shimano repeatedly refined the product. Its first major customer was a coup: America's oldest bike maker, Columbia, the successor firm to Col. Albert Pope's pioneering company. When Columbia's president, Ben Harding, landed in Osaka to visit the factory, a high school band was on the tarmac to welcome him. Shimano soon was supplying large U.S. manufacturers such as H. P. Snyder, Huffman, and Murray Ohio. Bob Huffman was impressed when he toured the plant—until he read the packaging for a front derailleur. "It's the name," he explained. The Japanese translation to English called the part the "Little Pecker." Shimano hastily renamed it "Thunderbird," but Yoshi is still abashed thirty years later. "It was a bad mistake."

By 1965, Shimano was having enough success to open a U.S. headquarters in New York under Yoshi, who would prove to be a determined salesman. Yoshi pitched prestigious Schwinn for years without success, first calling longtime general manager Bill Stoeffhaas, then Al Fritz. "Many of our dealers were adamantly opposed to anything Japanese,"

Fritz says. "And in those days, Japanese products had a very poor quality image."

Nevertheless, Schwinn's European suppliers didn't always have the answers. During the bike boom, the company was receiving complaints, mostly from the West Coast, about noisy freewheels on its Varsitys and other ten-speeds. "We were replacing freewheels left and right," Fritz says. A closer examination showed that the noise was caused by sand and dirt kicked up during the ride. Fritz contacted the sales representative from Maillard.

"I'd like to have a sealed bearing freewheel," Fritz said.

"We can't do that," the rep replied. "It would cost too much."

"I'm willing to pay," Fritz persisted.

"Can't do it, Al. We'll give you the replacement part, no charge."

Mere replacement wouldn't solve the problem. There still was the cost of the dealer's labor and the damage from a customer's annoyance. Several months later, Yoshi and his technologically savvy brother Keizo dropped by on one of their goodwill calls.

"Keizo," Fritz said, "this is bugging the hell out of me. I want a sealed bearing freewheel. And Maillard turns me down."

Keizo made a note, and not long after their visit, Fritz received a sample. Soon Schwinn was buying freewheels and derailleurs from its accommodating new supplier. Keizo and Yoshi would brainstorm with Fritz and engineer Frank Brilando, often jotting drawings on a napkin in a Japanese bar or restaurant.

Yoshi, especially, was close to Fritz, serving as his interpreter during Schwinn's early bargainings with Japanese bike makers and government officials. That gave him access to precious market intelligence on Schwinn's future plans, but the benefits were personal, too. Fritz arranged internships for Shozo's son at Schwinn and Murray Ohio. Brownie entertained Yoshi and his family, along with the Fritzes, at the ranch in Wyoming. And before Fritz left Schwinn headquarters in 1980 to launch the Excelsior exerciser division, he made a farewell trip to Asia bicycle suppliers, including a sentimental sojourn with the Shimanos. After dinner, the group repaired to Shozo's impressive home for drinks, where they presented Fritz with a watch. Shozo's wife, Aiko, beckoned

Fritz to a room where she displayed her paintings. "Al-san, please take one for your Florida home and one for your Northbrook home," she said. He selected one of flowers, another of a bamboo forest.

The warmth chilled after Ed's ascension within Schwinn—and Shimano's within the industry. Ed was mistrustful, suggesting that Schwinn was not getting the best prices and that any supplier was lucky to have his business. The new administration, under John Barker and Bill Austin, also wanted a more arm's-length relationship. By this time, Schwinn no longer was seeking exclusives, because few of its 1980s customers cared. Component makers—not just Shimano, but also Japan's SunTour and Italy's Campagnolo—were the ones that now enjoyed the broad recognition among more serious consumers who wanted those names on their bikes, not just Schwinn's. Ed, of course, was dutiful in maintaining the corporate relationship—he and Yoshi went fishing off the coast of California during the late 1980s, and Shimano invited Ed to its festive seventieth anniversary celebration in 1991—but this was a shadow of the old affiliation. Where a dinner or golf outing with Fritz or Ray Burch usually would cover nuances of design, production, or marketing, Yoshi was disappointed on such occasions to find Ed uninterested in talking shop. "A nice fellow," Yoshi concludes, "but he had a lower degree of interest for the business."

Shimano in the 1980s was growing larger and more powerful every year—it no longer needed Schwinn. "Our attitude was that Shimano should have helped Schwinn," says purchasing manager Mark Marusarz. "Help us because we helped them. They were getting so popular, they didn't have to play the game."

At the start of the '80s, Shimano was not yet the dominant player. It had a substantial rival in the SunTour brand owned by Japan's Maeda Industries, a privately held manufacturer that got its start making gear sprockets for agricultural machinery. SunTour, under its longtime chairman Junzo Kawai, had a leg up on Shimano in the dealer market, commanding as much as 65 percent of sales of the drive-train sets (gears, brakes, and other components) that propelled bikes. Shimano's Dura-Ace group of components for racing bikes had been launched to good reviews, but U.S. dealers couldn't get enough of them on time. And it was derided for its 1981 line of sleeker "aerodynamic" bicycle components. The company maintained the idea was ahead of its time, but sheepishly acknowledged that components played a minor role in minimizing wind resistance, especially when compared to the cyclist's body.

Both Shimano and SunTour hopped on the Northern California mountain bike craze early, producing lines of components that facilitated a wider range of gearings to withstand dirt, rocks, and the general rough-and-tumble of a race down Repack Road. Shimano even began importing mud from the United States and Europe to test parts designed for off-road use. Then, SunTour stumbled with a design flaw in its second series of components. "SunTour tried to improve, but there was no way to change design and catch up," says Nai-Wen Kiang, who was purchasing Schwinn's mountain bike parts in 1982. "Meanwhile, Shimano came to me—'Oh, we have this model. Try to use it. If the dealer rejects it, return it. We charge only for what you use.' "

What really catapulted Shimano into the big time was its 1984 introduction of index shifting, which enabled a cyclist to shift neatly and accurately instead of hearing and feeling the friction of the gears. Some compared it to tuning a radio station with an electronic push button, instead of dialing manually. "It just felt good," says California framebuilder Steve Potts. "Shimano components are like sex. There's no way you could talk to someone about it. You have to get on the bike and feel it." Shimano marketed its innovation methodically, starting with top-of-the-line models and instructing bike makers just how precisely they needed to install the parts, before gradually expanding the system to less expensive bikes. Based on Shimano's success, SunTour brought out its own version of index shifting, called Accushift, and prematurely tried to leapfrog Shimano and market the full range of components at once—with disastrous consequences. "SunTour's reputation was badly damaged," says former SunTour consultant Tom Franges. Market share dropped like a stone, and by the time Accushift finally worked, Shimano was far ahead. SunTour continued to try matching Shimano products, but it was too late.

Many manufacturers, including Schwinn, sought to bolster SunTour as a buffer against Shimano hegemony, but it was a lopsided market. A humbled SunTour was acquired first by a Japanese conglomerate then by a management group that moved the components maker to Taiwan. The Europeans were in no better shape: "Shimano came out with new models; they stuck with the old," says Fred Todrys, a former independent sales rep in the States for components by both Maillard and Huret. Just as a boutique might sell complete ensembles of hat, belt, and shoes, Shimano by 1986 was selling its hardware in complete "groups." The matched pieces looked sharp on the bike. The shifter, for instance, connected perfectly with the derailleur, which fit nicely with the crank-set. Schwinn and other manufacturers, worried about a consolidation of power, tried to roust the somnolent Europeans. "This is what we need—what *you* need," purchasing manager Mike Marusarz remembers warning. "We're trying to help. The ball already is rolling for Shimano." Europe didn't seem to want to bother. "We have six different internal coaster hubs," was the indifferent response. The European industry, in fact, was already consolidating, as Germany's Fichtel & Sachs, a producer of internal hubs and a unit of the conglomerate Mannessman AG, acquired derailleur giant Huret in 1982 and Maillard, the producer of hubs and freewheels, in 1986. "When Shimano came to dominate in groups, Sachs decided it had to acquire everyone else," says John Neugent, president of California-based Sachs Bicycle Components.

There was good reason for Shimano's success. The parts were well made, fairly priced, and smartly marketed. The company convinced buyers that the heart of the bicycle no longer was the frame—it was the drive-train. By 1988, Shimano practically had a monopoly in components, with about 85 percent of the dealer market and 60 percent of the mass market. Shimano also simplified the job of designers at manufacturers like Schwinn. All they had to do was specify the Shimano group corresponding to the planned retail price of the bike. A $300 mountain bike? That called for Shimano 100 GS parts, a $50 package containing nearly twenty pieces, including the derailleur, brakes, brake levers, pedals, and shifters (representing about half the retail price of the bicycle). "It was a drug," says Stanley R. Day, president of Chicago-based parts maker SRAM Corporation, which sued Shimano in 1989, alleging restraint of trade. Day had a promising business selling a product called

Grip-Shift, which allowed riders to change gears by a simple twist of the handlebar, instead of a lever. Buyers were interested, the suit alleged, but they faced a 10 percent surcharge if they tried to exclude a single piece, such as the shifter, from the Shimano package they ordered, and customers who ordered the complete groups would be shipped first. In addition, SRAM charged, Shimano refused to warranty parts that were not purchased as an item in a group. SRAM settled the suit out of court in the United States for an estimated $3 million to $5 million. Shimano wrote a letter to various bike companies' product managers stating there would be no penalty if they used Day's Grip-Shift. It even reduced the surcharges if buyers declined to purchase entire groups. "It's like a bully on the block that beats the crap out of you until another bully comes and saves the kids," Day boasts. Yet Shimano, which went public in 1972, remained powerful. (It earned $54 million on sales of $1.3 billion in 1995.) U.S. entrepreneurs preferred to graze in areas where they wouldn't have to butt heads, such as rims, tires, saddles, and handlebars. "To get in their face is a serious thing," says California parts designer Keith Bontrager, whose firm was acquired by Trek in 1995.

Schwinn (along with its U.S. competitors) was hurt by the standardization fueled by Shimano, because it offered one less incentive to buy any bicycle brand over another. Moreover, by the late 1980s, Schwinn had become a minor purchaser of components. Ed said otherwise—he liked to point out that his company controlled production of nearly one million bikes—but it was actually Giant and China Bicycles that negotiated directly with Shimano for the volumes it purchased for Schwinn and other labels. Tony Lo and Jerome Sze wielded the influence, not Ed. Schwinn bought components directly only for its Greenville plant (between 100,000 and 200,000 Shimano groups annually) and for the deluxe Paramount framesets (a measly 1,000 groups) that were built at a tiny satellite operation in Waterford, Wisconsin, after the Chicago factory was closed. By 1989, Shimano again was upgrading its components (to the distress of dealers who'd be saddled with obsolete inventory), but this time, there were shortages. That lacerated Schwinn, which had 80 percent of the parts it needed in Greenville soaking up money while it waited for the missing pieces to complete the bikes. Schwinn dispatched

Mark Marusarz to Japan to find out if it had been relegated to the back of the pack. "I'd get on their doorstep and ask for delivery," Marusarz says. "Nothing was done maliciously—they showed me the bottleneck, they did have problems—but it hurt us good."

Thus marked the beginning of a series of shortages that would plague Ed in his final three years at the company and send dealers scurrying to other brands. The center of the bicycle industry long had left Chicago; it was now outside Osaka. The most important family name was not Schwinn; it was Shimano.

18

MISSISSIPPI CHURNING

In the early 1980s, Southern California dealer Chris Travers had a nagging problem with many of the bicycles from Schwinn's Greenville factory. "The pieces didn't fit," he explains. When Travers toured the Mississippi site with product manager Carl Cohen, as part of a corporate plan to prop up sagging dealer support for Greenville, his fears were confirmed: "We took a bike and put it together. The wheels were bad, the seams were bad . . . after riding the bike for a mile-and-a-half, they were wobbling."

Even diehard Schwinn retailers quickly branded the Made-in-America product as inferior. At first, it was basic start-up glitches: wheels weren't true; kickstands were missing; colors were mismatched; bikes arrived without seatposts, their saddles tagged with IOUs. "My mechanics would tell me, 'Don't buy any more of that bike,' " says Gary Sirota of Wantagh, New York. "But Schwinn was such a strong name, you had to buy." Similar complaints could be heard 3,000 miles west. "My mechanics didn't like putting together a Schwinn," recalls Marin County dealer John Lewis. A dangerous dynamic, he notes. "A dealer's sales force is also the mechanic and assembly force. If they don't want to put together a Schwinn, they won't want to sell one, either."

Production crises reared year after year. In the summer of 1986, the factory shipped thousands of models that became chipped in transit because someone had neglected to strap the wheels and handlebars so they wouldn't rotate inside the box—a routine packing procedure. Dennis Kilfoy had just started working at Schwinn's elite Paramount frame shop in Wisconsin as a painter, when he was ordered to the Midwest warehouse to touch up mutilated bikes. Kilfoy spent the next two weeks applying aquamarine paint with a special spray gun. He estimates, conservatively, that at least 10,000 bikes were damaged. Based on Greenville's production rate at the time (some 700 to 1,000 bikes a day), that suggests the oversight went undetected for at least two weeks. "All they needed was string," Kilfoy notes, to secure the parts in shipping.

There were other snags. Greenville didn't have equipment for the frontside alignment known as the fork, so Chicago had to order the correct number in the correct sizes. Easier said than done. The plant sometimes found itself with a deficit of long forks and a surplus of short forks. "I threw out so many forks for scrap metal," says purchasing manager Mark Marusarz. Once, Schwinn goofed on an order for 10,000 brake levers, according to former marketing director Byron Smith: "They found they had ten thousand for the right side, when they needed five thousand for the right and five thousand for the left."

The logistical nightmare of receiving timely shipments from Shimano and other suppliers was also part of Greenville's curse: How could the Mississippi factory compete with large Asian manufacturers a mere hub and spoke from Osaka? In addition, late shipments threw the design process into disarray. Carl Cohen, a thirty-year-old product manager at the time, was saddled with leftover 1984 parts while planning 1985's line. Hired by Bill Austin in 1982, the Boston native found it tough to apply the lessons he'd learned in his MBA classes at the University of Michigan—this case study wasn't academic. Unfortunately, it was repeated in 1986, when Cohen had to use up old 1985 components. No wonder dealers were sniping that Schwinn was behind on the latest innovations, such as index shifting, alloy rims, or new seatpost designs.

Another difficulty lay in the way Schwinn tried to differentiate the lines being manufactured at various factories. Initially, Taiwan's Giant produced lower-priced road bikes, such as the World at $149, the World Sport at $179, and the Traveler at $199. Greenville manufactured mid-priced models, such as the LeTour at $249, the LeTour Deluxe at $279, and the Super LeTour at $299. Matsushita's National built the higher-priced SuperSport and Voyageur road bikes. But Giant's Traveler, with an alloy rim and chrome-moly frame, was a better value—and probably underpriced—compared with the inconsistent quality of Greenville's bikes. "There was not a clear distinction," observes Trek product manager Harry Spehar. "For the same components, Giant would be $50 less. They were competing with themselves." Similar thinking ruled the higher ends of the Schwinn line. In 1984, Carl Cohen set out to design pricier bikes made at National and aimed at the upscale Trek customer. "I was gonna put Trek out of business," Cohen recalls, acting out his enthusiasm at the time. "We had them nailed!" But the models didn't fare well because, he says, at about $400 they were overpriced by $50. Upper management insisted that, just as in the auto industry, more expensive models should bring more impressive profit margins. Moreover, they wanted to maintain a wide berth—about $100—between Japanese-made and Greenville-made products. It was a self-defeating distinction, in Cohen's eyes. "They didn't want a National bike selling well at $350 and a Greenville bike not selling at $299. A rational organization would say, 'Let the chips fall where they may.' " With its Greenville-centric policy, Cohen adds, Schwinn essentially surrendered the upper tier of the market to Trek, having proved to itself that the high-end adult market didn't really exist, since those consumers weren't bothering to buy Schwinn's offerings.

Trek would grow and show that bikes could be made successfully in America, although in 1984 and 1985, the young Wisconsin firm was floundering. Product manager Spehar was awed by the Greenville setup: Schwinn was purchasing top-notch components from Shimano and SunTour, while Trek only had access to cheaper French parts. Schwinn seemed to be taking advantage of its size. "I couldn't hit their price," Spehar says. "Were they running the factory at a loss?" Spehar didn't know it, but the answer was a resounding yes: Greenville never made a dime. Losses mounted during the 1980s—the plant would lose $7.6 million in 1990 alone—and the total would surpass $30 million before the site was shuttered in 1991. Ed Schwinn asked his partner in Hungary, Willy Ehrlich, what he thought of Greenville after a visit there. Ehrlich's response: "It's a very expensive American address."

Trek showed Schwinn how it should be done. At Trek, executives and assembly-line workers toiled under one roof. At Schwinn, top managers (including tool and die specialists) shuttled between their Chicago-area homes and a $49-a-night Hampton Inn in Greenville. "How can you run a plant in Mississippi from Chicago? You've got to live and eat and breathe there," scoffs John W. Graves, president of the Bike Line retail chain based in West Chester, Pennsylvania, the nation's No. 1 Schwinn seller in 1991. In addition, Trek was located more conveniently to receive parts and ship bikes. And Trek separated its line production more precisely than Schwinn: manufacturing expensive (and more profitable) bikes—starting at around $500—in Wisconsin and importing less expensive models—around $300—from Taiwan.

In 1986, some Schwinn executives, including Cohen, pressed for change. The Greenville factory wasn't competent enough to produce five models in seven frame sizes, they argued, and it was constantly retooling. Why not simplify things and just produce the basic Traveler? Schwinn's mass market competitors, like Huffy, made money selling inexpensive bikes, Cohen noted. Others even suggested hiring a Japanese or Taiwanese manufacturer to manage the plant—an intriguing idea, but not quite right for a factory meant to showcase American thinking. Ed said no, Schwinn needed to keep itself up to date in technology. If we don't manufacture our better bikes, how can we design them?

Instead of shifting production to less expensive bikes, Ed moved in the opposite direction. Schwinn licensed technology from hot frame builder Gary Klein to make $500 to $700 aluminum bikes. But the move was late, and it was difficult to catch up with new market leaders Trek and East Coast upstart Cannondale. "There was no business strategy to match what Greenville was capable of," Cohen says. "The factory specialized in what it did worst."

At headquarters, Greenville was the subject of continued intra-management sniping. Executives in the marketing and finance departments, such as Gerard O'Keefe, counseled pulling the plug. Others also were pessimistic. "It's hopeless," Bevil Hogg told John Barker in early 1989. (Ex-Trekker Hogg had sold his carbon-fiber bike venture to Schwinn the year before and now was a Schwinn manager.) "John," Hogg suggested, "you need to shut it down and get out of the business." Hogg was astonished a short time later, when Ed's brother, Richard, announced that the company's future was in Greenville—and that the younger Schwinn personally was going to oversee it.

Ed had considered closing the besieged plant, which was run by a succession of three general managers, but Richard had persuaded him to give Greenville another shot. Richard's premise: putting the family name behind the plant would strengthen internal support for it. Richard proved to be passionate about his project. Hoping to lower the average cost of making a bike, he expanded Mississippi production to more than 100,000 units in 1990 from 75,000 in 1988. Richard transferred less expensive models from Giant, but that only turned once-profitable bikes into money losers. The losses, which Schwinn officialdom euphemistically called "variances," did not narrow with higher output. In fact, improvements at Giant and other foreign bike makers led to an ever-widening cost gap between domestic production and buying finished bikes overseas. Richard and director of engineering Mike Fritz (who had survived the abrupt departure of his father, Al) agreed that the tooling department should be shifted to Greenville. In the summer of 1989 Mike Fritz offered the tooling engineers—mostly old-timers—the opportunity to relocate. "To a man, they resigned," he says. Fritz rented a house and moved to Mississippi in January 1990.

Greenville's quality under Richard improved, to acceptable from horrible. "His heart was in the right place," says Mark Marusarz. "But the level of commitment was a little late." Soon, Schwinn would have no choice but to cut its losses. With its bicycles being produced in the United States, Taiwan, Japan, China, and Hungary, the company was juggling too much. None of the bigwigs seemed to have the time to devote to the struggling factory in the South. Worse, Schwinn was so absorbed in global sourcing issues that the most fundamental part of its business—devising innovative, marketable bikes at competitive prices—got short shrift.

It wasn't just the Greenville bikes that suffered. To many dealers, Schwinn was not providing the best component for the money. It seemed to be specifying the parts, or "speccing" its bikes, too cheaply everywhere. Quality problems and late deliveries throughout the operation had pressured profit margins, so the company maintained prices higher than they should have been. That hurt Middle American dealers like John Pelc, who has sold Schwinns for more than forty years in tree-lined Lincoln, Illinois. "When people came in here and saw the price—boom!—out the door they went," Pelc says.

Michael Mulrooney, vice president of a family-owned chain in status-conscious Orange County, California, applauded a Schwinn bull's-eye one year with a High Plains mountain bike that sold for $299. "A killer mountain bike; they hit it right on the money. We couldn't get enough." The following year, however, Schwinn charged $50 more for the same Taiwanese-made bike (exchange rates were a factor) and the model no longer was competitive. To Chris Travers, who once worked for the Mulrooney family and later opened his own shop in blue-collar La Mirada, Schwinn seemed half a step behind. Instead of using a wider seat, Schwinn tacked on a narrow vinyl saddle; Schwinns would have steel, instead of alloy, handlebars. By the mid-1980s, "dealers [were] starting to get really torqued," Travers says. That's when he added Giant and Diamond Back to his offerings. Travers could make a 36 percent profit margin on a $199 entry-level mountain bike from Giant. To make the same profit, he'd have to sell a comparable Schwinn for $240. Yet the Giant was a better value, he says, with its additional features, such as mounts for a rack and two water bottles. Often, Schwinn would flop on colors and graphics. Travers says it produced a Day-Glo yellow Paramount a year after the hue was popular. Mulrooney recalls unveiling a new model with patterned seats. "We all stood looking at this stuff—it was the most ugly thing you'd ever seen," he says. "We laughed. It was sad." Mulrooney, who had been one of the country's largest Schwinn dealers, brought in other lines. Schwinn's share of his business dropped from 35 percent in 1984 to a puny 10 percent by 1991—a far cry from the days when the company could demand at least 50 percent of a store's attention. "In a highly competitive market, you couldn't just be Schwinn," Mulrooney explains. "No question—the name had high recognition; it's impressive. But you have to have the product right." For other dealers, delays and cancellations prompted them to look elsewhere. "We just couldn't get the right bikes when we needed them," says Joe Russell, owner of Russell's Cycle & Fitness in Washington, Illinois, about 10 miles from Peoria. Schwinn could deliver only half of the 400 mountain bikes Russell wanted for his 1987 season, spurring him to increase his business with Specialized and others.

In Chicago, product managers were frustrated. They had to produce a line of bikes at a range of prices that theoretically would hit a 30 percent profit margin for the company. A persuasive manager might be able to argue he needed an alloy rim and, accordingly, a 28 percent margin; otherwise, the accountants would prevail. Their argument: take the higher markup, because Schwinn still was so big its bicycles were bound to sell on their own reputation, even if models were a year behind on a particular component that only a small percentage of the market truly cared about. But, in truth, Schwinn was on the defensive, trying to fend off the guerrilla marketing tactics of competitors who made a point of touting their superior brake or shift lever. "We didn't anticipate enough of those moves," concedes former product manager Brad Hughes, who departed for Western States in 1991.

Schwinn's decades-long orientation to kids was one reason for its foot-dragging in the growing market for sophisticated super-lightweight adult bikes. Many old-timers never could quite believe it, but by the mid-1980s, half of all dealer bike sales were to adults. Mike Fritz remembers chatting with a weathered engineer on the latest bonding technology in aluminum cycles. "You can't glue a bike," the engineer jeered. Actually, you could—with the right new materials. Carl Cohen recalls pushing for the introduction of special handlebars for triathlon bicycles around 1986, after five-time world champion Mark Allen (whom Schwinn had sponsored) mentioned that the new design might be more comfortable following the rigorous swim in the first stage of a race. The old guard, however, was geared to traditional road racing. *What does some guy who rides in a teeny bathing suit know about bikes?* was the general thinking. Engineers dismissed the proposal after playing around with the design on a computer screen rather than testing it on a bike. The market, however, embraced the special handlebars made by others, which not only were more comfortable but were aerodynamically superior. To Cohen, it was another example of the company's stubbornness.

In Waterloo, Wisconsin, Trek product manager Harry Spehar waited for Schwinn to make its move. "It's a matter of time before they wise up," he figured. In 1986 Trek had imported its first moderately priced mountain bikes (about $300) from Taiwan's Merida, making inroads on Schwinn turf. "We were beating them on price," Spehar says. Strong lines that year and in '87 and '88 helped yank Trek from its slump. Dealers who used to order 1,000 Schwinns were now cutting their Schwinn count to 900 and taking 100 Treks. Pat Sullivan, Trek's national sales manager, noticed Schwinn-only stores picking up one competitor or another because of dissatisfaction with specs. "We were the beneficiary," Sullivan says. "Anyone was. At first, we got the feeling we were a stopgap measure until Schwinn came back, then we'd be out the door. Each year that feeling declined."

Schwinn was butting against formidable opponents in both Trek and Specialized. The competitors were choosing the right components and paying the right prices for them. Schwinn was inconsistent and, of course, still dogged by its image as a maker of kids' stuff and the heavy Varsity. Trek and Specialized were leaner and younger operations. Schwinn was bloated with a disproportionately larger and older staff and headquarters. Trek and Specialized were aggressive in their sales terms: take it now, pay us much later. Schwinn was a stickler on payments. Trek had Richard Burke and Specialized had Mike Sinyard, both highly focused and driven first-generation entrepreneurs who had everything to gain and less to lose. "Schwinn was a little more relaxed," says Tom French, who had helped Bevil Hogg start Trek and then worked for Schwinn after the pair sold their start-up to the Chicago company. "There was no killer instinct at Schwinn for a long time."

The differences were also reflected in the pool of dealers. Schwinn still had merchants from the old school—"the Coke-and-cigarette guys," as competing reps called them—and some even sold lawnmowers. Ray Burch would have disapproved. Even the Total Concept Stores were looking dated, with their '60s typefaces, orange and avocado carpets, Naugahyde seating, and wood-grain laminate counters. The larger and more successful Schwinn dealerships, often upgraded by the fitness-friendly children of their founders, had to diversify to survive in a market that demanded more choices. They were turning not just to Trek and Specialized, but to Giant, Diamond Back, Cannondale, and GT. Other retail formats hurt, too. Schwinn was nowhere during the rise of Erehwon, REI, and other hip, outdoorsy sporting goods stores that offered expensive bicycles and the appropriate clothing and camping gear for a trip to Yellowstone or even Nepal. Schwinn's market share eroded—from 12 percent of the U.S. market in 1979 to 7 percent in 1991, and 5 percent the following year—and the dealer defections caused friction, especially when his or her Schwinn offerings dipped below the 50 percent standard. Yet Schwinn discovered it had less clout. Cutting off big-volume dealers would boomerang and hurt Schwinn's own distribution. "Sometimes we didn't raise hell, sometimes we did," recalls former manager of dealer relations Bill Chambers, who remained at Schwinn until retirement age in early 1992, chafing at the marketplace slide. "It depended on the dealer."

The company attempted to make examples of a few errant merchants. One was Charles Bonten, a second-generation dealer in the prosperous Detroit suburb of St. Clair Shores. Bonten always was something of a maverick: his cyclery, which was about 80 percent Schwinn, also did a booming business in skateboards. He was an early supporter of the Air-Dyne exerciser and developed a strong area following through referrals from cardiologists he had courted. By mid-decade, he was the nation's seventh-largest Air-Dyne dealer. Other local Schwinn sellers, however, were demanding a piece of the Air-Dyne action and pressuring headquarters to step in. The company may have found an opening when Bonten picked up Raleigh, the illustrious British brand that had fallen on hard times during the 1970s and was sold to Ohio-based Huffy. Now, Raleigh was waging an energetic campaign to regain U.S. market share, underselling Schwinn's $120 Sprint road bike by $10 and offering dealers both advertising dollars and trips to Australia. "If someone hands you one hundred–dollar bills," Bonten explains, "you don't say why, as long as they're not counterfeit." Picking up old archrival Raleigh infuriated Schwinn, especially because parent Huffy pinched on the other side by selling to chain stores. Bonten began having difficulties. Salesmen were counting his inventory to determine if it was 50 percent Schwinn, and two other local dealers were allowed to move closer to his store. "I was livid," Bonten says. Tensions heightened. When Schwinn started buying tires and tubes from a Taiwanese supplier, Bonten snatched a batch from the forsaken domestic supplier at 75 percent off. "A loyal Schwinn dealer wouldn't do that," Midwest sales manager Bruce Sikora scolded him. Then, in January 1985, Bonten committed a cardinal sin in Schwinn-land—he bootlegged 250 Air-Dynes, selling them to other retailers. "I did it to spite them," Bonten offers as explanation, citing "the way I was treated."

It wasn't until the spring of 1986 that Schwinn confronted Bonten on the trans-shipping issue. Ed and Bill Austin flew to Detroit and lunched with Bonten at a bar across the street from his shop. Bonten would not admit to wrongdoing. Instead, he poured out a stream of complaints.

"You took Huffy," they pointed out.

"You wouldn't support me," he countered.

"Chuck, why do you complain so much?" Ed demanded. "If it wasn't for Schwinn, you'd be nothing."

Ed looked directly at Bonten, Austin recalls, and said, "You're finished as a dealer."

Bonten says he was canceled the following September. Sales dropped by 10 percent the following year, mostly due to the loss of Air-Dyne, but rebounded as he picked up Specialized and Giant. In retrospect, Bonten says, the only way to remain a Schwinn dealer "was to shut up and buy a few more Schwinns."

Bonten was one of four Michigan dealers canceled around the same time. In Flint, a town ravaged during the 1980s by auto plant closings, Gary Chenett says he took on Raleigh because he couldn't get enough Schwinns. The nine-year Schwinn dealer doubled his sales by selling more than 1,000 Raleighs. "Those could be Schwinn sales, if you could get more product," he told his sales rep. The next year, he sold 1,200 Schwinns and 1,600 Raleighs. "The Raleigh numbers are going up and Schwinn can't supply me." Chenett returned from a Raleigh junket to Brazil to find his franchise had been pulled. (Bill Chambers says Chenett didn't pay his bills; Chenett says he was current.) Chenett, Bonten, and the two other Michigan dealers axed by Schwinn later went on a Raleigh-funded trip to the Caribbean and raised their glasses to Ed Schwinn in a satirical toast.

Bonten and other sacrificial lambs were merely reflective of a new breed of more assertive dealers who operated large stores, and sometimes many large stores. By handling a number of bicycle brands, they were not dependent on a single manufacturer and not easily controlled. Selling big volumes, they pushed Schwinn and other suppliers for special consideration: volume discounts, better terms, priority shipments. Yet Schwinn felt abused. These dealers displayed large Schwinn signs, which generated traffic, but devoted perhaps only 30 percent of floor space to the line. Once in the store, the customer could be swayed to try the higher-margin Trek, Giant, or Cannondale. Ray Burch had argued decades earlier that if a dealer couldn't make a living off Schwinn—if the company couldn't "offer the chance to make him a millionaire"—the name would have no pull. Now, dealers didn't need Schwinn to make a living. There were too many other options available.

John Graves is illustrative of the change. His bustling Bike Line chain outside Philadelphia was growing rapidly—to 18 stores by 1988. Graves owned his market, but Schwinn feared he was too dominant, perhaps even a threat. "Schwinn held him at arm's length," says former marketing director Byron Smith. "Schwinn's historical attitude was, 'Better to sell twelve to fifteen new accounts.' " (Indeed, Graves soon expanded dramatically by franchising his Bike Line concept. By 1996, more than 70 stores in 17 states collectively generated nearly $30 million in sales—with about 4 percent of franchisee sales flowing to him as a royalty. A typical Bike Line shop grosses $450,000 to $750,000 annually, he claims, versus $350,000 for the average bike store.)

Some dealers gnawed at Schwinn by feasting on closeouts. In a typical transaction, an opportunistic dealer would buy for $150 a bike that at the start of the season would have cost him $200. The dealer might advertise it for $50 off—selling it for $250 instead of $300, but still make good money. While Schwinn aimed for an average profit margin in the range of 30 percent from bicycles and exercisers, its margin from dealers like this was around 14 percent. That was punishing for Schwinn, but the merchants simply were capitalizing on the company's missteps.

Headquarters finally decided it was missing out on some of the bigger profits being enjoyed by retailers and in 1988 pushed to open its own stores. The cycleries could become showcases for bikes, exercisers, and fitness gear and serve as a potent marketing tool. They also could become something of a tourist attraction, much like house-owned shops operated by Sony, Nike, or Ralph Lauren.

Byron Smith helped launch the company stores. Smith had joined Schwinn in 1987, working under Gerard O'Keefe, who had run marketing for Al Fritz at Excelsior and assumed the top corporate marketing post in 1987 after Bill Austin's departure. O'Keefe came to bicycles late in his career, having held a series of sales and marketing jobs in the sporting goods industry and the presidency of Brunswick Corporation's MacGregor golf division in the early '70s. O'Keefe was inclined to hire marketers from the package goods industry and tapped Smith, who had blue-chip credentials: an MBA from the University of Chicago and ten years at the buttoned-down Quaker Oats Company in Chicago, where he worked his way through the product management ranks, from oatmeal to Aunt Jemima pancake mix. Smith was accustomed to substantial markups in package goods, which usually left lots of dollars for advertising and marketing, and was dismayed at the low profits in bicycle distribution—a 3 percent return on sales, compared to 9 to 12 percent in food products. Smith's frequent comparisons to his old industry didn't sit well with technically oriented product managers or longtime dealers like George Garner, who called him "Oatmeal Man." Successful strategies in the food industry hinged on advertising, promotion, and pricing; the actual products didn't change much from year to year. But in the swift-moving bike industry, marketers overhauled their models each season, racing to be first with a new innovation. To the gearhead product managers, bikes couldn't be sold like cereal. And to the established dealers, Schwinns shouldn't be sold by anyone but them. They were incensed, especially at marketing director Smith, when the company in 1989 opened a showcase store on Chicago's North Side. "The dealers lost faith," says Oscar Wastyn, Jr., whose West Side shop was less than a mile away. Even Schwinn's own sales reps observed that the company didn't have enough inventory to supply its 1,700 dealers. Why add even more outlets?

Smith today says Schwinn had no intention of plopping company-owned stores near its dealers. The outlets were devised to help raise awareness of the brand in a given market and thereby boost all local dealer sales. Better sourcing, he argued, could solve the inventory shortfalls. Besides, the Chicago store was a knockout: sleek, carpeted, loaded with flashing videos and high-intensity lighting. It performed well, too. Annual sales soared to more than $1 million by 1991, with a gross profit margin of 46 percent. Near the end of 1990, Schwinn opened a second store, this time in Denver, which the company believed was an underdeveloped market, and planned to open five stores a year in selected cities through 1996.

Although Schwinn had been religious in its dedication to the independent bicycle store, a nagging question remained: Could the company make more money selling its bikes through mass merchants? Sears, Montgomery Ward, and newer chains handled about 70 percent of U.S. bike sales. Some observers say Schwinn, by refusing to sell in this arena, passed up a golden opportunity—a miscalculation fueled by management's misunderstanding of the true nature of Schwinn's name in a changing market. "Their image became down-market to people buying better bikes," says Felix Magowan, publisher of the cycling magazine *VeloNews*. "Schwinn's brand equity was with the Wal-Mart and Kmart crowd."

There were no lack of overtures. Companies like Sportmart, a regional sporting goods chain based in the Chicago suburb of Niles, made numerous pitches to Ed and other executives, only to be rebuffed. "We gave all kinds of ideas," says Sportmart CEO Larry Hochberg. "At first, they were mum. Then they said, 'We do have a dealer organization.' Pity. [Schwinn] could have been a major Chicago corporation. . . . I never felt we had a meaningful discussion."

But there was much internal discussion of the issue around 1990. Executives like Byron Smith noted that the brand was missing substantial exposure by not being at Target and other big retailers, alongside such powerful brands as Nike and Apple. Industry consultants estimated that only two-thirds of the population ever visits a bike shop, and only 3 percent of consumers buy there in a given year. Meantime, almost everyone trolls through a Sears, Ward's, Kmart, Wal-Mart, or Target at least once a year. "There was no exposure of the brand to casual shoppers," Smith says. Schwinn went so far as to hire a consultant to survey mass merchants and consider how the product might fit into the larger market. Could the company juggle both channels by perhaps using different brand names? Could it find a home at the regional specialty chains, such as Sportmart and Oshman's, while avoiding huge outlets like Wal-Mart? One strategy floated at headquarters was to sell the Schwinn brand name—at a premium—to chains that wanted to offer a first-rate $200 to $350 bike, then distribute the finer and pricier Paramount cycles under that name to the better independent dealers. The cost, of course, would lie in snatching away the coveted Schwinn name from dealers, since mass merchants wanted only the famous brand. That move would decimate up to 500 of the less successful mom-and-pop shops, according to one source, but much of the sales force, as well as many members of the family, had no interest in ending relationships with dealers that stretched back ten, twenty, thirty years and more. The logistics of selling to mass merchants also would be far different. Working on a slimmer markup of 18 percent, the chains would undersell remaining dealers (who need a margin of 35 percent or more) and inevitably eat into their sales. It also would be difficult for Schwinn to make much money on bikes that retail for less than $200, a popular price at the chains. Moreover, many thought Schwinn was not a powerful enough company to stand up to the demanding mass merchants, who might ask for even bigger discounts or for unsold inventory to be taken back. And there were matters like timely delivery, which Schwinn couldn't control because its bikes were being made overseas. Finally, to feed a hungry chain with the hundreds of thousands of bikes needed, Schwinn would have required substantial new financing, perhaps through an outside investor or public offering, something the family was loath to consider.

In the end, Schwinn worried most about tarnishing its name. Top management agreed: there was no point in alienating dealers just to speculate on a new channel. The independent retailer, after all, was an essential part of the company's history and culture. Nevertheless, some observers argue that Ed might still control Schwinn today if he had sold his goods to mass merchants. He'll never know.

19

"AN IMPORTANT GUY"

Shortly after Schwinn acquired his high-tech exerciser company in 1987, Bruce Sargeant found himself in a Chicago bar slugging oyster "shooters" with John Barker. Chasing down raw bivalves with whiskey was an uncomfortable experience for the thirty-seven-year-old entrepreneur from Irvine, California, who was more interested in fitness and his company's computerized exercise bike, which simulated a Tour de France race. "We didn't do that kind of stuff," Sargeant says, still blanching at the taste. "Sometimes you go along, but it was kind of weird."

Sargeant's Frontline Technology featured the Velodyne exerciser, which used a computer and screen to help the user pretend he or she was in the middle of a pro race. It was a hit at a 1987 trade show in Long Beach. "Schwinn's fitness people came over—one, two of them, four of them, eight," Sargeant says. Frontline merely had wanted an order. Barker and Ed eventually flew out to meet the partners. "Why don't we just buy you guys?" Ed proposed over dinner.

Having posted three years of earnings, Schwinn was rolling. It paid $840,000 for Frontline, including $150,000 in cash. Nevertheless, management was clueless about what to do with their gizmo. "They thought they were buying technology, but Schwinn never had an overall plan for coordinating Frontline into Schwinn strategy," complains former chief financial officer Mike McNamara. "Barker and Ed Schwinn told Marketing, 'We got this. What can you do with it?' " The Velodyne hardly fit into Schwinn's Main Street approach. The product was expensive ($1,300 to $1,700 retail) and few dealers were capable of selling it. Product manager Carl Cohen, who had moved from bikes to exercisers, regrets that Schwinn didn't aggressively position the Velodyne as a less expensive alternative to the Lifecycle, which mostly was sold to health clubs. Yet Schwinn at the time would not consider moving outside its traditional distribution. According to Sargeant, the company even turned down an opportunity to sell 1,000 Velodynes to The Sharper Image, the trendy retailer of gadgets. The high-tech Californians also never meshed with Schwinn's heartland culture. Sargeant's group had no responsibility for marketing their invention and remained in California functioning as a kind of cycling think tank—a luxury Schwinn could ill afford. A disappointed Sargeant resigned in the spring of 1989. "It's pointless to hang around, it's costing you money," he told Ed, who tried to persuade him to stay. "It wasn't going to work," Sargeant explains today. He was right: Schwinn lost $1.5 million on Frontline before the undertaking was abandoned two months later. Looking back, Sargeant says, Schwinn had no business making this kind of investment. "It was too new, too off-the-track."

Schwinn's other stake in California technology, Cycle Composites, fared somewhat better, although it, too, floundered under Barker's and Ed's stewardship. The enterprise was founded by Bevil Hogg, who had headed west in 1986, after being nudged out at Wisconsin's Trek, and was determined to tackle some unfinished business: to develop and market a super-lightweight carbon-fiber bicycle with the sleek name Kestrel. Hogg and fellow Trek pioneer Tom French believed carbon fiber was the future of the high-end market. They settled in Silicon Valley, birthplace of Apple Computer and other high-tech start-ups (as well as headquarters of Specialized), and raised venture capital, including a stake from Japanese trading giant Mitsui & Company.[1] The pair purchased frames from a subcontractor in the aerospace industry, then painted, machined, and assembled the bikes, first in mellow Santa Cruz and later in the sunny artichoke capital of Watsonville. Hogg and French shipped their first Kestrels in the summer of 1987 and quickly built a network of two hundred dealers. Selling at $3,000 a pop, Kestrels turned out to be a minor phenomenon. Dealer Ron Boi, for example, developed a flourishing business in Kestrels, selling to doctors, commodities traders, business executives, and other weekend triathletes from the posh Chicago lakefront suburbs of Winnetka and Lake Forest. Soon, Hogg and French were looking for a deep-pocketed buyer to help them expand. After Hogg's unsatisfying experience at Trek (which he calls "agony, with little ecstasy"), he wanted to make real money this time around.

French called Ed in September 1987. "We've got this wonderful bike," he said, "and we plan to be acquired. We want to be the research-and-development arm of a major bike company."

"Yes," Ed replied. "We're interested."

The partners signed the deal at Keck Mahin & Cate's law office in June 1988. Schwinn paid $1.4 million for a 51 percent stake in Cycle Composites, with payments spread over five years, and loaned the company another $1.7 million. Hogg and French received three-year management contracts and went to work for Ed. Kestrel dealer Ron Boi was skeptical of this new relationship. "They're in great shape," French insisted. Indeed, both he and Hogg saw Schwinn riding high and credited Ed with the turnaround.

Once again, Barker was the director of the transaction. The sizzling Kestrel brand was meant to strengthen Schwinn's miserable following among cycling enthusiasts, yet matching Barker's grand vision with reality was another matter. Schwinn's elite Paramount line confused the issue: Which would be the company's best label? It was a troublesome detail that was never resolved. Another obstacle: Barker wanted to manufacture Kestrel models in China, but Schwinn was barred at the time from exporting carbon-fiber technology, which also was used in the U.S. defense industry. While Kestrel developed a select following, it, like Frontline, was never blended into Schwinn. As with other investments, Schwinn lacked both the funds to sink into a cash-hungry enterprise and the manpower to steer it along. In addition, Chicago's headquarters was not open to innovation. In the late 1980s, for instance, product manager Bill Corliss won an exclusive for a mountain bike suspension fork called Rock Shox—a product that would become popular in the '90s. "I couldn't get the interest out of the sales force," Corliss says. "It was beyond [their] scope why bikes needed suspension forks." Fifty years earlier, the company had touted its introduction of the knee-action spring fork, and a stroll through Schwinn's collection of antique bicycles, lined up in a warehouse just a block away, also would have explained the need for such technology. Plenty of 1890s cycles had variations of suspension forks to help smooth the ride over the era's rough roads.

Some of Schwinn's bankers, still scrutinizing the flow of assets as part of their loan agreement, raised concerns about Kestrel and the other deals, but Barker was persuasive, smoothly explaining the rationale of each deal, the cost, and the projected payback. And the initial outlays were never eye-popping—a million here, a million there. "The banks never rejected them," says ex-CFO McNamara. "We were making money when we did those."

Barker was admired by many inside and outside the company for his energy, perceptiveness, and ability to get things done. He talked the language of banks and adopted a tough stance in negotiations. He served as lieutenant and teacher to his boss, who heartily subscribed to Barker's enthusiasm for spending money. Both men enjoyed the chase, the intrigue, the glamour of deal-making. Barker also seemed to manage Ed expertly, telling him, for example, which meetings to attend and which to skip. "Barker was always looking for projects to get Ed occupied and out of the way," says Carl Cohen. (Ed liked the globe-trotting, too, and once described himself as a "citizen of the world," according to Bruce Sargeant.) Barker buffered Ed from much of the day-to-day decision-making—he was running the company.

While Barker reveled in the deals, he often didn't have a detailed game plan as to how Schwinn's various acquisitions and joint ventures would be integrated into headquarters. "Barker was astute, experienced, and worldly," Hogg observes, "but not a good operating manager." On one occasion, Cohen was surprised to find Barker unaware that

Schwinn's bike sales were off by 30 percent for a particular quarter. "He threw so many balls in the air, he forgot the colors." By 1989, Barker's first-class lifestyle also was becoming an issue, especially among Schwinn family members who viewed him as too high a roller, sapping funds at their expense. Annual dividends were lower than the payouts during the company's heyday; worse, they now were spread among fourteen shareholders. Brownie Schwinn's six children, especially, were "beside themselves," says former controller Don Gilliard. Although some held jobs at Schwinn, none had a top management role, and many seethed at the executive perks. Brownie's son-in-law, Brad Bailey, a Schwinn sales rep in the South, was among the more vocal. "I remember comments he made about John's extravagance," Gilliard says.

Brownie's side of the family may have found an ally in Ed's brother, Richard, who at the time was manager of dealer development and made a point of living modestly. ("We have an old family saying—nothing exceeds like excess," Richard said in a 1994 speech.) In February 1989, Barker invited Richard and his wife, Robin "Shoe" Shoemaker, to travel with him to Paris, where Barker entertained in his usual style. Company lore has it that Shoe was shocked when Barker ordered a $60 bottle of wine. "If you knew Richard and Shoe, that's not their style," says Mike Martinsen, former director of international business development. "They're more comfortable with backpacks. I have to believe that after going on the trip, Richard felt too much was being spent on travel and entertainment."

The ax fell the morning of April 25. Martinsen, a recent recruit to Schwinn (he had started two weeks earlier), was strategizing with Barker when Ed walked by at 9:30 A.M. and summoned Barker.

"John," Ed said after closing his office door, "I'm going to take you out of here."

"Fine," Barker responded. "Bring your wallet."

Martinsen was in the men's room when he was paged by his secretary.

"Ed would like to see you," she said.

"Ed's with John," Martinsen replied.

"No he's not," she insisted, pointing him toward an office containing an antique desk that had belonged to Ignaz Schwinn.

Ed strode in. "Congratulations on your career move," he sarcastically told the baffled Martinsen. "John's no longer here. The mission is still the same."

"I couldn't believe it," Martinsen recalls. "I was shocked. Ed was nonchalant, joking."

General counsel Daniel Garramone joined the meeting. Martinsen watched Garramone's jaw drop when the house lawyer was told the news.

"I want you to know, Mike," Ed consoled, "that just because this happened doesn't mean we don't have international vision."

Ed hastily called a meeting of Schwinn's executive committee for 1:00 P.M. the next day. Managers flew in from out of town—Bevil Hogg from California, distribution chief Al Durelli from Schwinn Sales East in New Jersey, among others—and as they waited for Ed, committee members joked that nobody wanted to sit in Barker's usual chair.

The proceedings failed to shed much light. "I was going to tell you why John is no longer here," Ed said, "but he's too good a friend of mine to do that. It doesn't really matter. We're going to move forward without him."

Although Barker remained outwardly cool at being let go, he was "devastated," says longtime friend Joe Glunz, Sr., the Chicago wine distributor. "He felt he was instrumental in turning [Schwinn] around." Since Ed never publicly explained the dismissal, the ouster has generated only conjecture. Barker says he never was given a reason. On the matter of expenses, he adds, "Richard seemed to make it an issue. I don't think my spending was bad. The only time I spent heavily was with the Schwinns, picking up their bills. Richard never said a word to me." Barker confirms he was asked to file expense reports for advances he had drawn. "I don't remember how much, but it was definitely less than $100,000. It was expenses over a couple of years. I had all the receipts. And that took care of it." Expenses were just part of the story. It was Ed, after all, who had set the standard for travel and entertainment and frequently accompanied Barker, who'd often pick up the CEO's expenses. "Ed likes the better things in life," Barker told Martinsen before his departure. "He knows that to keep good people, you've got to take care of them." Perhaps family members raised a larger issue: Just who was running the company? The argument that Barker was in charge and Ed was not might have stirred the Schwinn chief's ego and prompted him to make a dramatic gesture to regain control. As with Al Fritz, the image of a non-Schwinn overseeing things may have been intolerable to Ed and other family members.

When Schwinn's executive committee was notified formally of Barker's exit, its members also learned of a promotion. Thirty-five-year-old Richard—"through a miracle of nepotism," the younger brother quipped to the group—was being elevated to vice president in charge of domestic manufacturing operations, and later would assume responsibility for engineering and product development. His primary task: turning Greenville around.

Some of the managers were astounded by Richard's elevation. "He had never run a hot dog stand," Bevil Hogg says. So, too, were major dealers. "That was a big boo-boo," observes John Graves, president of the Bike Line retail chain. Although most observers found him friendlier than his often-detached brother, Richard was too ethereal, too intellectual, for many bike people's tastes. He was known to go off on tangents, saying in 15 minutes what could be said in three. Imagine William F. Buckley, Jr., running a factory floor, is the way one former employee puts it. "Richard seemed to love to hear himself talk," Graves adds. "He talked a different language than me—theorizing, idealistic-type talking." Still, he knew how a bike was made. Veteran employees remember the high school–age Richard working in the Chicago factory far more than Ed had. His first job was sweeping floors, and he later labored on the assembly line and learned to braze Paramounts. Like Ed, Richard was educated at the University of Denver, where he received degrees in psychology and economics and an MBA. He worked at Schwinn during college breaks in the '70s as a part-time management trainee and finally joined the family fold in 1986, following a stint at a Colorado software company. With his collar-length hair and casual attire, he was quickly branded a hippie by old-timers.

Richard's new responsibility for Greenville added another dimension to the company's problems: the blood connection inevitably softened the hard decisions every business has to face, making even tough managers timid in their recommendations. "To attack Greenville looked like you were attacking Richard," says a former Schwinn insider. "It became emotional."

Such is life at a family company, at least at this family company. Richard was fortunate enough to have been born on the favored branch of the tree. As vice president, he would earn $135,000 a year and become one of two family trustees on a three-man oversight board. (The other trustees were Ed and First Chicago banker James Kiel.) Yet the Ignaz Schwinn Trust, governed by primogeniture, was stifling the company seventy years after its formation. Perhaps most damaging was the absolute power of the trustees. Other beneficiaries had no formal say in business matters, and there was no real outside check and balance on management, no fresh air. Only a majority of the trustees could oust the president—highly improbable, in this case.

Ed should have been dismissed, his cousins and aunts would argue later, but that is debatable. For all of Ed's management failings, he towered as CEO material over many of the other thirteen beneficiaries of the trust. And Ed had much at stake as the helmsman. Despite his executive status, he was a minor beneficiary of the trust, with an ownership stake of about 3.4 percent, compared with the nearly 18.3 percent stakes owned by his aunts, Betty Dembecki and Shirley "Pepper" White.[2] Ed's greatest financial attachment to the company actually was his positions as president and trustee and his $250,000 annual salary. "Ed didn't have anything if he didn't have the company," contends Jeff Marwil, an attorney for unsecured creditors during the bankruptcy.

Some beneficiaries may have been at peace with their powerlessness, but many more were dissatisfied. If they were going to be boxed out of decision-making, they still should be provided for properly—as their parents and grandparents had been. It was a birthright.

Schwinn, however, was not as flush as it had been in Brownie's era. Like Cousin Ed, Brownie's six children grew up knowing they'd have dividends waiting for them when they became adults. They certainly could have afforded college, but, unlike Ed or Richard, most didn't earn degrees. Few, if any, formally trained themselves to win influential positions at Schwinn—or elsewhere, if the company should leave family hands. "The kids had that attitude—'I'm a Schwinn,'" says Stan Natanek, former head of the service school. Some cousins resented Ed, with his quarter-million-dollar salary and world travels, but Ed tried to help, sending cousins to job counselors and encouraging them to go to school. There also were perks for shareholders, such as company-paid medical insurance. Schwinn picked up lease payments for a year on Betty Dembecki's Cadillac, and eight of the trust beneficiaries and spouses held jobs at the company during its latter years, ranging from Richard to Brownie's daughter, Barbie Schwinn Jacobs, who earned $28,080 a year as a receptionist. Brad Bailey, the husband of her half sister, Deborah Schwinn Bailey, was a longtime salesman in the South, while Betty Dembecki's husband, Stan, sold fitness equipment to schools and hospitals. Executives estimate that corporate perks to family members, excluding jobs and salaries, cost some $250,000 a year. "These are the kinds of things that go on in a family-owned business," says Bill Chambers, former manager of dealer relations.

Brownie's oldest son, Ignaz Schwinn III, also known as Ricky, admired his father and coveted his legendary job of glad-handing and living the high life on the road. He did handle public relations–type functions for a time, presenting a bicycle to Chicago Mayor Michael Bilandic in the late '70s, for instance, and appearing on *The Bozo Show*, a local televsion program for children, to discuss bicycle safety in 1983. But Brownie's position had died with Brownie. "Ricky was a nice kid—friendly—but he couldn't settle down," says former national sales manager Jack Smith. "They put him in a department and he'd take off for a week or two." In 1988, at age forty-two, Ricky was convicted of driving under the influence in Chicago's suburban DuPage County, sentenced to a year's probation and ordered to attend alcohol counseling. He withdrew from the industry and has spent recent years at the family's Wyoming ranch.

Brownie's youngest son, Thomas Schwinn, was convicted of a similar charge in 1991, at age thirty, and was sent to counseling. Nevertheless, Tom was viewed by many at Schwinn as more down-to-earth and pragmatic than Ricky. As a teenager, he was the victim of a freak accident—witnessing a car accident, he became entangled in a high-tension wire.

Tom lost a leg and a portion of his sight and was scarred severely. He worked for years in customer service and quality control at Schwinn's Midwest distribution center, where he was considered dependable and hardworking.

Robert Schwinn fell somewhere between his brothers—more demanding than Tom, more willing than Ricky to put in the hours needed to assume his rightful place. Bob had worked in the Chicago factory on production and time-study duties, and many colleagues considered him to be bright, someone who'd offer ideas to anyone who'd listen. Still, he was frustrated, believing he had paid his dues. Why couldn't he get ahead at headquarters?

Mississippi offered him an opportunity. Bob volunteered for duty at Greenville, where he served a seven-year stint as an engineer overseeing quality control. Few employees shined through the uncontrollable mess that was Greenville. Bob was recalled to Chicago in 1989—he wasn't getting along with the newest general manager in Mississippi—but things weren't any better up north. Ed didn't offer the expected headquarters position and Bob, according to his former wife, Rychie, took to spending long evenings at the bar in the suburban hotel that was his family's temporary home. "The bartender would call me, 'Come and get him,' " she says. Rychie pleaded with Ed to find her husband a post at Schwinn. The president subsequently assigned his cousin to Schwinn's first company-owned store, but Bob was again disappointed when Ed hired someone else to manage it. Later, Bob handled a computer project for Brian Fiala in human resources. Soon he would become one of the most outspoken of Ed's disgruntled cousins. "He stuck his nose into things," Rychie says. Like his father, Bob had a tempestuous marriage. At one early juncture, he filed for divorce, charging Rychie with "abusive and humiliating treatment," although the pair reconciled. By 1992, the year of the Schwinn bankruptcy, their seventeen-year marriage was again unraveling. In August, Rychie won a court order barring Robert from "harassing" her and their two children. She had complained of abuse: one argument, she alleged, culminated when "Robert grabbed me and threw me, headfirst into the side of the car. . . . My mother took pictures of my bruises." Rychie repeatedly filed complaints large and small charging that Bob had violated the order, citing threats such as "you will pay dearly and be very sorry," and twice Bob was found guilty of violating the order. The couple finally divorced in early 1994.[3]

Bob and his siblings were either too mired in personal problems to really rock the boat at Schwinn or they were too timid. They had few tools at their disposal for forcing change, although they might have made more noise, lobbying the trustees or threatening legal action. In 1989, however, things didn't look so bad. The shareholders sat tight and hoped that the financial picture would improve.

Unfortunately, it did not. Barker's departure had left a power vacuum, and top managers broke into factions, each competing for Ed's attention.

On one side was Jay Townley, perhaps the strongest personality remaining. Townley had been close to Barker and shared in his global orientation and his belief that Schwinn should buy equity in its suppliers. He also had excellent relations with Schwinn's Asian vendors. As vice president of materials management, Townley headed purchasing and developed his department into a force that some former executives complain was too bureaucratic. There was a rule, for example, that product managers couldn't call or visit a supplier without the involvement of a counterpart from purchasing. Trips to negotiate with Asian vendors required an entourage, including managers from marketing, purchasing, engineering, and finance. "They'd all tag along and spend tons of money," says Sargeant of Frontline. While some companies are considered marketing-driven or technology-driven, Schwinn now had become purchasing-driven.

On the other side was the quieter Gerard O'Keefe, who, along with his right-hand man Byron Smith and some in the finance department, believed that Schwinn was stretched and ready to snap. O'Keefe and Smith didn't see the need to buy equity in manufacturers. Just buy intelligently, they suggested, and use the available funds where they were needed most—at this point, Greenville. "It was always contentious," former product manager Chuck Gillis says of the politics. "A lot of finger-pointing. There was no one at the top to pull together a team."

In California, Bevil Hogg and Tom French suspected Chicago was in chaos. "Once John Barker left, the lights were on, but there was nobody at home," Hogg says. With Barker gone, there suddenly was little enthusiasm at Schwinn for Hogg's carbon-fiber technology, especially considering the company's many mounting problems. "We acted as caretakers."

Many of the managers remaining at headquarters mourned the loss of Barker, who had acted as a filter between them and the boss, talking their talk, yet keeping Ed at a proper distance from the troops. Expensive wines and hotel rooms, some mused, were a small price to pay for a semblance of organization.

The first casualty of the post-Barker era was thirty-eight-year-old controller Don Gilliard. His recent number-crunching had revealed a troubling trend he thought Ed ought to understand: the Air-Dyne cash cow was masking the ills of the bike business. Other executives had tried to suggest the same thing in the past, but Gilliard had prepared a thorough analysis showing that, although Schwinn was in the black, it actually was losing money on its bikes.

Gilliard fought too hard on that and other strategic issues when nearly a dozen senior staff members began a three-day brainstorming retreat at the Chicago Club on a Monday in June, just two months after Barker's exit. The group checked in around 4:00 P.M. Some played squash and others relaxed before all settled down to a leisurely dinner in the 1871 Room, an enclave bedecked with newspaper clippings and memorabilia from the Great Chicago Fire. The group met all day Tuesday in a conference room at the club. Barker had always done the talking at gatherings like these, but now it was Gilliard who assumed the lead. He began by noting that bike sales during the first half of the year were disappointing because of bad spring weather. Then there were all those trouble spots: Greenville, Kestrel, Csepel. The committee agreed that Frontline should be closed. The big picture was equally gloomy. How long could Air-Dyne prop up the bike business? It was not a new tune; Gilliard simply sang it louder, with bleaker financial projections if current trends continued.

Ed seemed mostly interested in how Schwinn could shore up 1989 results; he clearly was cold to the discussion about long-term prospects.

Ed left the room as the conversation continued. "Why isn't he here to hear this?" Martinsen wondered. "This is music he doesn't want to hear, so he leaves."

On Wednesday morning, the group revisited several of the troubling issues. Again, Ed exited the room, this time beckoning Richard, human resources head Brian Fiala, and chief financial officer Mike McNamara. "I'm not comfortable with Gilliard," he told them.

Ed returned to the conference room at 11:30. "Guys," he announced, "this is not going in the direction that I wanted it to. We'll have lunch and head back. We'll pick this thing up at a later date."

The group ate a quiet lunch. Back at headquarters, junior managers were surprised to see the big shots' cars pulling into the parking lot a day earlier than expected. "What's the deal?" muttered purchasing manager Mark Marusarz.

Gilliard was asked to resign a week later. His colleagues concluded the obvious—their chief executive did not want to hear bad news.

Today, the former controller says he had believed naively that once he outlined his case, Ed, as a rational manager, would see the light. "Individually, the [other executives] agreed with me," Gilliard says. "Collectively, they knew it was not what Ed wanted to hear. I charged into a buzz saw."

Ed later dismissed the incident. "There's only so much room in the boat," he said. It all seemed so capricious: Barker gone in a flash, and now Gilliard, too. Corporations aren't assumed to be democratic, yet Ed didn't handle dissent gracefully. "You had the impression he didn't want an honest answer," observes one veteran dealer. "You could have small talk. But on a serious issue, like Schwinn's prices not being competitive, you couldn't have a conversation on it." He just wasn't interested in the details. The Kestrel founders note that Ed never visited their factory, and, unlike Grandfather F.W., Ed wasn't known for dropping in on dealers and picking their brains. "I'd be amazed if Ed walked into more than ten stores," says Byron Smith, who once had to convince the CEO to travel with him to Denver to examine a market where Schwinn was lagging. While Ed fancied himself a behind-the-scenes strategist and manipulator, he fell short on that score, too. He wasn't deft at anticipating opponents' moves or closing all the loopholes—as he showed in his dealings with China Bicycles. He also was bored easily: During meetings, Ed was known to pace, stare out a window, or simply leave. On sunny summer afternoons, often he was gone by three or four o'clock. In Hong Kong, he'd gladly escape a parley and bolt for the hotel swimming pool. "Ed was happy distracting himself," says Bevil Hogg. Some found it hard to engage him in real business talk. "He would turn the conversation off the salient issue, and talk about another topic, like boating on Lake Geneva," Smith says. "He would leave things hanging."

Some suggest Ed overcompensated for his shortcomings by alternating between flippancy and forcefulness. Mike Martinsen recalls arriving for his second interview at Schwinn and hearing Ed quip, "Still looking for a job?" Martinsen wasn't sure if Ed was being sly to catch him off guard, or merely nonchalant. "Sarcasm was the norm," he later concluded. Other times, there was bombast. Even if Ed's logic was flawed (such as his premise that Taiwan no longer was competitive, so production should be shifted quickly to China), he was an articulate speaker with a domineering style. "He had a bluff attitude that masked insecurities," observes Arnold Dratt, Schwinn's turnaround specialist after the bankruptcy. Ed found he could deflect anxiety in the ranks by being charming and chatty, smoothing ruffled feathers by dispensing salary hikes and perks. "You came out of a meeting feeling quite good," says a former top executive. Ed often held court at a table in the cafeteria at lunchtime. It made for awkward moments—nobody could walk away with Ed at the table, yukking it up with the boys. "You pretty much had to sit there and laugh," Martinsen recalls. "Finally, he'd be ready to go, and everyone would get up. It would be the last table to leave the cafeteria."

What Ed seemed to enjoy most was the ceremony. He socialized with counterparts from the Chicago Young Presidents' Organization, a collection of local businessmen, most under forty, who ran their own companies. And he was a regular at prestigious Economic Club of Chicago functions, buying a table for eight to ten other Schwinn executives; they'd have drinks at the Chicago Club before walking over to the formal dinner and mingling with the city's capitalist cognoscenti. Like his predecessors, Ed was not one for prominent civic causes (although he was recruited to serve on local hospital boards and once donated nearly fifty Cruisers and other bicycles to the city's Lincoln Park Zoological Gardens). Nonetheless, some observers feel he was obsessed with his role as the public face of the family's company. When Willy Ehrlich worked with Ed alone, the Hungarian-born partner saw "a regular guy, down-to-earth." In a larger group, Ed became pretentious, as though he felt he had to project a "high and mighty" image, Ehrlich says. Adds Stephen Codron of China Bicycles, "He was wrapped up with the image of Schwinn. 'We are Schwinn. We are Number One.' "

Ed indeed bore a heavy burden. Once again, the family business was developing serious problems, yet this time he didn't seem disposed to put in the sweat equity that was needed—nor was he willing to cede authority to a professional who was not a family member. "He just liked being Ed Schwinn," Martinsen says. "An important guy."

20

DOWNHILL, FAST

Not long after Don Gilliard's warnings of vulnerability went unheeded, old nemesis Sears finally flattened Schwinn's Air-Dyne profit cushion. The retailer was selling a similar exerciser for as low as $300—some $400 less than the Air-Dyne. Schwinn's response was a pathetic attempt to sue the manufacturer of the competing product for "willfully and knowingly misappropriat[ing] . . . the configuration and appearance of the Air-Dyne . . . for the sole purpose of trading on the goodwill Schwinn has generated in that appearance, and thereby increasing its profits." U.S. District Judge James B. Moran almost hooted the charges out of court. Schwinn, he ruled, had this particular market to itself for almost a decade and now was "using this suit primarily to parlay its marketing advantage into a product monopoly."

Insecurity reigned at headquarters. "We were naked," says former CFO Mike McNamara, "and someone pulled the sheet down." Schwinn had sold a record 124,000 Air-Dynes in 1989, thanks to a last-quarter push to boost the year's sagging earnings and remain on good terms with the company's lenders. But many of Schwinn's marketers, meeting in

January to plan their 1990 strategies, knew the ride was finished. "Anyone sitting there could see the company was not going to make it in the next three years," says Carl Cohen, the product manager in charge of fitness equipment. Cohen figured the best survival strategy would be to cut the Air-Dyne's price from $700 to $450. Marketing chiefs Gerard O'Keefe and Byron Smith resisted, noting that Schwinn didn't have a high enough volume to compensate for the lower price, and that a retail price of $450 still wouldn't come close to what Sears was advertising. Yet Cohen had become outspoken, even belligerent, on the subject. "You have to control yourself if you expect to last," Richard Schwinn urged him over lunch. Cohen still seethed, thinking, "It's *your* company that's not going to last." An equally worried Mike McNamara urged Cohen to take up the matter directly with Ed. Cohen appealed O'Keefe's decision, but the boss didn't want to hear it. The product manager said farewell several months later, taking a new job in the baby products field. Meantime, Schwinn said goodbye to $8 million in gross profits in 1990, as Air-Dyne sales plunged more than 35 percent to less than 80,000 units.

Cohen followed fellow product managers Bob Read and Bill Corliss, who had recently exited their posts in the company's parts and accessories segments. All three had been close to Bruce Sargeant of Frontline and were discouraged when the Velodyne was abandoned. "That symbolized that the company was not going forward," Cohen explains, "that it was pruning itself down." Another notable departure in 1990 included veteran Jay Townley, who was said to be disillusioned by the course of events, as well as Richard's rise in influence. The vice president of purchasing, legendary for his workaholic habits, resigned after a trip to Asia and moved into consulting. (Today, Townley says "no one thing" pushed him out. "I was taking stock of Schwinn's outlook—the company's culture and direction. I wanted to do something new.") The following year, Brad Hughes, a product manager for bikes (and a Schwinn employee since 1971), defected to competitor Western States. Headhunters, smelling blood, started calling. Throughout 1991 and 1992, "our phones were ringing off the hook," says purchasing manager Mark Marusarz. Most stuck it out, Marusarz strains to explain, because, well, "because it was Schwinn."

As earnings slid in the first quarter of 1990, Schwinn violated a covenant in its lending agreement that set a maximum ratio of debt to net worth. Once again, McNamara was forced to give up the Schwinn trade name as collateral. The family's unwillingness to seek financing through sources other than its banks was coming home to roost. Schwinn could sustain high borrowings as long as business was thriving, but now sales were slow, aggravated by the various snags with its foreign suppliers, and inventories were rising. "The business was thinly capitalized for many years," concedes Ed's brother-in-law and former director of corporate planning, Peter Davis. By the end of 1990, Schwinn would again be in the red, losing $2.9 million. It owed its banks more than $64 million, and its total debt of $80 million was more than three times shareholder equity of $24 million. Moreover, Schwinn had high costs: sales and administrative expenses exceeded 18 percent of revenues, compared with the industry standard of 13 percent. As total 1990 revenues slumped 5 percent to $189.2 million, more than 350 people worked in regional sales and distribution and at corporate headquarters, where the engineering and information services divisions seemed especially bloated. Schwinn's mainframe computer system, for instance, cost $1.2 million a year to maintain.

An anxious lending syndicate, which included Chicago's Harris Bank and LaSalle National Bank, New York's Chemical Bank, and Detroit's NBD Bank, demanded to know what Ed was up to. At first, the exchanges were low-key, but as the problems worsened, the bankers insisted on learning more about Csepel, China Bicycles, Greenville, Cycle Composites, and what was happening to sales and market share. Schwinn's skirmishes with its lenders soon escalated into battles—a nasty little war in which each general loathed the other side.

In 1990, Schwinn invited its bankers to a meeting at headquarters. Ed sat in the back of the room, yakking with underlings and ignoring the visitors to whom he owed more money than his company technically was worth. "The guys from the banks were looking at him in disbelief," McNamara recalls. Art Littlefield, a first vice president for NDB Bank, appeared particularly irked. By mid-1991, his institution was the first to send the Schwinn loan to its workout department—"The Roach Motel," as Schwinn's bankruptcy workout specialist, Arnold Dratt, describes it. "You go in, but you don't come out." Workout was a dark and unwelcome new world, where cheerless officers don't take the client to ball games or lunch. Their unstated assignment—squeeze repayments from the offending customer and reduce the bank's exposure as quickly as possible. "They all had the same job—get the money out," says Schwinn's bankruptcy attorney, Dennis O'Dea. "Nothing personal."

O'Dea had helped Ed navigate his first financial crisis a decade earlier and now the lawyer was back at Schwinn. In the interim, the brash O'Dea had gained legal stardom by helping end an epic oil patch feud between Texaco and challenger Pennzoil. Texaco had filed for bankruptcy protection in 1987, after a Texas jury slapped it with an eye-popping $10.5 billion judgment for thwarting Pennzoil's planned acquisition of Getty Oil. O'Dea represented Texaco shareholders frustrated by management's intransigence (including famed corporate raider Carl Icahn) and went over the executives' heads to negotiate directly with Pennzoil and hammer out a $3 billion settlement. The episode earned O'Dea a reputation as an aggressive and confrontational lawyer—traits he'd exhibit frequently during the Schwinn bankruptcy. O'Dea preached defiance to Ed and top managers: "They're out to get you," he counseled. "If you give them this, they'll ask for that." Unlike multibillion-dollar Texaco, however, Schwinn had little leverage. It was embattled and, increasingly, without friends, as other members of the banking syndicate rerouted the Schwinn loans to their own Roach Motels.

The workout process had a life of its own. Each time Schwinn violated a covenant—by performing below expectations in a particular quarter, for instance—the banks would tighten the noose, demanding swifter payment of the loan, a lower credit line, or a higher interest rate. There was no give, only take. "It's one-way," McNamara says. "The main focus is to reduce the bank's exposure and grind it down any way they can." (O'Dea talked resistance, but whenever the inevitable unpleasant concession had to be made tended to disassociate himself from the others at Schwinn. "You're the guys doing it, not me," McNamara recalls him saying.) The banks chose their words carefully and moved cautiously, lest they be accused of provoking a financial crisis and expose themselves to a lender liability lawsuit. Nonetheless, they increased the pressure. In the summer of 1991, the banks suggested Schwinn hire a workout specialist, then engaged their own consultant, Mike Silverman, and lobbied Schwinn to seek outside equity. Ed remained noncommittal. He didn't appear concerned—one bank executive was surprised to see Ed arrive for a session wearing sneakers—and sometimes didn't appear at all. McNamara remembers Chemical and NBD flying in their executives for a 2:00 P.M. meeting at Schwinn, only to be told by Ed's secretary that he had left for the day. Such actions made McNamara nervous. The former staff accountant at Peat Marwick had joined Schwinn in 1966 and risen through the ranks of the finance department before being named CFO upon John Barker's ouster. Yet he was a stark contrast to his former boss. McNamara was mild-mannered, an accommodating accountant who wasn't comfortable with conflict and wanted to stand behind the numbers. Where Barker wouldn't have cared what the bank executives thought, McNamara preferred to smooth things over between the company and the lenders whenever possible. However, frustrations soon boiled. "We're not afraid of a Schwinn bankruptcy," Patrick McDonnell, Harris Bank's officer on the credit, told McNamara. Schwinn no longer had access to McDonnell's superiors at Harris or its parent company, Bank of Montreal, for appeals. Still, Ed's advisers concluded that any decision on Schwinn's fate would have to be made at the bank's highest level, because Harris had the power to push an American icon over the cliff.

Throughout 1990 and 1991, others in the bike industry suspected something was wrong at Schwinn. The dealer exodus swelled, and Trek moved swiftly from the No. 4 brand in the independent market to No. 3 then No. 2, by capitalizing on Schwinn's shortages of bikes and parts. "By 1990," recalls Trek sales manager Harry Spehar, "Trek realized that if we continued to improve, we would have staying power. It wouldn't be a flash." In the Chicago suburb of Crystal Lake, the economy was slowing and sales were ebbing for Schwinn dealer Jeff Crittenden. Customers were asking for other lines. Crittenden added Specialized in 1990, then

Diamond Back. He had turned down Trek during the booming 1980s, but in 1991 sought the line. Too late: Trek already had opened another shop nearby.

Many dealers, angry over late shipments, couldn't get answers from Schwinn. Eight customers at two of Kestrel seller Ron Boi's stores had put down deposits for the $3,500 carbon-fiber bikes before Christmas 1990. It now was April 1991, but whenever Boi called headquarters, there was another excuse. "The mold broke," he mimics, "or the paint booth fell over." Boi's wife offered a solution to the mystery: the framesets were sitting in a Mitsui warehouse in California until Schwinn paid the Japanese shipper for its services.

Boi telephoned Richard Schwinn, whom he had befriended after recently opening a Schwinn dealership in the family's weekend haunt of Lake Geneva. "I want my Kestrels released out of California," Boi told him. "I just talked to my bank—they'll work [the financing] with me."

Richard pleaded ignorance: "I don't know anything. I'll get back to you."

Next, Boi called a Kestrel salesman. Bluffing, he said he had seen U.S. Customs documents that showed the bikes had arrived in the United States and were in a warehouse.

The salesman choked up. "It's true, but don't tell anyone," he pleaded. "I'll lose my job."

Boi phoned Richard the following day.

"They're missing hubs from Shimano," Richard told him.

"I got hubs," Boi answered.

"Maybe a few other pieces are missing, too," Richard said.

"Just ship me the frames!" Boi screamed.

The Kestrel operation, in truth, was in disarray. The only company left to pick up the pieces was Mitsui, which had continued to hold its minority position in the venture. With Schwinn unable to fund the high-tech project, Mitsui converted Schwinn's Kestrel debt to its own equity, turning Mitsui into the majority owner of Kestrel. Citing financial burdens, Schwinn and Mitsui also asked Kestrel founders Bevil Hogg and Tom French to defer payment of their final installment on the original buyout—around $300,000—due at the end of 1991. Wait one more year,

Schwinn and Mitsui pleaded. "Like a bunch of dunces, we said yes," Hogg rues. Soon, he would be forced to conclude another mistake: his carbon fiber vision for bicycles had been flawed. The super-lightweight material lent itself to road races and triathlons, but those sports had been eclipsed by mountain biking. Carbon fiber, at the time, could not survive a downhill assault. Only in the years after Hogg left the industry did manufacturers make the material strong enough for mountain bike use.

Financial troubles also battered the Waterford, Wisconsin, frame shop where Schwinn produced Paramounts. Builders were running out of the special oversized tubing they needed to make the handcrafted models, and they couldn't get a straight answer from the purchasing department in Chicago. "We were pulling the last run off the shelves," says former frame builder Dennis Kilfoy. "We were a week away from being dry." A Paramount employee decided to call the Ohio-based fabricator directly. "The damn tubes are sitting on the loading dock," was the answer. "Where's the check?"

That spring, headquarters was involved in a massive juggling act. Whom to pay next? Giant or China Bicycles for their finished bikes? Other suppliers for replacement parts? What about components for Greenville? Parts for the Mississippi operation were stuck in a Memphis warehouse. Mitsui would release the inventory only after it was paid. Schwinn cherry-picked the pieces it needed most. Over the Fourth of July weekend, Mark Marusarz was preparing for a trip to Japan to expedite a shipment of parts for Greenville when he received a call from Nai-Wen Kiang, who now was Schwinn's head of purchasing, as well as its director of Asian operations. "Don't bother," Kiang told Marusarz. "Greenville is going to be closed."

Under pressure from the banks, Ed finally pulled the trigger. Richard had the unenviable task of breaking the news to some 240 Greenville employees as they returned from a scheduled two-week summer shutdown. The factory would be closed within 60 days. "It was the best job I ever had," fifty-seven-year-old Janie W. Johnson, who worked in personnel, told the *Los Angeles Times* that September. "I felt that the floor was swept out from under me."

And so ended Schwinn's near-hundred-year legacy of making bicycles in the United States. The only remaining domestic production was the tiny Paramount machine shop in Waterford, with a staff of a dozen. The company had an "emotional attachment to manufacturing," Richard explained to the *Chicago Tribune*, but Richard's heart wasn't enough to make up for the years of poor management and corporate neglect of Greenville. He did grow a beard, telling colleagues, "I'm grieving" for the doomed factory.

Marusarz was charged with closing the plant. He packed up containers of parts and shipped them to Giant or China Bicycles, which picked up the Greenville models. He sold the rest for scrap, including all those mismatched forks that never could be cut to the proper size. Yet shutting off the lights didn't end the curse of Greenville. The closing of the old Chicago plant nearly ten years earlier had obliterated Schwinn's equity, but the company gradually had rescued its balance sheet. Now, by closing Greenville and taking various accounting charges, Schwinn's net worth of $23.8 million was virtually wiped out, and there were still mortgage payments to be made: more than $15,000 a month to the Ignaz Schwinn Trust that had guaranteed the bond issues. When Schwinn filed for bankruptcy protection, it left the Schwinn Trust—the family—holding the bag.

21

A SERIES OF AGGRAVATIONS

Ralph Day Murray was at home in Minneapolis, preparing to move to his new job in Chicago as vice president of marketing and sales at Schwinn, when Ed telephoned before Labor Day in 1991 and invited him down to Lake Geneva. Over drinks on the patio of Ed's weekend home, Murray shared some of the strategies and procedures he had learned during his seventeen years at lawnmower maker Toro Company. He also raised concerns about Schwinn's corporate hierarchy. Crucial departments, like purchasing and product development, were isolated, and that stifled teamwork.

"You're right," Ed said. "I'd like to make you chief operating officer."

Murray was pleased, but puzzled. "It was odd," he recalls, "to be given a promotion before you start."

He was forty-six and a bright professional—senior vice president at Toro—yet Murray's promotion wasn't simply a matter of his insights dazzling an impressionable Ed. In reality, Schwinn's banks were breathing down the top executive's neck; perhaps Ed could appease them by bringing in a chief operating officer to help him oversee a turnaround.

Murray would witness many odd moments between that Labor Day weekend and Schwinn's bankruptcy filing thirteen months later. In fact, the new COO turned to keeping a diary to help him make sense of the unfolding crises. Murray knew going in that Schwinn wasn't profitable, but he figured, "What consumer products company hasn't lost money?" He soon learned that Schwinn's difficulties were anything but routine. Drafted to prepare a cost-cutting plan for a September 18 bank meeting, Murray was alarmed by the animosity between the new boss and the lenders. "There was bad karma," he says. "You could see it. Ed didn't hide it." By November, the truth was clear. "This company is in worse shape than I thought," he told Ed. "Maybe you didn't know. I won't sell my house [in Minneapolis]; you keep paying for my apartment here, and I won't bitch."

Other people were complaining, however. Bowing to pressure from family members, in October Ed added three relatives to Schwinn's advisory board: brother-in-law Peter Davis, aunt Betty Dembecki, and cousin Deborah Bailey. They joined Bruce Chelberg, chief executive of Chicago's Whitman Corporation, and two other outside business experts recently recruited to the board: Peter Guglielmi, president of Tellabs International, in suburban Lisle, and John Ward, a small business consultant and professor at Loyola University of Chicago. The three had no governing authority; they were advisers only—professional wise men who could do little to steer the company, other than use their powers of persuasion. The same was true for the board's new family members, thanks to the restrictive bylaws of the original Ignaz Schwinn Trust. It had been an agreeable enough arrangement over the years; by the 1980s, the trust's fourteen beneficiaries had been receiving $800,000 to $1.2 million in total dividends annually for nearly a generation, according to several sources with knowledge of the company's financial history. The payments stopped during the early-1980s flirtation with bankruptcy, but dividends resumed in 1987, though they were smaller than in the past, totaling just $1.5 million over the next four years. The well was running dry: beneficiaries shared a final $125,000 in 1990 and received nothing the following year.

The resentments erupted during a late summer family meeting at headquarters where Ed acknowledged Schwinn's dismal prospects. "How could this happen?" his cousins and aunts demanded. "Why didn't you tell us sooner?" They had been planning a Hawaiian celebration for Schwinn's centennial in four years; now Ed was impassively presenting less sunny options: Should the company sell bikes to mass merchants such as Sears? Sell part of Schwinn? Sell stock to the public? According to Rychie Schwinn, family members worried that Ed, as the chief executive controlling such a stock offering, might have the opportunity to acquire more shares and increase his ownership stake at their expense.

Horrified by Schwinn's sudden downturn, Betty Dembecki and Deborah Bailey became more outspoken that fall, often calling Murray and other senior executives for financial information and complaining that Ed hadn't been forthcoming. "Debbie had a lot to say," recalls former CFO Mike McNamara. "She railed at Ed that he mismanaged." Dembecki's husband, Stan, was wistful. Standing by Ralph Murray's desk one day, he remarked, "We used to get a quarter-million dollars a year in the 1960s." But the shareholders could only watch that fall as Ed, under further pressure from the banks, hired Continental Partners Group, the investment banking arm of Chicago's Continental Bank Corporation, to help find an equity infusion for Schwinn. By the following March, family members would be asked to sign waivers that ended their rights of first refusal in any sale. Murray had the unpleasant task of explaining the details to the angry shareholders during a daylong meeting at Chicago's Knickerbocker Hotel. (Ed had called in sick that morning.) "There was some yelling," Murray recalls, although "not as bad as it could have been." Brownie's middle son, Robert Schwinn, strongly opposed the idea. He simmered with rage at Ed, whom he felt hadn't given him his due. Robert suggested that *he* might lead a bid for the company. Murray was surprised—representatives of Continental Partners were shocked. "You'll bring down the family," a panicked relative cried, begging Robert to sign the waiver. "This is our one chance for survival." Ed tried to enlist Rychie's help: "Robert could be sued," he warned. Most family members acquiesced over the next few weeks. Robert was the last holdout, finally signing the document in May, not long after being rehired at headquarters.

Ed had overtures from outside investors in the past, but had never taken them seriously. Several years earlier, he had discussed a sale with Mort and Edward Finkelstein, two brothers in their early fifties who had sold their regional retail chain, MC Sporting Goods of Grand Rapids, Michigan, and were flush with cash. The two sides talked, on and off, for more than six months. The Finkelsteins proposed acquiring control, with the Schwinn family retaining a minority stake. The name had great potential, the brothers reasoned, and annual sales could be pumped by taking the mass-merchant route, while Ed Schwinn could handle public relations. "A super nice guy," Edward Finkelstein says. "He would have made a good spokesman." The Schwinn chief acknowledged his company was troubled, but wasn't prepared to admit defeat. "The biggest problem was giving up family control," Finkelstein says.

(Apparently, not all family members knew about the proposal. Mike Martinsen, head of international business development, mentioned the Finkelstein offer to Stan Dembecki during an industry trade show in September 1992, when the company's finances were far bleaker. "Too bad the family is in this situation," Martinsen said, describing what he and other managers had understood to be a $115 million offer. "I saw Stan's jaw drop.")

The question of control would repeat itself to the excruciating end. Continental Partners attempted to find Schwinn a junior partner, but no outsider was going to sink money into such a troubled enterprise without gaining authority over the operation. "They were trying to sell a minority stake at a time when you ought to be running for the lifeboats," scoffs Schwinn's bankruptcy attorney, Dennis O'Dea, who contemptuously viewed the Continental investment bankers as innocents. The Continental team had no fondness for the confrontational O'Dea, either. They were a young unit of an old bank that had been among the nation's largest financial institutions—until the federal government bailed out the bank in the early 1980s, after multibillion-dollar loans in Texas and Oklahoma went sour. A humbled Continental had launched its investment banking operation in 1990 by recruiting Michael A. Smith, the managing director of Bear Stearns & Company's Chicago office and a man with a homespun approach that played well at middle-market companies in the Midwest. Crafting an equity deal for a household name like Schwinn would help put Continental Partners on the map.

Although Ed clearly preferred marketing a minority stake, he didn't formally rule out the alternative of selling the company. Ed and Richard even prepared for that possibility by drafting golden parachute agreements that would cost a potential buyer nearly $1 million to oust the brothers. (The brothers would redraft the parachute on the eve of the bankruptcy, an exercise creditors found particularly galling.) Still, it's difficult to know if Ed ever seriously meant to sell any part of Schwinn—suitors would come and go.

At the start, Continental Partners had no trouble identifying potential mates: Michael Smith and colleague Barry Craig presented Ed with a list of several hundred possible investors or purchasers. The Schwinn chief, however, seemed determined to control the process, crossing out the names of competitors or prospects he considered nosy or those he just didn't like. Ed also limited communication between Continental and the lending group, which didn't know who the investment bankers were contacting and how Schwinn was being marketed. But perhaps Continental's biggest problem was that, from the start, Schwinn's numbers were tumbling, sometimes by dramatic amounts. Potential buyers found it difficult to calculate a value. The company was a moving target.

One of the most promising early investors was Virginia entrepreneur William H. Goodwin, who had purchased some of the broken assets of sporting goods giant AMF in the wake of a corporate raid and moved them to his hometown of Richmond. The secretive Goodwin, worth an estimated $250 million, had amassed an empire that included companies making equipment for bowling, golfing, boating, and billiards, and was always looking for brands to acquire. He flew to Chicago to meet Ed.

"What will it take to do a deal?" Goodwin asked.

Ed drew a blank. "What do you mean?" He wasn't looking for a buyer, just an investor.

"Come on, Ed. With this financial picture? You're not serious." Goodwin rose from the table. "If you figure this out, give me a call."

(Goodwin today says he arrived virtually with checkbook in hand. "I would have bought the business.")

Ralph Murray suggested his boss develop more cohesive responses for potential suitors. Perhaps a minority sale wasn't realistic, he prodded.

In the spring of 1992, Schwinn received an overture from a venture capital unit of the New York investment banking firm Donaldson Lufkin & Jenrette. The chemistry with Donaldson Lufkin seemed good, at first.

"What if they make you an offer?" Murray asked Ed on the way to a Chicago Club dinner on March 31.

"I never thought of that," Ed responded.

"Take it," Murray urged.

The two met with the Continental team and Jim Milligan, a consultant to and investment partner with Donaldson Lufkin, at one of Ed's favorite spots, the 1871 Room, with its Great Chicago Fire theme. Sure enough, during the meal, Milligan leaned over to Ed. "We have an erection for this company, but we can't keep it up forever. What will it take?"

On the way home, Ed confided to Murray that he was uneasy at the prospect of working for someone as hard-driving as Milligan. After all, he never really had a boss. Could he adapt?

"You'll have the biggest culture shock of anyone," Murray said.

Donaldson Lufkin proposed a $90 million deal that would acquire between 85 and 90 percent of Schwinn. Most of the money actually was assumption of debt, but the price also included $25 million in cash to reduce debt and serve as working capital. The family would keep the old Schwinn's 18 percent share of China Bicycles (worth at least $15 million, according to Continental Partners) and retain a 10 to 15 percent stake in the healthier new Schwinn.

Ed was not impressed. "They wanted too much," was his cursory answer to Murray. An even bigger stumbling block would have been Donaldson Lufkin's request that Schwinn's lending group take a "haircut," or a discount, on its loan in return for an immediate, guaranteed partial payment. The proposal was never formally presented to the bank group; instead, Ed cast his lot with a competing suitor that offered a potentially sweeter package for the family. Acadia/Bain, a New York partnership affiliated with Texas investor Robert Bass, offered a complex package that would allow the family to pocket $10 million to $15 million in exchange for 50 to 80 percent of the company. The Schwinn family also would keep 75 percent of the shares in China Bicycles, while the new Schwinn company would hold the balance of the stake. Schwinn signed Acadia to a three-month exclusive bargaining period at a July 18 meeting at the Chicago Club. (Even after he signed, Ed still hoped for something better, Murray says. "He was always looking for the next thing over the horizon that was going to save him.") The same day, Acadia presented its plan to Schwinn's bankers and asked them to make a "contribution" (albeit a less severe hit than Donaldson Lufkin would have sought). The lenders were unsympathetic. They were confident of recovering their loan in full. In fact, they already were.

During the first nine months of 1992, the banks quietly swept cash from Schwinn's revolving credit line. As money came in, it was snatched by the banks as payment for their loans. The action cut their exposure in half, to about $32.5 million, but it forced Schwinn to run up nearly $30 million in debt with suppliers China Bicycles and Giant. Faced with Acadia's request for concessions, the banks tightened their grip, reducing Schwinn's credit line by $6 million during the next 30 days. That all but ensured Schwinn would enter bankruptcy. "It was like being on a runaway train," says attorney O'Dea. "It was horrific."

Although the lending syndicate dismissed talk of a haircut, some thought Continental Partners might have been able to at least explore the possibility if Schwinn had maintained better relations with its banks. Others, such as O'Dea, argue that the bottom-fishers at Acadia were trying to provoke the lenders and force a crisis that could result in an even lower price down the road. The bigger damper, however, was Schwinn's disclosure—just days after signing with Acadia—of its burgeoning debt to its Asian suppliers. The company's finances were eroding faster than anyone had realized.

Schwinn had recorded a net loss of $23.3 million in 1991, largely reflecting the shutdown of Greenville. Although it broke even for the first half of 1992, it lost $1 million in July, then another $2 million in August. As the business deteriorated, so did the prospective selling price that Acadia, or any buyer, would pay. Mike Smith and his Continental Partners were furious. Ed had an agenda other than a sale, they concluded, because potential deals had been torpedoed at every turn. Now, with the value of the company withering daily, Ed had even less incentive to sell and more reason to wait for a miracle.

By late August, Acadia's ardor had cooled. The New York firm withdrew, citing the banks' unwillingness to make concessions as well as an "ongoing deterioration of the business of the company." Like the Finkelstein brothers earlier, and the Donaldson Lufkin venture several months before, Acadia would have relegated Ed to a ceremonial position—a role that might have suited him well, although Ed did not want a title that stripped him of real power.

At the same time, Schwinn's bank group suggested in a letter that Ed step aside as chief executive, according to sources who say they read the document. The lenders had long since lost confidence in Ed, but that didn't mean they had lost confidence in Schwinn. Murray and other members of the executive committee understood the message: the banks would consider refinancing Schwinn if it were placed under new management, but they wouldn't allow the company to survive until there was a change at the top. "The banks wanted his head," says Peter Davis. "They would have been happy to put it on a stick and parade it down La Salle Street."

Ed kept his counsel. He was tight-lipped with bankers, and didn't say much to dealers, or even the corporate staff. Calls for his resignation only produced indignation. "If I thought that was the solution, I'd do it," he once told Murray. Another time Ed said, "I'll do it before I let this company go down the tubes."

Nevertheless, Schwinn employees and advisers had concluded that Ed's need for control was paramount. He had gone along with the search for buyers, when in reality, it seemed he didn't want a deal at all. To hand over the family's company to a non-Schwinn was more than he could bear. That, more than anything, would define defeat for Ed. "He never called us in and said, 'This is the big picture,' " Mike McNamara says. "We figured that out ourselves."

Following Acadia's withdrawal, rumors of a Chapter 11 bankruptcy filing swirled through headquarters. Ed tried to squelch such talk. "It's sanity-check time," he insisted to the executive committee. "Chapter 11 has nothing to offer us." Still, the longer Schwinn waited to petition for court protection, the more money its banks would recover and the less Schwinn would have to fund its business. As long as the lending syndicate continued sweeping cash from the revolving loan, both Murray and O'Dea reported to the advisory board on August 26, a bankruptcy filing was inevitable. Outside directors Bruce Chelberg, John Ward, and Peter Guglielmi swiftly resigned, in part, perhaps, to limit their liability in any potential lawsuits by disgruntled family members, but also because there were few, if any, options left for Schwinn. "It was very sad," Peter Davis remembers. The resignations, he adds, reflected the trio's own frustrations. There was nothing they—or anyone—could do. "At this point, we were hitting a wall."

During a financial crisis, a borrower often can look to its suppliers as allies who can ship the goods needed to generate the cash to pay its banks. Giant and China Bicycles were not ordinary suppliers, however; they were rivals of Schwinn in the U.S. market.

The two firms had been shipping on a so-called "open account" that accepted payments after delivery (instead of a stricter system requiring letters of credit, which demand payment before cargoes are released). With the banks grabbing Schwinn's loan repayments whenever cash was deposited, it didn't take long for the Chicago company to run up big debts: $9 million at Giant and $18 million at China Bicycles. More cynical observers hypothesize that Schwinn was being lured into a debt trap by suppliers who must have at least suspected it was having trouble paying bills elsewhere in the industry. But executives of the Asian firms angrily reject that scenario, each saying they were surprised—then incensed—to discover the level of the exposure during the summer of 1992. "What Schwinn . . . has done to Giant is totally unfair," Tony Lo argues. "They mismanaged the company, went bankrupt, and Giant suffered from all this credit [it had extended]." In Hong Kong, an equally peeved Stephen Codron speaks for China Bicycles. "Schwinn let [the banks] take it—our money," Codron says, adding that when Ed asked him and founder Jerome Sze to continue the more liberal payment terms, "he lost absolute respect from this end."

Ed tried to enlist Lo's support when the Giant president visited Chicago that summer. Perhaps Lo would come to his aid, as had happened a year earlier, when Schwinn was short of bikes from an overburdened China Bicycles and Giant stepped in to meet production. This time, Lo hung tough. He would ship bikes that already had been built, but only for cash. As for starting new production? "No," Lo answered. "There is no assurance we will get paid."

Schwinn strained to set up a mechanism that would guarantee payment, but Lo didn't seem interested. He had supported Schwinn many times in years past, but Giant already was taking too big a hit with the $9 million debt. If Lo continued to throw money down a hole, he would lose face. Lo also was becoming skeptical about Schwinn's prospects of resurfacing. Just look at its overhead, Taiwanese managers clucked. Schwinn sold twice as many bikes in the United States as Giant did, but its corporate staff was eight times the size of Giant's efficient U.S. sales arm.

Like Giant, China Bicycles was willing to ship finished bikes as long as payment was secured with a letter of credit, but wasn't inclined to begin any new production for Schwinn. In September, Ed and in-house attorney Daniel Garramone checked into Hong Kong's Regent Hotel prior to talks with Sze. There, they linked up with Nai-Wen Kiang. Perhaps the company's stock in China Bicycles somehow could be used to jump-start the flow of bikes—or serve as the capital to bring about a broader financial restructuring of Schwinn.

"What's the plan?" Kiang asked Garramone.

"We don't know what we're going to do," Garramone said.

Kiang was incredulous. "You flew seven thousand miles and you don't know the plan?"

The next day, Ed met with Sze and his recently recruited executive director—John Barker.

After being fired by Ed some two and a half years earlier, Barker had become chief executive of a California window coverings company. He had stayed in touch with Sze, however, and moved to Hong Kong in February 1992 to work for China Bicycles. Now Barker was in a position to enjoy sweet revenge.

The talks were inconclusive, and Ed headed home. Nevertheless, Sze wanted to explore the possibility of a takeover of Schwinn by his California-based Western States Imports—the competitor that Ed once thought he'd control through China Bicycles before it was acquired independently by Sze in 1990. Sze dispatched Barker and Western States president Michael Bobrick to negotiate a merger. The duo suggested that Schwinn move its operations to Southern California, where the combined company would be run by Bobrick. Ed would receive a chairman emeritus–style title and an annual salary of about $100,000. "Ed was not interested," Bobrick says. "He didn't believe it would happen." Indeed, many Schwinn insiders found the financial details sketchy and a merger with the smaller Western States impractical. "It was like a mouse trying to eat a lion," says ex-CFO McNamara.

The stress and uncertainty were gnawing at employees. In late 1991, McNamara had been hospitalized for nervous exhaustion. "I took things too seriously," he says today. His wife tried to help: "Don't worry so much," she advised. "It's not like you own the company." But McNamara couldn't help but worry. "It seemed like every day was a war," he explains. "Ed wasn't supportive. It was like I was doing it myself." By the time McNamara returned to work, there were new players: the bank's workout departments, Ralph Murray, Continental Partners. "The battle lines were drawn," he says.

The following summer, engineer Rene Mraz traveled to Taiwan to work with Giant on a new exerciser. "Something was strange," Mraz recalls of the difficult discussion. He just couldn't get the job done. At a dinner with Giant engineers and several Schwinn colleagues, Mraz suddenly collapsed, blacking out for almost half a minute. Back in the States, his doctor told him he was merely exhausted and should take it easier, but the Czech-born engineer was discouraged by what he perceived to be a professional failure and considered retiring. Only later did friends at Giant disclose it was Schwinn's unpaid bills that had prevented them from cutting a deal. "We don't have anything against you," they assured him. Mraz wondered why he hadn't been given some kind of warning by headquarters. "It could have saved me a lot of embarrassment."

By June and July, vendors stopped returning the faxes of Schwinn's product managers. "Everything came to a screeching halt," says Chuck Gillis. Rumblings of an impending bankruptcy now were shaking both headquarters and the industry. Surely, a buyout deal was imminent—Schwinn still was such a powerful name—yet no announcement came. Workers were obliged to conduct business as usual. "We were telling things I knew weren't going to happen," Gillis admits. "That containers [of bikes] were on the water. What could I do?"

The marketing department also had to continue the charade as dealers and sales reps from around the country convened at a Schwinn sales meeting at the Abbey resort in Lake Geneva to view the 1993 season's models. Recalls Byron Smith: "My job and Ralph Murray's was to hold the dealers together, to shore up the sales guys, though we were on a precipice. Everyone was worried. Some had worked at Schwinn for thirty years. Would they have a job?" As the salesmen fretted, Ed buoyantly cruised into the hotel's harbor at the helm of his vintage wood racing boat. The grand entrance seemed inappropriate to some—and generated considerable derision among workers. "Could anyone be more out of touch with the feelings of employees?" Smith wondered. Nevertheless, Ed strutted from the dock and struck a confident note throughout the meeting. "You would never believe that Schwinn was in deep, deep, deep doodoo," says Mike Martinson, former director of international business development. The Abbey resort also never suspected the worst—it was stiffed, through Schwinn's Chapter 11 filing, for the event's $120,000 tab.

The sense of unreality continued at a September trade show in Anaheim, California, where the Schwinn booth was the hottest attraction—for about twenty minutes. Movie star Arnold Schwarzenegger was making an appearance as thanks for the company's sponsorship of his body-building contest. Whispers of a pending Schwinn bankruptcy filing had been sweeping the convention hall all morning. Now, here was the Terminator, posing for publicity photos with a grinning Ed. The scene was more than a little surreal to the cheerless Schwinn crew manning the booth. *Hasta la vista, baby.*

Although several passers-by quipped, "Is this a closeout sale?" the general reception for Schwinn's 1993 line on display was the best it had received in years. The bikes had better components, competitive prices, and up-to-date graphics. The new child's Z-bike—a sharp little number with a low, sweeping frame—was being touted as the first new kids' cycle since the BMX. Many dealers were impressed. Maybe Schwinn finally *was* getting its act together. "I was the most excited puppy you'd ever seen," says Joe Russell of Washington, Illinois. Unfortunately, Schwinn had few bikes to ship, since its suppliers were demanding cash before delivery. Dealers were getting restless. "They couldn't fill two-thirds of their parts orders," notes Orange County's Michael Mulrooney. "It didn't take a genius to figure it out." Even the few hundred diehard Schwinn dealers who hadn't yet diversified their lines finally faced the facts: They needed new brands—fast.

George Garner found the realization especially painful. For four decades, he'd been "Mr. Schwinn"—the dealer's dealer, the nation's No. 1 seller for almost twenty years—and he still was a regular on the company's annual top ten list. But the past three seasons had offered little but a series of aggravations. "No matter how much I complained," Garner says, "we just weren't getting enough Schwinns." He was tired of waiting for phone calls to be returned, angry at the stupid mistakes coming out of headquarters, hurt by the chilly receptions from Ed and those MBA hotshots who acted like they knew everything. "Quit being so loyal to Schwinn," old friend Elmer Sorensen told Garner. Sorensen was a long-established Schwinn seller in Minneapolis who had become Trek's charter dealer in the late '70s. For several years, he had urged Garner to broaden his base. Now, in Anaheim, with Schwinn failing to deliver what he needed, Garner pulled aside Sunnyvale, California, dealer Jim Burris and asked for his help in getting an introduction at the Trek booth. Burris shakes his head at the memory. "I had to tell this kid from Trek, 'Don't you know who the hell this is?' " Garner soon hooked up with Trek's national sales manager, Pat Sullivan, who immediately recognized the potential for a coup. Sullivan visited Garner's shops—those pioneer "ultra-modern" cycleries that had sold more than 100,000 Phantoms, Sting-Rays, Varsitys, and latter-day models over the years—and quickly signed up the dean of dealers. Garner's move had the industry buzzing. "I got a lot of phone calls, that this was the last nail in

Schwinn's coffin," Sullivan says. "Mr. Schwinn is now a Trek dealer." Trek soon accounted for 30 percent of Garner's sales, yet he remained queasy about jumping ship. "Schwinn had built me up as a good image," Garner explains. "I felt guilty, because that's what I used to preach—one hundred percent Schwinn. But it was hurting my business."

Schwinn was hurting, too, and the pain was about to prove unbearable. On the morning of October 7, Schwinn's banks swept more cash from the credit line. Suddenly, the company's checks were bouncing. "It was like the shooting of Archduke Ferdinand, the trigger that started World War I," Murray says.

Dennis O'Dea was ready to file for Chapter 11. A court petition would stanch the hemorrhaging, yet Ed was hesitant during a conference call late that afternoon.

"What are my orders?" O'Dea asked Ed.

"There's no alternative," added CFO McNamara, "you've got to file."

Ed's brother, Richard, concurred.

"Ed," O'Dea urged, "are you telling me to file?"

"Yes," Ed replied weakly.

"What?" O'Dea pleaded.

"*Yes.*"

22

THE GREASE FOR A DEAL

In the weeks leading up to the Chapter 11 filing, Ed had reluctantly authorized Continental Partners to open talks with potential buyers he wouldn't have considered earlier. One such suitor was Michael Sinyard's Specialized Bicycle Components. The California mountain bike monster was represented by John Jellinek, a cagey investor from Chicago's North Shore who owned stakes in several bicycle and accessory companies, including helmet maker Bell Sports. Preliminary talks were encouraging. "Sounds promising," Ed said after his debriefing. A delighted Continental arranged a session between Jellinek and representatives of the lending syndicate at Harris Bank on the afternoon of October 7. The Continental group was upbeat when they returned to Schwinn headquarters early that evening.

"This one could bear fruit," one investment banker told Ed.

"You're an hour late," Ed said. "We've just filed for bankruptcy."

The Continental bankers were flabbergasted. Ed had jettisoned his company into bankruptcy without pausing to check whether an eleventh-hour deal could be settled. But Ed's position was in character. Mike

Sinyard was not going to offer him any role of substance; Ed had a better chance of protecting his position in bankruptcy court.

News of Schwinn's Chapter 11 filing precipitated a flood of publicity nationwide, from the *New York Times* and the *Washington Post* (where a writer bemoaned the end of "the era when boys were boys and bikes were bikes and nobody went pedaling around wearing stupid little helmets") to smaller newspapers that frantically telephoned dealers to localize the story. "You'd have thought it was Joey Buttafuoco who'd filed for Chapter 11," cracks Long Island dealer Gary Sirota of Wantagh, New York. In the prosaicly named central Illinois city of Normal, dealer Terry Gibson and his wife, Patty, were watching television in their home behind their store when ABC's Peter Jennings reported that Schwinn was in bankruptcy. "Folks came out of the woodwork, calling us up," says Patty Gibson, "asking if they could buy a bike—two bikes, three bikes—to help save the company."

Ed labored through the obligatory interviews and photo shoots the day after the filing, but he was unwilling to reflect on the management decisions that had brought Schwinn to such a state. "Do we have perfect decision-making?" he asked defiantly in an interview with *Crain's Chicago Business*. "No one does." Instead, he faulted the weakened economy and his bankers' recalcitrance. "We couldn't go further with these guys."

Life quieted a bit after the burst of attention, and Ed's disposition brightened. Perhaps the bankruptcy petition really could buy the time needed to fix Schwinn. If it didn't, well, there was always the new golden parachute agreement Ed and Richard had signed the day of the filing—this time stipulating a $636,000 payout upon a sale or change in control during a Chapter 11 proceeding.

The management team, however, was demoralized. The group, including Ralph Murray, Mike McNamara, Mike Martinsen, and Byron Smith, huddled in a sixth-floor conference room late on a Friday afternoon the week after the filing to ponder the company's sorry fate.

Schwinn couldn't go on with Ed in charge, someone said.

True, another noted, but what are our options?

Suddenly, Ed and Richard walked in.

"Whatcha talking about?" Ed asked.

Had he overheard? They attempted to finesse the moment.

"Oh, just stuff in general . . ."

"Yeah, like, what are we going to do about all this, Ed?"

"Should we even bother coming to work?"

Ed reassured them. "There's a lot to hold on to, guys."

But bankruptcy has its own inertia. Soon, the process—the judge, the creditors committees, the lawyers, the paperwork, the scrutiny—would consume the company, leaving management powerless.

Chicagoan Arnold Dratt was sipping coffee on a sunny October morning at a cafe in Aix-en-Provence, when an *International Herald Tribune* story popped out at him: Schwinn files for bankruptcy. Dratt had the sour feeling of being in the wrong place at the wrong time. His specialty was helping troubled companies, and he had chatted with Ed and Richard shortly before leaving for a long-delayed anniversary trip to France. Dratt hadn't known the brothers were so close to the end of their rope. Now, he faxed Richard: "Can I help? I'm coming back next week."

A jet-lagged Dratt started work on the Schwinn case on October 19, adding a new dimension to the company's saga. The forty-eight-year-old workout specialist was controversial in some financial circles. As an investment banker at Chicago's Rodman & Renshaw Capital Group, Dratt helped finance a commuter start-up called Chicago Airlines and an Italian ice company named Mama Tish's Enterprises. Both deals failed, and Dratt took the heat, perhaps unfairly, in some quarters of the local investment community. He left Rodman in 1988, but a reputation for being clinical, and sometimes cynical, followed him. Dratt doesn't reject the description, noting that the business of salvaging distressed companies requires a certain amount of detachment and, sometimes, black humor. "I call myself an unlicensed mental health care professional," he says. "I have to give bad messages. . . . You need to develop a little shell."

Dratt had a bad message for his new clients. "Let's face it," he told Ed and Richard. "If this were a public company, you'd be out of here. Thank your stars you are Schwinns."

"Sure, we know that," Ed replied. Richard laughed nervously.

Dratt and Schwinn's executives goaded Ed to slash costs to improve credibility with the banks. As talk of impending firings raced through headquarters, Ed dryly delivered the final word at a meeting in the Schwinn cafeteria on November 6. About 160 workers—almost half the staff—would be laid off. He couldn't promise severance payments. Any questions? "It was short, not very sweet," says Byron Smith. "It's a rough thing for a guy to get up and tell his employees, 'We have to let a lot of people go.' "

Schwinn family members no longer were immune, either. Ralph Murray had told Ed earlier, "I can't fire people unless you get rid of the Schwinns lying around." Some half-dozen relatives still worked at the company, and cousin Robert Schwinn, who'd been rehired earlier that year to conduct a computer inventory, was in the first wave of layoffs. Another casualty was Rush Smith, the family's longtime chauffeur, whose time with Schwinn stretched back to the 1950s, when he drove F.W. and Gertrude. "I thought I had fired him in December 1991," Murray says. "We gave him a retirement party in January 1992. But he kept showing up. I asked Ed, 'Did your dad tell him he had a job for life?' " Ed continued to pay Smith on an hourly basis, according to Murray, until the driver left for good in October.

A phone list soon circulated, the names of employees presumably due to receive pink slips highlighted. The kiss of death: an announcement over the intercom to "Call extension 6522"—the line to the "Hollywood" conference room on the second floor (named after an old Schwinn model), where the sentences were being dispensed. Gallows humor ruled. "You're still here?" managers quipped at the water fountain. "I thought I heard your name being paged."

Business prospects were just as grim. Byron Smith asked product manager for parts Chuck Gillis, "What would your line look like if we did $25 million [in sales] instead of $40 million?" Gillis devised several scenarios, but found the exercise too depressing and departed for a new job in the sporting goods field. Strategically sprinkled incentive payments kept other managers from jumping. "Still," says Mike Martinsen, "the attitude was, 'If you hear of something better, take a close look.' "

The bankruptcy filing also strapped hundreds of businesses that were owed money—an especially traumatic experience for small shops, such as Chicago's Magnani & Associates Advertising. Owner Rudy Magnani designed Schwinn's catalogs and brochures and depended on the bike company for half his sales. The adman had strong ties to Schwinn: His father had worked at the company and Magnani had spent two summers in high school painting the rims of Pixies. Now his longtime client owed him $150,000, while he in turn owed his suppliers $100,000. "It was painful to us," says Magnani, who subsequently worked out a plan to pay off his bills at $2,000 a month.

As employees, creditors, and dealers grieved for their fallen company, the parade of prospective buyers continued through headquarters—this time without the expertise of Continental Partners. The investment bankers had wanted to continue their search, and Ed was willing, but a judge's approval was needed because Schwinn was now under the jurisdiction of Bankruptcy Court. Arnold Dratt argued that Continental's monthly retainer of $35,000 was too rich. Continental responded: Let the judge decide. Ed signed a document seeking court approval for Continental's request, yet Dratt won the day. "I got Ed to withdraw it," he says, "to the undying enmity of Continental Partners."

Plenty of potential bidders, such as Chicago-based components maker SRAM Corporation, the developer of shifters that had taken on mighty Shimano, expressed interest. One of the more persistent visitors to headquarters was Specialized, the suitor that had huddled with Schwinn's bankers on the day of the filing. Investor John Jellinek appeared in Bankruptcy Court for Specialized, although his agenda was a mystery. "My interest," he coyly told *Crain's Chicago Business*, "is in helping the survival of the Schwinn name." Ralph Murray says Specialized's founder, Mike Sinyard, wanted to introduce the Schwinn brand to large sporting goods chains. Sinyard, however, won't reveal what he had in mind. "Obviously, we thought the name was very good," he says. This, too, passed. Ed and his staff worried that Specialized was gaining access to competitive information and ended the talks.

Exasperated creditors concluded that Schwinn wasn't serious about a sale and pushed the company to conduct a public auction. The banking contingent, led by Harris Bank, championed a hard line. In Bankruptcy

Court, they contested Schwinn's right to use cash in the bank on an emergency basis, arguing that the bike maker was deteriorating so swiftly it would be better off liquidating than remaining unsold and continuing to lose money. For several weeks, the bankers refused Schwinn's attempts to obtain debtor-in-possession financing (or DIP financing, the standard source of working cash for companies in Chapter 11) until Schwinn agreed to sell its assets through public bidding. That stance embittered Schwinn representatives. "There was never a question that the banks would get paid," says attorney Dennis O'Dea. "But they did it [recovered the loan] in the most painful way."

O'Dea explored an intriguing alternative: Harris rival American National Bank, a unit of First Chicago Corporation, offered DIP financing of $10 million. It would be enough to tide Schwinn over and position it for sale, with American National vaulting to the head of the repayment pack. Lawyers involved in the case doubted that such an antagonistic move—appropriately called "hostile DIP financing"—had been done before in Chicago banking, a still-gentlemanly world where larger players were loath to mess with each other. Winning acceptance for American National's plan would have required a courtroom brawl, since Harris would have fought any attempt to subordinate its standing. American National was ready to battle, but O'Dea worried that a Harris victory would leave Schwinn with nothing but Harris' vengeance. He decided to stick with the enemy he knew best.

The bank syndicate finally prepared to lend Schwinn $7 million on the unyielding condition that it hold a public auction. The restriction showed "the level of distrust," Dratt says. "They felt Ed was gonna squelch it." Adds David Schulte, partner in Schwinn suitor Zell-Chilmark Fund: "I've never seen DIP with a stipulation to sell. That spoke volumes about the way people felt."

Schwinn's largest unsecured creditors, China Bicycles and Giant, were no more friendly. Their confusing mix of roles—suppliers? creditors? competitors? buyers?—made many of the other players in the drama uneasy. (Sometimes it seemed there were no degrees of separation: Even China Bicycles' John Barker was a Schwinn creditor, with a claim of nearly $700,000 for insurance and retirement benefits.) Chicago attorney

Mark Thomas in particular was suspicious of the two suppliers. The Katten Muchin & Zavis lawyer represented the unsecured creditors committee, a standard body in the bankruptcy process. He questioned whether it was appropriate for China Bicycles and Giant even to have seats on the committee. The two companies had already hired their own lawyers, he noted, and their claims far exceeded those of other unsecured trade creditors, almost all of whom were owed less than $1 million each. Although China Bicycles and Giant conceivably would gain by Schwinn's demise, executives of both companies insist they tried to help the beleaguered debtor. Nevertheless, they were wearing so many different hats, it was difficult to gauge their motives. "They wanted Schwinn to liquidate," O'Dea insists.

At least one of them wanted more than that. Soon after the Chapter 11 filing in October, China Bicycles hired the Chicago investment banking boutique Fort Dearborn Partners to prepare a possible bid for Schwinn. Fort Dearborn had conducted due diligence for an aborted deal several weeks before, so it was able to swiftly launch a campaign to raise local equity and line up a replacement management team. Having had the earlier access to Schwinn's numbers, Fort Dearborn partner Stephen Coates told the bank syndicate and unsecured creditors that Schwinn's position was much worse than was being disclosed in Bankruptcy Court. "This is hemorrhaging," Coates warned. If the lengthy formal bidding process were followed, "the patient will be dead" by the time it's sold. Even the banks, he added, would be unable to recoup anywhere near the $32.5 million they still were owed. (China Bicycles never offered a formal proposal, but the numbers it was considering were low—about half the price ultimately offered. "We were preparing creditors for a brutal hit," Coates says.)

Of course, China Bicycles, as Schwinn's biggest supplier, had a tremendous say in whether the patient revived, depending on its willingness to ship or withhold bikes. It soon became apparent that Jerome Sze and Stephen Codron weren't going to lift a finger to help. China Bicycles said it couldn't; others insisted it merely wouldn't.

"The facts are that China Bike is running at capacity for clients who will be there and have been there and will continue to pay their bills,"

China Bicycles' lawyer Jill Ann Coleman of Chicago law firm Neal Gerber & Eisenberg said in Bankruptcy Court. "There is full production already, and to put Schwinn in, we would have to dislodge that."

Ralph Murray testified to a different story. China Bicycles had continued to ship bikes, despite threats to the contrary by John Barker. Murray said in court that he had spoken to Sze, who told him he would consider producing for Schwinn as long as the components were available. "He said, 'I will support you. I don't know about the component question, but I will support production.' "

Stephen Coates of Fort Dearborn Partners explains that China Bicycles didn't mind shipping finished bikes, but had no desire to gear up new production for Schwinn, which involved too high a degree of financial exposure. The manufacturer might have looked at the situation differently, Coates concedes, if there wasn't so much bad blood between the parties.

Who knew what was real? There was bluff and bluster, dissonance and confusion that China Bicycles hoped would help it in its ultimate goal: retrieving Schwinn's 18 percent share of the joint venture. "Our agenda was to survive ourselves—keep a customer and get our stock back," Barker explains. Sustaining a Schwinn outlet for its Shenzhen factory's production was a priority. A potential buyer, after all, could shift all that business to archrival Giant. Yet the stock was even more important for China Bicycles' future. "We didn't want it in unfriendly hands," Barker says. "It only had value to us."

Computing that value would require more art than science. Schwinn's initial one-third stake in China Bicycles had been diluted over time, first by Stephen Codron's purchase of a portion of Schwinn's share and then further by the Asian company's going public on the Shenzhen Stock Market in April 1992. Schwinn still owned some 37 million shares, or 18 percent of one of the world's largest bicycle manufacturers. Ed's detractors must credit him for at least one thing: He had made a prescient investment in the Shenzhen factory five years earlier. The chunk of stock would be key to any resolution of the bankruptcy. It was the one big chip that every bargainer would try to play.

Tapping the stock was another matter. Michael Smith, senior managing director at Continental Partners, had testified that the China stock was worth between $15 million and $40 million. Others weren't as sure. These were founders' shares scribbled in a ledger in China, where a real commercial code barely existed. How liquid—how sellable—were they? Attorney O'Dea hoped to use Schwinn's shares to propel a reorganization of the Chicago company with Ed and the family still holding some measure of control. His biggest barrier, however, was that under the original purchase agreement, Schwinn couldn't dispose of the shares without the agreement of its partners: Sze's holding company and the government-controlled Shenzhen Municipal Power and Light Company. The latter answered the question when Schwinn received a letter from the agency explaining that the stock couldn't be sold until the $18 million owed to China Bicycles was paid—essentially slapping a lien on the shares. Given's China's still-primitive economy, the unsecured creditors committee was persuaded that it couldn't go to Shenzhen, sell the stock, and transfer some $30 million to Chicago. "A fantasy," says attorney Mark Thomas of that scenario. China Bicycles appeared to have the biggest stick and it was being wielded by John Barker. Some Schwinn managers couldn't help wonder: If Barker still were playing on their team, might the outcome be different?

The unsecured creditors committee was inclined to support the formal bid process, yet China Bicycles had a point in pushing for a faster sale. The longer the company dragged its feet, the more the value of the Schwinn estate would dissipate. In addition, waiting to conduct an auction still left open the possibility of a Schwinn reorganization without a sale—an alarming prospect to creditors, who probably would be left behind to eke out an even smaller return on their claims. Nevertheless, to expedite a sale without a public auction, the creditors needed the cooperation of the Ignaz Schwinn Trust.

David Heller, attorney for the suddenly potent Schwinn Trust, opened a tab at City Tavern, around the corner from Bankruptcy Court, and held his own courtroom session. Over Diet Cokes and coffee, Heller told creditors and other parties in the case, "If you want us to forgo the opportunity to reorganize, then pay us for that opportunity." Though the family legally wasn't entitled to any money, and the chance of a reorganization was slim, could the creditors live with some sort of payout to the Schwinn Trust . . . in the interest of hastening a sale of the company? "We believe in miracles," Heller said. "If you want us to stop believing, pay us."

Heller's faith in engineering a payout lay in an obscure and overlooked license held by the Schwinn Trust—a license to use the heralded Schwinn name. It had been established quietly by the company's Keck Mahin & Cate lawyers in 1984 after Schwinn had endured the private humiliation of hocking its name to its lenders. Here was the family's way to hold on to the valuable trade name if the banks ever again moved to take the assets. The license hadn't been used much, except for a line of miniature model bicycles. Revelation of its existence, however, caused consternation in Bankruptcy Court.

"Assuming that all the assets of the company were sold . . . would you then be able to license products in competition?" Judge Jack B. Schmetterer asked Ed during his testimony.

"I suppose that would be the case," Ed replied.

The license was an impediment to a sale. "It's not in the best interest of this estate that it be marketed with that type of cloud," argued Mark Thomas for the unsecured creditors. "What will happen is, anybody that wants to buy the Schwinn name will not come in and make a good offer for it, knowing Mr. Ed Schwinn can go and start making bicycles with his name on it somewhere else."

The license was suspect, and might have been invalidated with enough challenges, but that wasn't the point. Here was the grease for a deal—a way to bring in the Schwinn family. "It worked," O'Dea says, "because they had nothing else to sell."

23

THE VULTURE SWOOPS

Investor David Schulte sidled up to lawyer David Heller outside the courtroom.

"I have wampum," Schulte said.

"I have shit," Heller replied.

"What do you want?" Schulte asked.

"A lot of your wampum."

Schwinn's corporate bankruptcy attorneys had already drawn up documents for a public auction and were preparing to seek bids when Schulte and partner Sam Zell, owners of a $1 billion vulture fund that targeted troubled companies, swooped in on December 7 with a surprise offer to buy most of Schwinn's assets for $40 million. The only catch: a deal must be completed by Christmas. A refinancing would have to be turned quickly, an attorney for their Zell-Chilmark Fund argued in court two days later, so that Schwinn's dealers could receive bikes in time for the spring selling season. "If the company is not sold by the last week in December," he warned, "its value will diminish rapidly."

Sam Zell's interest in Schwinn was mostly financial, yet a small part of it also stretches back to his childhood. "My parents wouldn't step up for the extra fifty bucks," he says with a smirk. "They bought me a Huffy." Zell certainly could afford a Schwinn now. His net worth in late 1992 was an estimated $625 million, and the bicycle company would be but one bauble in a shopping spree that Zell-Chilmark had started two years earlier and included purchases or controlling stakes in such names as California's Broadway Stores, the Revco drugstore chain, the Sealy mattress company, and Midway Airlines.

David Schulte was the strategist of the fund, but Sam Zell was the marquee name who attracted the project's investors. Among the wealthiest men in Chicago, and a regular on *Forbes* magazine's annual rankings of the 400 richest people in America, Zell enthusiastically embraces the nickname the "Grave Dancer" (derived from a 1976 article about his investment style) and even has installed a near-life-size statue of himself, jigging atop a tomb, on a landscaped terrace outside his downtown office. The son of a Jewish grain trader who fled Poland on the eve of the Nazi invasion, Zell was born in 1941, raised in the affluent Chicago suburb of Highland Park, and studied business at the University of Michigan. Starting in the 1970s, Zell and a fraternity brother, the late Robert Lurie, amassed a real estate empire by snatching up distressed properties at bargain prices. He attracted considerable attention over the years, not only for his unorthodox investments, but also for a bad boy image that includes eschewing suits for jeans, commuting by motorcycle, and speaking bluntly and sarcastically, usually punctuating the finer points with four-letter words. The short and burly Zell and a collection of high-powered businessmen and dealmakers depart each year for Nepal, Europe, or some other travel spot for two-week motorcycle escapades—"real male bonding," as he once described the experiences to the *Chicago Tribune*. "Harleys are for paraders," he later told a *Chicago* magazine writer. "We ride on Ducatis and Hondas as a sport. Those are high-performance crotch rockets for serious folks." Zell and his wild ones, dubbed "Zell's Angels," are rich enough to flaunt convention. They power up to posh hotels and dine in splendor—in jeans and leather jackets. "The Jewish American Prince Tour," a friend calls it. Another macho Zell pastime is "War at Four," where up to twenty guys gather in the woods below his Sun Valley, Idaho, vacation home on a Saturday afternoon, split into competing armies, and shoot each other with paintball guns.

Zell owns stakes in the Chicago Bulls basketball team and Chicago White Sox baseball franchise, but the cornerstone of his holdings was Itel Corporation (now Anixter International), a railcar leasing firm that emerged from bankruptcy in 1984. Zell gradually increased his holdings—he owned 26 percent of the company by the early '90s—and rode the federal tax code to turn Itel's annual losses into huge tax breaks that helped generate money to diversify the company's base. He also teamed up with Wall Street powerhouse Merrill Lynch & Company to form two real estate vulture funds that invested in vast numbers of financially wobbling shopping centers, office buildings, apartments, and mobile home parks, betting that tumbling real estate values would recover.[1]

In the midst of his Itel overhaul, Zell hooked up with Chicago workout specialist David Schulte, who recently had opened his own debt restructuring boutique, Chilmark Partners. The two are only five years apart in age, but the younger Schulte's preppy investment banker look contrasts sharply with Zell's iconoclastic demeanor. Schulte's extracurricular activities are more conventional, too: golf, tennis, sailing off Martha's Vineyard. Although Schulte is the son of a New Jersey retailer, he developed a royally blue-chip résumé: Williams College with top honors, Yale Law School, editor-in-chief of the law review, clerk to U.S. Supreme Court Justice Potter Stewart. He didn't aim for a career practicing law, however; instead, at age twenty-seven, he went to work in 1973 for Chicago conglomerate builder Ben Heineman and learned the game of acquisitions and financial restructurings. In 1980 Schulte convinced Salomon Brothers to hire him as a workout specialist, and a prestigious assignment almost immediately surfaced: the ongoing federal bailout of Chrysler Corporation, for which Schulte became Salomon's point man. With a bronzed tombstone ad marking the 1983 reclassification of $1.1 billion in Chrysler preferred stock, Schulte decided to strike out on his own. He launched Chilmark Partners in 1984, naming his company after the town on Martha's Vineyard where he had a summer home. Schulte soon became involved in another high-profile case, advising independent directors of Resorts International against a lowball bid by New York real estate magnate Donald Trump. "Tangling with Donald has been real hard—and real fun," Schulte told *Crain's Chicago Business* in 1988.

Zell approached Schulte to work on debt restructuring at Itel. "When I first met Sam Zell, I didn't know what to make of him," Schulte reminisced to author Hilary Rosenberg. "There before me was an exuberant Jewish leprechaun emitting lots of energy. I wasn't sure if he was real or a figment of my imagination." The two went to work on other projects. Their restructuring of Apex Oil, a St. Louis oil refiner and marketer, produced big profits. "If we're going to do this kind of thing," Schulte suggested, "we ought to have our own source of equity." Zell and Schulte raised $1 billion pledged by investors and let the world know they were ready to shop.

Zell-Chilmark had passed on a Schwinn deal when the bike maker was on the market through Continental Partners. At the time, Schulte recalls, he and Zell lacked a partner with the experience to oversee a bicycle company. But Schwinn's tumble into Bankruptcy Court created new opportunities. "We wouldn't have to deal with the Schwinn family," Zell explains tartly, "particularly the guy that was running it." The pair also had found someone who could run Schwinn: Charles T. Ferries, chairman of Sun Valley–based Scott Sports Group.

A Schwinn deal had long been coveted by the gutsy and competitive Ferries, who for most of his life had been more inclined to schuss, rather than cycle, down a mountain. A twenty-one-year-old Ferries had raced in downhill and slalom skiing events at the 1960 Winter Olympics in Squaw Valley, California. Four years later, he competed at Innsbruck. Ferries worked as a sales rep for Head, which had developed the metal ski and was the top U.S. brand during the '60s, and went on to become executive vice president and a minority owner in K2 Corporation, an up-and-coming company that pioneered the use of lightweight fiberglass. He left K2 in 1977, moving to Sun Valley to launch a high-end ski business, and saw his big break four years later, when Scott, pioneer of the modern ski pole, filed for bankruptcy protection in Salt Lake City. Ferries put together a group that bid $4.1 million for the firm at a court-sponsored auction, barely beating a Canadian rival with ties to the prominent Bronfman family. Annual sales were $5 million. To diversify, Ferries and his European partner, Tom Stendahl, sought another endeavor in 1986. "We wanted a 'summer' business," Ferries says. "A lot of our people biked at noon. Everyone was out riding mountain bikes." Scott decided to start selling mountain bikes in the United States and, by Ferries' admission, "did everything wrong," selling to ski shops using sales reps oriented to that business. Scott changed direction, but it was more successful in cycling accessories, such as an aerodynamically positioned handlebar that was used by Greg LeMond in one of his later Tour de France victories.

Although it stumbled in the States, Scott's timing was perfect in Europe, where the mountain bike was becoming popular. This time, Scott set up a separate sales force to court specialty shops, which have a proportionally larger market share compared with U.S. cycleries. There were no pan-European brands in the field, either, and American names, such as Trek and Specialized, were only beginning to target Europe. Scott "had strong recognition through skiing," Tom Stendahl says. "We got a good head start on everybody." Sales soared from 8,000 bikes in 1987 to 200,000 in 1991. A year later, Scott was one of the top bike brands in Europe and had total sales of about $110 million. The company also was at a crossroad: Scott was a U.S. firm, yet it didn't have the capital to expand the domestic bike business because the larger and cash-hungrier European operation was gobbling up much of the resources. "We felt we had to grow to go forward, to be a worldwide player," Ferries says.

Schwinn was a logical fit. Nevertheless, Ferries says, Continental Partners had disqualified him from bidding earlier in 1992 because he was a competitor. When Ferries heard rumors late in the summer that Schwinn was preparing to file for bankruptcy protection, he contacted his longtime skiing pal, Sam Zell. (The two had vied on the slopes since the '70s, and Ferries often showed up for War at Four. "If there was an issue with Scott, I'd give him a call and spend half an hour," Ferries says of Zell. "He can look at a problem and come up with a solution quicker than anyone.") In early October, Ferries outlined his ideas for a deal over dinner with Zell, who was intrigued by the potential of turning around one of America's great brands. ("An extraordinary nameplate with an extraordinary franchise that was allowed to deteriorate," Zell explains.) By November, Ferries was crunching data with Zell-Chilmark's whizzes, using Bankruptcy Court filings and documents that Continental Partners had offered Schulte a year earlier. "The numbers kept moving around," Ferries recalls, "but we kept coming up with $40 million."

Their initial strategy was to purchase the bank debt at a discount, which would give it a powerful influence in Bankruptcy Court. Schulte and Zell-Chilmark analyst Marcy Rosenberg visted the Loop office of Harris Bank executive Pat McDonnell. Schulte proposed purchasing an option to buy the bank group's $30 million Schwinn debt—and even said he was ready to write a check for $500,000. McDonnell seemed leery. It was one thing to play hardball with a family business, another to cut deals with a major league vulture fund. Confident that its loan was fully covered, the bank group declined Schulte's help. "You hold on to it," McDonnell told Schulte. "We'll get back to you."

Rebuffed from acquiring Schwinn's secured debt, Zell-Chilmark and Scott fashioned a bid that would be difficult for others to preempt. They asked the court for control of Schwinn by December 24 and built in "bid protection" of $4 million (meaning a competitor would have to offer at least $44 million to best them). In addition, Zell-Chilmark would receive a $1 million consolation prize, or "breakup fee," if its bid initially was accepted but turned out not to be the highest offer. The joint proposal generated plenty of publicity, which is what Zell-Chilmark intended. "We created an event and got everyone's attention," Schulte says. "If we could shine a spotlight with a real offer, we could remake the timing [of the bankruptcy process]." Schwinn, however, was not moved. "We reject your offer," a melodramatic Dratt told Schulte at a December 9 court hearing, insisting there was potential for better offers through the standard auction process.

Yet Schulte was already working behind the scenes. He cut a side deal with Schwinn Trust attorney David Heller to pay the family $2.5 million for the license to their name. "It was a way to get the family in," Schulte says about the deal. "No one had offered them money before." More than 1,200 creditors stood in the bankruptcy line, from China Bicycles to small businesses with unpaid bills of several hundred dollars. Considering that legally the Schwinns weren't entitled to a dime after having stiffed creditors, the licensing payoff was richer than many had expected. "It was a holdup," John Barker says, "but everybody does that in the bankruptcy process."

The unsecured creditors committee also was inclined to support an expedited sale to Zell-Chilmark, but then came a courtroom surprise—and suspicions of betrayal.

On December 17, Ferries disclosed under questioning by a Giant attorney that Barker, working on behalf of China Bicycles, recently had asked to join Zell-Chilmark's and Scott's run for Schwinn. Although China Bicycles was already a supplier to Scott, the Zell group passed on Barker's proposal. "It didn't make any sense," Ferries testified. "We couldn't be involved with China Bicycles Company in any way . . . because they were also a creditor in this action. But more importantly, we had a financial partner that we had lined up and it made sense for the two of us to do it together."[2]

Barker wanted a piece of the action from the start, Ferries says today. "But we never gave it credence. There was a perception that we were working together. That was not true." As Schwinn's supplier history had shown, it was poor business for a distributor to ally itself with a single vendor. And China Bicycles had been marching with Fort Dearborn Partners, drumming up a bid of its own. "We were never sure where China Bicycles was," Ferries says.

Giant, too, had wanted a cut of the proposed deal. The No. 2 creditor, with $9 million in unpaid bills, sought to buy Schwinn's Air-Dyne business, but the Zell group held Giant at bay, explaining that bankruptcy ethics prevented it from talking separately to creditors.

Ferries' disclosure of the Barker solicitation angered China Bicycles' already-suspicious counterparts on the unsecured creditors committee. Here was China Bicycles voting to accept the Zell offer, then maneuvering to be part of the deal. China Bicycles was in a conflict and should have recused itself from voting, the other committee members agreed, chalking it up to Barker's gamesmanship. (For his part, Barker claims he disclosed his actions to the committee and simply was trying to expedite a deal.) Lawyers polled the group overnight and this time turned thumbs-down on the Zell package and its promise of paying creditors between 15 and 20 cents on every dollar owed.

Schulte was furious at the turndown, according to creditors attorney Jeff Marwil. Entering the courtroom, he shook Marwil's hand and said, "You scabrous motherfucker." Schulte withdrew his team's offer on December 18—and went skiing in Vail.

As Christmas approached, creditors' stockings still were empty. Most began to reconsider. Perhaps they had chased away real money. "During the next week," Schulte recalls, "it became clear that the parties did not want us gone."

By now, it was obvious that China Bicycles, which coveted the chunk of its shares in Schwinn's hands, was going to be instrumental to the entire deal. "They wanted the stock," Ferries says, "and if they had to buy the company [to get it], they would have." Yet if China Bicycles was going to get its stock back, creditors attorney Mark Thomas argued, the company would have to relinquish its $18 million claim against Schwinn. That would cut the unsecured debts by a third and leave a bigger pie for the remaining creditors to share. For the Zell group, however, the stock was a bogus commodity. "The only value of the shares was in gaining the cooperation of China Bicycles," Schulte says. Schwinn's legal and bankruptcy advisers had insisted for months the stock had value. It did, but not in saving Schwinn.

Barker met Schulte for a 7:30 breakfast at the Chicago Club on December 28. The dining room was nearly empty on a Monday after Christmas weekend. "You don't have to whisper," Barker notes, "when there's no one else in the room." China Bicycles, he told Schulte, was willing to waive its $18 million claim in exchange for the stock. The two sides carved a deal on the spot: China Bicycles would get a three-year supply agreement with the new Schwinn and provide favorable payment terms.

To oil the bankruptcy machinery further, China Bicycles subsequently agreed to sell about 2.8 million of the nearly 38 million Schwinn shares and return the proceeds to the Schwinn Estate (the remains of the bicycle company under the jurisdiction of the Bankruptcy Court). The unsecured creditors would pocket the proceeds, with a guarantee of

$2.5 million. By waiving its debt claim and tossing that little extra into the pot, China Bicycles had left the remaining creditors a more lucrative payout projected at 25 to 30 cents on the dollar. The vote was swift. "This time," lawyer Marwil says, "Schulte sent me a bottle of champagne." Schwinn's bankruptcy attorneys also could join the toast. Counting the $43.25 million in cash and the waiver of the China Bicycles claim, they could proclaim they had won a deal valued at more than $61 million.

Schulte had his ducks lined up. All except Ed Schwinn.

From the start of the bankruptcy, the chief executive had seemed to pursue two agendas: Schwinn's and Ed's. Whether the company was sold or broken up made little difference to his career plans, so, as outside offers and counteroffers swirled, he continued seeking a savior. As late as December, Ed tried to formulate a reorganization by teaming up with friend Don Schumacher, chairman of small-town department store operator Spurgeon Holding Corporation and a fellow member of Chicago's Young Presidents' Organization. But time ran out. Zell-Chilmark went to court on New Year's Eve seeking approval of its new proposal. Participants could reach only one conclusion: Richard Schwinn and bank trustee James Kiel—seeing no place else to go—had opted for a sale, with or without Ed. Observes Ferries, "Ed was never on board, right to the end." Schulte agrees: "He was instructed by the trustees to sign; he had to be ordered. The beneficiaries put pressure on Ed and the other trustees to sign."

Schwinn executives and advisers say relations between the two brothers frayed in the final weeks. Even when Richard had ascended to vice president years earlier, Ed continued to treat him as the kid brother. Richard had tolerated the attitude until the crash, but by the time of the bankruptcy, Richard was more concerned about morality than money, doing what he thought was right for the family and the creditors they owed money to. He didn't expect a white knight and he wanted to end the whole horrible mess with some degree of dignity. The friction became evident to many. "I had the feeling at the end they were not on good terms," says an attorney in the case. "Maybe they reconciled. Richard realized what he had to do."

Advisers credit Ed with maintaining a strong front during the final days, never showing weakness, intimidation, or panic. Nevertheless, for all his arrogance and bluster, in the end he was not really a fighter. Ed continually sought alternatives, yet didn't pursue a "scorched earth" policy that might have terrified creditors into negotiating a better deal—battling to the death for the right to reorganize the company, for instance, or rendering it even more unattractive through such tactics as refusing to lay off workers or reducing the value of inventory by selling bikes and parts to dealers on extended terms. True, Schwinn's value had already deteriorated enormously prior to bankruptcy, as the half-hearted search for a buyer dragged on for almost a year, but as long as Ed held the top spot after the filing, he had the power to make things miserable for creditors and buyers. This late in the game—with no assets left for shareholders—there was no incentive for him to make things better. After the onset of the bank crisis and the search for a buyer, he stalled as long as possible, then acquiesced without an open confrontation. "Ed had no stomach for real warfare," says attorney Dennis O'Dea. Observes Stephen Codron of China Bicycles, "Ed was a domineering character who never used [that trait] to his potential."

Ed now was isolated. Cousins and aunts were talking about lawsuits. Employees were appalled at his seeming lack of compassion for their straits. Ed had assumed that people would help him and felt let down when they didn't, his advisers say. He failed to understand the need to build a consensus and was unaware of the deep anger and hostility he generated until it was too late. George Garner had tried to reach out at a regional dealer meeting that November, pulling Ed aside and counseling: "I wish you would thank the sales people for hanging in and the tremendous way they've stuck with you. There's a lot of bitterness." Ed didn't respond. Instead, he wandered away. Observes O'Dea, "He lost his sense of empathy and communion." Indeed, Ed seemed to be in his own world. "He was combative, conciliatory, philosophical, argumentative," Dratt says. "Then, he'd shrug and walk out and go to lunch. He was caught in a hard squeeze—nothing he ever prepared for. It's an overwhelming task for anyone. But control was real important to him. This was the only job he ever had. He realized his phone might not be ringing off the hook."

One last, desperate grab for the company was made in the final weeks before the closing of the Zell deal, when Giant announced in court on January 5 that it intended to make a $45 million bid, with a superior payout for unsecured creditors.

The possibility of a Giant acquisition of Schwinn stirred rival Trek to action. As a defensive measure, Trek developed a financial package by teaming up with its main supplier and Giant's Taiwanese foe, Merida. "We could live with Zell owning them," explains Trek chairman Richard Burke. "But a Schwinn/Giant [combination] would be lethal."

Burke was able to save his pennies, because Giant never delivered a formal proposal. Schwinn's China Bicycles stock likely posed a problem for Giant—Jerome Sze would have fought any attempt by Giant to own a piece of his company. Still, Giant might well have pulled off a deal if it had begun working on a bid earlier. Instead, it snoozed through the bankruptcy, assuming that all creditors were on common ground while China Bicycles was cutting its own deal. Sze all along held the chip no other creditor had. With the help of Barker, he was able to cover his losses—and then some. Some observers suggest Giant lost sight of such subtleties because it relished the prospect of Schwinn's demise and a clearer path for its U.S. subsidiary. Not so, says Giant's Tony Lo, noting that his company continued to supply Schwinn with bicycles up to the bankruptcy filing. "We feel very sorry about the potential that was lost," Lo says. "We think we were the victim trying to help Schwinn." Whatever its aims, Giant was left with little: partial repayment from the old Schwinn and no success in buying the Air-Dyne unit, no bike orders from the new Schwinn, and a China Bicycles that was stronger than ever.

In fact, some argue, China Bicycles made out like a bandit. If it sold the roughly 37 million shares recouped at an average share price of about $1, China Bicycles could net some $12 million, after subtracting the $18 million debt that was waived, the $2.5 million paid to the creditors committee, and several million dollars in expenses during the bankruptcy. "They came out terrific," says an impressed Dratt.

And no one seemed to come out better than John Barker, the solo figure onstage holding the winning ticket. The man who had been fired only three years earlier had returned in triumph to slice up the company that had wronged him. Despite countless opportunities to do so, Barker never took cheap shots, yet he surely must have taken satisfaction in the way the case panned out.

But among members of the Schwinn family trust, there was only sorrow and anger. "This has been devastating for the family," says Peter Davis, Ed's brother-in-law and former director of corporate planning. No more dividends. No more jobs. No more ownership of an American icon. No more extra beat of the heart when a cyclist pedals by on a Schwinn. *We make those, you know.* After nearly one hundred years of work, the most respected family name in the business—and one of the most celebrated in any business—finally was worth a paltry $2.5 million.

Ed apparently had trouble accepting the idea that it was over when the court put its final blessing on the Zell-Chilmark purchase. On January 19, 1993, moments before Judge Schmetterer brought his gavel down on the deal, Ralph Murray says he walked with Ed in the hallway outside the courtroom.

"Is that what you want, Ed?" he asked. "This is going to happen. It's over."

Ed failed to grasp the moment. "I appreciate your support, Ralph. I've got a couple of things working. I'm going to come in with a proposal. There will be a spot for you."

24

A FINAL SPIN

On January 21, Chuck Ferries and Tom Stendahl began digging through the rubble that was Schwinn. Employees who had survived the bankruptcy and sale were like shell-shocked wartime survivors. "People were hiding under their desks, figuring if they didn't say anything, they could stay alive a little longer," Stendahl says. No such luck. The new regime swept out most of the old employees on the premise that anyone associated with Schwinn was tainted. Among the few initial survivors: Ralph Murray, who was promoted to president, and Byron Smith. Although Ferries had assured everyone that Schwinn would remain in Chicago, he and Stendahl soon decided the company would benefit from a fresh start in the trendy sports capital of Boulder, Colorado. Ferries had always managed to conduct business in some of the country's most scenic settings, and downtown Chicago, he wryly explained, "is not conducive to the outdoor sporting goods industry."

Schwinn now was better capitalized, thanks to a $6.75 million cash infusion from Zell-Chilmark, and it attracted fresh talent, like Skip Hess, Jr. (son of the BMX pioneer), who had spent the past five years managing product development in the United States for Giant. Schwinn moved swiftly to shed its Main Street image, although some outsiders thought it was trying a tad too hard to be cool. "Schwinns are red. Schwinns are blue. Schwinns are light and agile, too. Cars suck. The end," read one magazine ad. *We get it!* was the message from Schwinn's intense new marketing director, Gregg Bagni, a cycling enthusiast and former sales rep for Scott. By mid-decade, Bagni was attempting to woo "top-knots," ultra-hip cyclists who wear their hair samurai-style, with a little ponytail atop the head, and he was marketing to the younger cyberspace crowd with gimmicks like tagging an aluminum mountain bike model with a name reminiscent of an e-mail address: s(9five).1.

Ferries at first had given Murray and his team latitude to quickly develop and market 1994 models that would be unveiled at late-1993 trade shows. At center stage was the children's Z series, wheeled out before the bankruptcy. Geared for dirt trails or city streets, Schwinn press materials hyped it as the Sting-Ray of the '90s. Kids who had tested it called it "totally rad," but the Z-bike flopped. "Nobody wanted it," Ferries explains.

Relations between the new regime and the holdovers withered following the move to Boulder. Ferries and Stendahl showed up almost every day; including Murray, there were too many chiefs. "It became clear we were a transitional team," says Byron Smith. There were philosophical differences, too. Murray and Smith wanted to use extensive national advertising and promotions to jump-start the company and win back customers quickly. But Scott had been successful with a grass-roots approach, heavily backing star racers and using their endorsements to distinguish the rest of the line. Schwinn returned to sponsoring BMX racers. "If you don't have winning teams—heroes riding bikes—how do you appeal to kids other than price?" Ferries asked.

Just months after transferring to Colorado, Smith and national sales manager Ken Lesniak left Schwinn; Murray resigned two months later. CEO Stendahl assumed day-to-day responsibility. "I needed to get down and dirty—understand what was happening and why," he says. A native of Sweden who speaks several languages, Stendahl was Scott's European licensee in 1981 when Ferries purchased the company in Bankruptcy

Court. The two sparred over the rights to the name in Europe for several months, then agreed to join forces. Stendahl had been instrumental in building the Scott bike brand overseas; now he set out to get Schwinn's finances in order. Nose-deep in Chapter 11, Schwinn had lost at least $18 million on sales of $147 million. "We needed to get sales down to where we could be profitable," he says. In its first fiscal year, Schwinn reached an operating break-even, generating revenues of $110 million and claiming sales of about 350,000 bikes (many of them unprofitable closeouts), and in its second fiscal year, ended August 1995, Schwinn may have even registered a profit: revenues rose to an estimated $135 million on sales of nearly 450,000 bikes in the U.S.

By 1995, Schwinn's centennial year, the revamped company was gaining recognition for an overhauled line that included better mountain bikes. Although long associated with $199 to $299 models, Schwinn began pushing into new territory—$300 to $700 bicycles—that could yield more profits and broaden its appeal. To gain credibility with cycling's movers and shakers, it subcontracted with small U.S. frame shops for a domestic line called Homegrown (price: $1,400 to $3,800 each) and acquired Yeti, a tiny but high-end frame builder in Durango, Colorado. Schwinn was among a handful of firms licensing technology for front and rear suspension in $2,000-plus mountain bikes. Schwinn hardly was alone in this area, but Steve Frothingham, executive editor of *Bicycle Retailer and Industry News*, credits the company with foresight for jumping on the suspension craze. "They executed it well."

Suspension forks (to soften the shock of a rocky ride) were just one of the hot trends at mid-decade. When it came to frames, chrome-moly steel was beginning to look dowdy. Bike companies were experimenting with defense industry-inspired materials, such as strengthened carbon fiber, titanium, and exotic metal matrixes. Fortunately for adult consumers, prices were tumbling. A steel bike with front suspension could be had for about $550 in 1995; similarly equipped carbon fiber bikes sold for about $800. Favored colors were neutral, like silver, black, and dark shades of green. The children's market, however, was heading in a different direction, with wild cherries and other candy-colored themes, often accented with holographic decals. The two biggest fads both emulated the motorized world. For the under-ten crowd, zoomy re-creations of motorcycles ruled the field; some featured mag wheels and sweeping plastic shields, tanks, and bodies, while others offered extended forks and smaller front wheels to mimic Harley-Davidsons. For older children, the extreme craze was "low rider" bicycles. Again, the customized wheels first rolled out of California garages, and, again, old and beat-up Schwinns were the medium of choice. Only this time, the pioneers were Chicano kids inspired by *muy macho* adults who cruised main drags in hydraulically pumped low-rider cars, and their bikes were late-1960s Sting-Rays whose frames and forks had been chopped and molded into long, low vehicles of almost unrideable proportions. The pedals barely cleared the pavement. The best banana seats (preferably upholstered in velour) rose just high enough to meet the knees. The colors were riotous and the accessories ultra-glamorous—multiple lights and horns, rearview mirrors, steering wheels, and other auto-like ploys plated with chrome, silver, even gold. Whether white suburbanites would embrace a proudly Hispanic urban phenomenon remained to be seen, but children's bike designs at mid-decade (including Schwinn's brief Z series) were hugging more and more ground each season.

Schwinn had been one of the few bike makers to capitalize on a 1990s retro wave among adults. The new management redesigned the Cruiser based on 1954 drawings that were unearthed in the days after the acquisition. The fat-tire coaster-brake Cruisers, always popular in beach towns, remain a funky part of the company's heritage. Schwinn sales staff even sported bowling shirts at the fall 1994 trade shows, and the company hosted centennial bashes the following year that would have made Brownie Schwinn proud, including a "SchwinnDig" at a Las Vegas event that featured 100 cycling Elvis Presley impersonators. A limited-edition run of 5,000 Black Phantoms based on the original model sold for $3,000 each and were snapped up by collectors and fans, including comedian Jerry Seinfeld and publisher Hugh Hefner.

Both old and new designs were winning praise from long-skeptical dealers, such as Doug Stiverson of Westside Cycling and Fitness in Lakewood, Colorado, who once thought that a Schwinn "could be free and you're not going to get the twenty-two-year-old mountain biker to ride it." But Stiverson cleared floor space for the '95 models. "There are some very sharp people at Schwinn now," he told *Biz* magazine. "I'm not used to that." Many veteran dealers seemed to be willing to give the new management the benefit of the doubt. After all, they had prospered by the name, and some still express deep loyalty. "It's kind of like a son and a father," explains Jeff Allen from his store in the Chicago suburb of Villa Park. "A father can do a lot of wrong things. But he's still your father." Still, some worry about the corporate emphasis on currying elite markets with thousand-dollar bikes. "Schwinn should target the nine- to ten-year-olds on MTV," advises suburban Chicago dealer Jeff Crittenden. "I feel they're neglecting the low end."

The company also expanded its fitness line. To lessen dependence on the aging Air-Dyne (whose annual sales had dropped over the years to a mere 50,000 by mid-decade), Schwinn began marketing treadmills and stepping machines. Even before the sale to Scott, executives had been grappling with ways to widen distribution without alienating established dealers. The reorganized Schwinn dabbled unsuccessfully in direct marketing and by the summer of 1994 started selling exercise wares to retail chains specializing in fitness equipment. It also tested some fifteen mall kiosks operated by franchisees, including an entry at the mega-Mall of America outside Minneapolis. "We could not compete by only that [dealer] channel," Ferries explains. Some dealers may tremble at this move outside the traditional retail network, but for now, many seem to buy into management's premise that expanding distribution will improve consumer awareness of the brand.

A weak link for Schwinn was in parts and accessories, which can yield higher profit margins than bikes. In September 1994 Zell-Chilmark explored one diversification tactic by purchasing a 9.5 percent stake in Bell Sports Corporation, the leading maker of helmets. The deal sparked speculation that Zell-Chilmark would combine Scott, Schwinn, and Bell into a sporting goods powerhouse, but preliminary talks faltered, and publicly traded Bell found another merger partner in New York–based American Recreation Company, owner of the Mongoose brand. Although the merger diluted Zell-Chilmark's stake in Bell, the investment group still could attempt to combine its bicycle holdings. "We have no present plans for Bell," David Schulte told *Crain's Chicago Business* in mid-1995, "but we wouldn't have bought it if we were not in the bike business. Stay tuned." Bell and Schwinn remain small pieces of the billion-dollar Zell-Chilmark vulture fund, whose returns to investors were dampened by the financial woes of the fund's biggest investment, California department store chain Broadway Stores. Schulte and Sam Zell deftly extricated themselves from their doggy deal and cut their losses by selling the property, but the affair didn't squelch Schulte's appetite for buying troubled businesses as he prepared to launch a second fund—this time without Zell, who was focusing on other opportunities, such as an unsuccessful bid to buy Rockefeller Center. Since Zell-Chilmark must eventually unwind its investments, the shape of the future Schwinn still must be fashioned. The new owners must improve returns if they hope to take their company public.

Meantime, Schwinn is a vastly different company. "Now it's more entrepreneurial," says Mark Marusarz, one of the few Chicagoans to survive the move to Boulder. "There are hungry young people. Before it was sedate. You could sit on your laurels." Although Schwinn's owners have stabilized the operation and begun paving the way for a recovery, the question remains, Can Schwinn ever again be Schwinn? A 1990 consumer survey rated it the most powerful brand name in the sports equipment field, ahead of Wilson balls and Remington guns. Among all goods and services, Schwinn's recognition among shoppers falls between that of United Airlines and Wrigley's Doublemint gum. Ferries notes that Schwinn still sold nearly a half-million bikes in 1992, when all the mistakes of past years drove the company into bankruptcy. Imagine how many it could sell, he argues, "if you could just be as good" as the competition.

Schwinn in its final years as a family company was easy pickings for antagonists like Trek, Specialized, and Giant. But by 1996, the new owners were demonstrating that they could be as good as the competition, as Schwinn actually gained on Specialized and Giant. Trek still rules the independent market, outdistancing itself from its nearest competitor by 500,000 bikes, but in early 1996, No. 2 Schwinn was "fending off others who have pretensions for second place," says industry consultant Bill

Fields. Competitors had been skeptical that Schwinn ever could make a dent in the market for bicycles above $500, yet marketing director Bagni was courting a new generation that didn't remember the bad old days.

Trek was one of the biggest winners in the Schwinn crack-up; in 1995 it generated $330 million in revenues and sold about one million bikes worldwide—the kind of volume Schwinn enjoyed in its heyday. The Wisconsin company expanded domestic production, building a second plant 40 miles southeast of Waterloo, and its strategy was to grow by adding new lines. After the 1993 acquisition of the Gary Fisher brand, Trek bought other hot names in companies owned by components maker Keith Bontrager and aluminum bicycle pioneer Gary Klein. A licensing deal with three-time Tour de France champion Greg LeMond helped Trek remain the bicycle brand of the hour. "Trek is riding a tremendous wave of designer labelism," grouses dealer Jeff Crittenden. "If you're fifteen years old and not on a Trek, don't bother riding a bike."

With its highly crafted image, Specialized gained its share of the pie during Schwinn's fall, and the California company remained more deeply associated with racing and the oh-so-hip elements of biking. Corporate marketing and press materials regularly touted the company's almost maniacally with-it bike designers, from "Insane" Wayne Croasdale to a colleague who annually pedaled 140 miles across Death Valley on the latest Specialized model. "Nobody designs better bikes than a bike fanatic," sniffed a catalog. But Specialized, which sold an estimated 350,000 bikes a year in the United States during the early 1990s, was losing market share at mid-decade, according to consultant Fields. In a move that some observers interpret as a prelude to a sale, Specialized owner Mike Sinyard in 1995 formed a joint venture with adversary Tom Ritchey, whose early designs for MountainBikes were cribbed by Sinyard.

Plenty of other winners and losers emerged in the aftermath of Schwinn's Chapter 11 filing. A supplier shuffle followed the Zell-Chilmark purchase as Schwinn aligned itself with Trek's Taiwan vendor, Merida, for the models that China Bicycles didn't produce. Giant completed the game of musical chairs by partnering with Trek. The reason for the split was simple. After collecting only a portion of its $9 million debt, "Giant would always be billing Schwinn for the past," observes former Trek purchasing manager Fred Drenhouse. "Schwinn had to make the move." Some at Giant looked at the $9 million philosophically: it was the cost of repaying Schwinn for spectacular growth. In 1995, Giant became a publicly traded company, with earnings of $12 million on worldwide sales of more than $380 million. Later that year, the blue chip investment banking firm Goldman Sachs purchased a 7 percent stake in Giant for an estimated $12.5 million. The bike maker constructed a second plant—this one on mainland China, east of Shanghai—whose capacity of 1.5 million bikes doubles annual output to 3 million bikes.

Business wasn't going as smoothly in the United States. Bill Austin, who had launched Giant's American drive in 1988, left his post in late 1993, after a falling out with Tony Lo. Giant was unable to sustain its early sales gains. Although the company had sold as many as 300,000 bikes a year around the time of the Schwinn bankruptcy, sales slipped closer to the 200,000 level in 1995, according to consultant Fields. In contrast to Trek, Giant was saddled with a middle-market image, acquired no doubt through its unwitting mentor, Schwinn. Former executive turned consultant Jay Townley, who had engineered Schwinn's shift in production from Chicago to Giant in the early 1980s, served a one-year stint heading Giant's U.S. operations until Tony Lo moved to the States in early 1995 to assume the presidency of Giant's flailing U.S. arm. Many Schwinn veterans remained, including former product managers Fred Teeman, David Karneboge, and Chuck Gillis. Walking into a Giant booth at an American trade show often felt like entering a Schwinn exhibit ten years earlier.

After leaving Giant, Austin resurfaced six months later as head of the renamed Raleigh USA Bicycle Company in Kent, Washington, part of Derby International Corporation of Luxembourg, which also now owns the Nishiki name. Derby bought the lagging brand from Huffy in 1988, but Raleigh was plagued by steep losses and declines in dealer loyalty. Austin's task is not unlike that of Schwinn's new owners: attempting to restore a venerable brand to its former glory.

Austin's old rival John Barker continued globe-trotting for China Bicycles, which earned $16 million on sales of almost $191 million in 1994.

A year later, Jerome Sze and Stephen Codron moved to sleek offices on the thirty-seventh floor of a new Hong Kong tower with a spectacular 360-degree view of the city. The offices scream, "Let's show the world how well we've done," says one frequent visitor. Like Giant, China Bicycles also built a massive second factory complex—this one in Longhwa, less than an hour from the original Shenzhen plant, and stretching nearly fifteen city blocks; slated production of 2.5 million units would boost China Bicycles' overall capacity from the two locations to 3.5 million, but the plant was operating well below capacity at mid-decade.

Bikes are just a part (and a dwindling one at that) of Sze's thriving empire. China Bicycles in recent years has invested in real estate, construction, and printing, both in Hong Kong and on the mainland, and bicycles are expected to fall to 20 percent of total sales by the year 2000 from about 40 percent in 1996. In joint ventures with the Chinese government, for example, China Bicycles began constructing a power station and a water treatment plant, investing $500 million in the projects.

Nonetheless, China Bicycles was dogged by the bankruptcy. The liquidation of the Schwinn Estate, under the jurisdiction of the unsecured creditors committee, presented a way for Giant (head of the group after China Bicycles' lucrative exit) to get even. As part of the deal to appease unsecured creditors, China Bicycles in the spring of 1993 had remitted to the estate about $2.5 million from the sale of a slice of the Schwinn-held stock it had retrieved. That added up to an average stock price of nearly 91 cents a share. In the following months, however, members of the committee received copies of Asian newspaper articles reporting that China Bicycles stock subsequently traded elsewhere at $1.27 a share. The committee, led by Giant's attorney, won approval from Bankruptcy Court Judge Jack Schmetterer to investigate, which included a one-hour telephone grilling of John Barker, and later sued both China Bicycles and Barker for $1 million it said it should have received, along with $3 million in punitive damages. Barker had engaged in "inequitable conduct relating to Schwinn and its assets," the creditors charged. (They subsequently won a court order halting distribution of $44,380 in employee benefits that Barker had been owed by Schwinn.) Giant had nothing to lose; a judgment against China Bicycles could recoup more money for it and other unsecured creditors. In early 1996, China Bicycles agreed to pay $700,000 to settle this and an unrelated dispute. Barker's creditor status was restored and he was slated to receive the previously withheld distribution—with interest.

The scuffle with China Bicycles was but one sideshow in the bankruptcy wrap-up, a seemingly never-ending process that proves, again, that lawyers and consultants often are the biggest winners in such proceedings.

Schwinn counsel Keck Mahin & Cate earned fees and expenses exceeding $1.1 million—a tidy sum, considering that the Schwinn family received only $2.5 million for the entire business. The unsecured creditors committee was impressed, too. It sued Keck to recover $486,000, but received only $45,000 in a settlement; still, the aggressive posture was part of a strategy to recoup more funds for creditors, with the hope of raising the final payout to as much as 35 cents on the dollar. Attorney Dennis O'Dea moved to New York in 1994 to expand his firm's bankruptcy practice, but Keck Mahin & Cate hit hard times following an overly ambitious expansion. By the mid-1990s, it was cutting costs amid lawyer defections and declining revenues and was forced to pare back to the smaller partnership it once was.

Workout consultant Arnie Dratt made about $260,000. "Administrating in a bankruptcy is a feeding frenzy—a lineup of lawyers," he observes. But "I don't think any of the fees were unusual. It's miraculous the family got anything."

Chapman & Cutler, the law firm representing the bank syndicate, was awarded some $433,000 in fees and expenses. (And embarrassed not long after when its top bankruptcy partner was discovered to have billed his numerous clients, including Harris Bank, more than 5,400 hours in a single year—a figure that averages out to near-15-hour days, every week, weekend, and holiday, for 365 days.)

Katten Muchin & Zavis, attorney for the unsecured creditors committee, was paid $609,000 through January 1994, the month that Judge Schmetterer signed off on most of the lawyer and consultant fees, although the firm continued to make money handling creditor claims. Shortly after the Zell-Chilmark sale, Katten hired a new head of its bankruptcy practice, David Heller, the lawyer who represented the Ignaz Schwinn Trust and helped negotiate Zell-Chilmark's $2.5 million payment for the license to the family name. Heller already was well known in local workout circles for his representation of secured creditors, but the Schwinn case burnished his reputation.

The task of engineering the optimal payout to unsecured creditors fell to Katten's Mark Thomas, who worked to reduce the size of questionable claims and negotiated to get the best deals possible for the assets of the Schwinn Estate not picked up by Zell-Chilmark. One of those unwanted holdings was Schwinn's Paramount machine shop in Waterford, Wisconsin. Shortly after the close of the Zell-Chilmark deal, the estate sold the Paramount Design Group to Richard Schwinn, who is forging his own path in the bike business. Richard and partners George Garner and former Schwinn designer Marc Muller paid $145,000 for the subsidiary that hand-crafted bikes. Yet even Richard cannot lay claim to the family's famed Paramount brand. The Zell group owns that name, too. Garner bailed out one year after the purchase, following disagreements with Richard. Ed's younger brother—the only Schwinn left in the bicycle manufacturing business—must make the diminished enterprise spin with a new handle, Waterford Precision Cycles.

Then there was the matter of disposing of Schwinn's stake in Hungary's Csepel factory. Zell-Chilmark wanted no part of the Budapest fiasco. It was up to liquidator Arnie Dratt to wring the most he could from Schwinn's 41.5 percent stake. His strategy: make a nuisance of the Schwinn Estate as a shareholder. He opposed managers' bonuses, for example. "I gave [General Manager Gyorgy] Podolak incentives to get me out of his hair," Dratt says. In 1992, as Schwinn unraveled, Podolak had found a new investor in Hanti Limited, a venture between a colorful Russian oilman who had hit it big in Siberia and traveled with an entourage and a Hungarian entrepreneur who operated an oil field service business and drove a Mercedes. Hanti paid an estimated $2 million for an initial 41.5 percent stake in Csepel, which enabled Podolak to pare debt and obtain bank credit. In December 1993, Dratt sold the Schwinn Estate's equal stake to Hanti for about $330,000 during a long session at the country home of Hungarian partner Sandor Molnar. The closing featured three-way translations and frequent vodka toasts to friendship and eternal peace. The factory continued to use the name Schwinn Csepel on its bikes sold in Hungary. Willy Ehrlich continued as a shareholder, too, albeit with a reduced 3 percent stake. But Ehrlich had his own problems: The company he had founded, Bicycle Corporation of America, filed for Chapter 11 protection in August 1994 and Ehrlich retired as chairman several months later.

The 1,000 former Schwinn employees with traditional pensions had nothing to fear from the bankruptcy: Their retirement benefits were assured by the government's Pension Benefit Guaranty Corporation. Still, the Schwinn plan was underfunded by 55 percent, or $9 million, according to the federal oversight agency. As an unsecured creditor, the government is set to get about $2 million through the Bankruptcy Court, while the Pension Benefit Guaranty Corporation, funded by employer-paid premiums, will cover the remaining $7 million shortfall.

A handful of former top executives, including Barker, Al Fritz, Lee Meader, and Frank Brilando, filed six-figure claims in Bankruptcy Court for life insurance or supplementary retirement benefits that weren't covered by traditional pension protection laws. Former senior vice president Gerard O'Keefe was hardest hit. Having joined Schwinn late in his career, he opted for an alternative plan that offered accelerated payments after retirement. Unfortunately, it wasn't insured by the government. O'Keefe and the other executives went for more than two years without a Schwinn benefit check and they, like other unsecured creditors, were slated to collect only about 35 cents on every dollar owed.

There were other familiar faces in the unsecured creditors line. Bevil Hogg and Tom French, who had agreed to defer their last payment for Kestrel, were stiffed in the bankruptcy and asked the estate for $300,000. They, too, negotiated the size of the claim and ended up receiving about $50,000 each. Hogg and French again moved on, but managed to remain in a business with spokes and hubs. In early 1994, Hogg was named chief executive of Everest and Jennings International, a St. Louis manufacturer of wheelchairs that had fallen on hard times, while French became head of Everest & Jennings' West Coast–based R&D department. That same year, Japan's Mitsui sold Kestrel to a management group headed by outside investor Bill Gilliam, a North Carolina triathlete and bicycle devotee.

Lawyers for the creditors committee wrestled with Continental Partners, the investment banking unit that had sought to sell Schwinn in the months before the bankruptcy. Continental filed a claim for $450,000 after the family's business was sold to Zell-Chilmark. Citing its 1991 contract, Continental said it was entitled to its fee if it was terminated and Schwinn was sold within one year. Moreover, Continental argued, it had made the initial contacts with the Zell group when marketing Schwinn. After negotiations, Continental accepted a claim of $200,000. It is expected to receive about $40,000.

The committee also tangled with Ed and Richard to invalidate their claims of $636,000—the golden parachutes drafted several hours before the Chapter 11 filing. The brothers had the effrontery, the creditors contended, to sign this agreement and "claim with straight faces" that they weren't required to seek court approval for an obligation that would load Schwinn with more than $500,000 in additional debt on the day it entered bankruptcy. The creditors blamed the brothers for rendering the company insolvent and not intervening at critical junctures to accept offers to buy the company or hire a crisis manager—moves that could have resulted in a better payout for creditors. Lawyers for Ed and Richard denied the committee's accusations, calling them "unspecific attacks" on the brothers' business judgment. Ed and Richard "exercised due care, judgment, and skill in the management of the company and at all times acted in good faith," the lawyers argued. In 1995 the brothers negotiated settlements with the unsecured creditors—Ed agreed to a $20,000 payment, while Richard will receive $12,000.

Ed and Richard faced legal problems on another front. Ten months after the Zell-Chilmark sale, eight of the family trust beneficiaries, led by cousin Deborah Schwinn Bailey, sued the brothers and First Chicago for a whopping $200 million. The suit alleges numerous infractions, including fraud, self-dealing, breach of trust and fiduciary duty, mismanagement, and reckless misconduct. Those and other lapses by the trust officers, the disgruntled relatives charged, had led the company into bankruptcy and depleted the trust's value.

The case was filed in Bailey's hometown of Mobile, Alabama. She was joined by her three brothers and two sisters, each of whom owns about 7.1 percent of the trust's stock, and their aunts, Betty Dembecki and Pepper White, who each have about 18.3 percent. The group controls nearly 80 percent of the trust. Attorneys for Ed and Richard called their lawsuit groundless, and the defendants sought to dismiss the action, arguing that Alabama had no jurisdiction in the matter. Illinois would be a more convenient forum, the brothers' lawyers said, since records pertaining to the Schwinn bankruptcy were in Chicago, as were many of the potential witnesses in the case. "I have physically been in Alabama for approximately 15 minutes as a tourist," Ed said in an affidavit.

(First Chicago, which declined to comment on the charges, resigned as bank trustee in 1994. The Ignaz Schwinn Trust was relocated to Lake Shore National Bank, which subsequently was acquired by First Chicago, and was moved again, this time to another Chicago institution, Cole Taylor Bank.)

An Alabama judge dismissed the case in December 1994, without ruling on the merits of the charges. He agreed with Ed and Richard that the matter would be more conveniently contested in Schwinn's former home state of Illinois. The Bailey group appealed to the Alabama Supreme Court, rejecting, for the time being, the option of bringing the dispute to Illinois. As of early 1996, the petitioners vowed to pursue their charges. The original complaint argued that Richard and First Chicago trustee James Kiel could have voted to fire Ed "and install competent management." The pair could have accepted an offer for all or some of the stock or otherwise acted "to forestall and to mitigate and to redress and recover the losses of the company, the Trust, and the beneficiaries." Ed frustrated opportunities for new capital in 1991 and 1992 because he couldn't bear to give up his job, with its salary, benefits, and control, according to the suit. The family cited as a breach of duty Ed's 1985 investment in the partnership that owned Schwinn's downtown headquarters building and leased the space to the bicycle company—a potential conflict, they say, that wasn't disclosed to beneficiaries until six years later.

The move that really came back to haunt all fourteen beneficiaries was the 1981 financing of the Greenville plant. The trust had guaranteed a bond issue of about $2 million to build the factory; closing Greenville in 1992 hadn't ended that obligation. Since the bankruptcy, the Bailey group said in its lawsuit, the trust has been funding the failed factory's amortizations, insurance payments, and other obligations that total more than $17,000 per month. Papers filed in Robert Schwinn's 1994 divorce peg the assets of the trust at $5 million or more. (The trust, of course, does not reflect any personal wealth of the individual beneficiaries, including properties they may have inherited over the decades.) Ignaz Schwinn's vehicle for distributing the family's corporate wealth dissolves in 2008. Whatever assets remain presumably will be divided among shareholders.

More pain stung the family following the bankruptcy. Betty and Stanley Dembecki began divorce proceedings. Rychie Schwinn sought a court ruling that would compel her ex-husband, Robert, to help with insurance and college tuition in addition to child support. Robert's younger brother, Tom, also divorced.

There was a consolation prize, of sorts. A century in the bike business had offered plenty of time for the family to collect the world's best cycles. And collect they did—amassing more than 600 two-, three-, and four-wheelers of various makes and sizes, plus several thousand components, signs, decals, accessories, and other memorabilia. Fortunately for the family, nostalgia meant nothing to Zell-Chilmark, so the family's antique bikes and cycling knickknacks were excluded from the final sale agreement and remained the property of the Schwinn clan. "We called it the 'tchotchke clause,' " quips David Schulte.

The Schwinns did nicely by their collection. In July 1993, the family sold most of it for an estimated $700,000 to the Bicycle Museum of

America, a nonprofit organization started by former Schwinn curator James Hurd. Among the directors was Peter Davis, who has pursued a career in computers since his departure from Schwinn. The museum, housed in a renovated pier on Chicago's downtown lakefront, opened during the summer of 1993. Its offerings range from an early draisienne to an 1870 wood-wheeled "boneshaker," from a 1950 Rollfast Hopalong Cassidy bike (with toy pistols holstered at the handlebar) to a 1972 lemon-yellow Sting-Ray. Various Schwinns stop by every once in a while with their children to remind them (and perhaps themselves) of the family's role in the industry.

And what of the rest of the cast? Friends gathered for the funerals of Keizo Shimano, lawyer Bob Keck, former executive Keith Kingbay, and longtime California dealer Bill Hill. Yet life rolls on. Most of the members of Schwinn's executive committee, such as Mike McNamara, Brian Fiala, and Mike Martinsen, fanned out into management jobs in the Chicago area. After his ill-fated transfer to Boulder, Byron Smith moved back to Chicago to handle marketing for a company that makes glass for cars. Consultant Jay Townley joined a bicycle components startup. Al Fritz, champion of the Air-Dyne, is seeking a partner to help him market an exercise machine he developed. Once a month, he and other old-timers, including Bill Chambers and George Garner, get together for lunch. Ray Burch visits from California once a year. Inevitably, they reminisce about the good times. And the bad. Ed bears the blame in their book: they were the ones who helped Ignaz, F.W., and Frank V. over the decades build the greatest name in bikes, while *he* ran it into the ground in just over ten years.

It's not that simple. When Schwinn reached the fourth generation of management, it was running on borrowed time—a rare family enterprise that had lasted even that long. "It was a miracle that our business survived for ninety-seven years," Richard Schwinn told *Bicycle Retailer* in 1994. Indeed, studies show that only 10 percent of family-owned companies survive even the *third* generation. Grandchildren are bequeathed the company, observes consultant and University of Chicago instructor Bob Calvin, but "nobody inherits the ability to make these things go." What Ed inherited in the 1970s was a company with outdated manufacturing, an entrenched bureaucracy, and an extreme case of corporate arrogance that blinded him and other top managers to the realities of a changing market. "Schwinn is a story about complacency," says Sam Zell. "It thought it was bulletproof." The company nearly died during the early-1980s financial crisis, yet because Schwinn had so much going for it—its name and reputation, its dealers and sales strength—the family won a second chance from lenders. The tragedy was that they couldn't capitalize on the opportunity, and in this respect, the fault lies not only with Ed but with the structure of the family trust, which offered no mechanism for a change in leadership if current management failed. In the end, the family business suffocated.

Still, Ed is left with the blame. There can be no other ending, for he was the man in charge, the Schwinn who lost Schwinn. It's not clear, however, how Ed is faring with that judgment. In the months after the bankruptcy, he fled from public view, selling both his home on the North Side of Chicago and the family's grand old mansion on Lake Geneva (the latter for $1.2 million to a developer who bulldozed the property to build another residence). A yard sale in Chicago offered little for Schwinn scavengers: a couple of electric fans from Ignaz's days; some cycling posters from the 1970s; the usual ashtrays and similar trade show gear stamped with corporate logos. Many of the prices seemed high. His wife, Leslie, was overheard explaining, "Ed walked around this morning putting ones in front of my prices." A few weeks later, sources say Ed was asked what the future held for him. "I run companies," he responded matter-of-factly. "I'm looking for a company to run."

Ed soon settled in the familiar surroundings of Lake Geneva. His new enterprise: a cheese shop and mail-order business. "The Cheese Box—carrying on a tradition of excellence," a local shopper's guide reported in mid-1994, after Ed and a partner bought out the owners of Walworth County's oldest cheese store. "For over fifty years, a landmark at the southern gateway of Lake Geneva . . . the only place in the area you can find fresh mozzarella." To visitors and Internet customers, Ed sells gift baskets, jams and jellies, pickled vegetables, "Summer Sausage that comes 'Mit' or 'Mitout' Garlic," wax-coated cheeses in the shape of cows, and "Just Say Moo" T-shirts. In this pastoral setting that inspired great-grandfather Ignaz, Ed seems to have enough time to think about the past, to wonder, perhaps, how he could have done things differently. How he might have changed the course of the final days; how he might have prevented a Great American Company from slipping through his fingers.

NOTES

1: "EVERYTHING IS BICYCLE"

1. Family lore also has the young Ignaz Schwinn inventing the coaster brake in Germany. "However, somebody stole his invention," great-grandson Richard C. Schwinn said in a 1994 speech at the Mountain Bike Hall of Fame in Crested Butte, Colorado. "Angry, Ignaz traveled to America." Yet there's no evidence to support such a claim, according to James Hurd, former curator of the Bicycle Museum of America in Chicago, adding that the New Departure Company and Eclipse Bicycle Company, both based on the East Coast, received the first U.S. patents for coaster brakes in 1897, two years after Ignaz had founded his business.
2. Despite his early fame and wealth, Major Taylor died alone in the charity ward of Chicago's Cook County Hospital in 1932, his death noted only by a local black-owned newspaper and the French cycling press. Sixteen years later, Frank W. Schwinn paid to exhume Taylor's remains from an unmarked grave and bury the man properly, with a eulogy by 1932 and 1936 Olympics runner Ralph Metcalfe (a Chicago alderman at the time) and a bronze plaque that read, "A credit to his race who always gave out his best. Gone but not forgotten." Former executive Keith Kingbay told bicycle historian and Taylor biographer Andrew Ritchie that if Frank W. had "known in 1932 that Major Taylor was in a hospital, and in a county hospital like

that, he would have been over there, to give some help, some assistance. . . . Frank Schwinn would do an awful lot of those kinds of things, without ever tying his name or his company's name to them."

2: A BUST—AND A COMEBACK

1. "People still ask me if I am related to Arnold Schwinn," Richard C. Schwinn joked in 1994.
2. Such as Huffman, H.P. Snyder Manufacturing Company (later known for its Rollfast models), and the remnants of Colonel Pope's once-mighty firm, reorganized as Westfield Manufacturing Company after the bicycle trust failure, and as Columbia Bicycle Company in 1961.
3. Besides Frank V. and Edward R. Schwinn, F.W. and Gertrude had two children who died at early ages. Helen Virginia Schwinn was born in April 1926 and died in December 1930. John Robert Schwinn was born in November 1921 and died in July 1925.

5: COOL? AND HOW

1. "In a few short paragraphs," *Business Week* huffed, "the high court went far beyond anything it had said previously about manufacturers' controls over distribution." Yet for all the sturm und drang over the antitrust fight, Schwinn's position was upheld a decade later in a 1977 case involving GTE Sylvania. A more conservative Supreme Court agreed that the television manufacturer had the right to cancel a bootlegging San Francisco dealer who had shipped sets to an unauthorized second store in Sacramento after Sylvania had refused his request to open a franchise there. That overturned the Schwinn Doctrine and gave a nod to manufacturers who wanted greater power to control their distribution. The reversal helped Schwinn, too, because it could crack down on dealers who similarly trans-shipped goods. Twenty years after F.W. told Ray Burch he had done nothing wrong, Schwinn's position finally was vindicated. Antitrust prosecutor Richard Posner today is chief judge of the 7th Circuit Court of Appeals in Chicago and a prominent University of Chicago professor known for his vigorous free-market views. Judge Posner looks back on his role and says the concept of restricting distribution gained academic respectability in the ten years between the Schwinn decision and the Sylvania ruling. "I was unsympathetic at the time," he says, "but now I think [Schwinn's marketing approach] was good."

7: THE HANGOVER

1. Weight was a relative thing. Schwinn called its 37-pound Varsity a "lightweight" because the model was not as heavy as its old 50-pound paperboy bike with coaster brakes.

8: "WEIRD AND FREAKY STUFF"

1. Changed from Huffman Manufacturing Company in 1974.
2. The competing GT brand, founded by drag-racer Gary Turner, would later overtake Mongoose as the biggest force in the BMX market.

9: "JUST BEING A KID"

1. Breeze says he never was a stoner. Fisher says he "never smoked before a race."
2. A July 1983 *New York Times* article described one mountain biker in Central Park as an urban oddity, drawing stares from ten-speed cyclists and questions at stoplights. "It's meant to be abused," said the rider, an East Village artist. "I also look more ominous on the bike—pedestrians get out of your way because it seems heavier than a racer."
3. The '70s mountain bike pioneers still squabble over who deserves credit for "inventing" the vehicle. Gary Fisher generally is considered the first to add gears to a clunker. He also introduced thumbshifters, which had been used on Schwinn ladies' five-speeds, so that a mountain biker didn't have to risk losing control in mid-ride by groping for a gear-shifter, and he added an important mechanism for adjusting the height of the seatpost that was crucial in creating a safer, sturdier perch. Nevertheless, there is lingering controversy over the timing of his innovations. Fisher says he completed his first mountain bike in 1974. Charles Kelly and Joe Breeze suggest he actually got some of his ideas from now-forgotten riders who showed up at a cyclo-cross race in December 1974; therefore, Fisher couldn't have completed his mountain bike until 1975 at the earliest. In any event, the other riders didn't publicize their innovations; Fisher did, and continues doing so, frequently exhibiting his original mountain bike at trade shows. As for Breeze, his first Breezer model is on display at the Oakland Museum's Cowell Hall of California History. And Kelly's Breezer No. 2 rests in the Mountain Bike Hall of Fame.

13: THE DIFFERENCE O'DEA MADE

1. Northern Trust found itself in an interesting conflict. For decades, the bank had been custodian of the Ignaz Schwinn Trust, which was the ultimate owner and financier of the bike company. How could Northern be involved in strategic decisions of the Schwinn Trust, yet on the other hand demand payment of its loan from the family business? Northern's answer was to resign as trustee. The Schwinn trust was transferred to Oak Park Trust & Savings, later purchased by First Chicago Corporation.
2. Wilson, now a Northern Trust senior vice president, and Lyman, now a Harris vice chairman, declined to comment.
3. Disgruntled beneficiaries of the Ignaz Schwinn Trust later would charge they weren't informed until 1991 that the new headquarters building was leased from a partnership in which Ed, Barker, and Brilando held interests. The building was rented at an "exorbitant" cost of more than $635,000 in 1992, according to a lawsuit filed a year later by Schwinn family members. The lawsuit charged a "breach of duty," arguing that Ed, as a Schwinn officer, was bound to pursue the best interests of the company—a mission that could conflict with his additional role as landlord to Schwinn. An attorney for Ed's brother, Richard, called the entire suit "completely without merit." Barker says the building shares were offered to all senior executives, and the three paid the same price as nonaffiliated buyers who knew Schwinn would be the tenant. "It was a straight deal," he says.

15: SCHWINN MEETS CENTRAL PLANNING

1. Ross later was plagued by intrafamily squabbling. The company filed for U.S. Bankruptcy Court protection in 1987 and the forty-two-year-old Ross bike name was acquired by Rand International, a Long Island importer of cycles for mass merchants.
2. After an initial interview, Ehrlich did not return phone calls seeking comment on his Ross departure.
3. Nogradi and Podolak could not be reached for comment.

16: THE CHINA SYNDROME

1. Codron says China Bicycles never planned to sell Schwinn more than 30 percent of its capacity (1.5 million units at the time) because it needed to tend to more than a dozen other customers around the world—a point he believes Ed, as a shareholder, understood.

19: "AN IMPORTANT GUY"

1. Mitsui was a behind-the-scenes force in the industry, shipping parts for many companies, including Schwinn. Having provided early financing for Trek, Mitsui was impressed with the young Bevil Hogg and offered to buy into his next venture when its management learned he was exiting the Wisconsin bicycle maker.
2. Dembecki and White each owned 18.2540 percent of the Schwinn Family Trust, according to court documents. Ed's cousins, Ignaz Schwinn III, Robert Schwinn, Thomas Schwinn, Terry Ann Schwinn, Deborah Schwinn Bailey, and Barbie Schwinn Jacobs each owned 7.1428 percent. Ed; his brother, Richard; their sisters, Lisa Schwinn Thynne, Mary Katherine Schwinn Davis, and Susan Benett Schwinn; and their mother, Mary Coad Schwinn, each owned 3.4392 percent.
3. Robert Schwinn, Thomas Schwinn, and Ignaz Schwinn III did not respond to requests for comments.

23: THE VULTURE SWOOPS

1. Zell ran into a liquidity problem in the early 1990s because of his high debt load and the continuing market slump. Making matters worse, he had personally guaranteed real estate loans with an estimated value of between $300 million and $500 million. At the time of his bid for Schwinn, Zell was busy restructuring his portfolio by selling assets—including many of the Itel acquisitions he had engineered—and using a bull stock market to float a series of initial and secondary stock offerings whose proceeds were used to reduce debt. But by late 1993, a *Barron's* article found Zell in a more jovial mood: "Jesus," he told one telephone caller, "did you see the new high on Itel? Just [expletive] fabulous."
2. Charles Ferries was also a courtroom target of Schwinn attorney Dennis O'Dea, who needled the suitor (a former executive of ski maker K2 Corporation) by pointing to his lack of experience in the bicycle industry. "How many wheels were there on the K2?" O'Dea asked Ferries.

SOURCES

Despite numerous invitations, Edward R. Schwinn, Jr., declined to be interviewed for this book. The eight beneficiaries of the Ignaz Schwinn Trust who sued Edward and his brother, Richard C. Schwinn, also declined to discuss the family business, citing the pending litigation, although Robert Schwinn's former wife, Rychie Schwinn, provided a window on family dynamics. Edward's brother-in-law Peter Davis was interviewed for a 1993 article in *Crain's Chicago Business* but declined to cooperate for this book, and Richard voiced contempt for the project in 1994, telling the trade magazine *Bicycle Retailer and Industry News*, "I am calling on the thousands of people who have benefited from the work of the Schwinn family, and the hundreds of suppliers and thousands of employees whose wealth we helped increase, to not cooperate."

More than 160 people were interviewed in the course of this work, from family friends and longtime dealers to current and former executives. Their recollections, observations, notes, documents, and photographs helped make this story come alive, and for that the authors offer our deepest gratitude.

Ray Burch, Bill Chambers, and Al Fritz were instrumental in reconstructing the glory days of Schwinn Bicycle Company. F. W. Schwinn's nephew, Rudolph Schwinn, provided perspective on the family. Jack Ahearn was insightful on the decline of the Chicago factory. Other Schwinn alumni who were especially generous with their time include Bill Austin, Carl Cohen, Brian Fiala, David

Karneboge, Nai-Wen Kiang, Mike Martinsen, Mike McNamara, Byron Smith, David Staub, and Fred Teeman.

Uberdealer George Garner was key to our tale, and dealers Jeff Allen, Ron Boi, Jim Burris, Jeff Crittenden, Terry and Patty Gibson, John Graves, John Lewis, Ralph Litten, Mike Mulrooney, John Pelc, Joe Russell, Gary Sirota, Chris Travers, and Oscar Wastyn, Jr., took time from tending to their busy stores to assist us. Dale and Allen Martin of Martins Bike Shop in Ephrata, Pennsylvania, provided photographs of their bicycle collection.

Joe Breeze, Gary Fisher, and Charlie Kelly helped recount the early Marin County mountain bike years. Trek founder Richard Burke, managers John Burke, Harry Spehar, and Pat Sullivan, former manager Fred Drenhouse and departed co-founders Bevil Hogg and Tom French offered valuable insight. SRAM President Stanley Day provided a useful industry perspective. Bankruptcy attorney Dennis O'Dea was unsparing with his time, as were turnaround specialist Arnold Dratt and attorney H. Slayton Dabney, Jr. Industry consultant Bill Fields and other professionals were helpful; some spoke only on condition of anonymity, and we appreciate their guidance. Schwinn's new owners—Charles Ferries, David Schulte, and Sam Zell—illuminated the final stage of the drama. And special thanks to two experts who provided much of our early education in the workings of the industry: former Schwinn executive Jay Townley and Gregg Bagni, a former sales representative for Scott in Chicago who is the new Schwinn's marketing director.

Additional assistance and research materials were provided by the Alaska Historical Society, the American Motorcyclist Association, the Art Institute of Chicago's Ryerson Library, the Bicycle Museum of America, *Bicycle Retailer and Industry News*, the Chicago Historical Society, the Chicago Public Library, Crain Communications, Inc., Katten Muchin & Zavis, the National Museum of Man, Northwestern University Library, the Oak Park Public Library, the Ohio Historical Society, Spalding Sports Worldwide, the Chicago office of the U.S. Bureau of Labor Statistics, the University of Wyoming, the Winnetka Police Department, and the Women's Christian Temperance Union.

Chapter 1: "EVERYTHING IS BICYCLE"

The two most useful bicycle histories were published more than twenty years ago: Robert A. Smith's exhaustive *A Social History of the Bicycle: Its Early Life and Times in America* (New York: American Heritage Press, 1972) and Andrew Ritchie's excellent *King of the Road: An Illustrated History of Cycling* (London: Wildwood House, 1975). Another important source for this and other chapters was the trade magazine *American Bicyclist and Motorcyclist*, with issues under various titles (including *Bicycle News* and *The Wheel*) stretching back to 1879. Most helpful were issues from 1895 to 1899, as well as December 1955 (75th anniversary issue), October 1969 (90th anniversary), and December 1979 (100th anniversary).

Other sources that offered information on the development of the bicycle, the 1890s boom, the founding of Schwinn, and the collapse of the market include:

Alderson, Frederick. *Bicycling: A History.* Newton Abbot, England: David & Charles, 1972.

Avis, Frederick Compton. *Cyclists Reference Dictionary.* London: George Marshall, 1954.

The Book of Chicagoans (directory). Chicago: A. N. Marquis. 1931.

Bushnell, George D. "When Chicago Was Wheel Crazy." *Chicago History: The Magazine of the Chicago Historical Society,* Fall 1975.

Caidin, Martin, and Barbree, Jay. *Bicycles in War.* New York: Hawthorn Books, 1974.

Casey, Louis S. *Curtis: The Hammondsport Era, 1907–1915.* New York: Crown Publishers, 1981.

Casey, Robert J. *Chicago Medium Rare: When We Were Both Younger.* Indianapolis: Bobbs-Merrill, 1949.

Chicago Bicycle Directory. 1898.

Chicago: The Great Central Market. Chicago: Chicago Association of Commerce, 1923.

Chicago's Thousand Dollar Book (directory). Chicago: L. C. Hurley, 1914.

Chapin, Louella. *Round About Chicago.* Chicago: Unity, 1907.

Clark, Herma Naomi. *The Elegant Eighties: When Chicago Was Young.* Chicago: A. C. McClurg, 1941.

Cole, Terrence, ed. *Wheels on Ice: Bicycling in Alaska, 1898–1908.* Anchorage: Alaska Northwest Publishing, 1985.

Cook, Frederick Frances. *Bygone Days of Chicago.* Chicago: A. C. McClurg, 1910.

Country Club of Evanston (yearbook). Evanston, Ill., 1895.

Crissey, Forrest. *Since Forty Years Ago: A History of the Fair Department Store.* Chicago: The Fair, 1915.

Crouch, Tom D., and Sharkey, Gerald S. "A Wrong or Two Wrights?" *Timeline,* August–September 1987.

Dollar, Charles M. "Putting the Army on Wheels: The Story of the Twenty-Fifth Infantry Bicycle Corps." *Prologue: Journal of the National Archives,* Spring 1985.

The Elite Directory and Club List of Chicago. Chicago: Elite Directory, 1889.

Engelhardt, George Washington. *Chicago: The Book of Its Board of Trade and Other Public Bodies.* Chicago: Chicago Board of Trade, 1900.

Fifty Years of Schwinn-Built Bicycles: The Story of the Bicycle and Its Contributions to Our Way of Life. Chicago: Arnold, Schwinn & Company, 1945.

Harrison, Carter H. *Stormy Years: The Autobiography of Carter H. Harrison, Five Times Mayor of Chicago.* Indianapolis: Bobbs-Merrill, 1935.

Herringshaw, Mae Felts, ed. *Herringshaw's City Blue Book of Biography.* Chicago: Clark J. Herringshaw; 1913, 1914, and 1919 issues.

Howard, Robert P. *Illinois: A History of the Prairie State.* Grand Rapids, Michigan: W. B. Eerdmans Publishing, 1972.

Humber, William. "Could Gretsky Have Done It?" *Canadian Heritage,* Winter 1988.

Hyde, Charles K. "The Auto in American Life." *Technology and Culture,* Winter 1989.

Kingbay, Keith. *Inside Bicycling.* Chicago: Henry Regnery, 1976.

Lakeside Annual Directory of the City of Chicago. Chicago: Chicago Directory Company, 1893–1917.

Levine, Peter. A. G. *Spalding and the Rise of Baseball: The Promise of American Sport.* New York: Oxford University Press, 1985.

Lindberg, Richard. *Chicago Ragtime: Another Look at Chicago, 1880–1920.* South Bend, Ind.: Icarus Press, 1985.

Longstreet, Stephen, *Chicago: 1860–1919.* New York: McKay, 1973.

Lucas, John. "A Romantic Moment in Cycling History." *The Bicyclist's Sourcebook,* eds. Michael Leccese and Arlene Plevin, Rockville, Md.: Woodbine House, 1991.

Marinoni, Augusto. "The Bicycle." *The Unknown Leonardo,* ed. Ladislao Reti. New York: McGraw Hill, 1974.

Marks, Patricia. *Bicycles, Bangs, and Bloomers: The New Woman in the Popular Press.* Lexington, Ky: Univ. of Kentucky Press, 1990.

McCoy, Michael. "Bicycles and Buffalo Soldiers." *Men's Journal,* September 1994.

McGonagle, Seamus. *The Bicycle in Life, Love, War and Literature.* New York: A. S. Barnes, 1969.

Mecredy, R. J., and Stoney, Gerald. *The Art and Pastime of Cycling.* Dublin: Mecredy & Kyle, 1890.

Moran, George E. *Moran's Dictionary of Chicago And Its Vicinity.* Chicago: Moran; 1903, 1909, and 1914 issues.

Musselman, M. M. *Get a Horse!* Philadelphia: J. B. Lippincott, 1960.

Nye, Peter. *Hearts of Lions: The History of American Bicycle Racing.* New York: W. W. Norton, 1988.

"One-Hundred Years of the Car in America." *AutoWeek,* 19 July 1993.

Palmer, Arthur Judson. *Riding High: The Story of the Bicycle.* New York: Dutton, 1956.

Palmer, Herman L. *Prominent Citizens and Industries of Chicago.* Chicago: German Press Club of Chicago, 1901.

Plumbe, George E. *Chicago, Its Natural Advantages as an Industrial and Commercial Center and Market.* Chicago: Chicago Association of Commerce, 1910.

Pratt, Charles E. *The American Bicycler: A Manual for the Observer, the Learner, and the Expert.* Boston: Houghton Osgood, 1879.

Pry, Mark E. "Everybody Talks Wheels." *Journal of Arizona History,* 1990.

Ritchie, Andrew. *Major Taylor: The Extraordinary Career of a Champion Bicycle Racer.* San Francisco: Bicycle Books, 1988.

Rush, Anita. "The Bicycle Boom of the Gay Nineties: A Reassessment." *Material History Bulletin/Bulletin d'histoire de la culture matérielle,* Fall 1983.

Schwinn, Richard C. "A Tribute to Ignaz and Frank W. Schwinn." Speech presented at Mountain Bike Hall of Fame, Crested Butte, Colorado, 22 July 1994.

Sinsabaugh, Chris. *Who, Me? Forty Years of Automobile History.* Detroit: Arnold-Powers, 1940.

Stallman, R. W., and Hagemann, E. R., eds. *The New York City Sketches of Stephen Crane.* New York: New York University Press, 1966.

Starrs, James E., ed. *The Noiseless Tenor: The Bicycle in Literature.* New York: Cornwall Books, 1982.

Walton, Bill, and Rostaing, Bjarne. *Bill Walton's Total Book of Cycling.* New York: Bantam Books, 1984.

Whiteside, James. "Bicycling in Gilded Age Colorado." *Colorado Heritage.* Spring 1991.

Willard, Frances Elizabeth, *How I Learned to Ride the Bicycle.* Chicago: Women's Temperance Publishing Association, 1895.

The World (catalog). Chicago: Arnold, Schwinn & Company, 1896.

The World (catalog). Chicago: Arnold, Schwinn & Company, 1897.

Chapter 2: A BUST—AND A COMEBACK

"Notes on Arnold, Schwinn & Company Merchandising," an unpublished manuscript by Frank W. Schwinn, dated July 1942, was the major source for reconstructions of the bicycle industry's post-1900 decline and the company's role in its resurrection during the Depression. *American Bicyclist and Motorcyclist* anniversary issues, as well as issues of February 1933 (introduction of cord balloon-tire bike); September 1948 (Ignaz Schwinn obituary); and May 1963 (Frank W. Schwinn obituary) also were helpful.

Other published sources:

"Albert Goodwill Spalding," *Spalding Store News,* 9 September 1915.

"Motorcycles that Never Were: And Other Secrets of the Schwinn Archives." *American Motorcyclist.* American Motorcyclist Association, December 1994.

"Pre-Trial Brief of Arnold, Schwinn & Co.," *United States of America* v. *Arnold, Schwinn & Co., Schwinn Cycle Distributors Association and the B. F. Goodrich Co.* U.S. District Court, Northern District of Illinois, Eastern Division, 18 August 1962.

"Post Trial Brief of Arnold, Schwinn & Co.," *United States of America* v. *Arnold, Schwinn & Co., Schwinn Cycle Distributors Association and the B. F. Goodrich Co.* U.S. District Court, Northern District of Illinois, Eastern Division, 12 August 1963.

Chapter 3: THE OLD MAN

Nearly 300 back issues of *The Schwinn Reporter,* a monthly newsletter for dealers published from 1951 to 1980, provided much of the information on the company, its people, its corporate culture, the industry, and the marketplace in this and many other chapters. Bicycle sales figures from 1895 to 1979 were published in the March 1980 issue. The September/October 1977 issue of *Schwinn Cycle News,* another company newsletter, offered details on the factory and its workers in the 1950s. Additional information came from *American Bicyclist and Motorcyclist* anniversary issues, Frank W. Schwinn's unpublished notes and the pre- and post-trial briefs of *United States of America* v. *Arnold, Schwinn & Co., et. al.*.

Descriptions of the homes and belongings of Ignaz and F. W. Schwinn were constructed with information in the men's wills and court records on the dispositions of their assets filed in Cook County (Illinois) Probate Court and Walworth County (Wisconsin) Probate Court. The Ignaz Schwinn Trust of 1920 was entered as evidence in *Deborah Schwinn Bailey, et. al.,* v. *Edward R. Schwinn, Jr., et. al.,* filed in Mobile County, Alabama, in November 1993. Brownie Schwinn's arrest was reported in "Keystone Cop Act Lands 'Quiet' Celebrator in Court," in the *New Orleans Statesman,* 24 October 1951.

Other published sources:

Halberstam, David. *The Fifties.* New York: Villard Books, 1993.
Larkin, Larry. *Full Speed Ahead: The Story of the Steamboat Era on Lake Geneva.* Published by the author, Lake Geneva, Wis., 1972.
Wolfmeyer, Ann, and Gage, Mary Burns. *Lake Geneva, Newport of the West, 1870–1920.* Lake Geneva, Wis.: Lake Geneva Historical Society, 1976.

Chapter 4: DEALER AND ÜBERDEALER

The Schwinn Reporter, especially issues from 1951 to 1973, and the pre- and post-trial briefs of *United States of America* v. *Arnold, Schwinn & Co., et. al.,* provided numerous details on the growth of the dealer network and the company's marketing efforts. Also quoted: company brochures, posters, and advertisements from the 1940s, 1950s, and 1960s, and the *Schwinn Sales Manual for Franchised Schwinn Dealers* (Chicago: Schwinn Bicycle Company, 1968).

Chapters 5 and 6: COOL? AND HOW; LET THE GOOD TIMES ROLL

Details on the development of the Sting-Ray and the market's response to the model came from issues of *The Schwinn Reporter* and "The Spyder (Sting-Ray, Screamer) Bike: An American Original," by Arthur Asa Berger, in *Side Saddle on the Golden Calf: Social Structure and Popular Culture in America,* ed. George H. Lewis (Pacific Palisades, Cal.: Goodyear Publishing, 1972).

Facts and observations on family members Frank W. Schwinn, Frank V. Schwinn, Ignaz "Brownie" Schwinn II, and Edward R. Schwinn, Sr., came from source interviews and obituaries and other articles in *American Bicyclist, Chicago Tribune,* and *The Schwinn Reporter.* Additional information came from a divorce complaint, *Jean Y. Schwinn* v. *Ignaz Schwinn II,* filed in DuPage County (Illinois) Circuit Court in March 1971, and the will of Brownie Schwinn, filed in the DuPage court in October 1983.

Background and testimony in the ten-year antitrust case came from pre- and post-trial briefs of *United States of America* v. *Arnold, Schwinn & Co., et. al.* Additional information found in appendices to briefs of Schwinn and its distributors in *United States of America* v. *Arnold, Schwinn & Co. and Schwinn Cycle Distributors Association,* Supreme Court of the United States, October 1966. High Court arguments and ruling are quoted from a transcript of the Supreme Court proceedings (20 April 1967) and Justice Abe Fortas's majority opinion, published 12 June 1967.

Information on the early-1970s bike boom and its effects on Schwinn and dealers were found in *The Schwinn Reporter* and *Chicago Tribune* articles ("Schwinn Bicycle Opens Northwest Center Factory," 16 April 1972, and "Schwinn Can't Pedal Enough to Meet Demand," 27 August 1972, by Leonard Wiener), as well as issues of *American Bicyclist.* Also useful: *Schwinn Bicycle Company Marketing Analysis and 1979 Marketing Plan,* an internal corporate report dated 31 August 1978, and a 1991 report to potential acquirers of Schwinn prepared by Continental Partners.

Other published sources:

Burgess, Harold D., *Sixty Years at the Bar: Anecdotes of a Corporation Lawyer.* Smithtown, N.Y.: Exposition Press, 1981.

Shanahan, Eileen. "High Court Cites Dealership Curbs." *New York Times,* 13 June 1967.

Keck, Robert C., A *Lawyer's Autobiography—*A *75-Year Odyssey.* Published by the author, Chicago, 1989.

"When bicycle maker peddles alone." *Business Week,* 1 July 1967.

Chapters 7 and 8: THE HANGOVER; "WEIRD AND FREAKY STUFF"

The company's 1979 marketing plan and its product catalogs helped show how Schwinn began to lag in the 1970s and failed to embrace the BMX trend, as did *The Schwinn Reporter* issues from 1973 to 1983.

Other published sources:

Chicago Tribune Sunday Magazine. "Motocross: Splendor in the Dirt." 3 July 1983.

Edgerton, Michael. "Schwinn Bicycle Studies Transfer to Plant in Tulsa." *Chicago Tribune,* 9 June 1977.

Make no little plans: Jobs for Metropolitan Chicago, Commercial Club of Chicago, 1984; and *Jobs for Metropolitan Chicago: A Two Year Report,* Civic Committee of the Commercial Club of Chicago, 1987.

Nash, Jeffrey E. "Expensive Dirt: Bicycle Motocross and Everyday Life." *Journal of Popular Culture,* Fall 1986.

Chapter 9: "JUST BEING A KID"

Videotapes of early Repack Road races highlighted the emerging culture of off-road cycling, as did issues of *Fat Tire Flyer,* a newsletter-turned-magazine that was published from 1982 to 1987 in Fairfax, California, by Denise Caramagno and Charles Kelly. Mountain Bike Hall of Fame speeches in 1994 by Richard Schwinn and Joe Breeze ("They Gave Us Our Tire") also were helpful. And Santa Ana, California, bicycle collector and historian Leon Dixon provided information on the Southern California side of the clunker trend.

The Japan-based industry publication *Cycle Press International* (later called *Cycle Press*) offered details on Fisher and his relationships with Taiwan's Anlen Bicycle Company and Wisconsin's Trek Bicycle Company, especially the April 1992, December 1992, February 1993, and March 1993 issues.

Other published sources:

Clifford, Tom. "Breezin'." *Mountain Biker,* February 1992.

Espinoza, Zapata. "Memories of Marin." *Mountain Bike Action,* May 1991.

Fuller, Charles. "King of the Mountain." *Entrepreneur,* April 1991.

Gamstetter, Michael. "Tom Ritchey: His Designs are 'Honest Pizza'." *Bicycle Retailer and Industry News,* 1 August 1994.

Giovannini, Joseph. "A Sturdy Mountain Bike Wins Hearts in the City." *New York Times,* 30 July 1983.

Hosler, Ray. "Pirates of The Bike Industry." *San Francisco Chronicle,* 17 August 1987.

Kelly, Charles. "Built to Take It." *Mariah/Outside* (later renamed *Outside*), September 1979.

Kelly, Charles. "The Pioneers of Mountain Biking." Published for Anaheim and Atlantic City Interbike trade shows, June 1991.

Kelly, Charles, and Crane, Nick. *Richard's Mountain Bike Book.* New York: Ballantine Books, 1988.

Nilsen, Richard. "History of the Mountain Bike." *The CoEvolution Quarterly,* Spring 1978 (later named *Whole Earth Review*).

Patrick, Kevin. "Mountain Bikes and the Baby Boomers." *Journal of American Culture,* Summer 1988.

Schwartz, David M. "Over hill, over dale, on a bicycle built for . . . goo." *Smithsonian,* July 1994.

Selz, Michael. "Mountain-Bike Firm Performs Tough Balancing Act." *Wall Street Journal,* 31 October 1989.

Vetter, Craig. "Fat Is Back: The Triumphant Return of the All-American, Indestructible, Balloon-Tire Bike." *Outside,* April 1984.

Chapters 10 and 11: TREKKING; ED TAKES CHARGE

Schwinn Reporter issues offered information on corporate changes during the transition from Frank V. Schwinn to Edward R. Schwinn, Jr., as did the in-house *Schwinn Cycle News* ("Corporate Changes Begin Fourth Generation Era!" September–October 1979), Robert Keck's autobiography, and Frankie's obituary (*Chicago Tribune,* 14 January 1988). Details on the aborted attempt to extort Edward's family were culled from Winnetka Police Department reports dated 11 December 1958 and 21 February 1959.

Chapters 12 and 13: ONE STRIKE AND YOU'RE OUT; THE DIFFERENCE O'DEA MADE

Unbylined *Chicago Tribune* articles were helpful in documenting the course of the United Auto Workers strike, the opening of the Greenville, Mississippi, factory, and the closing of the Chicago plant, including "Schwinn Co. Faces Its First Strike" (15 September 1980), "Schwinn Employees Go On Strike" (26 October 1980), "Labor Talks at Schwinn Break Off" (29 October 1980), "Schwinn Contract is OK'd" (2 February 1981), "Schwinn Moving Assembly Operation" (28 September 1982), and "Schwinn's Bicycle Production in Chicago Pedals into Sunset" (26 October 1983).

Other published sources:

Greenberg, Herb. "Schwinn Settles, Plans Miss. Plant." *Crain's Chicago Business,* 2 February 1981.

Gurevitz, Susan. "Schwinn Rejects Manufacturing, To Close Plants." *Crain's Chicago Business*, 24 October 1983.
Halberstam, David. *The Reckoning*. New York: William Morrow, 1986.
Jouzaitis, Carol. "Schwinn Lays Off 211 at Chicago Bicycle Plant." *Chicago Tribune*, 8 July 1983.

Although Schwinn as a privately held company had kept its financial statements under close wraps, extensive information is disclosed in the U.S. Bankruptcy Court filing by Schwinn Bicycle Company and its affiliates, Northern District of Illinois, Eastern Division, Case Nos. 92 B 22474–22482, as well as a 1991 report to potential acquirers of Schwinn prepared by Continental Partners.

Other published sources:

Lazarus, George. "Skater Eric Heiden Joins Schwinn." *Chicago Tribune*, 29 September 1980.
Snyder, David. "A New Heat: Restyled Schwinn Wins Over Dealers." *Crain's Chicago Business*, 21 January 1985.
Ziemba, Stanley, and Ibata, David. "Gears stick on stadium plan, Schwinn shifting its offices to proposed site." *Chicago Tribune*, 4 October 1985.

Chapters 14, 15, 16, and 17: LAND OF THE GIANT; SCHWINN MEETS CENTRAL PLANNING; THE CHINA SYNDROME; THE OTHER *S*

For backdrops of the China, Hong Kong, and Taiwan economies:

Galenson, Walter, ed. *Economic Growth and Structural Change in Taiwan, the Postwar Experience of China*. Ithaca, N.Y.: Cornell Univ. Press, 1979.
Gold, Thomas B. *State and Society in the Taiwan Miracle*, Armonk, N.Y.: M. E. Sharpe, 1986.
Goldstein, Carl. "Brand of Hope: Asian Firms Seek to Produce Own-name Goods." *Far Eastern Economic Review*, 3 October 1991.
Tanzer, Andrew. "The mountains are high, the emperor is far away." *Forbes*, 5 August 1991.
Vogel, Ezra F. *The Four Little Dragons: The Spread of Industrialization in East Asia*. Cambridge: Harvard University Press, 1991.

For background on Hungary and Schwinn's Csepel venture:

Arndt, Michael. "A Lot Is Riding on Tandem of Schwinn and Hungary." *Chicago Tribune*, 24 December 1989.
Ingram, Judith. "Hungary Warms Up to Ventures." *Chicago Tribune*, 2 September 1991.
McClenahen, John. "Light in the East." *Industry Week*, 2 March 1992.
Rocks, David. "Schwinn Kin in Europe Left to Fend for Self." *Chicago Tribune*, 25 August 1993.

Additional details on Giant Manufacturing Company came from articles in the trade magazine *Bicycle Dealer Showcase* and from "Manufacturing Bicycles for the World," a speech by Tony Lo at the Interbike Symposium in Anaheim, California (excerpted in the December 1992 issue of *Cycle Press International*).

Other *Cycle Press* articles were helpful in documenting Schwinn's shift from Giant to China Bicycles Company, including stories in the June 1987, August 1987, June 1988, November 1990, and September 1991 issues. The magazine also covered China Bicycles' acquisition of Western States International in its June 1990 and July 1992 issues, and excerpted a speech by Stephen E. Codron at the Interbike Symposium ("China, Hong Kong and the Global Market: How Strong is the Link?") in its December 1992 issue.

Jerome Sze discussed the Western States deal in a letter to *Forbes* after the magazine published a story by Andrew Tanzer that was critical of Schwinn's Asian suppliers ("Bury Thy Teacher," 21 December 1992). Terms of China Bicycles stock ownership, including stakes owned by Schwinn and Stephen Codron, are outlined in an appendix to the bankruptcy court filing by Schwinn. Other sources for the Hong Kong-based company include its 1992 annual report, Reuters news service stories dated 22 June 1993 ("Bicycle Giant Sets Pace in 'China Play' Rat Race," by Jeffrey Parker) and 21 October 1993 ("Times have changed in China, Bike-Maker Tells EC," by Alex Lam), and articles in *Bicycle Retailer and Industry News* (June 1994), *South China Morning Post* (20 December 1993), and the 19 October 1992 issue of the *Sacramento Bee* ("Riding with China: Booming Chinese Bike Maker Could Revive Ailing Schwinn," by Stephen Magagnini).

A seventieth anniversary corporate history published in English by Shimano in 1991 was helpful on the company's early years. Allegations of restraint of trade are outlined in *SRAM Corporation* v. *Shimano Industrial Company, Ltd.*, United States District Court, Central District of California, 27 September 1989. *Cycle Press* articles provided background on the decline of rival SunTour (December 1990, October 1991, March 1993, July 1993, and September 1994).

Other published sources:

Johnstone, Bob. "Riding High: Business Booms for Bicycle-maker Shimano Industrial." *Far Eastern Economic Review*, 14 December 1989.

Kanabayashi, Masayoshi. "Japan's Shimano Prospers Amid Gloom with Line of High-Tech Bicycle Gear." *Wall Street Journal*, 13 January 1994.

Katayama, Hiroko. "Three Men and a Derailleur." *Forbes*, 21 January 1991.

Martin, Scott. "King of Parts: Shimano is taking over the component market. Should you be worried?" *Bicycling*, November 1993.

Thisdell, Dan. "Shimano's Dream Machine." *Management Today*, March 1990.

Chapters 18, 19, and 20: MISSISSIPPI CHURNING; AN IMPORTANT GUY; DOWNHILL, FAST

The 1991 Continental Partners offering detailed losses from the Greenville, Mississippi, factory and financial results of Schwinn's first company store. Newspaper articles on Greenville's demise: "Schwinn Closing Southern Plant," *Chicago Tribune,* 6 August 1991; "Schwinn Finds Overseas Lure Potent, *Chicago Tribune,* 9 August 1991; and "Bike Maker Closes Plant, But Ex-Worker Says Thanks for Ride," by John Balzar, *Los Angeles Times,* 20 September 1992.

Family complaints against Ed Schwinn are aired in *Bailey* v. *Schwinn.* Documents filed in DuPage County Circuit Court in 1988 and 1992 provided information on DUI charges against Ignaz Schwinn III and Thomas Schwinn. Discussion of Robert and Rychie Schwinn's marriage is based on a divorce petition brought by Robert in August 1977 and a second petition in September 1992 that culminated in the couple's divorce in 1994. Complaints of harassment were filed by Rychie Schwinn between August and December 1992; she won a protection order against Robert on 10 August 1992.

Other published sources:

Schwinn Bicycle Co. v. *Diversified Products Corp.*, U.S. District Court, Northern District of Illinois, 17 August 1988 (Air-Dyne litigation).

Stevens, Mark. *King Icahn: The Biography of a Renegade Capitalist.* New York: Dutton, 1993 (Dennis O'Dea's role in the Texaco/Pennzoil case).

Stoff, Bruce. "Bike Line Shoots for 300 Shops." *Bicycle Retailer and Industry News,* 15 May 1995.

Chapters 21 and 22: A SERIES OF AGGRAVATIONS; THE GREASE FOR A DEAL

The earliest indication to the general public of Schwinn's worsening financial troubles and its search for an investor was "Beleaguered Schwinn Seeks Partner to Regain Its Luster," by Timothy L. O'Brien, *Wall Street Journal,* 20 May 1992. Also: "Schwinn Fighting to Keep on Rolling," by Adam Lashinsky, *Crain's Chicago Business,* 25 May 1992. Schwinn's Chapter 11 bankruptcy filing nearly five months later was national news, with 9 October 1992, stories in the *New York Times* ("Schwinn Files Under Chapter 11," by Kenneth Gilpin), *Los Angeles Times* ("Schwinn, Venerable Bike Firm, Files For Bankruptcy," by Donald Woutat) and the *Washington Post* ("Schwinn: It Was the Wheel Thing; Memories of the Rock-Solid Bicycle for Rough-Riding Kids," by Ken Ringle). Local newspaper coverage that day included stories in the *Chicago Tribune* ("A Tottering Schwinn Puts Kickstand Down," by Stanley Ziembia) and the *Chicago Sun-Times* ("Schwinn Files For Chapter 11," by Mary Ellen Podmolik and Frederick

H. Lowe). *Crain's Chicago Business* weighed in with "Schwinn Pedaling Furiously; Chap. 11 Workout to Be Rough ride," by Judith Crown, 12 October 1992.

References to dividends and golden parachutes are cited in litigation brought by unsecured creditors against Ed and Richard as part of the bankruptcy's administration: *Schwinn Plan Committee* v. *Edward R. Schwinn, Jr., and Richard C. Schwinn,* Adversary Proceeding No. 94A01641, 6 October 1994.

On the origins of Continental Partners: "Cont'l M&A Drafts Hurt Bear Stearns," by Christopher R. O'Dea, *Crain's Chicago Business*, 28 August 1989. Senior managing director Michael Smith declined to comment for this book, but details of Continental's marketing of Schwinn, the valuation of Schwinn's stake in China Bicycles, and the courtship of Acadia/Bain were outlined by Smith in an 30 October 1992 deposition as part of the bankruptcy case.

Background on various Schwinn suitors: Acadia/Bain ("Bass Fund Eyes Stake in Schwinn," by Judith Crown, *Crain's Chicago Business*, 10 August 1992), Mort and Edward Finklestein ("Comeback Kid," by Andrew Gaffney, *Sporting Goods Business*, 30 November 1991); and William Goodwin ("The Virginia 100," *Virginia Business*, July 1995, and "Goldman is Seen in Talks to Buy Bowling Giant," by Peter Truell, *New York Times*, 5 January 1996). John Jellinek was quoted in *Crain's Chicago Business* ("Schwinn Spin: Who Is This Guy?," 26 October 1992).

Chapter 23: THE VULTURE SWOOPS

All quotes from the U.S. Bankruptcy Court proceedings were gathered in person or from transcripts.

For background on David Schulte and Sam Zell:

Allen, J. Linn. "Riding with Zell's Angels." *Chicago Tribune*, 12 December 1994.

Barsky, Neil. "Sam Zell Was Right About Real Estate—And Still Overbought." *Wall Street Journal*, 9 July 1992.

Crown, Judith. "Sam's Latest Shopping Spree." *Crain's Chicago Business*, 8 February 1993.

Ferguson, Tim W. "Combat Veterans of Sorts Raise the Schwinn Flag." *Wall Street Journal*, 27 July 1993.

Laing, Jonathan R. "Dancing Again: After a Tough Slump, Sam Zell Is Riding High and Loving It." *Barron's*, 13 September 1993.

Rosenberg, Hilary. *The Vulture Investors*. New York: HarperCollins, 1992.

Shen, Ted. "Uneasy Riders." *Chicago*, March 1995.

Strahler, Steven R. "David Schulte: A Little Guy Doing Big Deals." *Crain's Chicago Business*, 11 July 1988.

Strom, Stephanie. "A 'Vulture' Looks Skyward." *New York Times*, 10 September 1995.

Taylor, John H. "Fishing in Foul Water." *Forbes*, 9 November 1992.

Chapter 24: A FINAL SPIN

Litigation that provided information included *Schwinn Plan Committee* v. *Edward R. Schwinn, Jr. and Richard C. Schwinn*, 6 October 1994, along with "Answer and Affirmative Defenses of Edward R. Schwinn to Complaint," 27 December 1994, and *The Plan Committee of S. B. Liquidating, Inc., f/k/a Schwinn Bicycle Co.* v. *Shenzhen China Bicycle Co. (Holdings) Ltd., Hong Kong (Link) Bicycles Ltd. and John W. Barker*, 16 May 1995. The family lawsuit *Bailey* v. *Schwinn* also was discussed in *Crain's Chicago Business* ("A Schwinn Family Feud: Blame Game Hits 1st Chi. in $200 Mil. Suit," 14 February 1994, and "Schwinn Lawsuit Dismissed," 23 January 1995, both by Judith Crown).

Other published sources on the new Schwinn, the players in the bankruptcy, and trends in the bicycle industry:

Anderson, Veronica. "Damage Control Shifts to High Gear at Chapman, A Quiet Firm in Spotlight of Legal Scandal." *Crain's Chicago Business*, 30 May, 1994.

Anderson, Veronica. "Exit Door Swinging at Keck." *Crain's Chicago Business*, 22 January 1996.

Barrier, Michael. "Wheels of Change in Bicycle Retailing." *Nation's Business*. February 1996.

Crown, Judith. "The Sam & Dave Show Reviewed." *Crain's Chicago Business*, 5 June 1995.

Fritz, Michael. "Sam-Dave Show: No 2nd Act." *Crain's Chicago Business*, 30 October 1995.

Frothingham, Steve. " 'Grave Dancer' Grabs a Piece of Bell Sports." *Bicycle Retailer and Industry News*, 1 November 1994.

MacDonald, Douglas. "Going Uphill but Gathering Speed." *Biz*, January 1995.

McRae, Michael. "The Cosmic Conception of Fat Boy." *Outside*, January 1994.

Sani, Marc. "Austin Faces Tough Choices as He Takes Reins at Raleigh." *Bicycle Retailer and Industry News*, 1 August 1994.

Stevens, Amy. "Top Chapman & Cutler Partner Chalked Up Astronomical Hours." *The Wall Street Journal*, 27 May 1994.

Stoff, Bruce. "Black Phantom Rides Again." *Bicycle Retailer and Industry News*, 1 July 1995.

INDEX